The Politics of Institutional Weak

Analysts and policymakers often decry the failure of institutions to accomplish their stated purpose. Bringing together leading scholars of Latin American politics, this volume helps us understand why. The volume offers a conceptual and theoretical framework for studying weak institutions. It introduces different dimensions of institutional weakness and explores the origins and consequences of that weakness. Drawing on recent research on constitutional and electoral reform, executive–legislative relations, property rights, environmental and labor regulation, indigenous rights, squatters and street vendors, and anti–domestic violence laws in Latin America, the volume's chapters show us that politicians often design institutions that they cannot or do not want to enforce or comply with. Challenging existing theories of institutional design, the volume helps us understand the logic that drives the creation of weak institutions, as well as the conditions under which they may be transformed into institutions that matter.

Daniel M. Brinks is Professor of Government and of Law and Chair of the Government Department at the University of Texas at Austin. Dan's research focuses on the role of the law and courts in supporting democracy and human rights. His most recent book (with Abby Blass) is *The DNA of Constitutional Justice in Latin America* (Cambridge University Press, 2018), winner of the Corwin Award for Best Book on Law and Courts awarded by the Law and Courts Section of the American Political Science Association.

Steven Levitsky is the David Rockefeller Professor of Latin American Studies at Harvard University. He is coauthor (with Daniel Ziblatt) of *How Democracies Die* (Crown, 2018), a *New York Times* best seller published in twenty-two languages. His other books include *Transforming Labor-Based Parties in Latin America* (Cambridge University Press, 2003) and (with Lucan Way) *Competitive Authoritarianism* (Cambridge University Press, 2010). He is currently writing a book on the durability of revolutionary regimes.

María Victoria Murillo is Professor in the Department of Political Science and the School of International Affairs and the Director of the Institute of Latin American Studies (ILAS) at Columbia University. She is the author of *Labor Unions, Partisan Coalitions, and Market Reforms in Latin America* (2001); *Political Competition, Partisanship, and Policymaking in the Reform of Latin American Public Utilities* (2009); and (with Ernesto Calvo) *Non-Policy Politics* (2019), all published with Cambridge University Press.

The Politics of Institutional Weakness in Latin America

Edited by

DANIEL M. BRINKS
The University of Texas at Austin

STEVEN LEVITSKY
Harvard University

MARÍA VICTORIA MURILLO
Columbia University

CAMBRIDGE
UNIVERSITY PRESS

University Printing House, Cambridge CB2 8BS, United Kingdom

One Liberty Plaza, 20th Floor, New York, NY 10006, USA

477 Williamstown Road, Port Melbourne, VIC 3207, Australia

314–321, 3rd Floor, Plot 3, Splendor Forum, Jasola District Centre, New Delhi – 110025, India

79 Anson Road, #06-04/06, Singapore 079906

Cambridge University Press is part of the University of Cambridge.

It furthers the University's mission by disseminating knowledge in the pursuit
of education, learning, and research at the highest international levels of excellence.

www.cambridge.org
Information on this title: www.cambridge.org/9781108489331
DOI: 10.1017/9781108776608

First published 2020

Printed in the United Kingdom by TJ International Ltd. Padstow Cornwall

A catalogue record for this publication is available from the British Library.

Library of Congress Cataloging-in-Publication Data
Names: Brinks, Daniel M., 1961- editor. | Levitsky, Steven, editor. |
Murillo, María Victoria, 1967- editor.
Title: The politics of institutional weakness in Latin America / edited by
Daniel M. Brinks, Steven Levitsky, María Victoria Murillo.
Description: Cambridge, United Kingdom : New York, NY : Cambridge
University Press, 2020. | Includes bibliographical references and index.
Identifiers: LCCN 2019058907 | ISBN 9781108489331 (hardback) | ISBN
9781108702331 (ebook)
Subjects: LCSH: Political culture--Latin America. | Government
accountability--Latin America. | Administrative agencies--Latin America.
| Latin America--Politics and government--21st century.
Classification: LCC JL966 .P636 2020 | DDC 306.2098--dc23
LC record available at https://lccn.loc.gov/2019058907

ISBN 978-1-108-48933-1 Hardback
ISBN 978-1-108-70233-1 Paperback

Contents

Figures

Maps

Tables

Contributors

Michael Albertus is Associate Professor of Political Science at the University of Chicago. His research interests include political regimes, redistribution, clientelism, and civil conflict. He has published two books, *Autocracy and Redistribution: The Politics of Land Reform* (Cambridge University Press, 2015) and *Authoritarianism and the Elite Origins of Democracy* (Cambridge University Press, 2018), and a host of articles in outlets such as the *American Journal of Political Science*, *World Politics*, the *Journal of Conflict Resolution*, and *Comparative Political Studies*.

Matthew Amengual is Associate Professor of International Business at the University of Oxford. A political scientist by training, he specializes in regulation and labor politics. His first book, *Politicized Enforcement in Argentina: Labor and Environmental Regulation*, was published by Cambridge University Press in 2016.

Daniel M. Brinks is Professor of Government and of Law and Chair of the Government Department at the University of Texas at Austin. He has a PhD in political science from the University of Notre Dame and a JD from the University of Michigan Law School. Dan's research focuses on the role of the law and courts in supporting and deepening democracy and human rights, with a primary regional interest in Latin America. His most recent book, *The DNA of Constitutional Justice in Latin America* (with Abby Blass), is on the politics of constitutional and judicial design. His other books address the experience with uneven democracies in Latin America, the judicial response to police violence, and the enforcement of social and economic rights in the developing world. He has published articles in the *International Journal of Constitutional Law*, *Perspectives on Politics*, *Comparative Politics*, *Comparative Political Studies*, and the *Texas Law Review*, among other journals.

Ernesto Calvo is Professor of Government and Politics at the University of Maryland, Director of the Interdisciplinary Lab for Computational Social Science (iLCSS), and Comparative Institutions Field Editor of the _Journal of Politics_. He holds a PhD from Northwestern University (2001). His work uses big data to study comparative political institutions, political representation, and social networks. He is the co-author of _Non-Policy Politics_ "(with María Victoria Murillo)" (Cambridge University Press, 2019), _Legislator Success in Fragmented Congresses in Argentina_ (Cambridge University Press, 2014), and over fifty publications in Latin American, European, and US journals. The American Political Science Association has recognized his research with the Lawrence Longley Award, the Gregory Luebbert Best Article Award, and the Michael Wallerstein Award. He is currently working on a book project on the activation of political content in social media.

Eduardo Dargent is Associate Professor of Political Science at Pontifical Catholic University of Peru. His main teaching and research interests are comparative public policy and democratization and the state in the developing world. He has published in _Comparative Politics_, the _Journal of Latin American Studies_, and the _Journal of Politics in Latin America_. His book _Technocracy and Democracy in Latin America_ (Cambridge University Press) was published in 2015.

Tulia G. Falleti is the Class of 1965 Endowed Term Professor of Political Science, Director of the Latin American and Latino Studies Program, and Senior Fellow of the Leonard Davis Institute for Health Economics at the University of Pennsylvania. Falleti is the author of _Decentralization and Subnational Politics in Latin America_ (Cambridge University Press, 2010), coauthor of _Participation in Social Policy: Public Health in Comparative Perspective_ (Cambridge University Press, 2018), and co-editor of _The Oxford Handbook of Historical Institutionalism_ (Oxford University Press, 2016) and _Latin America since the Left Turn_ (University of Pennsylvania, 2018), among other volumes.

Belén Fernández Milmanda is Assistant Professor of Political Science and International Studies at Trinity College. She holds a PhD in political science from Harvard University. Her work focuses on how agrarian elites influence politics in Latin America.

Candelaria Garay is the Ford Foundation Associate Professor of Democracy at the Harvard Kennedy School. She is the author of _Social Policy Expansion in Latin America_ (Cambridge University Press, 2016). Her current research focuses on labor and social movement coalitions, environmental institutions, and subnational health services and outcomes.

Juan F. González Bertomeu is Assistant Professor of Law at Instituto Tecnológico Autónomo de México (ITAM) (Mexico Autonomous Institute of Technology). He specializes in Latin American constitutional law, legal empirical studies, and legal theory. He received his first law degree from the National University of La Plata (1999) and obtained an LLM degree (2003) and a JSD degree (2012) at New York University.

Gretchen Helmke is Professor of Political Science at the University of Rochester. Her research focuses on political institutions, democratic consolidation and erosion, rule of law, and Latin American politics. Her most recent book is *Institutions on the Edge: The Origins and Consequences of Institutional Instability in Latin America* (Cambridge University Press, 2017).

Alisha C. Holland is Associate Professor of Government at Harvard University. She is the author of *Forbearance as Redistribution: The Politics of Informal Welfare in Latin America* (Cambridge University Press, 2017) and is currently writing a book on the politics of infrastructure provision in Latin America.

Mala Htun is Professor of Political Science at the University of New Mexico, where she is also Co–Principal Investigator and Deputy Director of ADVANCE and special advisor for inclusion and climate in the School of Engineering. She works on women's rights and the politics of inequality and is the author of three books, most recently *The Logics of Gender Justice: State Action on Women's Rights around the World*, coauthored with Laurel Weldon (Cambridge University Press, 2018). She serves as Chair of the Committee on the Status of Women in the Profession of the American Political Science Association and cochaired the Presidential Task Force on Women's Advancement in the Profession. She has been an Andrew Carnegie Fellow and a Fellow at the Kellogg Institute for International Studies at the University of Notre Dame and the Radcliffe Institute for Advanced Study at Harvard University, and she has held the Council on Foreign Relations International Affairs Fellowship in Japan. She holds a PhD in political science from Harvard University and an AB in international relations from Stanford University. She was an Assistant and then Associate Professor at the New School for Social Research from 2000 to 2011.

Francesca R. Jensenius is Associate Professor of Political Science at the University of Oslo and Senior Research Fellow at the Norwegian Institute of International Affairs (NUPI), specializing in comparative politics, comparative political economy, and research methods. She holds a PhD from the University of California, Berkeley (2013).

Steven Levitsky is the David Rockefeller Professor of Latin American Studies and Professor of Government at Harvard University. His areas of research include democratization and authoritarianism, political parties, and weak and informal institutions. He is the author of *Transforming Labor-Based Parties in Latin America: Argentine Peronism in Comparative Perspective* (Cambridge University Press, 2003), coauthor (with Lucan Way) of *Competitive Authoritarianism: Hybrid Regimes after the Cold War*

(Cambridge University Press, 2010), and coauthor (with Daniel Ziblatt) of *How Democracies Die* (Crown, 2018). He is currently writing a book on the durability of revolutionary regimes.

Victor Menaldo is Professor of Political Science at the University of Washington and affiliated with the Center for Statistics and the Social Sciences, Near and Middle Eastern Studies, and the Center for Environmental Politics. His books, *The Institutions Curse* and *Authoritarianism and the Elite Origins of Democracy* (with Michael Albertus), are published with Cambridge University Press.

María Victoria Murillo is Professor in the Department of Political Science and the School of International Affairs at Columbia University, as well as Director of the Institute of Latin American Studies (ILAS). She is the author of *Labor Unions, Partisan Coalitions, and Market Reforms in Latin America* (Cambridge University Press, 2001); of *Political Competition, Partisanship, and Policymaking in the Reform of Latin American Public Utilities* (Cambridge University Press, 2009); coauthor (with Ernesto Calvo) of *Non-Policy Politics: Richer Voter, Poorer Voter and the Diversification of Electoral Strategies* (Cambridge University Press, 2019); and coauthor (with Daniel M. Brinks and Steven Levitsky) of *Understanding Institutional Weakness: Power and Design in Latin American Institutions* (Cambridge University Press, Elements in Latin American Politics and Society, 2019). She received her BA from the University of Buenos Aires and her MA and PhD from Harvard University.

Gabriel Negretto is Professor of Political Science at the Institute of Political Science of the Catholic University of Santiago de Chile. He specializes in comparative constitutional politics, institutional change, and democratization. His most recent books are *Redrafting Constitutions in Democratic Orders: Theoretical and Comparative Perspectives* (Cambridge University Press, 2020) and *Making Constitutions: Presidents, Parties, and Institutional Choice in Latin America* (Cambridge University Press, 2013).

María Paula Saffon is Principal Researcher of the Institute for Legal Research at the National Autonomous University of Mexico (UNAM), a position she has held since 2016. She holds a PhD in political science from Columbia University (2015). She was the Race and Ethnicity Fellow at the Princeton University Society of Fellows in the Liberal Arts (2015–2017).

Andrew Schrank is the Olive C. Watson Professor of Sociology and International and Public Affairs at Brown University and a CIFAR Fellow in the Innovation, Equity, and the Future of Prosperity program.

Acknowledgments

This book is the outcome of a truly collective effort. We cannot overstate the value of working with a talented group of scholars of Latin America who are deeply knowledgeable about the region but who work on very different institutions and draw on very different literatures. The conceptual framework, the basic theoretical approach, and the internal chapters all were enriched by the collective insight of all the contributors to this volume. The volume also benefited from the suggestions and input of many discussants in successive conferences at Harvard (2015) and the University of Texas at Austin (2017), and in seminars in the Universidad de San Andrés and the National University of San Martín. In particular, we would like to thank Peter Hall, Ira Katznelson, Marcelo Leiras, Juan Pablo Luna, Jim Mahoney, Dan Slater, Kathleen Thelen, and the anonymous reviewers at Cambridge University Press. We are also thankful for the financial support of the David Rockefeller Center for Latin American Studies and the Weatherhead Center for International Affairs at Harvard University; the Bernard and Audre Rapoport Center for Human Rights and Justice at the University of Texas at Austin; and the Institute of Latin American Studies at Columbia University. Finally, we would like to recognize the excellent research assistance provided by Alexander Claycomb at the University of Texas at Austin.

The Political Origins of Institutional Weakness

Daniel M. Brinks, Steven Levitsky, and María Victoria Murillo

The third wave of democratization transformed Latin America. Across the region, regime transitions triggered a plethora of institutional reforms aimed at enhancing the stability and quality of both the new and the few long-standing democracies. Most states adopted new constitutions. Many of them extended new rights to citizens, including unprecedented social rights, such as the right to health care, housing, and a clean environment (Klug 2000; Yashar 2005; Brinks and Blass 2018). Electoral systems were redesigned – at least once – in every Latin American country except Costa Rica;[1] judicial and central bank reforms spread across the region (Jácome and Vásquez 2008); and governments launched far-reaching decentralization initiatives and experimented with new institutions of direct or participatory democracy (Falleti 2010; Cameron, Hershberg, and Sharpe 2012; Altman 2014; Mayka 2019).

Yet these new institutions often failed to generate the outcomes their designers expected or hoped for. Constitutional checks and balances did not always constrain presidents (O'Donnell 1994); nominally independent judiciaries and central banks often lacked teeth in practice;[2] electoral reforms failed to strengthen party systems (Remmer 2008); newly enshrined social rights were often not respected in fact (Gauri and Brinks 2008); presidential term limits were circumvented or overturned (Pérez-Liñán 2007; Helmke 2017); and civil service laws, tax laws, and labor and environmental regulations were enforced unevenly, if at all.[3] Put simply, political and economic institutions remained

---

[1] See Calvo and Negretto, this volume.
[2] See Cukierman, Web, and Neyapti (1992); Bill Chavez (2004); Helmke (2004); and Brinks and Blass (2017).
[3] See Bensusán (2000); Piore and Schrank (2008); Bergman (2009); Ronconi (2010); Murillo, Ronconi, and Schrank (2011); Coslovsky (2011); Grindle (2012); Gingerich (2013); and Amengual (2014).

poorly enforced, unstable, or both. Even after more than three decades of democracy, formal institutions only weakly shape actors' behavior in much of Latin America, creating a sizeable gap between the parchment "rules of the game" and their expected, or at least stated, outcomes.

That gap is consequential. Institutional weakness narrows actors' time horizons in ways that can undermine both economic performance (Spiller and Tommasi 2007) and the stability and quality of democracy (O'Donnell 1994). Democracy requires that the rule of law be applied evenly, across territory and across diverse categories of citizens. That is, every citizen should be equal before the law in spite of inequalities created by markets and societies. Institutional weakness undermines that equality – and it hinders efforts to use laws and public policies to combat the multifaceted inequalities that continue to plague much of Latin America. Institutions, of course, are not uniformly positive. They may exclude, reinforce inequalities, or – as Albertus and Menaldo (2018, this volume) show – protect authoritarian elites. In some cases, democratization may require the dismantling of such institutions. In general, however, no democracy can function well without strong institutions.

Although the problem of institutional weakness has been widely recognized in the field of comparative politics, it has not been adequately conceptualized or theorized. Researchers tend to treat it as a feature of the landscape rather than as a variable—or, importantly, as a political strategy. To build theories about the causes and consequences of institutional weakness we need a clear conceptual framework that allows us to identify, measure, and compare different forms of institutional weakness. This volume takes an initial step toward such a framework.

The volume focuses on Latin America. It does so because the region contains both an important set of shared characteristics and useful variation. With few exceptions, Latin American countries possess at least minimally effective states and competitive electoral (if not always fully democratic) regimes. Thus, these are not cases in which political institutions can be dismissed as predictably and uniformly meaningless. Moreover, the region contains within it substantial variation on the dimension of institutional strength – across countries, across institutions, and over time. A focus on Latin America allows us to exploit this variation, while simultaneously benefiting from the insights generated by a close-knit community of scholars with a shared knowledge of the region's history and cases.

Issues of institutional strength are of great consequence in Latin America. Given the region's vast inequalities and state deficiencies, the potential impact of institutional reform *on paper* is often strikingly high. If laws aimed at eliminating corruption, clientelism, racial discrimination, or violence against women, or rules designed to redistribute income to the poor, enforce property rights against squatters, or protect the environment, were actually complied with over time, the social and distributional consequences would be enormous. So the stakes of institutional compliance and durability are high.

Struggles over whether and how the rules are enforced, and whether or not they remain on the books, have prominent winners and losers. Scholars must understand what drives these struggles – and what determines their outcomes.

Although this volume focuses on Latin America, its lessons clearly travel beyond the region. Incentives to create and sustain weak institutions are endemic across the Global South. Indeed, they may be found in industrialized democracies as well. Thus, understanding the causes and consequences of institutional weakness is critical for comparative politics more broadly.

WHY INSTITUTIONAL WEAKNESS MATTERS FOR COMPARATIVE POLITICS

Recent research highlights the need for scholars of comparative politics to take institutional weakness seriously. Take Gretchen Helmke's (2004) study of executive–judicial relations in Argentina. Established theories of judicial politics – which draw heavily on the case of the United States – tell us that lifetime tenure security for Supreme Court justices should enable justices to act with political independence. But when rules of tenure security are routinely violated, such that justices know that voting against the executive could trigger their removal, judicial behavior changes markedly. Helmke finds that when institutions of tenure security are weak, as in Argentina during much of the twentieth century, justices are more likely to vote with presidents during the early part of their term. As the president's term in office concludes, however, justices tend to engage in "strategic defection," ruling in line with the party or politician they expect to succeed the outgoing president (Helmke 2004). Thus, Helmke identifies – and theorizes – a pattern of judicial behavior that diverges markedly from what would be expected in a strong institutional context.

Alisha Holland's (2017) research on forbearance and redistribution similarly highlights the importance of taking variation in enforcement seriously. Most analyses of redistributive politics in Latin America focus on formal social policies such as public pension and health-care spending. By such measures, redistributive efforts in the region are strikingly low: social expenditure as a percentage of gross domestic product (GDP) is barely half of the average for Organization for Economic Co-operation and Development (OECD) countries, and unlike most OECD countries, taxes and transfers only marginally reduce income inequality (Holland 2017: 69–70). In unequal democracies such as those in much of Latin America, the persistence of such small welfare states may seem puzzling. By adding the dimension of forbearance, or deliberate nonenforcement of the law, Holland offers insight into why such outcomes persist. The state's toleration of illegal activities such as squatting and street vending distributes considerable resources to the poor (Holland estimates that in Lima it amounts to around $750 million a year [2017: 9]). Thus, whereas most Latin American states do little, in formal terms, to support housing and employment for the poor, nonenforcement of laws against squatting and street vending creates an "informal welfare state," in which "downward redistribution happens by the state's leave, rather than through the state's hand" (Holland 2017: 11).

Forbearance has powerfully shaped long-run welfare-state development in Latin America. Because forbearance entails less taxation than formal redistribution, governments and their nonpoor constituencies may come to prefer it; and when the poor organize to preserve forbearance, popular demands for formal redistribution are often dampened. This "forbearance trap" can lock in informal welfare states for decades (Holland 2017: 237–276). A central lesson from Holland's work, then, is that understanding the politics of redistribution in unequal democracies requires a focus not only on policy design but also on enforcement.[4]

Alison Post's (2014) research on foreign and domestic investment in infrastructure in Argentina offers another example of how variation in institutional strength shapes policy outcomes. Foreign multinationals – with their deep pockets and long time horizons – are widely expected to hold an advantage over domestic firms in winning favorable infrastructure contracts where institutional veto points constrain governments (Levy and Spiller 1996; Henisz 2002) or international third-party enforcement is included in contracts (Elkins, Guzman, and Simmons 2006; Büthe and Milner 2008). However, Post (2014) shows that in weak institutional environments, this is often not the case. In a context of economic and political volatility, where governments are able to alter the terms of contracts regardless of formal rules, domestic investors with extensive linkages to local economies and politicians are better positioned to sustain and, when necessary, renegotiate contacts.[5] Such "informal contractual supports" may be less important in an institutional environment with strong property rights. However, in a context of institutional instability, they help explain why domestic investments often prevail over foreign ones. Post (2014) thus shows how the behavior of both governments and investors changes in a weak institutional environment, producing investment outcomes that differ markedly from those predicted by the existing literature.

Attention to institutional instability has also reshaped our understanding of electoral design. Most comparative scholarship assumes that those who design the electoral rules do so with a self-interested goal: to maximize their electoral advantage. The most influential work in this area assumes that politicians engage in *far-sighted* institutional design. In other words, they design electoral rules in pursuit of relatively long-term goals (Rokkan 1970; Rogowski 1987; Boix 1999).

[4] Variation in enforcement should also influence individual preferences over social policy, in line with Mares's (2005) finding that prior individual experience with state institutions affects policy preferences.
[5] Such renegotiation often entails cross-sectoral bargains that violate rules governing market concentration and conflict of interest (Post 2014; Post and Murillo 2016).

Boix (1999), for example, argues that conservative elites in much of early twentieth-century Europe replaced plurality electoral systems with proportional representation (PR) systems in an effort to minimize their losses in the face of the growing electoral strength of socialist parties. Such theories of far-sighted design hinge on some critical assumptions: for example, actors must believe that the rules they design will endure over time; and they must have some certainty that they themselves will continue to benefit from those rules. In other words, far-sighted designers of electoral rules must be able to "predict with some certainty the future structure of electoral competition" (Boix 1999: 622). Neither of these assumptions holds in weak institutional environments. Where electoral volatility is high, and where institutions are easily replaced, far-sighted institutional design is more difficult. In such a context, rule designers remain self-interested, but they are less likely to be far-sighted. Rather, as scholars such as Karen Remmer (2008) and Calvo and Negretto (this volume) argue, politicians will be more likely to design rules aimed at locking in short-term electoral advantages. Such short-sighted design may well have the effect of reinforcing institutional instability. Allowing for variation in rule designers' time horizons should, therefore, enhance the external validity of theories of institutional design, facilitating their application across different national contexts.

Finally, attention to variation in institutional strength has yielded new insights into the dynamics of institutional change. Recent work in the historical institutionalist tradition focuses attention on forms of gradual institutional change emerging from the reinterpretation or slow redeployment of existing written rules (Thelen and Streeck 2005; Mahoney and Thelen 2010; Conran and Thelen 2016). This scholarship was a useful response to an earlier literature that emphasized discontinuous change – moments of dramatic and far-reaching change, followed by long periods of path-dependent stasis (Krasner 1988). Yet the patterns of layering, drift, conversion, and exhaustion identified by Kathleen Thelen and her collaborators operate in a context of strong formal institutions. As we have argued elsewhere (Levitsky and Murillo 2009, 2014), the dynamics of institutional change can be quite different in a weak institutional environment. Rather than being characterized by "stickiness,"[6] institutional change tends to be rapid and thoroughgoing, often following a pattern of serial replacement, in which rules and procedures are replaced wholesale – without ever settling into a stable equilibrium (Levitsky and Murillo 2014).

Second, actors in a weak institutional environment may achieve real substantive change by modifying enforcement or compliance levels rather than changing the rules. Mahoney and Thelen (2010) have shown how gaps in compliance can serve as a mechanism of hidden change via the subtle reinterpretation of institutional goals, even as formal institutional structures remain intact. Building on this insight, recent scholarship shows how the "activation"

---

[6] For example, Streeck and Thelen (2005: 18) explicitly assume the "stickiness of institutional structures" in their discussion of economic liberalization in the advanced democracies.

of previously dormant institutions can be an important source of change (see Levitsky and Murillo 2014). At the same time, noncompliance may also be a source of formal institutional *stability*, especially when it tempers an institution's distributive consequences (Levitsky and Murillo 2013).[7] During the 1990s, for example, Latin American governments seeking more flexible labor markets weakened enforcement of existing labor laws while keeping them on the books (Bensusán 2000; Cook 2007).

Recent research thus suggests the need for a more conscious focus on institutional weakness as an object of study; as a conscious political strategy rather than as "random error" that obstructs proper institutional analysis. That is what this volume seeks to do.

DEFINING INSTITUTIONS

Before we conceptualize weak institutions, we must define institutions. Most institutionalists begin with North's (1990: 3, 4) definition of institutions as "the humanly devised constraints that shape human interaction ... [in ways that are] perfectly analogous to the rules of the game in a competitive team sport."[8] In previous work (Brinks 2003; Helmke and Levitsky 2006), some of us have argued that institutions are made up of rules, and, in the context of defining informal institutions, sought to differentiate rules from purely descriptive statements or expectations about behavior. For this project, we adopt the same starting point – the notion that (formal) institutions are made up of (formal) rules. This allows us to focus on formal constraints that are "humanly devised" and recognized as compulsory within a polity. Many definitions stop there, but for our purposes we must push beyond the implicit equation of institutions with stand-alone rules. In all cases, we are concerned with the effectiveness of sets of rules, rather than with single rules in isolation, even though a single rule may sometimes stand in as shorthand for the institution as a whole.

We therefore define a formal institution as a set of officially sanctioned rules that structures human behavior and expectations around a particular activity or goal. Elinor Ostrom (1986: 5) defined institutions as

the result of implicit or explicit efforts by a set of individuals to achieve order and predictability within defined situations by: (1) creating positions; (2) stating how participants enter or leave positions; (3) stating which actions participants in these positions are required, permitted, or forbidden to take; and (4) stating which outcome participants are required, permitted, or forbidden to affect.

---

[7] For example, during the debate in 2018 over Argentina's abortion laws, supporters of the existing ban argued that reform was not necessary because no women were actually penalized for terminating their pregnancies (www.lanacion.com.ar/2157341-aborto-no-faltar-a-la-verdad).

[8] See also Peters (2011: 146).

She later added to this classification, arguing that institutions are further defined by rules that specify (5) the consequences of rule violation, which in most cases we expect to be associated with a specific sanction (Crawford and Ostrom 1995).[9] We simplify Crawford and Ostrom's "grammar" somewhat, specifying a (formal) institution as a set of formal rules structuring human behavior and expectations around a statutory goal by (1) specifying actors and their roles; (2) requiring, permitting, or prohibiting certain behaviors; and (3) defining the consequences of complying or not complying with the remaining rules.

Our conceptual scheme relies on identifying the statutory goal of formal institutions – the second element in our definition, above. As we will see in the next section, a strong institution is one that sets a nontrivial goal and achieves it, whereas a weak institution achieves little or nothing, either because it fails to achieve an ambitious goal or because it never set out to accomplish anything. We set statutory goals as the benchmark rather than the (stated or implicit) policy objectives of institutional creators because we recognize that the ultimate policy aim of institutions – often a product of compromise among distinct and even competing interests – may well be ambiguous or contested (Moe 1990; Schickler 2001; Streeck and Thelen 2005; Mahoney and Thelen 2010). By taking the statutory goal itself as a starting point, we can more easily identify how the preferences and strategies of actors work to weaken or strengthen institutions. Whether the institution succeeds in achieving its policy objective or produces far-reaching unintended consequences can be analyzed separately under more conventional policy effectiveness rubrics.[10]

Institutions may be *transformative*, in that they seek to move outcomes away from the status quo, or *conservative*, in that they seek to preserve the status quo in the face of potential change. This volume focuses primarily on transformative institutions, both because they are more often the subject of political and policy debates in Latin America and because they are more often identified as being weak. Nevertheless, conservative or status quo–preserving institutions can be of great importance. Property laws are a clear example. Civil codes enshrining traditional gender roles and family structures are another. Albertus and Menaldo's work (2018, this volume) on the persistence of authoritarian constitutions that protect wealthy elites from redistribution by constraining democratic governments shows that conservative institutions are widespread in Latin America. The conceptual scheme we propose works in either case. Whether conservative or transformative, institutions are meant to make it more likely that social,

---

[9] Similarly, definitions of "law" or "systems of social control" highlight the role of coordinated classes of rules that define not just required, proscribed or permitted behavior, but also mechanisms for enforcement, actors, consequences and the like (see, e.g., Hart 1961; Ellickson 1991).

[10] It is thus entirely possible, in this conceptual scheme, for a strong institution to nevertheless fail to achieve the policy objectives that prompted its creation.

economic, or political outcomes will be closer to a defined statutory goal than to some less preferred alternative outcome.

Weak formal institutions should not be confused with informal rules, or those that are "created and enforced outside officially sanctioned channels" (Helmke and Levitsky 2006: 5). Informal institutions may coexist with either strong or weak formal institutions. When they coexist with weak institutions, they may either reinforce them by providing a second mechanism that promotes the expected behavior ("substitutive") or undermine them by promoting an alternative behavior ("competing") (Helmke and Levitsky 2006: 14). Although we recognize (and discuss below) the importance of informal rules in generating institutional strength or weakness, our focus here is on formal institutions.

Finally, it is important to distinguish formal institutions, or rules, from the organizations that are either the targets of those rules (e.g., political parties, interest groups, firms) or dedicated to enforcing or implementing the rules (e.g., bureaucracies). By keeping rules and organizations conceptually distinct, we can evaluate whether strengthening state agencies – hiring more inspectors, spending more on training bureaucratic personnel, or establishing meritocratic criteria – actually enhances compliance with the institution, as do Ronconi (2010), Schrank (2011), and Amengual (2016) in their work on labor regulations and the civil service.

The Concept of Institutional Weakness

We now turn to conceptualizing institutional weakness. We expect strong institutions to redistribute and refract power, authority, or expectations in order to produce an institutional outcome (*io*, in Figure 1.1) that diverges from what the preinstitutional outcome (*po*) would have been.[11] An institution may be designed to produce an outcome (shown in Figure 1.1 as *io'*) that is more ambitious than that which it actually produces. A strong institution, however, makes a difference because the distance between *io* and *po*, a parameter we call S (for strength), is greater than zero. S, of course, is a cost to those who prefer *po* and exactly the benefit sought by those who prefer *io* or *io'*.

We can use the following graph to illustrate this and set up a vocabulary to use as shorthand:

FIGURE 1.1. Strong institution – io–po>>o.

---

[11] We use "preinstitutional" here in the same sense in which people commonly use "prepolitical." It is not meant to imply temporality, but rather simply what might happen in the absence of the institution.

It is important to note that the move from *po* to *io* is not a move from the state of nature to an institutionalized context. Indeed, *po* could be (in the case of a conservative institution) a feared future outcome the institution is designed to prevent, and *io* may be the status quo it seeks to preserve. The idea is that the institution of interest has been added to the array of inter-locking institutions that impinge on any given social and political activity in hopes of producing a particular outcome that might not otherwise obtain, either presently or in the future. The comparison point is a counterfactual – our best estimate of what might happen if the institution were to disappear or be replaced.

Central to our understanding of institutional strength, then, is the institution's *ambition* – the degree to which institutions are designed to change outcomes relative to what they would otherwise be. In Figure 1.1, this is the distance between the statutory goal (io') and the preinstitutional outcome (po). Some institutions seek to do more than others – raise more taxes, offer greater protection to workers or the environment, more narrowly constrain the executive, or more radically protect private property, for example. Any comparison of the strength of two different institutions must therefore assess not only whether they endure or generate compliance, but also how much work they are doing to generate or prevent change.

We might have adopted a relative, rather than an absolute, concept of institutional strength. In Figure 1.1, this would mean a focus on the proportion of the institutional goal that is achieved ($S/(io' - po)$) rather than S itself. Although such an approach may be appropriate in some cases (e.g., when comparing identical institutions), it rewards institutions with meager levels of ambition. Institutions that propose to do little and achieve the little they propose would appear strong, while institutions that seek to produce or prevent radical transformations and accomplish much, but not all, of their goal would be scored as weaker – despite doing more work. Thus, an institution may still be relatively strong if it is consequential in terms of its goals, despite falling short of full compliance. Most of our analysis holds ambition constant and focuses on compliance with, and stability of, the formal rules. However, we also introduce (below) the concept of "insignificant" institutions to characterize formal rules with zero ambition, in that they do not alter the status quo (po) even when achieving perfect compliance.[12]

---

[12] This does not mean, of course, that the level of noncompliance (io'-io) is irrelevant. Even an institution that generates significant effects in the direction of its formal goals might pay an important price if compliance is low. The institution may lose legitimacy, and the consequent public cynicism may undermine support for the institution, leading to instability. Scholars have made this argument, for example, with respect to the inclusion of social rights in Latin American constitutions. Although by some measures these institutions have had important effects (Gauri and Brinks 2008; Brinks and Gauri 2014), their uneven application has gener-ated strong critiques (Mota Ferraz 2010; Langford et al. 2011).

Social Norms and Institutional Strength

This volume focuses on formal institutions. As noted above, however, formal rules always coexist with unwritten social norms and other informal institutions, and their effectiveness and stability may be powerfully affected by their interaction with those norms (North 1990; Helmke and Levitsky 2004; Levitsky and Ziblatt 2018). Social norms shape individual incentives to comply with laws or report violations, which, in turn, shape the behavioral effects of regulations (Acemoglu and Jackson 2017). Take dueling in the antebellum United States. Although antidueling laws "were on the books in all states" (Wells 2001: 1807), compliance with these laws varied by region: whereas dueling disappeared in northern states in the early nineteenth century, it remained widespread in the South. This variation has been attributed to differences in underlying social norms. In the North, public acceptance of dueling evaporated in the wake of the 1804 Hamilton–Burr affair, but in the South, strong social norms – which treated duels as "affairs of honor" – induced citizens and state officials to ignore the law (Wells 2001: 1818–1825). Thus, even though every southern state had adopted antidueling legislation by the 1820s, charges were rarely brought against duelists, and when they were, "[s]outhern judges and juries…were unwilling to enforce" the law (Wells 2001: 1830–1833). As Harwell Wells put it, enforcement "relied too heavily on men deeply embedded in the very social processes the laws sought to overturn" (2001: 1831). Ultimately, it was the Civil War – which weakened the social norms that sustained dueling – that led to the disappearance of dueling (and the enforcement of antidueling laws) in the South (Wells 2001: 1838–1840).

Understanding the strength of formal institutions thus requires attention to the normative bases of those institutions. This task is simplest in the case of transformative institutions that seek to move outcomes away from a status quo that is congruent with social norms – we can, for example, track movement toward the institutional goal over time. But norms often undergird formal institutions – especially conservative ones – in less discernible ways. For example, many formal institutions generate compliance because they are reinforced by congruent social norms (Levi 1988, 1997; North 1990). As is always the case when two potential independent variables are colinear, this complicates the empirical exercise of inferring institutional strength. In such a case, to be able to attribute causal efficacy to the formal institution rather than the informal norms, we would want to show some nontrivial likelihood that the outcome would be different absent the formal institution, in spite of congruent social norms – in other words, that po is distant from the social norms as well. We might find, for instance, that some powerful political, social, or economic actor would not be constrained by social norms but is constrained by the formal institution. Observers argue that this was the case with presidential term limits in Colombia in 2010. Broad public and political support for Álvaro Uribe's pursuit of a third term suggests that the Constitutional Court's interpretation and enforcement of the constitutional prohibition on a second reelection was determinative (Posada-Carbó 2011).

Many institutions are designed in an effort to bring social norms in line with the institutional goal, effectively making the institution irrelevant over time. This introduces a temporal dimension into the analysis of institutional strength. Perhaps the strongest institutions are those that shape social norms and expectations to the point that they essentially put themselves almost out of business. Seat-belt laws and antilittering laws may have had this effect in some places, creating the possibility that, at least for the short term, the institution could be removed with no consequent change in behavior. Whether those social norms would erode over time without formal institutional reinforcement is an empirical question.

Insignificance

If the strength of an institution is measured by how much difference it makes, then institutions without ambition – where S approaches zero despite full compliance – must be weak. We characterize such institutions as *insignificant*. An institution is insignificant when it simply blesses whatever equilibrium outcome the dominant actors would produce absent the institution. Under conditions of insignificance, everyone complies and the institution is stable, but behavior would be unlikely to change if the institution were taken away. In other words, the institution is superfluous, and plays no actual role in guiding the relevant actors' behavior. In 2014, for example, voters in the US state of Alabama adopted a resolution barring the adoption of foreign laws that were at odds with citizens' existing rights. The primary target was Sharia law, which was not exactly pervasive in Alabama at the time, nor is it likely that a rash of Sharia legislation was imminent and that the law was required to head it off. In short, the absence of Sharia in Alabama can hardly be attributed to the strength of the institution. Thus, although the law may have symbolic value for anti-Muslim constituents, it produces no behavioral effects. A more serious example is Peru's recent ban on mayoral, gubernatorial, and legislative reelection.[13] Given extreme party system fragmentation, electoral volatility, and low public trust, reelection rates were extraordinarily low in Peru during the 2000s (Weaver 2017). In practice, then, a formal prohibition of incumbent reelection produced little change in behavior or outcomes.

Although institutions sometimes drift into insignificance, many are purposely designed so that S is low. The courts Brinks and Blass (2013) call "Potemkin Courts" are designed to either reflect their creators' preferences, or to be unable to effectively express any meaningful disagreement with those

---

[13] Mayoral and gubernatorial reelection was banned via legislation in 2015. Legislative reelection was banned via referendum in 2018.

preferences. The executive may be able to appoint justices at will and remove them equally at will; or the court may need such a large super-majority to invalidate a statute or challenge an executive action that any one or two allies on the court can prevent a judicial challenge from succeeding. When this occurs, the court can be seen to be acting exactly as the law provides, without any extra-legal interference, but it will never function as a serious constraint on the other branches. In Peru, for example, President Alberto Fujimori sponsored a reform that ostensibly aimed to strengthen the courts. The 1993 constitution created a constitutional tribunal (TC) with attributes that would have made it a strong institutional check on power. But the legislature also passed a law specifying that the votes of six of seven justices – who were selected by the legislature – were required to strike down a law. In practice, then, any two of these seven justices could veto a judicial ruling, making it very unlikely that any measure the legislative majority truly cared about would be declared unconstitutional. With or without the TC, and without violating the formal rules of the TC, the Fujimori government's behavior would be essentially the same.

Some "prior consultation" laws in Latin America may also be characterized as insignificant. Most Latin American states adopted prior consultation laws in the 1990s and early 2000s under external and domestic pressure to implement ILO Convention 169, which calls for mechanisms to consult local indigenous communities prior to the initiation of natural resource extraction projects. In principle, such laws should give local indigenous communities meaningful influence over whether or not such projects go forward, and it is clear that some communities would prefer not to see extractive projects proceed in their territory (Hale 2005; Rodríguez Garavito 2011b). In practice, however, prior consultation laws in Mexico, Peru, and elsewhere included no provision that might allow "consulted" indigenous communities to actually stop the projects (Torres Wong 2018b: 254). As a result, the outcome of prior consultation in these countries is always the same: the projects go forward, albeit sometimes after negotiating some payment to the affected community.[14] This has led some observers to conclude that prior consultation laws are, in effect, insignificant. According to Torres Wong, for example, prior consultation laws "[do] not deter the advancement of extractive industries," even when they are fully complied with (2018b: 246, 256–257).

The actual operation of prior consultation schemes in Latin America appears to run the gamut from insignificant to strong, thus usefully illustrating how institutional ambition can relate to institutional strength. When prior consultation institutions are insignificant, companies and governments go through meaningless pro forma exercises in consultation on projects that have been decided in advance. Full compliance leads to no discernible change in the outcomes for firms, the government, or the affected communities. In fact,

---

[14] According to Torres Wong, "all 66 prior consultation procedures conducted in Bolivia, Mexico, and Peru over hydrocarbon and mining projects resulted in indigenous approval" (2018b: 247).

by channeling conflict into empty, powerless forums and demobilizing communities, an ostensibly transformative institution can become a conservative one, making it easier to continue long-standing practices of simply extracting at will from indigenous territories and protecting governments and firms from less institutionalized forms of protest (Rodríguez Garavito 2011b: 298–301).[15] In a sense, such institutions produce a negative S, by disempowering their purported beneficiaries. In other cases, prior consultation schemes generate substantial side payments to affected communities, even when they do not give indigenous communities a meaningful say over whether and how an extractive project will go forward. Here the institution is weak but nevertheless does something positive for the intended beneficiaries, placing it at the midrange for strength. At the other end of the continuum lies the doctrine of prior consent developed by the Constitutional Court in Colombia, under which some communities have secured the right to veto certain projects. This occurred, for example, in the case of the expansion of a dam in Embera territory (Rodríguez Garavito 2011b: 297; also Thompson 2016: 91; Brinks 2019: 361).

Institutions that are originally insignificant may, of course, take on significance if changed circumstances increase S. Such a transformation would, in effect, mirror the process of institutional conversion described by Streeck and Thelen (2005) and Mahoney and Thelen (2010). Yet, unless circumstances happen to move *po* far from its original location, it will often require formal institutional change to make an insignificant institution substantive in terms of its behavioral effects. Falleti (this volume) argues this is exactly what happened with prior consultation on hydrocarbon projects in Bolivia.

It is difficult to know in advance whether an institution designed to be insignificant will endure and be enforced should the day come when actors begin to violate its terms. As Mark Twain once wrote, "the weakest of all weak things is a virtue which has not been tested in the fire."[16] Because the behavior in question is overdetermined, the strength of an insignificant institution is unobservable until circumstances change so that key actors are confronted with a larger S – what if, for instance, Peru's legislature had suddenly changed hands (causing *po* to shift) and found itself at odds with a constitutional tribunal appointed by the previous congress? Such changes often result in pressure for institutional reform. Argentina's long-established (and long-insignificant) constitutional requirement that presidents be Catholic was eliminated once the non-Catholic population increased and became politically relevant.[17]

---

[15] Critics have made similar arguments about the ultimately disempowering effect of a range of indigenous rights, at least as currently practiced (Hale 2005).

[16] Twain (1905[1899]) puts these words in the mouth of the stranger in "The Man That Corrupted Hadleyburg," a short story that first appeared in *Harper's Monthly* in December of 1899.

[17] The reform was undertaken during the administration of President Carlos Menem, who had converted from Islam to Catholicism in order to further his political ambition. See www.britannica.com/biography/Carlos-Menem.

Similarly, originally strong institutions can become insignificant over time by shaping preferences to match the institutional goal.[18] The strongest institutions are those that establish new societal norms and achieve compliance by modifying actors' preferences over time. When a rule is so effective that actors internalize it as a norm and compliance becomes taken for granted, its active enforcement may no longer be necessary to achieve behavioral change. In such cases, the formal institution no longer does much work, although this is hardly a sign that the institution was always weak. Rather, the rules have generated a normative change in society that has resulted in essentially voluntary compliance.[19] Here, the evaluation of weakness is a time-bounded one: we might say, then, that the institution was strong enough to produce the outcome and an associated normative change, to the point where it has become insignificant. In this case, however, the original institution was ambitious and designed to produce significant change. Its own success, rather than a strategic calculation of rule makers, made it insignificant.

TYPES OF INSTITUTIONAL WEAKNESS

Institutions that are significant on paper – that is, their statutory goals are ambitious, such that $io'-po > o$ – may nevertheless fail in distinct ways to achieve those goals. Take, for example, a constitutional amendment that limits presidents to one term. If, before the rule, many presidents enjoyed multiple terms in office and after the rule none do (and ceteris is reasonably paribus), we can be fairly confident that the institution is strong. There is a great distance between the expected outcome absent the institution, as evidenced by historical events, and the one with the institution. An institution is weak, by contrast, when S approaches zero because the rule is ignored. Following the same example, consider Latin American presidents (e.g., Daniel Ortega, Juan Orlando Hernández, Evo Morales) who overstay their term in office despite preexisting constitutional prohibitions. This is one type of weakness, which we will call *noncompliance*. Here there is no S: the preinstitutional outcome continues to obtain, despite the existence and persistence of the rule.

Now consider presidents constrained by term limits who enact a constitutional amendment permitting one or more reelections. When the rules change to suit the preferences of every new actor that comes along, we have another type of weakness – instability. Take for instance, the case of Ecuador, where the 2008 constitution – pushed by President Rafael Correa – replaced a ban on reelection with a two-term limit. Correa was reelected in 2009 and 2013. Facing the end of his final term, Correa orchestrated a 2015 referendum that ended term limits for all officials beginning in 2021 – a move that would allow him to run again in 2021.

---

[18] Alternatively, an institution may "drift" into "insignificance" by not adapting to the context, so that what was originally a demanding standard no longer has any bite (Hacker 2005; Streeck and Thelen 2005).

[19] We thank María Paula Saffon and Alisha Holland for bringing this point to our attention.

However, his successor – seeking to prevent Correa's return to power – organized another referendum that reestablished term limits. Similarly, the Dominican Republic shifted from indefinite reelection to a ban on immediate reelection in 1994 to a two-term limit in 2002, back to a ban on immediate reelection in 2009, and then back to a two-term limit in 2015. In cases like these, the rules sequentially change to match the preferences of successive rule makers. Rather than forcing preferences to accommodate to the institutional outcome, the institution changes to ensure that the outcome matches the preferences of those who were meant to be constrained. In these cases, S disappears through rule changes that lead the institution to match the "preinstitutional" preferences of the key actors.

These two types of institutional weakness – noncompliance and instability – reduce the effective value of S, even for ambitious institutions. Insignificant institutions, by contrast, have a near-zero S despite high levels of compliance and stability. The distinction among these types of weakness is important because, although in each of them S approximates zero, the politics that produce each outcome are very different. In the section that follows, we discuss institutions that are significant on paper but are nevertheless weak in practice due to either noncompliance or instability.

Noncompliance

Noncompliance occurs when S should be greater than zero given the rules established by the parchment institutions, but relevant actors are able to disregard the institution rather than either comply with or seek to replace it, effectively reducing S to zero. Noncompliance may be rooted in failures at two broad levels: (1) state officials' decision not to enforce the rules; and (2) state officials' incapacity to enforce or elicit societal cooperation with the rules.

STATE NONENFORCEMENT

We often assume that state officials seek to enforce the law. Frequently, however, noncompliance occurs because state actors choose not to enforce the rules. In these cases, the institution is formally designed to make a difference – it prescribes costly changes in behavior, and the penalties for noncompliance, if applied, are significant – but the relevant state actors simply fail to enforce the rules. An example is what Levitsky and Murillo (2009, 2014) call *window dressing institutions*, or institutions whose rules state actors create without any intention of enforcing. Take environmental laws in Brazil. Brazilian governments adopted an array of environmental regulations in the 1980s that, on paper, provided Brazil with "unusually strong foundations for environmental law" (Hochstetler and Keck 2007: 51). Through the early 1990s, however, many environmental regulations were not enforced, leading scholars to describe them as "simply a smokescreen for a general abdication of environmental governance" (Hochstetler and Keck 2007: 37). Another example is utility regulation.

When cash-strapped Latin American governments privatized public utilities during the 1990s, most of them created nominally independent regulatory agencies in order to enhance investors' confidence (Levi-Faur and Jordana 2005). In practice, however, most of these agencies lacked authority and routinely failed to enforce their by-laws (Murillo 2009; Post 2014).

In other cases, executives or legislatures adopt rules with the intention of producing real change, but the bureaucrats or local governments charged with actual enforcement refuse to carry these rules out. The result is what Alisha Holland (2017, this volume) calls *forbearance*. As Holland (2017) shows in her study of squatters and street vendors in Chile, Colombia, and Peru, local politicians and bureaucrats with low-income constituencies often deem the human and political costs of enforcing the law to be prohibitively high.

State officials may also engage in *selective* enforcement, applying the law to certain individuals or groups but not others. The bases for selective enforcement vary, ranging from personal ties to partisanship, class, ethnicity, and region. In the post-Reconstruction-era US South, for example, literacy tests and other suffrage restrictions were enforced rigorously on African American voters but not poor white voters (Keyssar 2000). For decades in Latin America, anticorruption laws tended to snare government rivals or former government officials rather than those currently in office. And Mexico's 1856 Lerdo Law, which ordered the breakup of all landholdings held by corporate entities in the name of individual property rights, was applied forcefully to Church lands but less rigorously to communally held indigenous lands (Saffón and González Bertomeu, this volume). Liberal governments used the law to harass the Church, a political adversary, but ignored it when it came to indigenous communities that were potential allies.

Noncompliance is not always rooted in a lack of enforcement. Some institutions establish what are, in effect, nonpunitive sanctions for violating what is otherwise a meaningful behavioral restriction. In these cases, state actors dutifully impose sanctions for noncompliance, but these sanctions (e.g., a minuscule fine) are so low relative to S as to be a meaningless incentive for actors to change their behavior. In effect, the formal rules ensure that the cost of complying significantly exceeds the trivial punishment for noncompliance. For instance, France's 2000 "parity law" required that parties field an equal number of male and female candidates. Parties that failed to comply with the new quotas were forced to pay a moderate-sized fine – one that the larger and wealthier parties were able and willing to pay (Murray 2007: 575). As one conservative party leader put it, "We prefer to pay fines than lose elections!" (quoted in Murray 2007: 571). Female quotas in El Salvador, Honduras, and Panama were similarly designed so that parties might simply pay fines and run male candidates.[20] Likewise, as Fernández Milmanda and

---

[20] See, e.g., Mariana Caminotti's discussion of the difficulties of increasing the political representation of women in Latin America, at https://reformaspoliticas.org/reformas/genero-y-politica/mariana-caminotti/.

Garay (this volume) note, some Argentine provincial governments use non-punitive fines as a means of enforcing antideforestation regulations without triggering resistance from big landowners. For all intents and purposes, then, S disappears in these cases, because actors behave as if the institution did not exist (except that they pay a trivial penalty). In such a situation, even if enforcement – in the sense of applying sanctions for violations – is 100 percent, the relevant outcome is similar with or without the rule.

State (In)capacity and Societal Resistance

A different sort of compliance failure occurs when governments possess the will to enforce but lack the capacity to do so. This is partly a question of the state's infrastructural power (Mann 1984; Soifer 2015). Some states lack the fiscal and administrative capacity to enforce certain laws – particularly ones that seek large-scale behavioral change and require extensive monitoring. For example, governments may not enforce labor, immigration, or environmental laws because the state lacks a sufficient number of trained inspectors, or because, due to low public-sector salaries or lack of equipment, orders to enforce are simply not carried out on the ground. In some cases, states simply lack the capacity to uphold the entire framework of the rule of law (O'Donnell 1993, 1999b). As Yashar (2018) shows, for example, the spread of illicit organizations and rising homicide rates in much of contemporary Latin America can be explained, in part, by the sheer weakness of state (i.e., police) monitoring capacities.

Long-run state enforcement capacities are shaped by political choices. As the chapters by Schrank and by Amengual and Dargent in this volume show, levels of enforcement capacity at time *t* reflect investments in capacity made at *t* minus x. However, because the development of state capacity takes time (Kurtz 2013; Soifer 2015), and because investments in state capacity may be matched by the growing strength of state challengers (Migdal 1988; Dargent, Feldmann, and Luna 2017), it is reasonable to suggest that in some instances, governments possess the will to enforce certain rules but simply lack the infrastructural wherewithal to do so.

We exclude from our analysis failed states that lack even minimal enforcement capacity, focusing on those with at least some infrastructural power but that nevertheless lack the capacity to systematically uphold the law in some areas. These are what Amengual and Dargent (this volume), following Slater and Kim (2015), describe as "standoffish" states – states that can and do enforce some of the rules some of the time but lack the resources to enforce all the rules all of the time. Enforcement is thus *intermittent*, in that it does not follow an identifiable pattern, or *selective*, in that resource-constrained states target some individuals or groups more than others. As O'Donnell (1993) noted in his classic discussion of "brown areas," selective enforcement sometimes follows a territorial logic, with states enforcing the law at a higher rate in the metropolitan centers than in the hinterlands (see also Herbst 2000; Soifer 2015). Alternatively, it may follow a class-based logic, in which the wealthier and better-connected members of society evade the reach of a standoffish state, leaving the poor more vulnerable (Méndez , O'Donnell, and Pinheiro 1999; Brinks 2008).[21]

In their analysis of regulatory enforcement in Argentina, Bolivia, and Peru, Amengual and Dargent (this volume) illustrate how enforcement outcomes can vary in standoffish states. In Lima's construction industry, where the local construction chamber actively supported enforcement, government officials cracked down on illegal activities. In Bolivia's gold mining sector, where cooperative miners were political allies of the governing Movement for Socialism (MAS), state officials looked the other way. In the Argentine province of Córdoba, state officials applied labor safety regulations in the construction industry, where union pressure was strong, but ignored flagrant violations in brickmaking, where workers were politically and organizationally weak.

As the above examples suggest, compliance depends crucially on the degree of societal cooperation or resistance. Societal responses to institutions vary widely, from active cooperation where rules align with social norms and underlying power distributions (e.g., property rights laws in the United States) to outright resistance where the rules contradict dominant social norms (e.g., antidueling laws in the antebellum US South) or are opposed by powerful societal actors (e.g., voting rights in the post–Reconstruction US South). The level of state enforcement effort required to produce compliance will, therefore, be a function of the degree of societal cooperation or resistance. Since enforcement is a costly endeavor for resource-constrained states (Amengual 2016), governments can be expected to tailor enforcement to the degree of expected resistance. Faced with sufficient resistance, officials may look the other way rather than enforce the law (Amengual and Dargent, this volume). As Hochstetler and Keck show, for example, Brazilian anti-deforestation law is "ample and often well formulated," and the Brazilian state possesses the capacity to enforce it (2007: 51, 151). Because enforcement requires confronting a powerful network of corrupt politicians and criminal organizations, however, governments often exhibit a "lack of desire to expend the necessary political capital and resources to enforce the law" (2007: 151–154). When governments find societal partners that seek and even cooperate with enforcement, states are more likely to enforce and will secure similar results with lower effort (Amengual 2016; Amengual and Dargent, this volume).

The state's enforcement capacity is thus relational.[22] On the one hand, the cost of enforcement can be reduced considerably when, due to the alignment

---

[21] The distinction between this and the politically motivated selective enforcement described earlier is not always clear cut. In principle, selectivity in these cases is simply a product of prioritizing resources. In practice, however, a degree of political calculus – state officials' desire to reward supporters, punish rivals, or avoid costly social resistance – invariably weighs in.

[22] See Migdal (1988); Amengual (2016); Dargent, Feldmann, and Luna (2017).

of underlying norms or interests with the institutional mandate, societal actors cooperate in ensuring compliance – a phenomenon that is sometimes called enforcement "coproduction."[23] Where social norms reinforce the rules, "quasi-voluntary" compliance reduces the need for a heavy investment in state enforcement (save occasionally punishing deviant behavior) (Levi 1988: 72–70, 1997: 19–25);[24] indeed, compliance may be high even where state infrastructural power is limited.

On the other hand, when formal rules run up against competing social norms or resistance from powerful interests, compliance requires greater enforcement effort. Strong competing norms – sometimes enforced by nonstate actors such as traditional authorities or religious communities – may inhibit societal cooperation with enforcement (for instance, in reporting of noncompliance) and even create incentives for outright noncompliance (Migdal 1988; Helmke and Levitsky 2004; Acemoglu and Jackson 2017). Where state infra-structural power is limited, the result is almost invariably low compliance. Transformative laws created in pursuit of far-reaching behavioral change will, in such cases, be limited to "aspirational" status (Htun and Jensenius, this volume). Sometimes societal resistance is so pervasive that it can overcome almost any enforcement effort, resulting in low compliance despite high state capacity. A classic example is Prohibition in the United States, where a strong state and a substantial investment in enforcement still failed to eliminate the production and consumption of alcohol. Strong institutions, then, are those that produce actual compliance with a demanding standard of behavior. The level of state enforcement effort required to produce that compliance will depend on the degree of societal resistance or cooperation.

In sum, noncompliance is a product of the interplay between state enforcement efforts from above and societal responses from below. If institutions do not change behavior because the relevant state agencies will not or cannot act to compel individuals or firms to follow parchment rules, then S is small with the state's complicity. But compliance may be low even where state will and capacity is high. The state may invest considerable resources into enforcing a particular institution, but if societal actors still find ways to continue their proscribed behavior, then the rule is clearly not producing its intended effect. Strong institutions, then, produce compliance with a demanding standard of behavior when there exists the will and capacity to enforce from above *and* they achieve compliance from below.

---

[23] We take this term from Amengual (2016). Our usage is similar to Levi's concept of quasi-voluntary compliance, in which convergent social norms reduce the cost of monitoring and enforcement, thereby allowing state agents to focus on deviant cases. See also Ostrom (1996) and Sabet (2014).

[24] The model developed by Acemoglu and Jackson (2017) suggests that social norms explain coproduction of legal enforcement by shaping incentives to monitor and report deviant behavior.

Instability

Most variants of institutionalism take a minimum of stability for granted, either because institutions reflect an equilibrium outcome or because they generate positive feedback effects. Indeed, nearly all of our theoretical expectations regarding their effects hinge on the assumption that institutions are minimally stable – that they do not change at each round of the game. And many institutions are designed not so much to produce change as to protect the status quo and extend the preferences of powerful actors into an uncertain future. Institutions can therefore most clearly be seen to "matter" – in the sense of constraining and enabling political actors – when they endure beyond the spell in office of those who create them. Otherwise they may be easily dismissed as epiphenomenal. Institutions must, moreover, endure for some time if political actors are to develop the shared expectations and consistent strategies that institutionalist theories lead us to expect.

As Levitsky and Murillo (2009, 2014) have argued, however, institutions vary widely in their "stickiness." In Latin America, one observes instances of extreme institutional instability, or "serial replacement," in which political and economic rules of the game are rewritten after virtually every change in government (Levitsky and Murillo 2014). For example, Bolivia, Ecuador, and the Dominican Republic have changed constitutions at an average rate of more than once a decade in the nearly two centuries since independence (Elkins, Ginsburg, and Melton 2009). Latin American electoral systems are also subject to serial replacement; the rate of change in much of the region is considerably higher than in advanced democracies (Remmer 2008; Calvo and Negretto, this volume). Venezuela employed thirteen different electoral laws between 1958 and 1998 (Crisp and Rey 2001: 176). Ecuador underwent fourteen major electoral reforms between 1980 and 2015 – nearly two major reforms per elected president (Calvo and Negretto, this volume). This pattern is not limited to the federal level. Argentina's twenty-four provinces undertook thirty-four electoral reforms between 1983 and 2003 (Calvo and Micozzi 2005). Institutional stability, then, cannot be taken for granted. Rather, it should be treated as a variable – and another dimension of institutional strength.

We define institutional instability as an excessively high rate of institutional change that leaves political actors unable to develop stable expectations about how the rules work or clear strategies to pursue their interests through them. It seems obvious that institutions that change with every shift in the political winds cannot be called strong. The kind of instability that should be associated with institutional weakness is, however, harder to identify than noncompliance. The problem here is distinguishing instability – an *excessively* high rate of institutional change – from "normal" institutional reform. Sometimes change simply reflects the persistence of the original goals, which requires adaptation to new conditions, such as raising the minimum wage to match inflation. Or the aggregate institutional cost might eventually be revealed to be intolerably high, so that the healthy political response would be to amend or replace the institution. Here, institutions are adapting to new information about environmental conditions. Alternatively, environmental conditions and societal power and preference distributions may change, generating pressure for reform in even the most institutionally stable environments. Few observers would consider suffrage extension, the design of civil service laws, or the adoption of laws legalizing gay marriage in established democracies to be signs of institutional weakness. Rather than institutional instability, these are better thought of as cases of adaptation to changing societal preferences.

Nor is an institution's persistence always a sign of its strength. If S is decreasing over time – say, because inflation is eating away at the minimum wage, as it does in the United States – formal stability could mask a growing weakness. Scholars have labeled this process of institutional change "drift" (Hacker 2005; Streeck and Thelen 2005). For an institution to remain strong in such a context, it must be able to adapt – to undertake reforms that preserve S in the face of changes that threaten the institutional goal. If it maintains S within acceptable and meaningful levels, adaptation may well be a sign of strength. Keeping S as the conceptual touchstone for institutional weakness helps us distinguish adaptation from instability.

Distinguishing between instability and adaptation poses an empirical challenge. The point at which change becomes excessive is frequently a context- and institution-dependent (perhaps even a normatively informed) judgment, which makes comparative analysis difficult. In many cases, measurement will require some kind of counterfactual exercise or the use of comparative benchmarks based on historical rates of institutional change within the country or average rates of change in other countries.

In most contexts, widespread institutional instability is costly, for it narrows time horizons and undermines cooperation in ways that hinder governance and leave democracies vulnerable to abuse, crisis, or both.[25] Yet democracies also contain "bad" institutions whose persistence produces harmful effects for important parts of society. Those who are concerned with some of the negative aspects of the United States' electoral system – such as the Electoral College, gerrymandered districts, and the many impediments to registration and suffrage – are understandably frustrated by that country's institutional stability. In some cases, durable institutions also create problems in Latin America. As Albertus and Menaldo (2018) show, many Latin American constitutions maintain key authoritarian features, some of which have proven difficult to replace. Rather than take a normative position with respect to institutional instability, then, we simply seek to identify it and understand how it affects actors' expectations.

Table 1.1 summarizes the types of weaknesses we have identified here:

---

[25] See Levitsky and Murillo (2005) and Spiller and Tommasi (2007). For instance, political instability has been associated with lower economic growth (Aisen and Veiga 2013), especially in developing countries (Berggren et al. 2009), as well as with lower investment in infrastructure (Henisz 2002).

TABLE 1.1. *Types of institutional weakness*

Type		Description	Examples
Insignificance		Institution has zero ambition, in that it does not prescribe a meaningful change in actors' behavior even when fully enforced and complied with.	*Symbolic institutions*: designed to please an audience but without behavioral effects; for example, "Potemkin courts" (Brinks and Blass 2013).
Noncompliance	Type I: Nonenforcement	Institution prescribes significant behavioral change, but state officials choose not to enforce it systematically.	*Window dressing institutions*: created without intent to fully enforce (Levitsky and Murillo 2009); for example, early prior consultation laws (Falleti, this volume). *Forbearance*: strategic neglect of enforcement, usually driven by political incentives; e.g., street vending restrictions (Holland 2017, this volume). *Selective enforcement*: state officials vary in enforcement effort across territory ("brown areas," O'Donnell 1993) or across different societal groups (literacy tests in the American South, Keyssar 2000).
	Type II: Nonpunitive enforcement	Rule is enforced and sanctions are applied, but the sanctions are too weak to change behavior.	*Unsanctioned institutions*: strategically designed to be enforced without effect due to trivial penalties; e.g., some antideforestation laws in the Argentine Chaco (Fernández Milmanda and Garay, this volume).
	Type III: Weak state capacity relative to societal resistance	Government officials seek compliance with the institution but lack sufficient state capacity or societal cooperation to systematically enforce it.	*Standoffish states and intermittent enforcement*: follow path of least societal resistance (Slater and Kim 2015); e.g., labor regulations (Amengual and Dargent, this volume). *Aspirational laws*: created with expectation of low societal compliance but with goal of long-term change in social norms; gender equity laws (Htun and Jensenius, this volume).
Instability		Rules change at an unusually high rate and in contradictory directions, preventing actors from developing stable expectations around them.	*Serial replacement*: rules and procedures are replaced wholesale, without ever becoming entrenched or settling into a stable equilibrium (Levitsky and Murillo 2014); e.g., electoral laws (Calvo and Negretto, this volume).

Judicial Interpretation as a Source
of Noncompliance and Instability

In closing this section, it is worth highlighting one more – often hidden – form of both noncompliance and instability: judicial (re)interpretation. The judicial power of interpretation is often viewed as a source of institutional strength. Elkins, Ginsburg, and Melton (2009), for example, find that, all other things being equal, including a constitutional court with the power of authoritative interpretation considerably extends the life of a constitution. Authoritative interpretation in response to unexpected contingencies and arising exigencies can add needed flexibility to an institutional framework. At the same time, however, judicial interpretations may merely provide "legal" cover and legitimacy for what is clearly a rule violation, or may be manipulated to produce frequent changes in response to changing preferences. Indeed, in contemporary Latin America, powerful actors increasingly use courts to legitimize noncompliance or instability. This is an important phenomenon, but because judicial interpretation is simply an alternative means of generating rule changes (i.e., instability) or noncompliance, we do not treat it as a separate category of institutional weakness.

We have seen weakness through judicial interpretation feature prominently in presidential efforts to circumvent constitutional term limits. Under Alberto Fujimori, for instance, Peru's Congress passed an "authentic interpretation" of the two-term limit imposed by the 1993 constitution, allowing Fujimori to seek a third term in 2000 on the grounds that his first term began under the old constitution. Although most legal experts deemed that interpretation to be in blatant violation of the "true" meaning of the constitution, the Constitutional Tribunal – a Potemkin court – upheld it. Peru is not alone in this respect. In other cases, supreme courts (Nicaragua and Honduras) or constitutional tribunals (Bolivia) enabled efforts by powerful presidents to circumvent constitutional term limits via dubious rulings that interpreted term limits as a violation of a "higher" constitutional right to run for office. In these cases, then, judicial interpretations of the law by friendly (if not subordinate) courts allowed presidents to circumvent the law.

Whether interpretive claims by the courts are merely cover for noncompliance and instability on the one hand, or instances of legitimate adaptability and flexibility on the other, can, of course, be difficult to determine. As in the case of the impeachments examined by Helmke (2017, this volume), it is not always clear whether the use of a norm or interpretation to justify behavior is pretextual or legitimate. Nevertheless, we can identify some reliable indicators of weakness. These include (1) frequent flip-flops on the part of the court on the meaning of a provision, especially if they are clearly aligned with partisan sympathies; (2) a broad-based consensus on the part of disinterested legal or other experts that the interpretation lacks technical merit; (3) an all-too-evident pattern of interpretations that respond to the interests of powerful actors; and (4) interpretations that do not outlive the tenures of the judges who produce them. Some cases will be more obvious than others, but in each case, it will be the researcher's task to persuade the audience that a court is complicit in the production of institutional weakness.

This section proposes some initial hypotheses to account for the different types of institutional weakness we have identified. In our characterization of institutional strength, S is the cost of the institution to the actors who prefer what we call the preinstitutional outcome (*po*, in Figure 1.1) – that is, the outcome absent the institution, or under a different preferred institutional arrangement. Although we have alluded to other factors – such as voluntary compliance rooted in social norms – in generating institutional strength, our theory is, at its core, a coalitional one, in that it centers on political support for the institution and its enforcement. For the sake of simplicity, we assume that for every institution there exists one coalition of actors that supports it and another coalition of actors that opposes it and prefers an alternative outcome. Actors who oppose a particular institution have three options: (1) comply at cost S, (2) avoid compliance and face the cost of a violation (V),[26] or (3) change the institution at cost C to achieve a new S.

An institution is strong if the cost for opponents of either changing it (C) or violating it (V) exceeds S, the cost of the institutional outcome. Typically, this will depend on the capacity of institutional supporters to block change *and* produce enforcement. Institutions are weak, on the other hand, when the cost of either changing or violating them is lower than S, the cost of compliance, so that either or both options (2) and (3) are on the table. To explain institutional weakness, we need to understand what factors raise and lower the cost of V and C relative to S and relative to each other. That is, we expect institutions to be stable and regularly complied with when the cost of changing the institution (C) is higher than the cost imposed by the institution (S) or the cost of a violation (V). Conversely, noncompliance should be high when the cost of violating (V) is lower than the cost imposed by the institution (S) or the cost of replacing it (C). Instability should be high when replacing the rule (C) is cheaper than accepting its cost (S) or the cost of sanctions for violating it (V). To identify the source of institutional weakness, then, we should examine the conditions that shape the value of complying with a particular institution (S), vis-à-vis either changing it (C) or violating it (V).

Sources of (Non)compliance

One important dimension of institutional weakness is noncompliance: institutions set out ambitious goals but fail to make a difference because actors do not comply with them. As a result, an S that is large on paper (what we have

---

[26] V is, of course, a function of both the magnitude of the penalty for a violation and the probability of facing the sanction.

denoted as *io'-po*) may be dramatically reduced in practice (to a much smaller *io-po*). We argued above that institutional compliance might be limited by a lack of meaningful enforcement effort or lack of enforcement capacity relative to societal resistance. Here we briefly examine the political origins of these failures.

Weakness by Design: The Role of Audience Value

Some institutions are weak because state officials lack an interest in enforcing them. Why would politicians incur the cost (in terms of time and political capital) of designing institutions that generate no real-world effects? An answer lies in the potential audience value generated by institutional reforms. International norm diffusion, reinforced by the growth of powerful transnational advocacy networks (Keck and Sikkink 1998), and the promotion of institutional reform agendas by international organizations such as the World Bank, International Monetary Fund, and the United Nations, led many lower- and middle-income governments to perceive a high return on certain institutional reforms (Dobbins, Simmons, and Garrett 2007; Henisz, Zelner, and Guillen 2005). Governments often claim credit with international audiences for a substantive achievement when they have done nothing more than create window dressing institutions – i.e., institutions they have no intention of enforcing. Thus, the audience value, in terms of international prestige, external support, or sustaining the good will of religious establishments and other cultural elites, outweighs the cost of institutional design, turning C into a net benefit rather than a cost.

In short, window dressing institutions are created by governments seeking to secure the legitimacy gains of adopting an institutional reform without incurring more than a trivial S, the cost of compliance. In this scenario, rule writers do not seek to depart from the preinstitutional outcome, but nevertheless derive some benefit from the mere act of institutional creation. When audience value turns C into a net benefit, governments that prefer the status quo have an incentive to design rules in the expectation that they will lie dormant.[27] This is easiest when the primary audience – members of the international community, for example – lacks the monitoring capacity to reliably observe violations.

During the 1990s and early 2000s, for example, many Latin American governments responded to international pressure by adopting anticorruption laws or statutes to protect human rights, women's rights, or indigenous rights. In some of these cases, the costs of actual compliance would have been quite high – either for governments themselves (e.g., anticorruption laws) or for powerful private actors (e.g., environmental regulation). In reality, however, designers often had no intention of incurring the cost of enforcing or complying with

---

[27] Designers may, of course, be surprised later on, when these institutions are activated and begin to produce important effects. Indeed, as we will see below in the discussion of aspirational rules, this may be the intended strategy of proponents of the institutional goal.

them. An example is the prior consultation systems adopted following passage of ILO Convention 169. Fifteen Latin American governments adopted prior consultation laws during the 1990s (Falleti and Riofrancos 2018: 89), but at least initially, most of them were dormant. As Falleti (this volume) observes, Bolivia's first (1991) prior consultation law was "designed not to be complied with or enforced." Likewise, antidueling laws in the US South were often "sops to vocal minorities" (Wells 2001: 1827). For example, South Carolina passed its 1812 antidueling law in response to a public campaign by evangelical leader Philip Moser, even though the state's political elite "never intended it to be enforced" (Wells 2001: 1827).

Not all predictably weak institutions are the product of a cynical political exercise. Occasionally, political actors design rules that are unlikely to be complied with today in the hope that they will be complied with in the future. Rule writers may understand (or fear) that in the near term, institutional opponents will be able to avoid enforcement, perhaps because the institution competes with existing social norms or informal institutions. In these cases, the contemplated S may be substantial, but the cost of violation in the near term is limited by some combination of low enforcement capacity and limited societal coproduction. In effect, champions of the institutions bet on the future, hoping that changing conditions will permit increased enforcement, or "activation," of the rules in some future round. These are what Htun and Jensenius (this volume) call "aspirational" laws. Examples include many of the social rights included in recent Latin American constitutions and, as Htun and Jensenius show, laws against domestic violence in Mexico. According to Htun and Jensenius, aspirational laws are passed in full knowledge that they will not change behavior in the short term but nevertheless seek to establish "goal posts, stakes in future developments, and guides to the process of social change."

Aspirational laws may be activated – made effective through enforcement, rather than formal institutional change – when the coalition supporting the institution strengthens, such that it either gains control of enforcement or exerts greater influence over those who control it. Take the activation of individual property rights in Mexico, the subject of the chapter by Saffón and González Bertomeu (this volume). Mexico's Lerdo Law, which was passed under Benito Juarez's liberal government, was initially ignored by the courts, which deferred to long-established norms protecting collective property rights. This changed during the late nineteenth-century export boom, which increased the value of commercial land. As the distribution of power shifted toward agricultural exporters, the courts developed a preference for the once-dormant Juarez-era law. Thus, individual property rights laws that had been only selectively enforced for decades were activated via court rulings during the Porfiriato.

Activation of aspirational laws is frequently a product of social change and the emergence of political movements demanding enforcement. In the United States, for example, the right to vote regardless of race was enshrined in the Fifteenth Amendment to the Constitution in 1870 but was not enforced in much of the country for nearly a century. This constitutional right was not activated until demographic and political changes in the African American community gave rise to a powerful civil rights movement that, acting in tandem with the courts, produced a coalition capable of generating compliance.

As the above examples suggest, institutional activation may be driven, in part, by judicial interpretation. Courts across Latin America have activated previously ignored social rights provisions in their constitutions (Gauri and Brinks 2008; Langford 2009). Colombia is probably the best example of the activation of constitutional rights through judicial interpretation. Colombia's Constitutional Court essentially rewrote that country's civil code to eliminate gender discriminatory provisions in line with prevailing norms of gender equality, first between men and women (Oquendo 2006), but eventually opening a path for the legalization of same-sex marriage (Landau and Cepeda 2017: 232–235).

Implementation Gaps: Disjunctures between Rule Writers and Power Holders

A second source of weak enforcement is a disjuncture between rule writers, on the one hand, and those with the power to affect compliance on the ground, on the other. Whereas scholarship on bureaucracies in advanced democracies draws attention to the phenomenon of bureaucratic shirking when the preferences of rule writers and enforcers do not coincide, the degrees of freedom in this gap are usually constrained by the statutory goals of the parchment rule.[28] In a context of generalized institutional weakness, by contrast, rule writers do not necessarily constrain enforcers, even where parchment laws prescribe such control. The coalition in control of the rule-writing process (legislators, constituent assembly members, technocrats in the executive) may not control key agencies of enforcement, such as local governments, bureaucracies, courts, and the security forces, allowing these latter actors greater degrees of freedom in deciding even whether to enforce or not.

Diverging preferences over design and enforcement can often be especially pronounced in hybrid or transitional regimes in which elected officials do not fully control the state. Take, for example, hybrid regimes in which civilian governments exercise little control over the security forces. Governments may adopt human rights laws that the security forces do not comply with (e.g., Guatemala in the 1980s). Or consider cases in which nominally independent constituent assemblies or legislatures exercise little real power over executives (who, in most instances, control prosecutors, the police, and the armed forces) and thus design laws that they cannot make binding. For example, Mexico's 1917 constitution – drawn up by a relatively independent constitutional convention during the Mexican Revolution – was "one of the most radical of

---

[28] See Huber and Shipan (2002) and Carpenter (2001) for arguments in the rational choice and historical institutionalist traditions, respectively.

its time" (Knight 1986: 470), but the more moderate president Venustiano Carranza, who controlled the revolutionary armed forces, ignored its most radical clauses (Wilkie 1967: 56).

Even in relatively well-functioning democracies, decentralization and fragmented bureaucracies and security forces may hinder enforcement of laws and rules that national governments seek to enforce. Thus, where state capacity is uneven across the national territory (O'Donnell 1993, 1999b), decentralization may weaken some institutions. If enforcement is entrusted to multiple levels of government, each of which has different constituencies, certain institutions may be vulnerable to local-level forbearance – a dynamic that O'Donnell (1993, 1999b) highlighted in his discussion of "brown areas."

Disjunctures between distinct levels of government may also occur when the designers of national-level institutions hold preferences that diverge from those of local officials charged with enforcing them. As Holland (this volume) points out, there is often a greater public appetite for rules that require some desired behavior than for the difficult work and painful choices involved in imposing sanctions for their violation. Whereas the general public may prefer a large S, at least in the abstract, state officials who are closer to the targets of a regulatory scheme may be deterred by the social or political cost of enforcement. Thus, national legislatures may pass broadly popular laws against squatting or street vending, but government officials operating at the site of noncompliance are often reluctant to impose the costs that are required to actually change behavior. Mayors whose constituents would lose their homes or livelihoods if regulations were enforced, or local bureaucrats charged with carrying out orders to enforce, may thus hold preferences over enforcement that diverge markedly from the national officials who design the laws. The result is a "coercion gap," in which laws are written and passed by national officials but not enforced by local ones (Holland, this volume).

Fernández Milmanda and Garay's analysis of deforestation in the Argentine Chaco (this volume) also highlights the role of divergent orientations toward enforcement across levels of government. The 2007 Native Forest Protection Regime was spearheaded by national legislators with an environmentalist bent whose urban constituents stood to lose very little under new laws restricting deforestation in the Chaco region. By contrast, governors from the region had to deal with powerful agricultural producers who had much to lose and were an important part of their constituencies. The governors, who were responsible for enforcing new environmental regulations, faced considerably higher costs of enforcement, and found various ways to reduce the impact of the law on their constituents.

A disjuncture between rule writers and power holders may also emerge in democracies with high socioeconomic inequality. Democracy shifts rule-writing power further down the socioeconomic ladder – the median voter is likely to be well below the mean income – and in cases of extreme inequality, the median income earner is poor. If the burden of a particular institution lands primarily on the rich, wealthy individuals may well possess sufficient resources to lobby against enforcement structures, buy off the enforcers – for example, local mayors and judges – and otherwise prevent full enforcement. For such individuals, the real cost of V is reduced even though the rules on the books are nominally universal (Lieberman 2003; Brinks and Botero 2014). Additionally, inequality usually allows the rich to exert disproportionate influence at the design stage (in the executive branch or the legislature), leaving the poor with few options other than protesting at the site of implementation.

State Capacity and Societal Resistance

Nonenforcement is often attributed to state weakness. Rules are violated because state officials lack the skills and resources necessary to enforce them. But this structuralist view – state capacity as a slow-moving variable rooted in long-term historical processes (Centeno 2002; O'Donnell 1999b; Soifer 2015) – obscures a more complex (and politically interesting) reality. Most Latin American states possess at least a modest capacity to enforce laws. Indeed, even seemingly weak state agencies have at times demonstrated striking enforcement capacity: Mexico's nineteenth-century state was capable of seizing and breaking up Church properties in the name of liberal property rights (Saffón and Gonzáles Bertomeu, this volume); the Dominican state proved capable of enforcing labor regulations (Schrank 2011, this volume); some Latin American mayors cracked down effectively on squatting and street vending (Holland 2017, this volume); and local governments in crime-ridden cites like Santa Tecla, El Salvador; Medellín, Colombia; Ciudad Juárez, Mexico; and Rio de Janeiro, Brazil have at times dramatically reduced violence (WOLA 2011; Moncada 2016). Hence, we view institutional enforcement efforts as driven as much by political choices as by underlying state capacity. Indeed, there is simply too much variation in enforcement in Latin America – within states over time, or across comparably weak states – to ignore the role of political decisions in shaping both short-term enforcement efforts and longer-term efforts to build state capacity.

It takes time to build state capacity (Soifer 2015), and states that fail to do the work of enforcing a certain regulatory framework over time often find it difficult to suddenly generate compliance when the government's preferences change. Yet enforcement capacity can be built – and sometimes quite rapidly. For example, Colombia's Constitutional Court was strong almost immediately after it was established in 1992 (Cepeda Espinoza 2004), defying both Colombia's reputation as a weak state and existing theoretical expectations about the requisite maturation time for new courts (Epstein, Knight and Shvetsova 2001; Carrubba 2009). Likewise, Peruvian technocrats – operating in a notoriously weak state – created effective economic policy-making institutions within the finance ministry under President Alberto Fujimori (Dargent 2015). And as Schrank (this volume) shows, the Dominican government introduced a set of Weberian administrative reforms that quickly gave rise to a more effective labor inspectorate during the 1990s.

But if enforcement is possible in weaker states, it is nevertheless costly. The sheer logistical requirements of monitoring consume vast resources; and enforcement may trigger resistance from powerful actors or electorally consequential constituencies. Where public sector resources and political capital are scarce, then, governments that possess the raw capacity to enforce laws may nevertheless opt for strategic forbearance or the selective use of enforcement, following what is, in effect, a path of least resistance. According to Amengual and Dargent (this volume), the latter strategy is followed by "standoffish states." Standoffish states can – and sometimes do – enforce the law. But because enforcement requires costly investments of scarce resources and political capital, governments are only likely to take action when significant countervailing constituencies mobilize behind it (Amengual 2016; Dargent, Feldmann, and Luna 2017; Amengual and Dargent, this volume). Standoffish behavior is particularly likely in unequal democracies, where the rich (but also, as Holland shows, the poor) possess a range of tools with which to resist enforcement efforts. Sometimes opponents do not bother to mobilize to block the passage of particular laws, counting instead on being able to neutralize it at the time of application.

Standoffish states are widespread in Latin America. The region's unequal democracies frequently give rise to ambitious institutional reforms aimed at regulating the powerful or protecting the vulnerable. These reforms are often designed by a handful of state actors operating without strong societal coalitions. Thus, efforts to generate compliance often confront fierce resistance on the ground. Without societal support, systematic enforcement requires a vast expenditure of human and financial resources, which are hardly abundant in most Latin American states.

Although the state's default strategy is often nonenforcement (Amengual and Dargent, this volume), standoffish states may enforce the law when societal mobilization creates incentives for them to do so. In Bolivia, for example, social mobilization led to unprecedented enforcement of prior consultation laws in the 2000s (Falleti, this volume). Likewise, in Brazil, where extensive environmental regulation had been on the books since the 1960s but was largely unenforced, the mobilization of environmental activist networks led to greater state enforcement efforts in the 1980s and 1990s (Hochstetler and Keck 2007). International actors may strengthen proenforcement coalitions (Keck and Sikkink 1998; Hochstetler and Keck 2007). As Schrank's (this volume) study of Dominican labor inspectors shows, the US government's decision to allow unions and other nongovernmental organizations to petition the US trade representative on behalf of Dominican workers "externalized the costs" of monitoring the country's new labor standards and, by raising the specter of a loss of trade preferences due to noncompliance, created powerful new incentives for the Dominican state to invest in enforcement capacity.

Societal Sources of Compliance

The state's enforcement capacity is thus relational. Some institutions fail to achieve widespread compliance even though governments possess both the will and what appears to be a reasonable capacity to enforce them. These are often institutions that compete with preexisting societal norms and/or are difficult to monitor. Examples include Prohibition laws in the United States, labor and environmental regulations in much of Latin America (Amengual 2016), and laws regulating violence against women in Mexico (Htun and Jensenius, this volume). In such cases, state enforcement requires societal cooperation. Without societal partners to engage in reporting or monitoring on the ground, and thus to "mobilize and push an indifferent bureaucracy to action" (Amengual and Dargent, this volume), compliance may remain low despite state officials' enforcement capacity. An example is the effort to regulate the Santa Clara plant in Rosario, Argentina (Amengual and Dargent, this volume). Rosario's environmental regulations were routinely unenforced during the early twenty-first century, allowing the Santa Clara plant to pollute the local air and water with impunity. However, mobilization by community organizations and their allies in the municipal government generated public pressure on provincial officials to enforce the law. Civic groups such as the Vecinal Santa Teresita worked with provincial regulators to beef up monitoring of Santa Clara. Local activists and city council members formed a committee that reinforced state monitoring efforts and served as a source of pressure on regulators and the firm.

Societal coproduction may yield high levels of compliance even where states are quite weak. In Colombia, for example, the cooperation of local business interests enabled mayors in cities like Bogotá and Medellín to successfully implement participatory policies aimed at reducing criminal violence (Moncada 2016).

Enforcement is often most challenging when institutions seek to change deeply ingrained social norms and behavior patterns. Thus, in their study of laws against domestic violence in Mexico, Htun and Jensenius (this volume) found that the law was resisted not only by its targets – the abusers – but also by its purported beneficiaries. Their analysis of survey results suggests that many women do not report domestic violence because doing so runs counter to existing norms that treat domestic violence as a private, family matter. Others opt not to report out of fear of the potential costs of reporting, including retaliation or even material privation, when the abusers, who often are the family breadwinners, are removed from the home. Thus, both competing social norms and material interests may reinforce the behavior that domestic violence laws seek to proscribe. Such bottom-up resistance on the part of beneficiaries clearly robs the institution of the potential for societal coproduction.

Relatedly, Falleti (this volume) argues that for new institutions to elicit compliance in a context of state weakness, they must gain broad legitimacy, which may be achieved through the political incorporation of the affected groups. When an institution's beneficiaries become an important part of the political ecosystem – through direct participation or as a support base for institutional designers – it is more likely that governments will invest in enforcement and that societal actors will cooperate. Thus, in her analysis of mechanisms of prior consultation with indigenous communities in Bolivia's hydrocarbons sector, Falleti argues that these institutions eventually gained strength because the MAS government endowed them with greater legitimacy. Because the MAS had politically incorporated indigenous communities, MAS-sponsored institutions of prior consultation were broadly accepted and complied with by all parties in the hydrocarbon sector.

Sources of Insignificance

Institutions are insignificant when they require outcomes that simply mirror what would happen in the institution's absence. Insignificant institutions differ from window dressing institutions in that they actually appear to generate compliance, but their presence does little or nothing to change behavior on the ground. Why would rule makers design institutions that neither change the status quo nor address any significant challenges to it? As in the case of window dressing institutions, the incentive to create these institutions lies in audience values that turn C into a benefit rather than a cost. External or domestic actors may demand the adoption of laws or regulations resisted by rule makers or powerful stakeholders, leading rule makers to create purely symbolic responses with high audience value. But in these cases, the cost of a blatant violation is high, which precludes the adoption of window dressing institutions. As an alternative to noncompliance, state officials may design rules that, while maintaining an outward appearance of significance, render the institution toothless in its effects.

An example is the creation of "Potemkin courts" – constitutional arrangements that create seemingly independent constitutional courts to satisfy international donors but which include "poison pill" mechanisms that enable executives to control them or limit their effectiveness without actually violating the formal rules (Brinks and Blass 2013). Attacks on high courts are very visible, even to outside audiences, and they carry high reputational costs – the foreign audience, in a sense, is part of the enforcement regime. When the fine print of the rules themselves produces a weak or subservient court, however, it is much more difficult to muster the requisite outrage in the international community. In these cases, the courts do not impose a significant cost on incumbent governments, even when everyone plays by the rules, and they can actually legitimize behavior of dubious constitutionality. Thus, the cost of the institution is intentionally kept low by the designers because the cost of a violation is expected to be high.

Sources of Instability: The Cost of Change

What accounts for institutional instability? As noted above, we expect institutional instability where, for those in a position to craft new institutions, the cost of change (C) is consistently lower than the cost of accepting the institutional outcome (S) and the cost of violating the institution (V). Endemic institutional instability in a given region, such as what we observe in much of Latin America, suggests that key actors must frequently find S to be very high, or they must routinely find the cost of replacement to be very low – or both.

Economic Instability

We expect to find institutional instability in regions afflicted by frequent economic shocks. Pressure for institutional change emerges when an environmental change alters S, which is more likely in regions that are more exposed to economic shocks. Thus, an economic crisis that erodes public support for existing policy arrangements (e.g., Argentina 2001–2002) may lead elected officials to conclude that the cost of leaving those arrangements intact (S) is unacceptably high. Or a prolonged commodities boom could both lead highly popular presidents to view the cost of constitutional term limits (S) as unacceptably high and generate political capital needed for institutional change. In short, whenever an exogenous change dramatically increases S, such that it exceeds the cost of replacement, we can expect pressure for institutional change.

For instance, in their analysis of the instability of electoral institutions in Latin America, Calvo and Negretto (this volume) argue that economic shocks increase public discontent with the status quo and create electoral constituencies for institutional reform. Where economic performance is poor or unstable, citizens will be less attached to existing rules of the game and thus less inclined to defend the institutional status quo. Likewise, Albertus and Menaldo (2018, this volume) find that economic crises increase the likelihood that authoritarian constitutions will be dismantled. Similarly, Henisz and Zelner (2005) point to the impact of negative economic shocks on the survival of regulatory agreements in the Argentine and Indonesian electricity sectors. Economic crisis often leads to discontent with incumbents, producing high electoral volatility and affecting the stability of the government coalitions that would otherwise support institutional arrangements, as discussed in the next section.[29]

Unstable Coalitions

Another source of institutional instability is what might be called actor volatility, or frequent change in the rule writers and the coalitions behind particular institutions. Institutions may be unstable because underlying power

---

[29] Campello and Zucco (2015) suggest that dependence on commodities and foreign capital increases political swings in presidential popularity, which, in turn, can generate electoral volatility. Likewise, Remmer (1991) and Murillo and Visconti (2017) find that, in Latin America, negative economic shocks increase electoral volatility and anti-incumbent votes.

distributions are fluid. Perhaps those who bear the cost of S (and who may have been the losers in the last round of institutional creation) are suddenly placed in a position to change the institution. In this case, instability is not so much a function of a change in outside circumstances, but rather of changes in the preferences of the institution makers.

Frequent turnovers in power – from soldiers to civilians, from leftists to rightists, from populists to antipopulists – should increase the frequency of institutional reform attempts, particularly when turnover yields substantial change in the preferences of rule-writing coalitions. So, too, should extreme electoral volatility, in which political actors rise and fall quickly, with outsiders often ascending quickly to power and incumbent "insiders" declining rapidly and even disappearing from the political scene. There is some evidence that outsider coalitions are more likely to try to rewrite the rules when they win power (Weyland 2002). And when the coalition behind the old rules collapses and disappears, fewer actors will remain to defend them, leaving the institutional status quo highly vulnerable.

Calvo and Negretto (this volume), for example, find that electoral volatility is a major determinant of electoral rule change. There appear to be two reasons for this. First, parties seek to rewrite the rules whenever doing so would improve their electoral standing. Where electoral volatility is low, such that each party's share of the electorate remains relatively stable, parties will see fewer advantages in rule changes. By contrast, where parties' electoral fortunes change quickly and dramatically, politicians will rethink the rules with greater frequency. According to Calvo and Negretto (this volume), the rate of electoral reform is higher in Latin American countries with historically high levels of electoral volatility (such as Ecuador) than in countries with low electoral volatility (such as Honduras and Paraguay).

Electoral volatility also encourages institutional instability by undermining the coalitions that create and sustain the rules. In a context of extreme volatility, the partisan composition of governments and legislatures often changes dramatically. Dominant parties decline rapidly and even disappear, while new ones emerge out of nowhere and become dominant (e.g., Peru and Venezuela in the 1990s). The collapse of the coalitions that designed the rules and the ascent of new actors with no stake in the existing ones increases the likelihood of rule changes. For example, Ecuador's 1998 constitution was designed by a coalition that included established progressive parties and a then-powerful indigenous movement (De La Torre 2010). Soon after the constitution was approved, however, the established parties collapsed and the indigenous movement divided and weakened. This permitted the 2006 election of outsider Rafael Correa, who ran in opposition to the established parties and without the support of the indigenous movement. Correa called a new constitutional assembly in 2007, in which an entirely different balance of forces – in which Correa's newly created party was dominant – produced a different constitution. In short, there is good reason to think that persistent political volatility contributes to institutional instability. Short-term electoral gains result in the definition of new rules seeking to strengthen incumbent coalitions, which are then subject to replacement when challengers prevail.

Instability Traps

Institutional instability may also be self-reinforcing. Repeated instances of institutional replacement may generate feedback effects that help to keep the cost of change (C) low. Institutions usually need time to take root. Their persistence over time – through crises and changes in government – often generates greater legitimacy and even "taken-for-grantedness." Thus, a new institution's "susceptibility to pressures for change is greatest early in its life and declines with time" (Henisz and Zelner 2005: 367). Older institutions are also more likely to be embedded in a complex set of layered institutions, formal and informal, and to generate elaborate networks of interconnected actors. This interconnectedness generates a mutually reinforcing effect: when removing one institution affects the functioning of others, the number of affected actors increases, thereby expanding the size of coalitions with a stake in preserving the institutional status quo (Pierson 1994, 2000; Hall 2016). Institutional stability also creates incentives for actors to invest in assets and strategies specific to that institution, including, in some cases, coproduction efforts. Such investments strengthen the coalition behind the institution, as actors who develop a stake in particular institutions are more likely to defend them (Pierson 2000).

Where institutions are replaced frequently, by contrast, no such self-reinforcing dynamic emerges. Newly created institutions lack the time to develop widespread public legitimacy and interdependencies with other layered institutions. Moreover, when institutions change repeatedly, actors develop expectations of instability. Because they do not expect new institutions to endure, they are less likely to invest in assets and strategies specific to that institution or engage in coproduction efforts. And because actors do not develop a stake in the institution, or even in institutional stability per se, the coalition in favor of the status quo tends to be weaker, thereby reducing the cost of change (Hall 2016). By contrast, institutional instability generates incentives to invest in extrainstitutional skills and technologies to cope with uncertainty. Those resources, in turn, reduce the cost of institutional replacement and further weaken incentives to keep the institution alive given comparative advantages generated by extrainstitutional investment. Finally, unstable institutions may generate feedback effects by undermining economic and government performance, which creates further pressure for institutional change (O'Donnell 1994; Spiller and Tommasi 2007). Early rounds of institutional change may thus give rise to what Helmke (2017, this volume) calls an "instability trap" – a vicious cycle in which early rounds of institutional change lower the cost of replacement in future rounds.[30]

---

[30] For a related discussion in the context of high courts, see Kapiszewski (2012).

Elkins (2017) and Helmke (2017, this volume) offer examples of how the low cost of institutional change may be self-reinforcing. Elkins argues that constitutions strengthen with age, as citizens come to know, understand, and value them. Older constitutions such as those of Mexico and the United States tend to possess greater legitimacy, which increases the cost of assaulting or replacing them. Thus, repeated constitutional replacement, as we see in countries like Bolivia and Ecuador, may trigger a "negative feedback loop," in which constitutions are never able to develop the legitimacy and citizen attachments required to withstand executive assaults. Likewise, Helmke (2017: 155–160) suggests that polities may fall into an "instability trap," in which repeated constitutional crises erode public trust in (and support for) existing institutional arrangements, which in turn lowers the cost of their replacement in the future.

There is good reason to think, therefore, that institutional instability begets institutional instability. For a particular institutional arrangement to take root, actors must adjust their expectations and behavior to the new rules and procedures. Such adjustments require time (Grzymala-Busse 2011; Pierson 2004). Given a sufficient period of time, actors will invest in strategies appropriate to existing institutional arrangements, and those who succeed under those arrangements will develop both a stake in defending them and the capacity to do so. Early rounds of institutional failure and replacement, however, foreclose such a path. Actors fail to develop stable expectations or strategies appropriate to the existing rules and are thus less likely to develop a stake in their defense. As a result, the cost of institutional replacement remains low.

COMPLIANCE AND STABILITY

Compliance and stability are often viewed as complementary. This makes intuitive sense. As the previous section suggests, rules that are widely violated often lack public legitimacy, which leaves them vulnerable to contestation and eventual change (see Helmke 2017: 155–160). In their important study of constitutional stability, Elkins, Ginsburg, and Melton find that "fealty to the dictates of the constitution … and [constitutional] endurance are inextricably linked" (2009: 77). This is not always the case, however. Indeed, institutional stability is sometimes rooted in the *absence* of such fealty. Noncompliance lowers the stakes surrounding institutional outcomes, which can dampen opposition to those institutions. By shielding potential losers from an institution's effects, forbearance may enhance institutional stability by convincing powerful actors to accept rules that they would otherwise push to overturn. In effect, low compliance can inhibit the emergence of reform coalitions.

The relationship between low compliance and stability can be seen in the case of labor regulations in Latin America. During the 1990s, Latin American governments faced strong pressure to flexibilize their labor markets as a means of attracting investment. Although a few governments (e.g., Peru) dismantled existing labor laws (Murillo 2005), others, such as that of Mexico, opted to maintain the labor code intact while achieving de facto flexibility by instructing bureaucrats to reduce enforcement of labor regulations (Bensusán 2000; Cook 2007). Thus, a labor code established in the 1930s survived the pressures of the Washington Consensus because enforcement agencies could modify its application, permitting lower compliance. Similarly, Argentina's labor law, which enables industry-level collective bargaining, remained untouched in the 1990s. However, this stability was rooted in the labor ministry's decision not to call industry-wide collective bargaining and instead push for company-level agreements, which reduced private sector pressure for reform (Murillo 2005). When economic and political conditions changed during the 2000s, so too did enforcement, and the number of industry-level agreements increased (Etchemendy and Collier 2007; Etchemendy and Garay 2011).

The stability of weakly enforced institutions is often enhanced by the existence of parallel informal institutions that reduce uncertainty and stabilize actors' behavioral expectations (Helmke and Levitsky 2004). For instance, Mexico's 1917 constitution was both remarkably stable and weakly enforced. Throughout most of the twentieth century, clauses that threatened the vital interests of the ruling Institutional Revolutionary Party (PRI) and its allies – including free elections, limits on executive power, judicial tenure security, and various social rights – were routinely violated. This arrangement persisted, in part, because an array of informal institutions helped to stabilize politicians' expectations and guide their behavior. For example, the uncertainty generated by presidential succession in a context of noncompetitive elections and a ban on reelection (a rule that was strictly enforced) gave rise to an elaborate informal institution, called the *dedazo*, in which presidents unilaterally chose their successor from a select pool of candidates (cabinet members) who followed a set of clear rules (e.g., candidates would abstain from publicly seeking or campaigning for the nomination). Outgoing presidents would then retire from political life (Langston 2006). The *dedazo* structured leadership succession for half a century, contributing in an important way to the stability of a constitutional system that was formally democratic but weakly complied with.

Conversely, rules that are regularly enforced and fully complied with may be more vulnerable to instability. In democracies, for example, various aspects of the electoral system (e.g., timing of elections, district magnitude, electoral formulae) are, due to a combination of high visibility and technical necessity, almost always complied with. Losers, therefore, cannot be easily shielded from their effects, which means that they are likely to seek institutional change whenever they have the opportunity. Changes in political power distributions are thus likely to generate pressure for electoral reform. And because political power distributions changed frequently in much of third-wave Latin America, electoral institutional instability was quite high (Calvo and Negretto, this volume).

Finally, the activation of previously dormant institutions may permit substantive change – an increase in S – without actually changing the rules. Mexico's democratization, for example, was achieved through greater compliance with the 1917 constitution rather than through its overhaul. Activation may also be seen in the enforcement of social rights in parts of Latin America. Although a wide range of social rights – for example, to health care, housing, and a clean environment – were incorporated into new constitutions across much of Latin America and the rest of the Global South during the 1980s and 1990s, these rights were, for the most part, aspirational (Klug 2000; Htun 2003: 126). Yet in a few cases, including Brazil, Colombia, and South Africa, civil society organizations mobilized effectively for enforcement, using the legal system to activate constitutional social rights.

Of course, activation may generate new pressure for change from losers who were once shielded from S by forbearance, thereby undermining institutional stability. Arguably, recent moves in Brazil to amend its constitution to limit social guarantees are one example of instability prompted by the unexpected strength of the existing institution. An attempt in Colombia in 2011 to force the Constitutional Court to take into account the fiscal impact of its rulings on social and economic rights is another example. This was quite explicitly a reaction to a court that made social and economic rights a centerpiece of its jurisprudence in a way that was perceived as too costly in fiscal and political terms (Sandoval Rojas and Brinks 2020).

CONCLUSION

This introductory chapter has proposed a framework for studying institutional weakness. Rather than treat institutional weakness as an accidental or unintended outcome, we argue that it is often rooted in deliberate political decisions. The chapter conceptualizes institutional strength based on the actual effect of the institution – what we might call a causal notion of institutional strength. That is, our measure of institutional strength centers on the difference between what the institution actually produces and what would happen in its absence.

We classify institutional weakness into three types: insignificance, noncompliance, and instability. We then develop some initial, broad-strokes hypotheses about the conditions underlying the variation in institutional strength that we observe in Latin America. First, pressure by international donors and transnational activist coalitions generates high returns to institutional innovation per se, often with little attention to real-world effects. This encourages the adoption of formally ambitious but weakly enforced institutions. Institutions that seek to change dominant social norms face especially high challenges. Second, a disjuncture between rule designers and agents of enforcement may lead to low enforcement when the latter do not share the institution's goals.

Third, compliance often increases dramatically – even where bureaucratic capacity is relatively low – where state officials elicit the cooperation of key societal actors. Fourth, political volatility – rooted in things like frequent regime change and economic crisis – weakens institutions' coalitional foundations, which, in turn, limits their stability. Early instability, moreover, generates negative feedback, as institutions fail to develop strong constituencies of support. The result, in some cases, is a persistent politics of repeal and replace in which few actors have a stake in institutional preservation.

It is unclear whether Latin America is at a turning point in this respect. In some instances, changing social norms, increased political pluralism, and the growing autonomy of enforcement mechanisms have led to greater institutional compliance in contemporary Latin America. Moreover, increasing fragmentation of the political arena may well make it more difficult to muster the requisite majorities to change institutional arrangements as often as we have seen in the past. These changes may place a greater premium on the politics of design, as opponents cannot count on simply ignoring the institution. Instead, opponents will have to either lobby for less ambitious institutions or seek to place loopholes in the formal design.

The volume contains eleven chapters developing and illustrating the concepts presented in this introduction. Chapters 2 to 4 examine the causes and consequences of institutional instability. Chapter 2, by Calvo and Negretto, documents and seeks to explain the persistent instability of electoral institutions in Latin America. Variation in electoral institutional instability, Calvo and Negretto find, is associated with economic shocks, electoral volatility, and weak checks and balances. In Chapter 3, Albertus and Menaldo explore why some "bad" institutions – specifically, authoritarian constitutions – endure. Like Calvo and Negretto, their explanations point to the role of economic shocks and veto points, as well as the death of authoritarian elites. In Chapter 4, Helmke examines why interbranch conflict leads to interruptions of fixed presidential terms in Latin America. She finds that such outcomes are most likely when the executive possesses extensive constitutional power but lacks control over congress. Helmke's chapter also explores the phenomenon of "instability traps," in which early institutional crises lower the cost of institutional replacement in the future.

Chapters 5 through 10 focus on issues of compliance. Chapter 5, by Holland, explores the politics of forbearance, or nonenforcement of the law, toward the poor. She introduces the notion of a "coercion gap," showing that whereas national legislatures – often following public opinion – often have an incentive to approve punitive laws against squatters and street vendors, the mayors and street-level bureaucrats who are responsible for implementing those laws often find the human and political costs of enforcement to be prohibitive. Thus, they have a strong incentive to engage in forbearance. Chapter 6, by Htun and Jensenius, analyzes the fate of a law seeking to prevent violence against women in Mexico. They show that compliance with the law requires systematic coproduction – in the form of reporting violations – from below. In Mexico, social coproduction is limited by competing pre-existing norms and widespread economic insecurity, thereby relegating the law to aspirational status. Chapter 7, by Amengual and Dargent, examines the interaction between state capacity and societal cooperation in shaping enforcement outcomes. The chapter argues that in much of Latin America, resource-constrained states are indifferent toward enforcement, and that as a result, resistance or cooperation by relevant social actors is critical to determining whether laws and regulations are enforced.

Chapter 8, by Fernández and Garay, studies the design, implementation, and enforcement of federal deforestation laws in Argentina. The chapter shows how provincial governments influenced the design of federal legislation to secure discretion in implementing the law. Where big landowners were politically powerful, governments adopted nonpunitive sanctions and exercised higher discretion in classifying areas as protected, using a combination of noncompliance and insignificance strategies to weaken the institution. As a result, in those provinces, movement toward the overall goals of the legislation was minimal, whereas other provinces, in which environmental activists were stronger, made more progress. Chapter 9, by Saffón and González Bertomeu, examines the selective enforcement of Mexico's Lerdo Law, which established the primacy of individual over collective property rights. Initially, liberal governments enforced the law on the Church but not on indigenous pueblos. As Mexico's export boom increased land values, however, judges began to reinterpret the law to apply to indigenous communal lands (though often defending the individual property rights of indigenous peasants). Chapter 10, by Schrank, examines the conditions under which borrowed or imported institutions may succeed. Focusing on the establishment of a civil service regime for labor inspectors in the Dominican Republic, driven by the incentive to retain access to US markets, Schrank finds that borrowed institutions may well take root, essentially under the same conditions as domestic ones.

Finally, our conclusion first draws on the chapters to examine the principal mechanisms that reproduce institutional weakness in Latin America, and then discusses the possible relationship between increasing levels of the democracy and institutional weakness in the region. It also reviews the challenges involved in measuring institutional weakness. Finally, it goes partly beyond the lessons of this volume to speculate about the causes of the weakening of previously strong institutions.

2

When (Electoral) Opportunity Knocks

Weak Institutions, Political Shocks, and
Electoral Reforms in Latin America

Ernesto Calvo and Gabriel Negretto

Major electoral reforms have been strikingly frequent in Latin America since the beginning of the third wave of democratization. Such reforms include the adoption of runoff formulas for the election of the president, changes in tenure and reelection rules, the replacement of proportional representation by mixed-member rules, alterations in the number and magnitudes of electoral districts, and the creation or elimination of legislative chambers as well as modifications to their size, to name a few important instances of electoral change. Such major reforms have not been simply the result of regime change, nor have they slowed down as democratic regimes have become more stable in the region. Instead, the rate of reforms has remained constant since the 1980s – the result of cyclical crises and weak institutions, features of day-to-day politics in Latin America. In this chapter, we seek to understand what determines the enactment of major electoral reforms in the region.

To study changes in the rules of the electoral game, we focus on 112 major reform events that occurred in the rules that regulate voting and the allocation of representative positions in eighteen democratic countries in Latin America between the early 1980s and 2015. We show that the rate of reforms is remarkable, with over six reform events per country, on average, over a very short period. Our dataset includes changes to formulas, terms, and reelection rules for presidents; major reforms to house and senate electoral formulas; significant alterations to district magnitudes and assembly sizes; and changes in electoral thresholds and in the design of ballots.

In Chapter 1, Brinks, Levitsky, and Murillo describe three different types of institutional weaknesses: insignificance, noncompliance, and instability. In this chapter, we focus our attention on the third type of weakness, instability, which is the type most commonly observed in the study of electoral rules. The rules of the electoral game are the backbone of modern democratic systems and tend to be binding, explicit, and enforced. That is, they apply to all parties formally recognized to compete in elections, they detail most aspects of the electoral process, and they are enforced by a large number of legal decisions that rule on small and large challenges raised on or around Election Day. Consequently, weak electoral institutions are generally more likely to result from their high rate of amendment and replacement than from open non-compliance or insignificance. For the same reason, although there could be some level of discretion in the interpretation or implementation of electoral rules, their displacement – rather than more incremental or less visible forms of institutional transformation – is the usual strategy politicians follow to change the rules of the electoral game (see Mahoney and Thelen 2010: 19).

Using studies of the rate of electoral change in Western Europe as a comparative benchmark, we provide evidence that formal electoral systems have been highly unstable in Latin America. We also show that the level of instability in this region varies depending on the type of electoral regime. In conducting our analysis, we measure the durability of major electoral rules for the election of presidents and members of the house and senate. We note differences in the durability of these rules as we explain fifty-five major reform events for the election of deputies, thirty-four for presidents, and twenty-three for senators. Each *event* in our data may contain either a single major reform or multiple major reforms implemented by politicians in a given year. Consequently, the total number of reform events we analyze includes a much larger sample of actual reforms. Our study indicates that reforms do not necessarily (or even frequently) occur simultaneously across all representative institutions (e.g., the executive branch, the house, and the senate), but rather are introduced at different times to satisfy different political goals.

Politicians, we argue, are always willing to introduce reforms to better their institutional standing and improve the odds of future success. However, in the particular case of electoral rules, they can only do so when major shocks to the system provide them with an opportunity and when institutional oversight is limited and gives them discretion to control the outcome of the reforms. Electoral shocks, such as the decline in overall party support during economic crises or the emergence of new political actors, increase the rate of reforms by providing political entrepreneurs with incentives to alter the rules of the game. By contrast, strong constitutional constraints on the executive, such as judicial and legislative oversight, reduce the rate of electoral change because they prevent politicians from adopting a reform or from devising it in a way that provides them with clear benefits.

In all, our results show that electoral shocks and weak constitutional constraints facilitate electoral reforms while political stability and effective constitutional limits on executive discretion prevent them. In terms of the sources of institutional instability identified in Chapter 1, we find that economic crises and unstable political environments tend to increase the rate of electoral reform. At the same time, however, we emphasize that even in volatile contexts the effective implementation of constitutional constraints over successive governments would decrease the actual number of reforms we observe. We also find that electoral regime instability tends to become self-enforcing over time, sometimes leading to what Helmke (this volume) calls an "instability trap."

The organization of this chapter is as follows. In the first section, we provide a rationale for why politicians introduce what we call *offensive* and *defensive* reforms, which seek to augment a party's advantage or to prevent further losses. In the second section, we define our unit of analysis and provide an overview of electoral reforms in Latin America. The third section estimates a variety of survival models to explain the rate of reforms and its determinants. We conclude with a discussion of the relationship between the degree of implementation of constitutional constraints and institutional instability and the mechanisms underlying patterns of electoral instability in Latin America.

WHY DO POLITICIANS REFORM THE RULES OF THE ELECTORAL GAME?

It is part of the conventional wisdom within electoral studies that reforms are a rare event. Given the information costs and the learning required to successfully change the existing rules of the game, it has been argued that electoral reform should be infrequent and, when implemented, incremental. As Taagepera and Shugart (1989: 218) summarize, "familiarity breeds stability."[1] This assumption, however, is debatable.

First, whether we consider electoral rules as stable or unstable often depends on the indicators used to measure electoral change. There is a *modifiable areal unit problem* as in geography, where stability is observed only for reforms defined as electoral regime replacement (e.g., changes from single-member district [SMD] to proportional representation [PR]). Lijphart and Aitkin (1994: 52) find evidence of electoral stability in the fact that no country changed from plurality to PR, or vice versa, in their study of twenty-seven stable electoral democracies from 1945 to 1990. As noted by Katz (2005), however, reforms are considerably more frequent when considering key features of the electoral rules such as district magnitude, legal thresholds, term limits, primary rules, ballot designs, and major changes in the administration of the election, which may have equally – and sometimes more – dramatic consequences on party competition and the allocation of political posts. Considering such reforms leads to a more nuanced assessment of stability in electoral rules.

It is also important to note that predictions of electoral system stability are usually restricted to the analysis of established democracies. These predictions do not hold, however, in many new democracies. Between 1978 and 2008, new democracies in Latin America underwent forty-five major electoral changes in the system to elect presidents and house members

---

[1] A similar argument is found in Lijphart and Aitkin (1994: 52).

(Negretto 2013: 25–29). The data include only significant alterations of the electoral formula, the adoption or elimination of legal thresholds, and a 25 percent or larger change in the size of district magnitudes or assembly size. Other authors (Birch et al. 2002) have found a similar pattern of electoral system instability in Eastern Europe, particularly during the 1990s.

Strategic theories, particularly those that emphasize the distributive consequences of institutional arrangements, are well equipped to explain many of these reforms. If the creation and maintenance of institutions reproduce the existing distribution of power resources among self-interested actors, institutions should not remain stable if the interests or resources of these actors change. It follows from this perspective that governing parties would tend to replace existing electoral rules when these rules no longer serve their interests or when parties that lost under the existing rules gain sufficient influence to induce a reform. This framework of analysis has been developed by several authors, including Boix (1999), Benoit and Schieman (2001), Benoit (2004), and Colomer (2004, 2005).

In its more general, comparative formulation, the power-maximization model postulates that whereas large or ascending parties support restrictive electoral rules, small or declining parties tend to favor the adoption of inclusive electoral rules, such as PR for legislative elections (Geddes 1996; Colomer 2004, 2005) and more-than-plurality rules for presidential elections (Negretto 2006). The strategic model has also been specified in more substantive terms to explain the historical origins of major electoral reforms, such as the adoption of PR rules in Europe at the beginning of the twentieth century (Rokkan 1970; Boix 1999; Andrews and Jackman 2005; Calvo 2009).

We follow the basics of this model by assuming that politicians always want to improve their electoral position. To achieve this goal, party leaders try to anticipate voters' preferences and design electoral campaigns or formulate policies in order to win elections (Downs 1957). From time to time, however, they also attempt to alter key features of the electoral system. Politicians have incentives to do so when they believe they can increase or consolidate electoral gains or minimize electoral losses under alternative electoral rules.[2] Whereas the first type of reform may be called offensive or proactive, the second one can be labeled defensive or reactive. Each type of reform originates in observed fluctuations in the electoral market, which in turn derive from shifting voter preferences. When electoral support for a given party or candidate is growing, political entrepreneurs are likely to promote reforms to secure this advantage. When this support is declining, they are likely to promote reforms to hedge their bets. From this perspective, electoral system instability should increase in political environments where party allegiances among voters are weak and may be altered by economic and political shocks, such as economic downturns or corruption scandals.

[2] If we assume that politicians also care about policy or that reformers are not always partisan actors with the capacity to compete in elections, reformers may also want to increase the electoral gains or minimize the electoral losses of other actors.

In a democratic context, competitive pressures may also derive from citizen demands. To be sure, voters do not usually pay much attention to the details of the electoral system. However, when economic performance is poor, political crises are frequent, and the level of public trust in representative institutions is low, some electoral institutions may attract citizen attention through public debates in the media and campaigns promoted by opposition parties (see Shugart 2001; Negretto 2015). For instance, there may emerge a shared perception that reforms that seem to increase the influence of voters over candidate selection or strengthen the personal accountability of representatives will diminish the power of party leaders, reduce levels of corruption, and bring the preferences of elected officials closer to those of voters. In this environment, party leaders from both government and opposition are likely to propose and compete for the approval of electoral changes that appear to improve the control of citizens over representatives, thus contributing to the overall number of electoral reforms replacing or revising preceding rules.

Fluctuations in the electoral market and citizen disaffection with the political system account for the incentives to reform and, as such, provide an indirect explanation for the electoral changes one may observe in different environments. Yet the actual rate of reform should also be determined by the political and institutional constraints that politicians face in implementing their preferences. Party leaders must obviously have sufficient partisan power (either from their own party or from a coalition) to muster the number of votes necessary to adopt an electoral reform. At the same time, however, reforms must be legally and politically viable. This means that reforms must be allowed by the existing constitution and legal system, that the actors who did not participate in the reform coalition should accept them, and that the changes can be enforced with the support of judicial institutions.

Whereas some important electoral rules, such as district magnitude, assembly size, or electoral threshold, are usually left to ordinary legislation, many others, such as electoral formulas, length of terms, and term limits, tend to be entrenched in the constitution. In fact, it is likely that, in contexts of high electoral instability, the number of electoral rules included in the constitution will increase. Knowing that electoral systems are fragile, those who reform electoral rules at $t = 0$ may want to constitutionalize these rules to prevent other actors from altering them at $t = 1$. However, this strategy will only enhance electoral stability if future political actors comply with the constitutional restrictions placed on reforms or if judicial institutions enforce those restrictions in case of transgression. In a context where constitutional constraints are weak, the attractiveness of reforms will increase because they make it possible for successive governments to adopt new rules and control their implementation.

Changes in presidential reelection rules provide a good example of the way constitutional constraints might work to facilitate or hinder electoral reform. The constitution must first allow this reform. For instance, some presidential constitutions, such as the constitutions of Honduras or Guatemala, prohibit adopting the consecutive reelection of presidents.[3] In addition, even if the reform is allowed, the support of the judiciary may be necessary to implement it because citizens or political actors may activate a judicial review process to determine whether the formal and material requirements of the amendment process have been observed. In 2010, the Colombian Constitutional Court ruled that Congress lacked the authority to amend the constitution to allow the incumbent president to run for a third time. In the court's view, such a reform would be a substitution (rather than a mere amendment) for the existing constitution because it would eliminate the checks and balances system created in the 1991 constitution (Negretto 2013).

What this analysis indicates, then, is that electoral reforms are the product of specific incentives and constraints coming from the electoral market, public perceptions, and the institutional context. Whereas unstable electoral markets and citizen dissatisfaction with the performance of the political system should increase the incentives to propose electoral reforms, weak constitutional constraints should facilitate their approval and implementation.

ELECTORAL RULE CHANGE IN LATIN AMERICA

Whether one looks at the sheer number of reforms or their content, there is clear evidence of electoral system instability in Latin America. From the early 1980s to 2015, we count 112 major electoral reform events in the rules to elect house members (fifty-five), the senate (twenty-three), and the president (thirty-four). Within each category, we define as a major reform event a change in any or several of the central rules that make up the electoral regimes to elect deputies, senators, and president.[4] In the case of house and senate members, this includes the alteration of the electoral formula, an increase or decrease in at least 25 percent of the assembly size or average district magnitude; the inclusion or removal of an electoral threshold; and changes in the ballot structure, length of term, electoral cycle, and the existence of recall. For the president, reforms include changes in the electoral formula, length of term, permission or proscription of consecutive reelection, and the existence of recall. Table 2.1 summarizes these reforms by country and category.

---

[3] The attempt of the executive to transgress this restriction was presumably the cause of the coup that removed President Zelaya of Honduras from power in 2009.

[4] In other words, we distinguish "reform events" from the total number of specific reforms to rules. Freidenberg and Došek (2015) describe 249 reforms during a similar period of time. Several of these reforms, however, were introduced at a single reform event. For example, the constitutional reform of Argentina in 1994 enacted reforms that altered the formulas to elect the president and senators. For the purpose of analyzing the survival of electoral rules, we consider the 1994 reform, by category, as a single event that changed different features of the regime to elect president and senators.

TABLE 2.1. *Number of electoral reforms by country and category*

Country	Deputies	Senate	President	Total
Argentina	1	2	1	4
Bolivia	6	2	2	10
Brazil	2	2	4	8
Chile	3	3	4	10
Colombia	3	2	2	7
Costa Rica	0	–	0	0
Dominican Republic	3	2	3	8
Ecuador	10	–	4	14
El Salvador	3	–	0	3
Guatemala	4	–	2	6
Honduras	2	–	1	3
Mexico	4	4	0	8
Nicaragua	2	–	3	5
Panama	2	–	1	3
Paraguay	1	1	1	3
Peru	4	2	3	9
Uruguay	1	1	1	3
Venezuela	4	2	2	8
Total	55	23	34	112
Mean	3.0	1.5	1.9	6.2

Note: Our data.

Although we include a wide variety of electoral rules, they all determine when and how citizens cast their votes and how those votes are aggregated to allocate representative positions. We have also aimed to reduce the heterogeneity of reforms by including only changes that the literature considers significant in their potential effects on citizen representation, party competition, and party systems. For instance, in the electoral formula we code as reform all shifts between majoritarian, mixed, and proportional formulas. We also incorporate changes within proportional formulas, but only when according to electoral scholars the alteration is expected to affect the distribution of legislative seats between large and small parties (see Gallagher and Mitchell 2005). Also, in order to code reforms to the average district magnitude and assembly size, we use a relatively demanding threshold. Whereas Lijphart and Aitkin consider an alteration of 20 percent sufficient to code a reform in these dimensions as significant, we use a threshold of 25 percent (see Lijphart and Aitkin 1994: 13–14).

It is important to emphasize that we are only observing the formal alteration of electoral rules, not changes that result from a failure to apply existing rules or transformations that derive from judicial interpretations. By this count, Argentina has a relatively low number of electoral reforms, below the mean of the whole region. Moreover, most of these alterations resulted from a single reform event, the 1994 constitutional reform. Yet an alternative analysis is also possible. In 1983, an electoral college elected Raúl Alfonsín, the first democratic president, for a period of six years. In 1989, however, he was forced to resign six months before the end of his mandate in the midst of a major economic crisis. In 1999, Fernando de la Rúa was elected president by direct popular vote for a four-year term, which was reduced to two as he resigned in the midst of another economic crisis. The interim president, Eduardo Duhalde, proposed and won a major legal court ruling to reinterpret Argentina's electoral laws, allowing candidates to run their own tickets outside of the established registered parties. Under the new interpretation, Néstor Kirchner was elected president in 2003, thus preventing the return of Carlos Menem to the presidency. From this per-spective, Argentina's electoral rules look a lot less stable than we report.

To take another example, in our database we code Costa Rica as having no significant reform. Although this country would still qualify as extremely sta-ble in comparative terms, it is worth noting that in 2003 the absolute proscrip-tion on presidential reelection, in force since 1969, was removed by a decision of the Constitutional Court. This type of analysis could certainly enrich our views on electoral instability. However, the problem with taking into account changes in electoral rules that occur outside the formal channels of reform in a legislative or constitution-making body is that they are too difficult to observe and compare in a relatively large number of cases. In addition, those changes are likely to be too heterogeneous for a reliable comparison.

To make a comparative assessment of the level of formal electoral instabil-ity in Latin America, we may look more closely at the frequency of changes in basic electoral formulas, where reforms are usually considered rare events. Western Europe and established democracies provide a good standard for com-parison. Bartolini and Mair (1990) found only fourteen major shifts in legisla-tive electoral formulas in Western Europe from 1885 to 1985.[5] Richard Katz (2005: 58) counts the same number of electoral changes among established democracies in the world during the period 1950–2005, but he includes the wholesale replacement of the formula through which a strong president, or the chamber of parliament to which the national government is responsible, is elected. By contrast, we observe thirty-one reforms in the formulas to elect presidents and members of the lower or single chamber of congress in Latin America from 1978 to 2015. This is more than double the total number of elec-toral reforms among established democracies during a shorter period of time.

It is also important to note that within the Latin American region there is significant variation across countries. As mentioned, Costa Rica is clearly an extreme outlier in terms of electoral stability, with no formal electoral reform

---

[5] They included shifts from majoritarian to proportional electoral formulas and back, as well as changes in specific rules that increased or reduced proportionality. See Bartolini and Mair (1990: 147).

registered during this period in any of the categories of electoral regimes we analyze. Ecuador, on the contrary, had fourteen electoral reforms, of which ten were made to the system to elect legislators. Changes in the system to elect deputies were so frequent that out of thirteen legislative elections, the maximum duration of the same rules during the whole period was only three elections.

A salient feature of electoral reforms in Latin America is the legal channels through which they tend to take place. Although some reforms were implemented via changes in ordinary legislation, most required constitutional change. Specifically, whereas 56 percent of the electoral reforms for deputies derived from the amendment or replacement of the existing constitution, 96 percent of the changes for the senate and 100 percent for the presidency required formal constitutional alterations. In other words, basic aspects of each category of electoral regime in Latin America are entrenched at the level of constitutional provisions where change is supposed to be more difficult than at the level of ordinary laws.

When looking at the substance of electoral reforms, certain patterns can be discerned over time. For the election of the house, there is a trend toward maintaining or increasing proportionality that runs in parallel with the growing fragmentation of party systems in the region (Coppedge 1997, 1998; Negretto 2009). This trend results from the adoption or maintenance of an inclusive proportional formula and a medium-to-high average district magnitude. Although no system for the election of deputies has become fully majoritarian, there are important exceptions to the trend toward more inclusive rules, usually in response to the collapse of traditional parties and the emergence of a new dominant party. For instance, as the hegemony of the governing party consolidated in Venezuela after 2006, the mixed-member proportional system that existed since 1993 was formally replaced in 2009 by a mixed-member majoritarian system to elect deputies.

There has also been a trend toward the personalization of voting rules since 1978. Personalization increases when the election of party candidates shifts from single closed lists to multiple closed lists, flexible lists, and open lists.[6] The same happens when a proportion of legislators are elected from single-member districts. The degree of personal voting is important because it may foster greater voter participation in candidate selection as well as increase intraparty competition and the local orientation of policies (Carey and Shugart 1995, 1998; Shugart 1995; Shugart, Valdini, and Suominen 2005).

---

[6] Multiple closed lists (traditionally used in Uruguay and until 2003 in Colombia) allow party factions to compete against each other under the same party label. Flexible lists provide voters with a list and the rank of candidates, but voters have the option of altering the order using a preferential vote. Open lists provide voters with only the names of candidates so that who gets elected is entirely determined by voters (see Shugart 2005: 41–44). In Latin America, both open and flexible lists are termed "closed, unblocked lists" (*listas cerradas, no bloqueadas*) while the term "open lists" (*listas abiertas*) is reserved for the case in which voters can select candidates from different lists. (See Nohlen 1994: 61–63.)

Personalization has increased in some cases by combining single-member districts with party-list voting, and in others by adopting open or flexible lists. As a result of these reforms, by 2015 only five countries in the region – Argentina, Costa Rica, Guatemala, Paraguay, and Nicaragua – elected all members of the single or lower chamber of congress by single closed lists. These reforms, like others such as primary elections and the authorization of nonpartisan candidates, belong to a series of institutional transformations intended to placate growing public criticism and distrust of parties and party leaders (Negretto 2009).

When considering senate electoral rules, which are fewer in number, we do not find a unique type of reform across all cases. Most reforms, however, followed a similar logic, namely, that of making the upper chamber more democratic and pluralistic. Such is the rationale for reforms shifting from indirect to direct senate elections (Argentina in 1994); removing unelected (appointed) senators (Chile in 2005); including minority representation clauses (Argentina in 1994, Bolivia in 1995, and Mexico in 1993); replacing majoritarian with proportional formulas (Bolivia in 2009); or adopting a single national district for the election of the chamber (Colombia in 1991 and Paraguay in 1992). As a result of these reforms, most senates in Latin America have today lost some of their initial aristocratic features and weakened their role as representatives of the territorial interests of subnational units.

Two salient trends can be distinguished in the election of presidents. The first refers to the electoral formula. Plurality formulas to elect presidents were once predominant in Latin America (in the 1950s and 1960s), often combined with concurrent legislative elections. However, as a result of the constitutional reforms implemented since the late 1970s, most countries require either an absolute majority (more than 50 percent) or a qualified plurality threshold (below 50 percent but above some minimum, such as 20 percent) to win a presidential election.[7] As of 2015, only five countries in the whole region (Honduras, Mexico, Panama, Paraguay, and Venezuela) elect their presidents by plurality rule, of which only three (Honduras, Panama, and Paraguay) have concurrent congressional elections. Similar to the shift to proportionality for legislative elections before and after 1978, this reform has coincided with the increasing fragmentation of party systems.

[7] Specifically, there have been fourteen changes in the formula for electing the president between 1978 and 2015. Eight of these reforms replaced plurality by runoff elections, either with a majority or a qualified plurality threshold. In three cases, direct presidential elections with a majority threshold already existed, but a second round of voting in the runoff replaced the involvement of congress to determine outcomes. Only three cases have shifted from less to relatively more restrictive electoral rules: Ecuador in 1998, which adopted qualified plurality presidential elections after having used majority runoff since 1979; Nicaragua in 2000, which lowered the threshold of votes for winning the presidential election from 45 percent to 40 percent; and Bolivia in 2009, which shifted from a majority formula with a second round of elections in congress to a qualified plurality formula of 40 percent threshold with a difference of 10 percent over the second-most-voted candidate.

The second important reform trend in presidential elections refers to the consecutive reelection of presidents. Since the early 1990s, most constitutional reforms in Latin America have relaxed presidential reelection rules, shifting from the absolute proscription of reelection or reelection after one term to one consecutive reelection (see Zovatto and Orozco Henriquez 2008; Negretto 2009, 2013). Specifically, of the eighteen changes introduced to the rules of presidential reelection from 1978 to 2015, eleven have made it more permissive and seven less permissive. Moreover, the rule authorizing unlimited presidential reelections (which in the past was typical of authoritarian regimes) has recently been adopted in Venezuela (in 2009) and in Nicaragua (in 2014).

In relation to term limits, we can also mention the introduction of recalls as a set of reforms that may affect the duration in office of deputies, senators, and even presidents. These reforms do not constitute a trend in numbers because only a few countries have established them. In particular, the recall of legislators was adopted in Bolivia after 2009, in Ecuador after 2008, in Panama after 2004, and in Venezuela after 1999. The recall of presidents, in turn, only exists in Bolivia, Ecuador, and Venezuela. Although fewer in number, these reforms are interesting in that they are aimed at improving the accountability of elected officials amid growing public distrust of representative institutions.

The fact that established democracies exhibit a relatively low rate of electoral reform and the fact that most countries in Latin America have inaugurated or reinaugurated free and fair elections since the late 1970s bring to the fore the question of whether electoral instability is not itself the result of democratization. Table 2.2 shows the total number of reforms observed by year across Latin American countries from 1978 to 2015.

The temporal analysis of reforms does not indicate that electoral rule change in Latin America was primarily determined by democratization. Most countries in the region became democratic between 1978 and 1990. However, the average number of reforms by year for the whole period 1978–2015 (2.9) is virtually the same as the average number of reforms by year before (2.8) and after 1990 (3).

MODELING THE SURVIVAL OF ELECTORAL RULES

In the previous section, we have shown that electoral reforms in Latin America have been extremely frequent within a comparative perspective. This is true when considering the aggregate number of rules that make up the regime for electing the president, the house, and the senate (where there is one), or more specific rules, such as electoral formulas. Descriptive information showed that reforms to the electoral rules of the house were also more frequent than for both the president and the senate. Finally, we have shown that the rate of reform over time has remained relatively constant, rather than being simply a reflection of democratization. In this section we seek to explain the rate of electoral reforms as a function of a variety of covariates.

TABLE 2.2. *Number of electoral reforms by year*

Year	Number of Reforms	Year	Number of Reforms
1978	3	1997	3
1979	1	1998	4
1980	3	1999	3
1981	1	2000	3
1982	3	2001	1
1983	6	2002	2
1984	1	2003	3
1985	4	2004	3
1986	4	2005	4
1987	1	2006	1
1988	3	2007	0
1989	5	2008	2
1990	1	2009	6
1991	4	2010	3
1992	3	2011	0
1993	6	2012	1
1994	8	2013	0
1995	3	2014	4
1996	8	2015	1

Note: Our data.

Consistent with our argument in the previous section, we expect politicians to produce moderate to large changes in electoral rules frequently if the opportunity presents itself and if they are granted enough discretion to tailor reforms to their needs. Consequently, consistent with Rahm Emmanuel's maxim,[8] shocks endow politicians with "good reasons" to adjust the rules of the game while weak institutions provide them with discretion to profit from reforms that go unchecked.

The Dependent Variable: Time to Electoral Reform

To test our arguments, we take advantage of the data described in the previous section, which includes cross-sectional time series observations of all major electoral reforms introduced in eighteen countries of Latin America between 1978 and 2015. Using this dataset, we estimate a variety of survival models that explain the time that it takes to replace the current electoral rules (i.e., *electoral regime*) by new ones. We consider an *electoral regime* as a set of rules that govern an election and a *new regime* as a significant modification in at least some of the components of this electoral set (formula, district magnitudes,

---

[8] A Terrible Thing to Waste. Available at: www.nytimes.com/2009/08/02/magazine/02FOB-onlanguage-t.html?referringSource=articleShare [Accessed February 8, 2020].

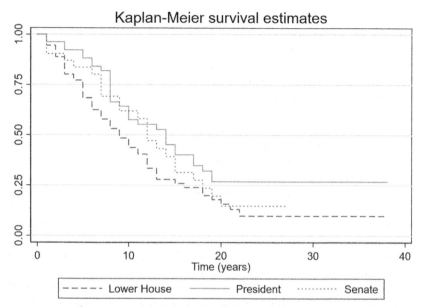

FIGURE 2.1. Kaplan–Meier survival plot by electoral category.
Note: Kaplan–Meier provides a summary depiction of the time to reform an electoral regime (change in electoral rules).

term limits, etc.). The dependent variable, consequently, takes a value of 0 every year that rules were kept in place and a value of 1 if a major electoral reform was introduced (regime failure). Once a new regime is in place, the dependent variable again takes the value of 0 until a new major electoral reform. Our survival models of electoral regime change consider differences across countries as well as across electoral categories (president, house, and senate).

Figure 2.1 provides a summary depiction of our dependent variable, as described by Kaplan–Meier survival lines for each of the three categories we analyze. As can be observed, between 75 percent and 80 percent of electoral regimes undertook major reforms within a twenty-year period. While the electoral rules for the election of deputies tend to be less resilient, over time the survival rates are not very different.

The Independent Variables: Electoral Shocks and Institutional Constraints

The most important variables for our analysis measure opportunities that result from shocks (both economic and political) as well as institutional constraints that limit discretion by reformers. We consider two types of shocks that may generate opportunities for reform. First, we examine political shocks as reflected by increasing electoral volatility and its impact on the distribution of partisan power.[9] We consider the potential of higher electoral volatility to provide new opportunities to adjust the rules of the game to the changing preferences of voters. Both significant increases and significant decreases in the vote for existing parties alter the preferences for electoral rules that reward growing parties or defend declining ones. Incentives to reform the current electoral rules, consequently, will follow the ebbs and flows of electoral preferences changes. Second, we consider two variables that describe economic shocks, (1) the share of income held by wage earners and (2) gross domestic product (GDP), both of which are expected to be negatively related to political disaffection and, consequently, should reduce the rate of electoral reform. We expect that both an increasing share of income held by wage earners and an increase in GDP will reduce political conflict and increase the stability of political institutions. By contrast, economic decline and a declining share of wages will provide incentives and opportunities to speed up the rate of reforms.

To measure constraints that limit the discretion of reformers over the adoption and implementation of electoral changes, we take advantage of new data collected by the Varieties of Democracy project (V-DEM). This dataset includes three index variables that attempt to measure the effectiveness of classic constitutional constraints on executive power. The first two (judicial constraints and legislative constraints) capture the extent to which the national executive abides by the constitution and respects court rulings and the extent to which the legislature is able to exercise oversight over the executive. The third variable, "liberal component," is formed by averaging the previous indices with another one intended to capture the actual implementation of equality before the law and individual liberties. Taken together, these variables provide an overall measure of the extent to which the constitution and its separation of powers system are effective in limiting the discretion of the executive.[10] As Table 2.3 shows, all three variables describing institutional constraints are closely related. Consequently, we include each of them in separate analyses.[11]

We have included a variety of control variables to account for possible alternative explanations of electoral reform. These variables are the GDP per capita (LN), population (LN), and controls for monetary shocks, such as variations in the exchange rate (LN). We also used a series of dummy variables capturing the presidential cycle (year prior to election, election year, and year

---

[9] Since the mechanical effect of electoral rules "filters" the impact of shifts in electoral support on the distribution of partisan power in current institutions, we use volatility in legislative seats rather than in legislative votes to measure the actual intensity of electoral shocks.

[10] See V-DEM codebook, version 2016. www.v-dem.net/en/data/data-version-8/

[11] A log-odds transformation of the original variables was used to obtain a normal distribution.

TABLE 2.3. *Correlation between judicial constraints, legislative constraints, and liberal component*

	Judicial Constraints (V-DEM)	Legislative Constraints (V-DEM)
Legislative Constraints (V-DEM)	0.6967	
Liberal Component (V-DEM)	0.9195	0.8276

after the election). Finally, we control for the category of electoral regime that is subject to change, using house election rules as the baseline for comparative assessment.

Results

Table 2.4 presents the estimates of five different specifications of Weibull survival models. Aside from the case of Costa Rica, all other countries in our sample have had multiple electoral reforms. Consequently, censoring is not a significant problem in our analyses, which was already clear from Figure 2.1. Alternative proportional hazard models gave similar results and are available upon request.

The different models indicate that the effect of political shocks is large and statistically significant, suggesting that large changes in seat shares across parties increase the rate of reform. Results also show that both a lower share of wages and a lower GDP increase the hazard rate of electoral regimes, thereby speeding up electoral reforms. All three variables we use to measure constitutional constraints show that the impact of these constraints is negative and significant, reducing the hazard rate and, consequently, the rate of reforms.

As expected, due to the larger number of reforms in the electoral regime for deputies, the rate of reform is faster for house election rules (baseline in the model) and declines for executive branch and senate election rules. Among the control variables, only the GDP per capita shows statistically significant effects, with higher growth being associated with fewer reforms. In all, results show that shocks reduce the time to reform while effective constraints on the executive slow down the pace of reform.

Figure 2.2 provides a visual description of the effect of judicial constraints on the survival of electoral institutions (Table 2.4, Model 1). For example, after ten years, close to 35 percent of countries with high judicial constraints engaged in major electoral reforms compared to almost 60 percent of countries with low judicial constraints. The effect of higher inequality between labor and capital (low share of wages) is also large and significant, with close to 20 percent of countries that display higher wage shares (1 standard deviation) reforming after ten years, compared to almost 50 percent for low wage share countries (−1 standard deviation).

TABLE 2.4. *Time to reform the electoral rules, Weibull models, Latin American countries, 1978–2015*

Variables	(1) DV Time	(2) DV Time	(3) DV Time	(4) DV Time	(5) DV Time	(6) DV Time	(7) DV Time	(8) DV Time	(9) DV Time
Judicial Constraints (V-DEM)	-0.338*** (0.0740)			-0.240** (0.104)			-0.116 (0.139)		
Legislative Constraints (V-DEM)		-0.165*** (0.0608)			-0.256*** (0.0906)			-0.224** (0.111)	
Liberal Component (V-DEM)			-0.425*** (0.142)			-0.425*** (0.142)			-0.304* (0.178)
Share of Wages			-0.830*** (0.320)	-0.707** (0.326)	-0.923*** (0.316)	-0.830*** (0.320)	-1.079* (0.550)	-1.166*** (0.419)	-1.054*** (0.339)
Seat Volatility			0.251* (0.135)	0.273** (0.139)	0.323** (0.132)	0.251* (0.135)	0.269* (0.151)	0.274* (0.140)	0.243* (0.139)
Category: President	-0.652*** (0.222)	-0.631*** (0.222)	-0.808*** (0.271)	-0.780*** (0.270)	-0.785*** (0.270)	-0.808*** (0.271)	-0.833** (0.337)	-0.836** (0.331)	-0.830*** (0.275)
Category: Senate	-0.391 (0.266)	-0.445* (0.266)	-0.313 (0.327)	-0.287 (0.328)	-0.365 (0.326)	-0.313 (0.327)	-0.286 (0.391)	-0.343 (0.373)	-0.277 (0.333)
Presidential Election Year							0.303 (0.284)	0.328 (0.290)	0.318 (0.277)

	(1)	(2)	(3)	(4)	(5)	(6)	(7)	(8)	(9)
Lag Presidential Election Year							0.188	0.194	0.208
							(0.297)	(0.296)	(0.292)
GDP (LN)							−0.651*	−0.634**	−0.478
							(0.386)	(0.316)	(0.346)
Population (LN)							0.773	0.789*	0.559
							(0.496)	(0.411)	(0.437)
Exchange Rate (LN)							−0.00374	−0.00552	−0.00847
							(0.0365)	(0.0373)	(0.0364)
Constant	−3.450***	−3.299***	−3.296***	−3.298***	−3.295***	−3.296***	1.441	1.212	0.158
	(0.307)	(0.300)	(0.422)	(0.424)	(0.419)	(0.422)	(2.809)	(2.428)	(2.684)
Observations	1,670	1,670	1,099	1,099	1,099	1,099	1,087	1,087	1,087
LogLik	−176.5	−183.7	−103.4	−105.2	−104.2	−103.4	−98.54	−96.72	−97.53

Note: Survival models, dependent variable (DV) time. Standard errors in parentheses. $^{***}p < 0.01$, $^{**}p < 0.05$, $^{*}p < 0.1$.

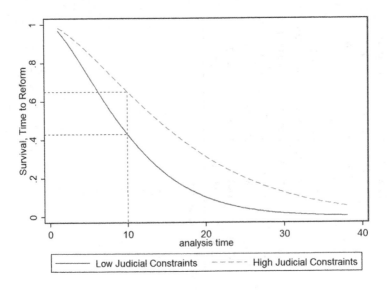

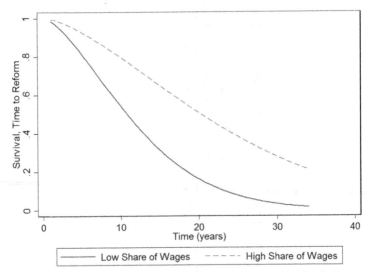

FIGURE 2.2. Time to reform, judicial constraints, and economic shocks.
Note: Plots from Models 1 (upper) and 4 (lower) in Table 2.4.

CONCLUSION

In this chapter we show that major electoral reforms have been a common occurrence in Latin America. In the past thirty years, countries in the region have consistently altered the rules of the electoral game. These changes have often made legislative and presidential electoral rules more inclusive, relaxed presidential term limit rules, removed undemocratic features from the senate, or increased the accountability of elected representatives to voters. Along its different dimensions, then, frequent electoral changes have made political representation more inclusive but, at the same time, allowed incumbents to extend their mandates and to gain critical electoral advantages to consolidate their position.

Our research also shows that the rate of reform has not slowed down since democratization. Rather than a "transitional moment," reforms are the result of opportunities that open up to political entrepreneurs. Political shocks and weak constitutional constraints are key determinants of the rate at which politicians alter the electoral rules. While political shocks provide opportunities to reform the rules of the game to benefit reformers, effective constitutional constraints limit the level of discretion and thus the attractiveness of reforms.

The implication of this analysis, however, is not that the benefits of electoral reform are exclusively appropriated by incumbent governments. Oftentimes, reforms are negotiated with the opposition, with incumbent presidents gaining the opportunity to trade concessions, such as making possible their consecutive reelection in exchange for making more inclusive the rules to elect deputies and senators. Reforms, in consequence, may often have different beneficiaries across electoral categories.

Our findings show that whereas economic crises and political instability contribute to electoral instability, the effective implementation of constitutional constraints over the executive is also a key factor in understanding whether and when electoral reforms take place. In this respect, the analysis provides valuable insights into the relationship between general institutional instability and the degree to which constraints at the constitutional level are observed in practice. If existing institutions inhibit or place obstacles to reform, the lack of compliance or weak enforcement of those restrictions would naturally increase the rate of reform. This is what we observe in the Latin American context, where many electoral reforms depended on overcoming restrictions imposed by formal constitutional rules.

Finally, this chapter also unveils the mechanisms of an "instability trap" (see Helmke, this volume) in electoral system reform, not only because frequent alterations lower the cost of changing electoral institutions by political actors but also because they affect the electoral preferences of voters. As we have shown, shifts in voters' preferences produce changes in the distribution of electoral support across parties and create incentives to introduce reforms among political actors. At the same time, however, frequent electoral

reforms also alter the structure of opportunities and constraints that voters face at each election. Just as a reform toward a more inclusive electoral
system would increase the opportunity of voters to opt for new parties, the
adoption of more restrictive rules would constrain individual voters to strategically switch their previous choices. In both cases, however, electoral reform
would lead to a more unstable electoral competition, which, in turn, would
shorten the duration of the existing electoral system. This constant tinkering
with electoral rules may not have a salutary effect on democratic governance.
Future research on this topic should explore whether and how different levels
of electoral instability affect the conditions of competition among parties, the
representation of voters' preferences, and the accountability of governments.

3

The Stickiness of "Bad" Institutions

Constitutional Continuity and Change under Democracy

Michael Albertus and Victor Menaldo

Most countries in the world operate under authoritarian constitutions. Historically, Latin American countries have been overrepresented in this group. Many of these authoritarian constitutions have proven remarkably sticky. The most long-lived ones not only govern the authoritarian regimes that pen them but subsequently constrain democratic successors long after the end of dictatorship.

On average, these constitutions are relatively strong as defined in this volume: they achieve their statutory goals and produce outcomes their authors and bequeathers intended them to produce. Historically, their authors and bequeathers have used them to satisfy a narrow set of objectives: secure the safety and welfare of outgoing dictators as well as safeguard the political and economic interests of their core supporters. These constitutions are also consequential, distorting democracy in favor of these former dictators and supporters. That is, without such constitutions, public policies and political and economic outcomes would have been quite different; it follows, then, that because they affect economic development, distribution, the provision of public goods, and the quality of democracy in general, these constitutions truly matter (see Albertus and Menaldo 2018).

This point is worth underscoring: authoritarian constitutions and the institutions they enshrine under democracy favor former authoritarian elites *even after* the de facto advantages they possessed start to fade post-democratization (see Albertus and Menaldo 2018). In other words, as authoritarian successor parties fracture or fade, or as civilians exert greater control over the military, former authoritarian elites still fare well under democracy due to the way in which institutions function. For instance, electoral rules prescribed by an authoritarian constitution can serve to overrepresent parties tied to the former authoritarian regime, an idea that resonates with Calvo and Negretto's chapter in this volume regarding the opportunistic shaping of electoral rules.[1] Furthermore, as we will explain, former authoritarian elites do not need to occupy the institutions inherited by a new democracy for these outcomes to obtain.

Of course, as with any institution, authoritarian constitutions are not always strong in an absolute sense. This is particularly the case in terms of stability; in respect to that dimension of institutional strength, holdover constitutions come in three varieties: The first are very stable and thus quite strong. The second are unstable on the surface but actually resilient despite frequent reforms. Then there are authoritarian constitutions that fundamentally change once democracy happens – and sometimes in short order.

The first set of holdover constitutions is very stable after democratization. Many holdover constitutions continue to linger for decades after a democratic transition.[2] Mexico's 1917 constitution is a quintessential example.

Authored during a civil war and intended to end a plutocratic and oppressive dictatorship by ushering in a republic with socialist characteristics, a dominant party made up of the victors of the Mexican Revolution then co-opted it, exploiting it to monopolize political and economic power for over seventy years. The 1917 constitution continues in force today and has allowed many of the forces that benefited under the single-party dictatorship to continue to thrive. The Institutional Revolutionary Party (PRI) secured political overrepresentation in the Mexican Congress, state governorships, and municipalities long after the first steps toward democratization began in the early 1980s, until President López Obrador's shocking landslide victory in 2018.

The reason for the type of stability evidenced by the Mexican constitution is simple: institutional supporters are able to induce enforcement and block change. Therefore, after a democratization stage-managed by outgoing elites,

---

[1] Many of our claims and conclusions coincide with Calvo and Negretto's contribution to this volume. We concur that when political actors are relatively strong, they lock in gains by way of crafting or changing institutions. One important difference, however, is that we examine higher-order institutions rather than just electoral reforms – and that we observe longer period of "lock-in" under these institutions. Another key difference is that we focus attention on both political incumbents and their economic allies under the previous, autocratic regime. Finally, in a point similar to Calvo and Negretto, we privilege the role of shocks in contributing to institutional change – including economic ones, as they also identify.

[2] Paradoxically, constitutions inherited from autocratic predecessors seem to help democracies endure. There were seventy-seven democratic breakdowns between 1800 and 2006. Only twenty-nine of these seventy-seven reversions were from elite-biased democracy – democracies that inherited constitutions from their autocratic predecessors. By contrast, forty-eight were episodes of backsliding from popular democracy – regimes that created new constitutions from scratch after free and fair elections. Furthermore, of these forty-eight episodes of breakdown from popular democracy, in nineteen cases democracy was reborn with an elite-biased constitution inherited from authoritarianism.

the new regime's institutions are insidiously strong: they depend to a degree on "coproduction" by regime opponents or those who would otherwise seek to change them. These authoritarian constitutions "create incentives for actors to invest in assets and strategies specific to that institution ... Such investments strengthen the coalition behind the institution, as actors who develop a stake in particular institutions are more likely to defend them" (Brinks, Levitsky, and Murillo, this volume).

Indeed, they contain the seeds of their own perpetuation by ushering in a host of crisscrossing checks and balances that steeply raise the transaction and collective action costs required to cobble together a broad coalition for change. Furthermore, they often incorporate provisions that call for supermajority vote thresholds for constitutional change, such as requiring two-thirds of both houses of congress to support amending the constitution. Therefore, while it might be easy to oppose specific elements of a constitution, it is far more difficult to agree on what to replace it with and even more difficult to marshal the support to make that change.

This helps create self-enforcing political stability that serves to undermine a dynamic that Helmke outlines in this volume as an "instability trap." Moreover, if succeeding democratic governments selectively enforce constitutional strictures they oppose – such as proscriptions against punishing former elites for crimes or corruption – they risk undermining their own authority and legitimacy or an authoritarian backlash. Consequently, actors begin to invest in assets and strategies such as party platforms and messages that are specific to the institution.

These obstacles effectively raise the costs of institutional change, as Brinks et al. highlight – in contrast to the relatively low costs of change in countries with high electoral volatility that Calvo and Negretto analyze in this volume. Authoritarian constitutions stand in sharp contrast to a prominent example of weak institutions that fail to compel compliance: when presidents overstay their term in spite of prohibitions to the contrary (Elkins 2017; McKie Forthcoming; Versteeg et al. Forthcoming 2020). It also contrasts with cases of institutional instability in which successors simply replace weak institutions at will to reflect their preferences.

Former autocratic elites can also bolster constitutional safeguards to their rights and interests under democracy by exploiting the power afforded by the constitution to cement in their political advantages. For example, they can gerrymander electoral districts to split opposition votes in a way that grants them more seats in the legislature, redraw districts, create or eliminate districts, or reassign the number of seats in each district to amplify the electoral voice of favored political allies.

Moreover, the constitution is itself a focal point that the military or other former autocratic elites can use to coordinate to oppose any threats to their interests and to forestall any attempts at punishing their misdeeds under dictatorship. Attempts by elected politicians under democracy to weaken or rescind elite-friendly measures left behind by autocratic political elites and their economic allies risk galvanizing those elites and inducing them to launch a coup.

In terms of stability, a second set of holdover constitutions are both strong and weak: they are bendable, but not breakable. Seemingly unstable, they nonetheless adapt to continue to advance their authors' objectives, rather than suffer from "serial replacement." This does not imply that their authors design and bequeath weak holdover constitutions so that future politicians and society will ignore, underfund, or fail to enforce them. Outgoing authoritarian incumbents care most about institutional persistence that lasts until their death. They are less concerned about what happens after they pass from the scene. Outgoing authoritarian incumbents who design these institutions are typically not normatively committed to them per se, but rather use them to safeguard their own well-being and parochial interests.

Take Chile's 1980 constitution. This autocratically imposed constitution has had a profound impact on Chilean politics since the return to democracy in 1990. The principal reason is that this elite-biased arrangement has been very stable: constitutional reforms in Chile are quite difficult to enact due to supermajority thresholds for change and the lack of a joint commission to resolve constitutional reform inconsistencies between the two houses of Congress. To be sure, there have been several amendments to Chile's 1980 constitution nonetheless; yet only a minority has adversely affected the autocratic regime's outgoing incumbents and their economic allies.

On the surface, many of these reforms appear consequential. This includes, in 2005, the elimination of designated senators and lifetime senate seats for former presidents, enhanced powers granted to Congress and a corresponding weakening of the military's political role, and the reduction of the president's term from six to four years without consecutive reelection. Perhaps more important was, in 2015, the elimination of the binomial electoral system that ensured the overrepresentation of conservative parties (see Albertus and Menaldo 2018).

Although perhaps better than the original constitution, upon closer examination it turns out that, by the time they were enacted, these reforms helped to advance the interests of conservative elements supportive of the Pinochet regime. Consider one of the most important reforms: the removal of designated senators and lifetime senate seats for former presidents. With the first three presidents drawn from the center-left Concertación, these governments began to appoint designated senators, and the balance of power in the Senate began to tilt away from former authoritarian elites and, absent a removal of this provision, promised to flip in the future. Both factors pushed the right to favor stripping these provisions from the constitution, lest their position in the Senate erode further under continued Concertación rule.

A similar scenario played out regarding reforms to the legislative branch, the executive branch, and the Constitutional Tribunal. In exchange for eliminating designated and lifetime senators, the Right obtained an important concession: weakening the powers of the presidency and enhancing those of the legislature. In particular, they sought minority powers to request ministerial accountability, enhanced powers to establish investigative commissions, and a stronger legislative veto role for the Constitutional Tribunal. As for the binomial electoral system: although the elimination of this patently unfair way of translating votes to seats may have weakened former authoritarian elites' political positions in the short term, it helped legitimize the authoritarian legacies that were not excised from the constitution. Moreover, left-leaning parties have spent decades moderating their platforms in order to be more competitive as coalitions during the tenure of the binomial system. This continued after 2015.

It is therefore not surprising that Chilean public policy has continued to evince considerable bias in favor of elites. In spite of a fairly large number of trials of lower-ranking officials, few top Pinochet-era officials faced punishment, inequality has barely budged, taxes remained modest, and the coddling of economic sectors such as banking and export-oriented agriculture has continued apace (see Albertus and Menaldo 2018).

Finally, there is a final set of authoritarian constitutions inherited from democracies that are relatively weak – at least from the perspective of stability. Institutional reformers usually upend them soon after the first free and fair election that ushers in a new democracy. In these cases, newly elected officials annul and fully replace them with alacrity. Prominent examples include formerly Communist countries that changed their constitutions shortly after the fall of the Soviet Union, such as Bulgaria and Romania.

While authoritarian constitutions are, for the most part, strong, they may perversely and ironically foster institutional weakness in other domains, such as social or environmental policy. This is especially the case in Latin America. The reason is that the institutions they engender perpetuate the factors that sustain general institutional weakness in this region. As Brinks, Levitsky, and Murillo argue in Chapter 1, institutional weakness has plagued this part of the world since the end of colonialism due to state weakness, inequality, and economic and political volatility. And authoritarian constitutions have certainly had an important role in perpetuating state weakness and inequality (see Albertus and Menaldo 2018).

THE OBJECTIVE OF THIS CHAPTER

Since 1800, only 29 percent of new democracies have begun with a constitution that they created themselves or inherited from a past episode of democratic rule in their country. Prominent examples after World War II include Greece, Argentina, the Philippines, and Mongolia. A total of 71 percent of new democracies inherited a constitution that was designed under dictatorship, and where outgoing elites dominated the transition process. Turkey, South Africa, Indonesia, Peru, and Guatemala illustrate this more common scenario.

In short, the prior dictatorial regime is almost invariably the birthplace of democracy. The importance we attribute to this observation parallels recent contributions by Slater and Wong (2013), Riedl (2014), Haggard and Kaufman (2016), and Ziblatt (2017) on the enduring legacies of former authoritarian regimes after democratization. But as distinguished from these authors, we argue that outgoing authoritarian elites do not just orchestrate favorable transitions but also design the core of democratic institutions and the terms of competition to their advantage before they exit dictatorship.

Figure 3.1 displays the ratio of democracies operating under an autocratic constitution versus those operating under a democratic constitution. We follow Przeworski et al. (2000) and define democracy as a regime in which the executive and legislature are elected, there is more than one political party, and control of the executive alternates between parties (i.e., the incumbent party does not always win). We use post–World War II data from Cheibub, Gandhi, and Vreeland (2010), who employ this coding scheme and update it to include data that is as current as possible. For the period 1800 to 1945, we rely on data from Boix, Miller, and Rosato (2013), who also adhere to this coding scheme.

In terms of measuring constitution making and constitutional engineering under autocracy that is then bequeathed to a democratic regime, we identify the type of constitution under which a democracy operates. We consider a country as inheriting an autocratic constitution if it operates with a constitution created under dictatorship. A country is identified as having a democratic constitution if it creates a new constitution upon transition, operates according to a prior democratic constitution that was in place before the previous period of dictatorship, or passes a new constitution sometime after democratization. Data on the origins of constitutions are taken from the Comparative Constitutions Project, which codes the formal characteristics of written constitutions for nearly all independent states since 1789 (see Elkins, Ginsburg, and Melton 2010).

Figure 3.1 allows us to draw attention to several interesting trends. The main takeaway is that elite-biased democracy – democracies that inherited a constitution that was designed under dictatorship and where outgoing elites dominated the transition process – is commonplace. Yet this has varied over time. With the exception of France, which operated under an autocratic constitution from 1870 to 1875, it was nearly unheard of for a democracy's social contract to have blatant authoritarian authorship prior to 1900. Beginning right around 1900, however, this pattern shifted definitively. Between 15 and 35 percent of the world's democracies have operated with autocratic constitutions since 1900. The number reached nearly 40 percent on the eve of World War I as democratic regimes in countries such as Argentina and Chile were

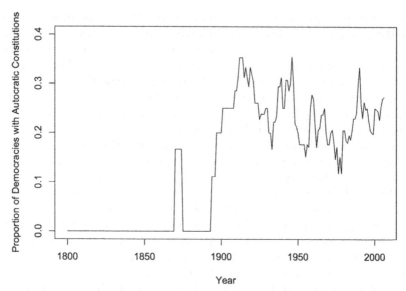

FIGURE 3.1. Proportion of democracies with autocratic constitutions since 1800.

burdened with constitutions penned under prior authoritarian regimes. This tendency decreased in the interwar period.

The predominance of elite-biased democracy becomes amplified after 1950, largely on the back of Latin American countries such as Costa Rica, Panama, and Venezuela, though not exclusively. Seventy percent of new democracies during this period adopted constitutions that had been created under autocracy. The proportion of democracies with autocratic constitutions declined throughout the 1960s and 1970s. Yet, since 1980, the proportion of democracies with autocratic constitutions has grown.

There is considerable variation in the stability of these authoritarian constitutions. While many last decades, until well after the old guard dies off, this is not always the case. Since 1950, 31 percent of the countries that democratized with autocratic constitutions went on to shed their inherited constitutions and replace them with new social contracts. A total of 15.4 percent of all democracy years from 1950 to 2006 are comprised of democracies with amended autocratic constitutions. Furthermore, a total of nineteen of the countries that democratized with elite-biased constitutions during this period subsequently shed their inherited autocratic constitutions for new social contracts. Countries such as Brazil, Madagascar, Poland, and Thailand are illustrative examples. As the pace of democratization slowed after 1990, many consolidating democracies began to shed the constitutions they had inherited from their autocratic predecessors in favor of new constitutions that more closely reflected the popular will.

An important puzzle that is relevant to the theoretical framework and hypotheses explored in this volume, therefore, concerns this question: under what conditions are autocrats and the oligarchs they represent able to design constitutions that endure over time, despite democratization and the changes in the balance of power it generates? In addressing this puzzle, this chapter engages with concepts such as the effectiveness of formal rules and the actors whose conduct is affected by these rules. It does so in a fashion similar to several other chapters in this volume, paralleling issues such as presidential term limits, non-discrimination laws, and rules governing mining and informal vending.

The rest of this chapter outlines the conditions under which this occurs. Elite-biased constitutions are much more likely to be overturned once the old guard from the former authoritarian regime is dead and gone. While this is a necessary condition, it is not sufficient, however. It must be followed by an organized opposition that exploits an economic crisis or a shift in the balance of power associated with globalization and trade. Important rivals to the economic elites who benefited under the initial democratic transition help mobilize everyday citizens to change elite-designed institutions.

In unpacking these ideas, we speak to the issue of why some normatively "bad" institutions such as holdover constitutions inherited by democracies from authoritarian predecessors are strong. Indeed, elsewhere we have shown that across most democracies these authoritarian constitutions are associated with less progressive social and economic policies and less representative and inclusive governance (Albertus and Menaldo 2018). This countenances the view that "laws create inequalities as often as they combat them. They may be exclusionary or discriminatory, reinforce inequality or other societal injustices" (Brinks et al. 2019). In short, not all "strong" institutions are "good" institutions.

FRAMEWORK

Autocrats and their allies seek to ensure that their rights and interests are protected after they hand over power to an incoming democracy. Most authors who write about this topic focus on the ways in which autocrats can safeguard their core interests through de facto "exit guarantees" (Dix 1982) such as military autonomy and the ability to bankroll conservative political parties (O'Donnell and Schmitter 1986; Przeworski 1991; Ziblatt 2017). In contrast, we focus on the role of institutions in protecting authoritarian elite interests through democratization and beyond. Indeed, we argue that the most typical and powerful way outgoing authoritarians and oligarchs can protect their core interests is by designing strong, biased institutions. More often than not, these are created by a constitution that also orchestrates a democratic transition on terms and via a timetable that best suit their interests.

Autocratic elites tend to introduce democracy when they have an advantageous position that they can leverage to their future benefit. The majority of democracies throughout history have been the product of a pact between out-going elites and ascendant political entrepreneurs (see Albertus and Menaldo 2014, 2018). The price of increased competition and pluralism is often the gaming of democratic institutions with laws and procedures that shield elites from the rule of law and that give them an unfair advantage. This has profound consequences for the way in which power is exercised under democracy as well as the economic and distributional effects of such power. And it often gives the democratic opposition strong incentives to try to overturn the institutions it inherits through transition pacts.

Outgoing authoritarian elites do not just orchestrate favorable transitions, but design the core of democratic institutions and the terms of competition to their advantage before they exit dictatorship. Constitutions matter, and constitutional design increases the stakes of politics because in many cases constitutions can indeed lock policy in, sometimes for decades, if not centuries (Elkins, Ginsburg, and Melton 2009).[3] However, rather than generating magnanimity in founding fathers, this creates a perverse incentive for constitution makers to focus more on their self-interest than they otherwise would (see also Hirschl 2004, 2009; Negretto 2013).[4] Instead of a veil of ignorance that militates in favor of the social good and the welfare of future generations, the timing and content of constitutions is, more often than not, opportunistic (Albertus and Menaldo 2018).[5]

Incumbent political elites design constitutions to protect themselves and their interests while holding down, if not crippling, their opponents and political enemies.[6] By designing a favorable constitution that is adopted by the new democratic regime as part of a transition pact, former autocratic leaders increase the likelihood that the representatives of the new political order will not implement harmful policies. They first and foremost seek to protect themselves from prosecution for crimes or corruption under the succeeding political regime.

---

[3] This point is consistent with Brennan and Hamilton (2001). It differs from scholars who believe constitutions reflect underlying power balances in society without shaping them in any fundamental way (Howard 1991; Posner and Young 2007).

[4] This point differs from that of authors who emphasize how founding fathers may be preeminently concerned about the future and their legacies, and thereby concern themselves with the social good and welfare of future generations (Buchanan and Tullock 1962; Elster 1995).

[5] To be sure, power is only one of the central animating features behind constitutions. Other important elements include values, aspirations, and the cataloging of citizen rights and obligations (see Galligan and Versteeg 2013).

[6] This point is somewhat consistent with Linz and Stepan (1996). However, they argue that holdover constitutions are always a ticking time bomb: such constitutions presage the failure of the new regime to consolidate, either because its institutions will be considered by citizens to be illegitimate or because they will be poorly designed. One of our goals is to explain variation in when these elite-biased constitutions endure versus when they are reformed to be more popular.

Incumbent economic elites are the manufacturers, large landowners, firm managers, and other private actors whose participation in economic activity generates rents and tax revenues that can be shared with incumbent political elites. Although incumbent economic elites are autonomous agents with their own interests and political agenda, they partner with political elites because they require favorable institutions and policies to thrive. They sometimes ally with political elites to attack or even eliminate outsider economic elites who are left to fend for themselves. Other times, they partner with political elites to exit a dictatorship on favorable terms.

Outsider economic elites do not depend on the political elites for their market share and rents – at least not in a direct sense. Their income and profits are not the by-product of rigged markets. Outsider economic-elite actors can thus constitute a distinct source of power and influence.

This leaves two options for the political incumbents: First, they can leave outsider economic elites alone. Alternatively, they may try to expropriate outsider economic elites, fearing that their power will only grow stronger in the future. Outsider economic elites under dictatorships therefore have an uneasy and possibly volatile relationship with both incumbent political elites and incumbent economic elites. Like incumbent economic elites, outsider economic elites are not passive bystanders. But, unlike incumbent economic elites, they are in a much more vulnerable position.

Under this framework, political incumbents do not always ally with the "oligarchy" or act as representatives of the Right or the upper classes. Indeed, these partnerships can be diverse (e.g., between communist party leaders and the bureaucrats of a command-and-control economy, where the latter are members of an economic elite but are not necessarily the large landholders or captains of industry usually associated with an aristocratic elite). Our general point is that political incumbents need economic allies and vice versa, and that these two actors sometimes face joint threats that motivate them to head for the exit and transition to democracy strategically, on terms that are favorable to their interests. Whatever economic sector these "economic elites" represent, they require favorable institutions and policies to vouchsafe their interests, even if these elites are newly rich or represent sectors that are not typically thought of as oligarchic.

Crafting the Deal

While the process by which a constitution is crafted and adopted may give political elites an upper hand on the eve of democratic transition, what they ultimately want through the process is a series of guarantees that their interests will be upheld in the long term. This requires considerable attention to institutional design, as well as the content of constitutional provisions.

Table 3.1 displays the constitutional means elites may pursue to ensure their dominance over the longer term, as well as the practical institutional

TABLE 3.1. *Elites' constitutional strategies for retaining influence*

Constitutional measures to ensure elite dominance	Practical manifestations
Vote Aggregation Rules	Electoral system design; malapportionment; gerrymandering; indirect elections
Military Integrity	Military vetoes; appointed military senators; parallel judicial organs for military
Defanging the Opposition	Selective party bans; lack of voter protections; lack of protection for unions; selective restrictions on the franchise
Protection of Former Regime Elements from Prosecution	Prohibition on retroactive criminal punishment
Safeguarding Assets and Rents	Constitutional guarantees to private property; allowing committee system to have input from special interests
Constitutional Stability	Federalism; bicameralism; prohibition on citizen-led legislation via referenda; supermajority thresholds for constitutional change

designs and constitutional provisions this entails. It is important to underscore that not all of these institutions and constitutional provisions are necessarily pursued by elites in the context of any given democratic transition; elites often tailor the design to fit the circumstances. For example, in the case of El Salvador, during the early 1980s the outgoing military regime implanted an idiosyncratic system of proportional representation with three member districts under quota remainders to overrepresent conservative parties; in the case of Chile, the one-of-a-kind binomial electoral system achieved a similar result during the 1990 transition.

The leftmost column of Table 3.1 outlines the most common constitutional means used to ensure elite dominance: vote aggregation rules and measures that govern military integrity, govern constitutional stability, weaken the opposition, protect the outgoing regime's political incumbents from criminal prosecution, and protect the property rights and rents of both incumbents and their economic allies. The rightmost column outlines examples for each of these categories. While we expand upon each of these lists further below and provide examples from actual constitutions inherited by democracies from previous authoritarian periods, here we briefly define some of the terms included in Table 3.1.

Let us begin with vote aggregation rules. Perhaps the most important element in the elites' strategy for gaining overrepresentation in the legislature or executive branch is to choose an electoral system design that maps votes to seats in a way that allows them to gain strong entry into the legislature, senate, or cabinet. This can include systems of proportional representation or outright quotas if elites fear they will be wiped out under majoritarianism. Alternative tools that can also yield the same end, or that can exacerbate the distortions of the electoral system to overrepresent elites, include malapportionment and gerrymandering to create political districts in which elites are overrepresented compared to the general population, or even to call for indirect elections (e.g., election of the executive by an elite-led senate) rather than direct elections.

For many outgoing authoritarian regimes, especially those composed of generals or other elements of the military, or that are strongly allied with the military, it is also important to protect the military's political, organizational, and economic interests. This enables the military to maintain leverage well after any individual dictator leaves office. Sometimes this means allowing the military to veto legislation that pertains to its interests (e.g., national security), or, in extreme cases, allowing it to intervene in national politics when "the national interest" is threatened – for example, by annulling elections. Furthermore, the military will often push for a parallel military judicial branch not subsumed under the civilian judicial system that is charged with adjudicating and punishing wrongdoing within the military. This ensures that military figures do not play by civilian rules, and it can provide cover for illicit military activity, such as cracking down indiscriminately on the opposition or cutting side deals with foreign investors in state-owned enterprises run by the military. More innocuously, military vetoes may also enable the military to choose and remove its own leaders and have power over its own budgets.

In terms of weakening the opposition under democracy, outgoing elites can seek to undermine measures that protect the integrity of the vote, making it harder for nonelites to exercise political voice and thus watering down the franchise and the accountability of citizens' elected representatives. One way to do this historically was by being a laggard in the adoption of the secret ballot, and thus allowing employers or other powerful actors to intimidate nonelites into voting for parties that did not represent their economic interests. Another mechanism with a historical pedigree is the implementation of restrictions on the franchise based on ethnicity, literacy, property, or social class. In modern times, voting restrictions have more to do with limiting access to voting through mechanisms such as voter registration requirements, provisions (or the lack thereof) for giving citizens time off from work to vote, or the failure to make available alternate means of voting, such as absentee balloting.

Table 3.1 also outlines other important constitutional measures to ensure elite dominance via a constitution, such as protecting former regime elements from prosecution, safeguarding elite assets and rents, and ensuring constitutional stability. The practical manifestations of these measures are perhaps more self-evident than the others.

Outgoing authoritarian elites often spend their dear – and rapidly diminishing – political capital, time, and resources to ink constitutions that they then foist on new, elected regimes. They craft these documents prior to inaugural elections, sometimes years, if not decades, before the actual transition. These constitutions tilt the rules of the democratic game in favor of outgoing elites in order to protect their most vital interests.

But as our discussion of Figure 3.1 suggests, that is not the whole story. Democracies sometimes escape the constitutional straitjacket they inherit from their autocratic predecessors. Some eventually annul their "founding" constitution and replace it with an entirely new document. Or they considerably amend it over time and thus eliminate its most egregious forms of elite bias. In other cases, a struggle between conservative elements and liberalizers begins almost immediately upon democratization, especially if the opposition wins the new regime's inaugural elections and can therefore appeal to a popular mandate to legitimize a precocious – and sometimes dangerous – attempt to reform the constitution. The latter scenario, embodied by well-known cases such as Egypt and Myanmar, has perhaps received the most attention from pundits and policymakers.

Despite the outsize attention they receive, brazen attempts by newly elected politicians to immediately rewrite the terms of a democratic transition dominated by outgoing elites are a relatively rare phenomenon. After all, outgoing authoritarian elites would not turn to constitutions to protect themselves after democratization if these constitutions were easily overturned.

The remainder of this chapter explores several facets of constitutional change. First, we examine the details that surround the annulments and amendments of elite- biased constitutions. Second, we look at the factors that explain why some elite-biased democracies with constitutions inherited from their authoritarian past discard those documents at some point down the line, whereas other democracies retain these charters. In other words, what explains the stickiness of this breed of bad institutions?

Looking under the Hood: Constitutional Annulments and Amendments

The table in the appendix to this chapter reports major changes to autocratic constitutions under democracy between 1800 and 2006. It identifies the full set of annulments to these charters. It also contains details of the first set of major amendments to authoritarian constitutions observed under democracy during this period. There are twenty-six cases of constitutions that are annulled at some point after democratization. While the appendix records whether an amendment to elite-biased constitutions occurred, this is a broad category that includes amendments that are unrelated to how popular the democracy is. There are only twelve major amendments to constitutions that made them more popular. Moreover, many of these amendments happen years, or even decades, down the line. There are also thirty-six cases of democracies operating with autocratic constitutions that were never amended at all after democratization. The bottom line is that elite-biased constitutions tend to be enduring deals between the political forces that were dominant before democratization and the opposition: they are rarely changed in ways that hurt the previous political incumbents and their economic allies, and, when they are, such changes tend to happen years after the constitution is inherited by the new democracy.

Of course, not all elements of constitutional reform serve to undermine elite interests, or have any effect, for that matter. Several dimensions of new constitutions (after annulments) and constitutional reform are therefore omitted from the table. Moreover, some changes to elite-biased constitutions actually reinforce elite advantages. Many of these changes, whether they are connected to annulments or to amendments of constitutions, help to solidify the political power of former autocratic incumbents. These include the introduction of bicameralism, for example, as well as the adoption of proportional electoral rules.

The appendix helps to demonstrate these points. It also contains a series of columns that highlight the features of constitutional change. If the autocratic constitution was annulled, it outlines elements of the constitution that replaced it. If the autocratic constitution was instead amended, it highlights the main structural changes and new features.

THE CAUSES OF CONSTITUTIONAL ANNULMENTS AND AMENDMENTS

What explains the durability of authoritarian constitutions? In particular, what explains the adoption of major reforms to elite-biased constitutions under democracy in the form of annulments and amendments that weaken these institutions' elite advantages? Similar to the dynamics highlighted in several other chapters of this volume (e.g., Brinks, Levitsky, and Murillo; Calvo and Negretto), the key to understanding this phenomenon is to identify the actors who want to modify the rules of the game under democracy, their opportunities for a favorable change to those rules, and the catalyzing reason that ultimately pushes them to it.

Whereas those who benefit from an elite-biased democracy are the former political incumbents from a previous autocratic period and their allied economic elites, it is economic elites unallied to the former authoritarian regime and the masses that are slated to benefit from a fundamental change to the rules of the game. Their ultimate goal is to make sure the country remains as a democracy, but they seek to transform it into a more popular one by reforming its elite-biased elements. Practically speaking, they can accomplish this objective by forcing a timetable for constitutional reform upon the government. This may include convoking a new constituent assembly and calling new elections, preferably culminating in a constitution that is more pluralistic, inclusive, and egalitarian. Alternatively, it may entail building broad support for consequential amendments to a country's political charter, and then crafting a plan to ensure that those amendments are realized.

What are the opportunities available to this latter set of actors to make this happen? First and foremost, they must be able to coordinate to agitate for political change. That means that the outsider economic elites who are the losers from the extant system of property rights, economic policies, and regulations must be able to organize citizens and civil society organizations to rally around the cause of constitutional reform. The outsider economic elites can catalyze this process by stoking a debate about the merits and justice of the current charter. They may spearhead outreach campaigns and espouse proreform propaganda. They may also stimulate media coverage that increases interest in their cause, or push opposition parties to adopt constitutional reform as an item in their political platforms. Importantly, due to their economic status, outsider economic elites have the financial wherewithal to bankroll these campaigns.

What might allow outsider elites to pull off such an ambitious agenda? After all, this is an agenda that threatens the rights and interests of the oligarchic elements that have heretofore held disproportionate sway over the democracy and benefited from its elite biases. The most important permissive condition is the death of the previous dictator, or, similarly, the death of key insiders in the previous regime.

Consider Chile. General Pinochet displaced the elected president, Salvador Allende, in 1973, and then imposed a new constitution in 1980. Among other elite-biased measures, it prescribed the appointment of unelected senators and a binomial electoral system that created parity between left- and right-wing parties; it also restored the property rights of landowners and other business interests who were expropriated under Allende. It was fully twenty-five years after the democratic transition, once Pinochet was on his deathbed or after he died in 2006, that the Chilean Left began to undo this legacy. After a rash of constitutional amendments, there are no longer unelected senators in the upper house, military officers from the Pinochet regime have been prosecuted, and the binomial electoral system that contributed to the overrepresentation of conservative parties in the legislature was scrapped in 2015. Given the passage of time, and the passing from the scene of the original actors, these changes were no longer as threatening to the interests of the Right as they might have been.

There are several reasons that the death of a former dictator opens up the playing field. First and foremost, autocratic constitutions designed by outgoing autocratic regimes and foisted upon new democracies often embed provisions that are explicitly intended to cover the lifespan of former autocratic elites. Most straightforwardly, many autocratic constitutions grant congressional posts to the most powerful members of the former authoritarian regime. Chile is again a good example of this phenomenon.

Even absent such provisions, former autocratic political elites can use other constitutional provisions that advantage them to block change. Take electoral system design. By constructing favorable vote aggregation rules, outgoing autocratic elites enhance the likelihood that they will be reelected to political office. This brings them the ability to forestall constitutional revisions; it also typically grants them immunity from criminal prosecution. Consider the PRI in Mexico. After allowing a transition to democracy in 2000, top members of the PRI captured congressional seats and key governorships. Indeed, the PRI even recaptured the presidency in 2012.

Electoral systems, while much stickier than ad hoc political posts created for outgoing autocratic elites, are nonetheless more fragile when their original designers no longer need them as shields. As a new generation of politicians comes to the scene, they may find tweaks to the electoral system to be to their advantage, and the stakes of individual losses are not as severe as for members of the prior autocratic regime.

Finally, if the most likely author of the democracy's constitution, the former dictator in place during the democratic transition, dies, he is no longer a natural focal point that the erstwhile autocratic elites can rally around. Furthermore, for members of the opposition that seek to overturn an elite-biased status quo, the death of the most prominent architect of that status quo can provide an impetus for broad organization across the ranks of the opposition in an effort to seize on popular ferment.

Yet holdover constitutions do not simply unwind as soon as the previous dictator dies. Change must be won by an organized opposition that seeks constitutional change. After all, these institutions are "sticky." So big changes often require a nudge. There are a host of precipitating factors that can facilitate the coordination of outsider economic elites and the masses. Some of these factors – such as major political scandals or bungled foreign wars – differ by country and time period, and therefore are idiosyncratic in nature. Others, however, are more likely to yield predictable shifts in the balance of power between allied economic elites, on the one hand, and outsider elites and the masses, on the other.

Sustained negative shocks to economic growth are one proximate factor that can provide the final trigger for outsider economic elites and the masses to coordinate and organize for constitutional change. Economic crises can set in motion two simultaneous dynamics that can catch allied economic elites flat-footed: First, a crisis can make it much easier for outsider economic elites to make the case to the masses that the economic status quo is fragile, unstable, and threatening to their basic livelihoods. Stimulating broad-based collective action against the status quo should therefore be considerably easier in such circumstances. Second, negative economic shocks can temporarily weaken allied economic elites, the major beneficiaries of the economic status quo. This again opens up an opportunity for outsider elites and the masses to push for change.

A second proximate factor that can trigger the outsider economic elites and the masses to coordinate and organize for constitutional change is a sharp shift in a country's economic openness. It is well documented that rapid shifts in economic openness can redefine the winners and losers in an economy (Rogowski 1989) and lead to substantial short-term economic dislocation. This again generates two dynamics that tilt in favor of the opposition winning changes to the constitutional status quo.

First, outsider economic elites can appeal to those groups who lose ground during a changing economy – in this case, who lose their jobs once tariff barriers come down – that the system is rigged against them. The newly unemployed, as well as those who take a hit to their economic bottom line, are easier to recruit in an organizational drive to topple the political status quo. Second, rapid shifts in economic openness can in some circumstances weaken allied economic elites or strengthen outsider economic elites. This shift in the balance of economic power can be translated to the political realm as outsider economic elites pour funding into opposition parties that espouse constitutional reform or use their relatively greater resources to lobby politicians to support reform in exchange for side benefits or to mobilize the masses.

The chief empirical implications that we can deduce from this discussion of constitutional change under elite-biased democracy are several. There should be a strong, positive relationship between the death of the previous dictator and the ability to change a holdover autocratic constitution. The reason for this "reduced form" prediction is that, although we cannot pin down all of the possible precipitating factors that galvanize the outsider economic elite and the masses to act together to overturn the status quo, we can say with considerable confidence that whatever the ultimate catalyst, when the day comes, these political outsiders will be more likely to coordinate and upend the status quo when the old autocratic guard is dead and gone and the constitution has already fulfilled its most important goals.

There are, however, at least two common factors that tend to weaken incumbent economic elites that were powerful in the previous authoritarian regime and any remaining autocratic political elites. One is prolonged economic crisis. Another is a major shift in economic openness that reconfigures the winners and losers in an economy. When such circumstances transpire, they are likely to precipitate consequential redesigns in the constitutional status quo that yield a reformed social contract.

MEASUREMENT STRATEGY FOR EXPLAINING CONSTITUTIONAL CHANGE

This section outlines our measurement strategy for testing the hypotheses laid out above.

Measuring Constitutional Change

The key dependent variable in the analyses that follow is the annulment or amendment of an autocratic constitution. This is a binary variable that is coded as a "1" in the year an autocratic constitution is annulled or amended under democracy and as a "0" otherwise.[7] Data on the origins of constitutions as well as constitutional changes are taken from the Comparative Constitutions Project.

Measuring Coordination Potential between Outsider Elites and the Masses

To understand why some countries reform elite-biased constitutions under democracy while others do not, we also need to operationalize and measure the structural and proximate factors that encourage constitutional reform as outlined above.

In terms of structural factors, the key variable that helps operationalize the conditions that make constitutional change more likely is the death of the former dictator. We identify the previous ruling dictator using data from Archigos (Goemans et al. 2009), and then track the year of the former dictator's death. Country years following the death of the former dictator are coded as a "1," whereas those in which the dictator remains alive are coded as a "0." The previous dictator is dead in 40 percent of all country years of democracy with an autocratic constitution in our data.

---

[7] As the appendix to this chapter indicates, there are far fewer major constitutional changes. We note that coding the dependent variable in this more inclusive manner biases against us, however, because it introduces noise: we are including both major and minor amendments in this measure, and many of these minor amendments are orthogonal to the interests of outgoing authoritarian elites, or only affect their interests in minor ways. Using major amendments produces similar, though somewhat weaker, results, given that the number of amendments that are coded in this way is reduced significantly.

In terms of proximate factors, we operationalize the concepts above in the following manner. To operationalize dramatic slowdowns in economic growth, we code economic growth shock as the number of years in a five-year lagged window when economic growth in a given country year is more than one negative standard deviation from the country's mean growth rate (dating back to either 1800 or, if the country was established after 1800, its year of independence). This measure is advantageous in that mean country growth rates differ substantially for structural reasons, and a relatively low growth rate for one country could be a relatively high growth rate for another. We use a window because it may take time for the opposition to organize and successfully push for change once an economic growth crisis hits. The mean of this variable is 0.38 across all country years of democracy with an autocratic constitution in our data, with a standard deviation of 0.71.

To measure rapid changes in economic openness that can empower outsider economic elites, we code trade openness shock as the first difference in exports plus imports as a share of GDP (percent) over a five-year period. Data on trade openness are from Penn World Table 6.2. We have coverage on trade openness between 1950 and 2006 for the entire world. The mean five-year first difference in trade openness is 3.33, and the standard deviation is 11.81.

Controls

We also control for several possible confounders across our models. These are all lagged by one period. We control for log(per capita income) and log(total natural resource income per capita). The former captures the idea that wealthier and more modern societies may be more likely to overturn elite-biased constitutions, in part because outsider elites and the masses are likely to be wealthier and therefore more likely to marshal the resources needed to solve the collective action problem than in poorer countries. The latter measures income generated from the production of all hydrocarbons and industrial metals and captures the notion that countries that are reliant on natural resources may be more – or perhaps less (see Menaldo 2016) – likely to overturn elite biases depending on the structure of ownership in the natural resource sector. We take both variables from Haber and Menaldo (2011) because they have coverage starting in 1800.

We also follow Albertus and Menaldo (2012) and measure coercive capacity as military size. Elite-biased democracies that have a greater ability to deploy an internal security force and project the regime's power via a larger, more powerful, military may be more able to forestall popular efforts to reform existing institutions, especially if these efforts play out in unorganized street demonstrations. We measure military size per 100 inhabitants and log it after adding 0.01 to address the zero values in the dataset.

EMPIRICAL STRATEGY FOR EXPLAINING
CONSTITUTIONAL CHANGE

We now turn to a statistical analysis that estimates the probability that a democratic regime will annul or amend an autocratic constitution as a function of the variables outlined above. Because we focus on changes to elite-biased constitutions, the analysis is limited to the set of country years in which democracies operate under an autocratic constitution. During the period 1800–2006, we observe eighty spells of elite-biased democracy in which a new democratic regime inherits a constitution from its autocratic predecessors. These episodes span forty-nine countries. Of these episodes, autocratic constitutions were amended in some way in fifty cases. In another eight cases, democracy gave way to dictatorship prior to any amendment or annulment of an autocratic constitution. That leaves twenty-two right-censored regime spells of elite-biased democracy; these are democratic countries with unamended autocratic constitutions that were still in operation as of 2006.

In order to test our hypotheses about the determinants of constitutional change, we estimate a series of hazard models that calculate a country's risk of succumbing to constitutional change as a function of the independent variables outlined above. In particular, we use competing-risks regression models.

For our purposes, we seek to examine the time it takes for an elite-biased democratic regime episode to "fail" into a more popular democracy. If an elite-biased democracy transitions back to dictatorship, then this new condition prevents that same regime from transitioning into a more popular democracy. Importantly, competing-risks models also account for right-censoring in a manner similar to other survival models. This is important because some regime spells of elite-biased democracy in our data are ongoing. These regimes could become more popular in the future, but had not done so as of the end of our sample period.

To estimate these models we pool the data, allowing us to exploit both its between and within variation. Robust standard errors clustered by country address heteroskedasticity and any intragroup correlation within countries. Furthermore, the results are robust to adding region-fixed effects to control for time-invariant and region-specific unobserved heterogeneity that may impact the likelihood that a country transitions to a more popular form of democracy. We include linear, quadratic, and cubic terms for time to rule out the possibility that some of our independent variables are merely proxying for secular trends.

EMPIRICAL RESULTS

Table 3.2 displays the results of these regressions. We report the raw coefficients from the regressions rather than the hazard ratios. Columns 1–5 test the hypotheses about structural factors that are conducive to reforms to elite-biased democracy. In Column 1, the key independent variable is whether the dictator from the previous episode of authoritarian rule is dead. The coefficient is, as expected, positive, statistically significant at the 0.05 level, and represents a fairly strong substantive effect. When all other variables are held constant, the condition of the former dictator being dead increases the estimated rate of failure into constitutional change by 156 percent.

Column 2 tests the idea that not all authoritarian legacies are created the same. For example, it could be the case that an extrication transition is different from a pacted transition and that these differences may have an impact on the opposition's incentives for change. We argue, however, that the key issue regarding the opposition's incentives for change is their role in the initial transition bargain. When the masses are left out – as they are in authoritarian constitutions – then they will have strong incentives to forge a new social contract regardless of whether that constitution was pacted or not. This does not mean, however, that all inherited constitutions elicit the same level of opposition.

Older constitutions, for instance, may be less likely to elicit strong preferences against them, despite their elite-biased measures or oligarchic tendencies, because they have proven the test of time and informal norms or legislative workarounds have weakened their most unpopular or anachronistic attributes. Conversely, constitutions foisted upon a democracy by an outgoing dictatorship that are of more recent vintage might be especially disliked by the populace and thus face pressures for reform.

To test this hypothesis, in Column 2 we add a variable, constitution age, that operationalizes how old the constitution is in year t. For example, in 2000 Mexico's 1917 constitution is coded as in its eighty-fourth year. Including this variable in the regression does not materially impact the main result of interest: previous dictator dead is still positive and statistically significant. Meanwhile, older constitutions are less likely to be annulled or amended, but the result is just short of statistical significance ($p = 0.11$).

Of course, a constitution's age is only one of several factors that may drive greater constitutional ferment during some periods versus others. The results from Column 2 suggest that constitutions have something akin to a lifespan (e.g., Elkins, Ginsburg, and Melton 2009) and, specifically, if they are able to brook challenges to their mortality early in their life, they are

TABLE 3.2. Annulments and amendments of autocratic constitutions under democracy

	No Oligarchic Constitutions						
	Model 1	Model 2	Model 3	Model 4	Model 5	Model 6	Model 7
Previous Dictator Dead	0.942** (0.383)	0.916** (0.366)	0.843** (0.423)	0.754* (0.435)		0.499 (0.503)	0.292 (0.334)
Previous Transitional Leader Dead					−0.223 (0.644)		
Economic Growth Shock						−0.286 (0.206)	
Previous Dictator Dead* Economic Growth Shock						0.792** (0.385)	
Trade Openness Shock							0.013 (0.011)
Previous Dictator Dead* Trade Openness Shock							0.113*** (0.038)
log(GDP per Capita)	0.602*** (0.228)	0.710*** (0.238)	0.599** (0.243)	0.836*** (0.229)	0.718*** (0.233)	0.680*** (0.260)	0.828*** (0.225)

log(Military Personnel per 100)	-0.249*	-0.220	-0.257*	-0.283*	-0.208	-0.283*	-0.438***
	(0.135)	(0.136)	(0.139)	(0.164)	(0.137)	(0.148)	(0.160)
log(Resource Income per capita)	0.213**	0.205***	0.131	0.170*	0.181**	0.187**	0.251**
	(0.088)	(0.079)	(0.083)	(0.088)	(0.084)	(0.080)	(0.106)
Age of Constitution		-0.009	-0.004	-0.014**	-0.009	-0.009*	-0.018**
		(0.006)	(0.007)	(0.007)	(0.006)	(0.005)	(0.008)
Third Wave			0.706*				
			(0.362)				
Time Trends	Yes	Yes	No	Yes	Yes	Yes	Yes
Observations	347	347	347	256	347	346	221

*p < 0.10, **p < 0.05, ***p < 0.01 (two-tailed). The dependent variable in all models is the annulment or amendment of an autocratic constitution. All models are competing risks regressions. Raw coefficients rather than subhazard ratios are reported. Standard errors clustered by country are in parentheses. Constants and time dummies are not shown. All independent variables except the status of the former dictator, constitution age, and third wave are lagged one period. Sample is restricted to democratic country years with autocratic constitutions.

more likely to survive into later periods. Similarly, it could also be the case that there are distinct global periods in which constitutional change is more likely than not. Indeed, this is the primary reason why we have introduced (nonlinear) secular trends into the regressions hitherto. It is particularly interesting to note that the cubic term (not shown) suggests a positive relationship between time and constitutional reform. In terms of theory, a possible explanation for this pattern is that the disappearance of the coup card during the third wave of democracy dramatically changed power distributions. This therefore should have made it easier to eliminate authoritarian constitutional legacies.

To find out if this is the case, in Column 3 we drop the secular trends and replace them with a dummy variable that is coded as a "1" during the third wave (between 1974 and 2006) and "0" otherwise. The results seem to corroborate our intuition. During this time period it was 103 percent more likely that a democracy that inherited an autocratic charter reformed its holdover constitution (p-value < 0.051). In the regressions that follow, we return to estimating secular trends, but note that this result strengthens the notion that the reason autocratic constitutions are retained in some democratic settings is not merely indifference by citizens or their relative impotence, but the fact that former political incumbents and their economic allies use their leverage and coercive capabilities to enforce these documents.

Of course, this does not mean that there are not some differences between constitutions that may be masked by our coding scheme. One might argue, for example, that authoritarian constitutions imposed by dictators, such as Pinochet in 1980 and Fujimori in 1993, are different from transitional constitutions in which the old regime has partially or fully collapsed, and that both of these types are, in turn, different from oligarchic constitutions: those drafted under limited suffrage and ushered in by governments that were civilian, pluralist, and often highly competitive. Examples are Chile before 1909, Argentina before 1912, and Costa Rica before 1946.

While it very well may be the case that the latter set of regimes already contained various protections for economic elites and their political benefactors, we theorize that the political dynamics driving opposition to constitutions inherited from nondemocratic regimes will nonetheless be similar across authoritarian constitutions and oligarchic constitutions. It is still the case that outsider economic elites and the masses are left in the political lurch during an episode of either "authoritarian" or "oligarchic" constitution making. Their best response in both cases is to bide their time and wait for a propitious context to seek to reform a holdover constitution in order to see their political preferences gain greater influence.

Columns 4 and 5 of Table 3.2 address these concerns. First, in Column 4 we rerun the regression represented in Column 2 after dropping democracies that inherit constitutions from an "oligarchic" regime. We code these regimes as oligarchic when they are characterized by multiparty competition among civilian politicians amid restricted franchise. The results of this experiment do not drastically alter our results, though the coefficient on previous dictator dead declines somewhat in statistical and substantive significance. Furthermore, in this model, constitution age reaches conventional levels of statistical significance.

In Column 5 we examine the effect of the death of transitional leaders on constitutional change. These are leaders who came to power on the eve of transition with the explicit intent of calling free and fair elections, and who ruled in office for less than one year. As anticipated, the death of transitional leaders has no statistically distinguishable impact on constitutional change. These leaders are unimportant when it comes to generating focal points or permissive conditions for scrapping or amending autocratic constitutions. This regression therefore serves as a "placebo" test that underscores the idea that a former dictator's death is critical to galvanizing a political movement based on coordination between opposition forces to change the political game.

While the death of a former dictator and his absence from the political scene might predispose an elite-biased democracy toward experiencing constitutional change, it does not explain the precise timing of change. Column 6 demonstrates that economic growth shocks following the death of the previous dictator make constitutional change much more likely. The hazard ratio for the interaction between the death of the previous dictator and economic growth shocks translates into a 123 percent increase in the estimated rate of failure to constitutional change. By contrast, an economic growth shock that occurs when the previous dictator is still alive has no distinguishable impact on constitutional change. Similarly, constitutional change is not more likely following the death of the previous dictator when economic times are good.

Column 7 demonstrates a similar finding for trade openness shocks. A trade openness shock following the death of the previous dictator increases the likelihood of constitutional change. The hazard ratio connected to this interaction term is 1.12, indicating a 12 percent increase in the estimated rate of failure to enact constitutional change. In contrast, a trade openness shock that occurs when the previous dictator is still alive has no statistically distinguishable impact on constitutional change. Similarly, constitutional change is not more likely following the death of the previous dictator absent a trade shock, though the coefficient is positive.

CONCLUSION

The seamless association between constitutions and democracy has a distinguished pedigree in political science. For many researchers, in fact, there is
no clear difference between adherence to the rule of law – which one might
refer to as constitutionalism – and democracy (Weingast 1997). In order for
free and fair elections to consistently guide political life, and for legislators to
govern in a manner that truly reflects the will of the citizens they represent,
they must abide by electoral and procedural rules that limit their own power,
keep the playing field level, and allow challengers to contest power (Dahl 1973;
Przeworski 1991).

Yet this volume raises critical questions about these guiding assumptions.
Political actors may simply change the formal rules when it is in their interests
to do so without fundamentally eroding democracy. They may also selectively
enforce rules. For example, they may allow anachronistic or draconian laws to
remain on the books, even if failure to enforce them signals the fact that these
laws are widely ignored by both citizens and their representatives.

Our chapter calls to attention yet another fly in the ointment of long-
standing theory: the formal rules of the game embedded in constitutions may
not reflect the will of the majority at all – and can even contravene it. Yet
given the strong, often self-enforcing, institutions that grow out of these documents, citizens may find it hard to change these rules. We find that this is
especially the case with constitutions written under dictatorships that persist
under democracy. The theoretical insights and empirical patterns we adduce
in this chapter also speak to a key feature of some of the institutions discussed
in the opening chapter of this volume. The constitutions we explore speak to
"a disjuncture between rule writers and power holders [that] may ... emerge in
democracies with high socioeconomic inequality."

This chapter takes an important next step in unpacking these issues by
investigating whether institutions under democracy will remain weighed
down by the legacy of their authoritarian past. Here we show that democracies can indeed reinvent themselves. A flawed social contract written by
dictators and for dictators can be renovated. This chapter also demonstrates
the conditions under which this occurs. Elite-biased constitutions are much
more likely to be overturned once the old guard from the former authoritarian regime is dead and gone. The most important institutional elements
are constructed to endure at least until generational change presents the

opportunity for a new dawn. A new beginning – if it comes – is usually initi-ated by an organized opposition that seizes on economic crisis or a shift in the balance of power. The origins of dismantling elite-designed institutions under democracy often reside not, paradoxically, with the majority of citi-zens, but rather with rivals to the economic elites that benefited under the initial democratic transition. New actors that arise on the political scene are often critical in this process.

APPENDIX

Country	Year	Annul-ment Year	Major Political Changes Linked to Annulments	First Set of Major Popular Amendments	Major Political Changes Linked to Amendments	Elite-Bias Change
Argentina	1912			No amendments		
Argentina	1946			1949	*Popular changes:* rescinded indirect elections and replaced them with plurality formula.	
Argentina	1958			No amendments		
Argentina	1963			No amendments		
Argentina	1973			No amendments		
Belgium	1894			1921	*Popular changes:* introduced universal male suffrage.	
Benin	1991			No amendments		
Bolivia	1979			No amendments		
Bolivia	1982			No major popular amendments	*Elite-biased changes:* introduced steeper supermajority requirements for constitutional change (1993, 1994).	
Brazil	1985	1988	*Popular changes:* allowed for popular referenda; ban on leftist parties lifted; amending constitution made easier.	No major popular amendments		
Bulgaria	1990	1991	*Elite-biased changes:* adopted proportional electoral system; strengthened protection of property rights.	No major popular amendments		
Burundi	1993			No amendments		
Burundi	2005			No amendments		
Central African Republic	1993	1994	*Popular changes:* civilian control over military increased; unicameralism adopted.	No amendments		
Chile	1909			No major popular amendments	*Elite-biased changes:* empowered the military in executive politics (1924).	
Chile	1934			1963, 1967, 1970	*Popular changes:* gave government broader powers to expropriate land (1963); nationalized mines (1967); allowed illiterates to vote (1970). *Elite-biased changes:* limited parliamentary initiatives on public expenditures (1943).	

Federal/ Unitary State	Bicameralism	Electoral System	Leftist Extremist Party Ban	Popular Initiation of Legislation	Prohibits Ex Post Punishment	Property Rights Protection	Miscellaneous
Federal	Bicameral	Majoritarian		No	Yes	Yes	Indirect elections for senate, restrictions on the franchise, no secret ballot
Federal	Bicameral	Majoritarian	Banned	No	Yes	Yes	Indirect elections for senate
Federal	Bicameral	Majoritarian	Banned	No	Yes	Yes	Indirect elections for senate, military veto
Federal	Bicameral	Proportional	Banned	No	Yes	Yes	Indirect elections for senate
Federal	Bicameral	Proportional	Banned	No	Yes	Yes	Malapportionment
Unitary	Bicameral			No	No	Yes	Indirect elections for senate, supermajority amend, restrictions on the franchise
Unitary	Unicameral	Proportional	No ban	No	Yes	Yes	Supermajority amend
Unitary	Bicameral	Proportional	Banned				Malapportionment, military veto
Unitary	Bicameral	Proportional	Banned				Malapportionment
Federal	Bicameral	Proportional	Banned	No	Yes	Yes	Supermajority amend, Malapportionment
Unitary	Unicameral	Mixed	No ban	No	Yes	Yes	Supermajority amend
Unitary	Unicameral	Proportional	Banned	No	Yes	Yes	Supermajority amend
Unitary	Bicameral	Proportional	Banned	No	Yes	Yes	Indirect elections for senate, supermajority amend
Unitary	Unicameral	Majoritarian	Banned				
Unitary	Bicameral	Majoritarian	Banned	No	Yes	Yes	Supermajority amend, restrictions on the franchise, no secret ballot
Unitary	Bicameral	Majoritarian	Banned	No	Yes	Yes	Restrictions on the franchise, no secret ballot

(continued)

Country	Year	Annul-ment Year	Major Political Changes Linked to Annulments	First Set of Major Popular Amendments	Major Political Changes Linked to Amendments	Elite-Bias Change
Chile	1990			2005	*Popular changes*: reduced military role in politics; eliminated appointed senators; opened door for electoral reform away from overrepresenting conservative parties.	
Colombia	1937			No major popular amendments		
Colombia	1958	1991	*Popular changes*: party ban lifted.	1968	*Popular changes*: lifted bans on electoral competition (1968); abolished two-thirds majority requirement to pass legislation (1968).	
Comoros	1990	1992	*Elite-biased changes*: bicameralism adopted.	No amendments		
Comoros	2004			No amendments		
Costa Rica	1946			No amendments		
Cyprus	1983			No major popular amendments		
Czechoslovakia	1989			No major popular amendments		
Denmark	1901	1915	*Elite-biased changes*: moved to proportional electoral system. *Popular changes*: universal suffrage extended.	No amendments		
Ecuador	1979	1984	*Popular changes*: prohibited ex post punishment.	No major popular amendments		
El Salvador	1984			1992	*Popular changes*: civilian control over military increased.	
Fiji	1992	1997	*Popular changes*: ethnic Fijians gave up guaranteed legislative minority in lower house. *Elite-biased changes*: protected landholdings of powerful ethnic Fijians.	No amendments		
France	1870	1875	*Elite-biased changes*: adopted indirectly elected senate.	No major popular amendments		
Georgia	2004			No major popular amendments		
Ghana	1993			No major popular amendments		

Federal/ Unitary State	Bicameralism	Electoral System	Leftist Extremist Party Ban	Popular Initiation of Legislation	Prohibits Ex Post Punishment	Property Rights Protection	Miscellaneous
Unitary	Bicameral	Binomial	Banned	No	Yes	Yes	Appointed Senators, supermajority amend, constitutional court can ban parties, malapportionment
Unitary	Bicameral	Proportional	Banned				
Unitary	Bicameral	Proportional	Banned				
Unitary	Unicameral	Majoritarian	No ban				
Unitary	Unicameral	Majoritarian	No ban	No	No	Yes	Supermajority amend
Unitary	Unicameral		Banned	No	Yes	Yes	Supermajority amend
Unitary	Unicameral	Proportional	Banned	No	Yes	Yes	Supermajority amend
Federal	Bicameral	Proportional	Banned				
Unitary	Bicameral	Majoritarian	Banned	No	No	Yes	Malapportionment, restrictions on the franchise
Unitary	Unicameral	Proportional	Banned	Yes	Yes	Yes	Supermajority amend, Malapportionment
Unitary	Unicameral	PR 3-seat districts under quota-remainders	Banned	No	Yes	Yes	Supermajority amend, military veto
Unitary	Bicameral	Majoritarian		No	Yes	Yes	
Unitary	Unicameral						No secret ballot
Unitary	Unicameral	Mixed	No ban	No	Yes	Yes	Supermajority amend, constitutional court can ban parties, Malapportionment
Unitary	Unicameral	Majoritarian	Banned	No	Yes	Yes	Supermajority amend, Malapportionment

(continued)

Country	Year	Annul-ment Year	Major Political Changes Linked to Annulments	First Set of Major Popular Amendments	Major Political Changes Linked to Amendments	Elite-Bias Change
Guatemala	1958			No amendments		
Guatemala	1966			No amendments		
Guatemala	1986			No major popular amendments		1993 amendments simply set the stage for new elections and redefined term limits, following an attempted *auto-coup*.
Guinea-Bissau	2000			No amendments		
Guinea-Bissau	2004			No amendments		
Honduras	1971			No major popular amendments		
Hungary	1990			No major popular amendments		Drafters finished up unfinished business.
Indonesia	1999			No major popular amendments		
Italy	1919			No amendments		
Italy	1946	1947	*Elite-biased changes*: quasi federalism adopted; stronger property rights protection put in place. *Popular changes*: party ban lifted; right to form trade unions introduced; universal suffrage enacted.	No amendments		
Kenya	1998			No major popular amendments	*Elite-biased changes: gave parliament, rather than civil society, the ability to enact constitutional change (1999).*	
Korea, South	1960			No major popular amendments		
Korea, South	1988			No amendments		
Kyrgyzstan	2005	2006		No amendments		
Liberia	2006			No amendments		
Madagascar	1993	1998	*Elite-biased changes*: federalism adopted.	No major popular amendments		
Mexico	2000			No major popular amendments		

Federal/ Unitary State	Bicameralism	Electoral System	Leftist Extremist Party Ban	Popular Initiation of Legislation	Prohibits Ex Post Punishment	Property Rights Protection	Miscellaneous
Unitary	Unicameral	Proportional	Banned				
Unitary	Unicameral	Proportional	Banned	No	Yes	Yes	Military veto
Unitary	Unicameral	Proportional	Banned				Malapportionment, military veto
Unitary	Unicameral		Banned				
Unitary	Unicameral	Proportional	Banned				
Unitary	Unicameral	Proportional	Banned	No	Yes	Yes	Supermajority amend, indirect elections for executive, military veto
Unitary	Unicameral	Mixed	No ban				
Unitary	Unicameral	Proportional	Banned	No	No	No	Supermajority amend, military veto
Unitary	Bicameral	Proportional	Banned				
Unitary	Bicameral		Banned				
Unitary	Unicameral	Majoritarian	No ban	No	Yes	Yes	Supermajority amend, malapportionment
Unitary	Bicameral	Majoritarian	Banned				
Unitary	Unicameral	Mixed	Banned	No	Yes	Yes	Supermajority amend, constitutional court can ban parties, malapportionment
Unitary	Unicameral	Mixed	Banned	Yes	Yes	Yes	Supermajority amend, constitutional court can ban parties
Unitary	Bicameral	Majoritarian		No	Yes	Yes	
Unitary	Bicameral	Proportional	Banned	No	Yes	Yes	Supermajority amend
Federal	Bicameral	Mixed	Banned	No	Yes	Yes	Supermajority amend

(continued)

Country	Year	Annulment Year	Major Political Changes Linked to Annulments	First Set of Major Popular Amendments	Major Political Changes Linked to Amendments	Elite-Bias Change
Netherlands	1897			1917	*Popular changes*: universal suffrage and corporatist bargaining introduced. *Elite-biased changes*: proportional representation introduced.	
Niger	1993			No amendments	None	
Niger	2000			No amendments	None	
Nigeria	1979			No amendments	None	
Pakistan	1972	1973	*Elite-biased changes*: federal form of government adopted; two-thirds majorities and assent of president required for constitutional amendment.	No amendments	None	
Pakistan	1988			No major popular amendments	None	
Panama	1949			No amendments	None	
Panama	1952			No major popular amendments	None	
Panama	1989			1994	*Popular changes*: standing armed forces abolished.	
Paraguay	1989	1992	*Elite-biased changes*: former presidents allowed to serve in senate for life; active-duty members of the military banned from political participation.	No amendments	None	
Peru	1946			No amendments	None	
Peru	1956			No major popular amendments	None	
Peru	1963			1964	*Popular changes*: facilitated land reform.	
Peru	1980			No major popular amendments		
Peru	2001			2004	*Popular changes*: popular initiation of legislation introduced, including popular recalls.	Decentralized structure of government (national, regional, municipal) (2002).
Poland	1989	1992	*Popular changes*: made it easier to reject amendments to legislation made by senate.	No major popular amendments		
Romania	1990	1991	*Elite-biased changes*: party ban introduced.	No amendments		

Federal/ Unitary State	Bicameralism	Electoral System	Leftist Extremist Party Ban	Popular Initiation of Legislation	Prohibits Ex Post Punishment	Property Rights Protection	Miscellaneous
Federal	Unicameral						
Unitary	Unicameral	Mixed	No ban	No	Yes	Yes	Supermajority amend
Unitary	Unicameral	Proportional	No ban	No	Yes	Yes	Supermajority amend
Federal	Bicameral	Majoritarian	Banned				
Federal	Bicameral	Majoritarian	Banned				
Federal	Bicameral	Majoritarian	Banned				
Unitary	Unicameral			Yes	Yes	Yes	Supermajority amend
Unitary	Unicameral	Proportional	No ban	Yes	Yes	Yes	Supermajority amend
Unitary	Unicameral	Mixed	Banned		Yes	Yes	Supermajority amend, malapportionment
Unitary	Bicameral	Mixed	Banned				Appointed senators
Unitary	Bicameral		Banned				Restrictions on the franchise, military veto
Unitary	Bicameral	Proportional	Banned				Restrictions on the franchise
Unitary	Bicameral	Proportional	Banned				Restrictions on the franchise
Unitary	Bicameral	Proportional	No ban	No	Yes	Yes	Appointed senators, supermajority amend
Unitary	Unicameral	Proportional	No ban				
Unitary	Bicameral	Majoritarian	Banned				
Unitary	Bicameral	Proportional	Banned				

(continued)

Country	Year	Annulment Year	Major Political Changes Linked to Annulments	First Set of Major Popular Amendments	Major Political Changes Linked to Amendments	Elite-Bias Change
Senegal	2000	2001		No amendments		
Serbia RB	2000	2003	*Elite-biased changes*: introduced bicameralism.	No major popular amendments		
Spain	1977	1978	*Elite-biased changes*: introduced bicameralism; devolved power to local governments; property rights strengthened. *Popular changes*: party ban dropped.	No amendments		
Sri Lanka	1989			No major popular amendments		Amendment intended to depoliticize the public service introduced (2001); no real changes made.
Sudan	1965			No major popular amendments		
Sudan	1986			No major popular amendments		
Sweden	1911	1974		1918, 1919	*Popular changes*: universal suffrage extended at local level, followed by national level.	
Thailand	1975			No major popular amendments		
Thailand	1979	1981	Constitution suspended	No amendments		
Thailand	1992	1997	*Elite-biased* changes: bicameralism enacted; proportional representation adopted. *Popular changes*: direct elections introduced in both houses of congress.	No major popular amendments		
Turkey	1983			1987	*Popular changes*: party ban lifted.	
Uruguay	1919	1933	Constitution suspended.	No major popular amendments		
Uruguay	1942	1952		No major popular amendments		
Venezuela	1946	1947	*Popular changes*: introduced direct elections for the executive; expanded workers' rights; introduced secret ballot.	No amendments		
Venezuela	1959	1961	*Popular changes*: popular initiation of legislation allowed.	No amendments		

Federal/ Unitary State	Bicameralism	Electoral System	Leftist Extremist Party Ban	Popular Initiation of Legislation	Prohibits Ex Post Punishment	Property Rights Protection	Miscellaneous
Unitary	Bicameral	Proportional	No ban				
Federal	Unicameral	Proportional	No ban				Military veto
Federal	Bicameral	Proportional	No ban				
Unitary	Unicameral	Proportional	Banned	No	Yes	Yes	Supermajority amend
Unitary	Unicameral	Majoritarian	Banned				
Unitary	Unicameral	Majoritarian	Banned	No	Yes	Yes	Supermajority amend
Unitary	Bicameral	Proportional	Banned	No	No	No	Restrictions on the franchise, indirect elections, supermajority amend
Unitary	Bicameral	Majoritarian	Banned				
Unitary	Bicameral	Majoritarian	Banned				
Unitary	Unicameral	Majoritarian	Banned				
Unitary	Unicameral	Proportional	Banned	No	Yes	Yes	Constitutional court can ban parties, malapportionment, military veto
Unitary	Bicameral	Proportional		Yes	No	Yes	Indirect elections for senate, supermajority amend
Unitary	Bicameral	Proportional	No ban				
Federal	Bicameral	Proportional	Banned	No	Yes	Yes	Indirect elections for executive, restrictions on the franchise, military veto, lack of secret ballot
Federal	Bicameral	Proportional	Banned				Indirect elections for executive

Sources: V-DEM, Comparative Constitutions Project, Database of Political Institutions, Gerring et al. (2005), Bakke and Wibbels (2006), Henisz (2000), Mainwaring and Pérez-Liñán (2013), and country-specific sources.

4

Presidential Crises in Latin America

Gretchen Helmke

INTRODUCTION

Presidential failure and Latin America have long been synonymous.[1,2] Although the specter of military coups that replaced elected leaders with generals largely receded during the 1980s, presidential crises, like the one that engulfed Brazil's political class and resulted in the impeachment of President Dilma Rousseff in 2016, continue to grab headlines. Following the Venezuelan Supreme Court's ruling to strip the opposition-led legislature of its authority in 2017, Congress voted to put President Nicolás Maduro on trial for plotting a coup against the constitution. A little more than a year later, Peruvian president Pedro Pablo Kuczynski resigned rather than be impeached on graft charges related to the widening Odebrecht scandal.

Fixed terms (along with separate selection of the executive and legislature) are at the very core of presidentialism, neatly distinguishing it from parliamentarism (Shugart and Carey 1992; Linz 1994). Although term lengths and reelection rules vary across countries and over time, each and every Latin American constitution calls for the president to serve at least four years (Corrales and Penfold 2014;

---

[1] This chapter draws on *Institutions on the Edge: Inter-Branch Crises in Latin America* (Helmke 2017, Cambridge University Press). I want to thank YeonKyung Jeong and Rabia Malik for their excellent research assistance and help in preparing the chapter. I am especially grateful to Jorge Domínguez, for comments on an early version of this chapter and to Daniel Brinks, Steven Levitsky, and Vicky Murillo for their editorial suggestions.

[2] Although the vast majority of Latin American presidents prior to the 1980s fell in military coups, presidential impeachments by the legislature were carried out in Cuba (1936) and Panama (1951, 1955, 1964). Self-coups took place in Uruguay (1933, 1942), Panama (1946), Colombia (1949), Honduras (1954), and Ecuador (1970) (see Pérez-Liñán 2007: 52–55).

Elkins 2017). Thus, according to the framework articulated by Brinks, Levitsky, and Murillo (hereafter Brinks et al.) in Chapter 1, deviations in the actual duration of presidential terms – whether longer or shorter, as this chapter discusses, seemingly offer prima facie evidence that such institutions are weak.

Yet most Latin American constitutions also provide for formal institutional mechanisms for impeachment, the declaration of mental incapacity, and/or the option of recall elections. Intended to provide citizens with a kind of safety valve, these are measures of last resort against the abuse of executive power. As in the Constitution of the United States, they are designed to "thread the needle" between preserving the separation of powers inherent in presidential systems and preventing tyranny or chaos in the event that a president cannot or will not serve the public interest (Sunstein 2017).

Precisely because one of the long-standing concerns about presidentialism is its rigidity, the relative normalization of impeachment and other related forms of early removal in the region has often been taken as a rather positive sign that these fraught systems are adopting parliamentary traits (Carey 2005; Pérez-Liñán 2005, 2007; Marsteintredet and Berntzen 2008). Consider recent events in Guatemala. Caught in the middle of a corruption scandal uncovered by the International Commission against Impunity (CICIG), pundits applauded the stunning early resignation of Guatemalan president Otto Pérez Molina in 2015, touting his downfall as a sign of a "democratic spring" in Central America.[3]

Indeed, when it comes to assessing the relative weakness of institutions surrounding executive fixed terms in Latin America, the optimistic view for invoking such mechanisms of early removal might even be taken a step further. If we suspect that many leaders in the region are prone to just the sorts of bribery and corruption scandals that have taken some of these presidents down (witness the unfolding Odebrecht scandal that has implicated multiple current and former presidents in Brazil, Peru, Ecuador, Colombia, Panama, and Venezuela), then it may be that the failure to oust other such compromised presidents is the real problem. Perhaps undue forbearance, to borrow Holland's terminology, not constitutional hardball (cf. Tushnet 2003; Fishkin and Pozen 2018; Levitsky and Ziblatt 2018), is the real sign of institutional weakness?

OUSTERS AND OBSERVABILITY

When it comes to classifying forced presidential exits (or their absence) as indicative of weak institutions, we instantly run up against a common problem of partial observability (Bas and Stone 2017). The basic dilemma is that we observe easily enough the universe of premature presidential ousters, but often have incomplete or conflicting accounts about whether ousted presidents committed an impeachable

---

[3] *BBC Monitoring Latin America*, September 7, 2015.

TABLE 4.1. *Ousters and inference*

	Crime	Not Crime
Ousted	A	B
Not ousted	C	D

offense, and/or whether full-term presidents did not. In other words, among the former group, we do not know for sure whether any given case lies in cell A or cell B. Or, among the latter group, whether a case fits in cell C or cell D.

If the rule of law is operating as it should and institutions are strong, most administrations most of the time should be located in cell D, although a few might land in cell A. Impeachment is thus serving the intended safety valve role and performs primarily as a mechanism of deterrence. The threat of early removal, in other words, operates off-the-equilibrium path and presidents obey the rule of law (and fulfill their term) as a result (Helmke 2017). Until recently, most comparative scholars would have classified the United States as fitting just this sort of pattern. Of the forty-five presidents that have served in last 240 years, only four have faced impeachment by Congress and none have been removed by the Senate.[4]

Note that even in this fortuitous scenario, it is hard to know for sure whether we should attribute the pattern to the strength of the formal institutions constraining presidents and their opponents. Politicians may be complying with the rule of law due to other normative commitments that have little do with how the formal rules for removal are structured or enforced (Levitsky and Ziblatt 2018). To this point, the editors' discussion of insignificant institutions reminds us that simply observing an outcome consistent with the formal rules does not always tell us which, if any, formal institutional mechanism is driving it. The relative frequency of presidential ousters across contemporary Latin America, of course, suggests that unpacking the potential problem of institutional insignificance is hardly the most pressing conceptual concern. The bigger problem of interpretation rather lies with the partial observability mentioned above both for those presidents that complete their terms, but suspicions abound over whether they violated the rule of law, and for those who exit early. Among the latter, citizens and elites may vehemently disagree over what exactly constitutes an impeachable offense and whether the president committed one.

Witness the debacle in Brazil during 2016 over Rousseff's impeachment. Although the procedural rules were followed at each instance (a point I return to below), the basis on which the president was impeached was far murkier.

---

[4] Recently, however, critics of the Trump administration have raised the question of whether the standards for impeachment in the United States are too high and whether the mechanism has been under-used (see Ezra Klein, "The Case for Normalizing Impeachment," *Vox*, November 30, 2017).

She and her supporters had good reasons to argue that the crime of which she was accused – breaking fiscal laws by using funds from a federal bank to mask government deficits in the run-up to her reelection in 2014 – was not a crime at all, and had long been a standard practice for former presidents. To be sure, Rousseff was deeply unpopular at the time of her ouster, but many saw her removal as a coup against democracy and the rule of law.

Fueling this concern was the subsequent revelation of secret tapes suggesting that Rousseff was removed to halt Operation Car Wash, which has become the largest corruption investigation in history.[5] This interpretation has only been made more plausible by the fact that many of her accusers in congress have been repeatedly linked to the unfolding scandal. Most notably, her main accuser, former speaker of the lower house, Eduardo Cunha, was subsequently convicted and is currently serving a fifteen year sentence for taking bribes from the giant state oil company Petrobras.[6] Meanwhile, Rousseff's successor, President Michel Temer, managed to stave off numerous corruption charges and retained his tenuous grip on power until he handed over power to Jair Bolsonaro in 2019. But if Rousseff's supporters were right, the country suffered the fate befalling leaders in cell B, whereas, under President Temer, Brazil was entrapped in cell C.

As the Brazilian example also nicely illustrates, whether the formal rules for removal are followed is not dispositive that institutions are working as they should. To be sure, instances where procedural rules are clearly skirted – for example, the 2012 snap impeachment of Paraguayan president Fernando Lugo, which took place in approximately thirty-six hours and left the president no time to mount a defense – obviously raise red flags.[7] But cases such as Rousseff's are harder to interpret from the standpoint of institutional weakness, not because the procedures are flouted or evaded, but because the standards for removal are often unclear. U.S. constitutional scholars routinely debate what exactly constitutes a "high crime" or "misdemeanor," or who, and on what basis, determines the president's "mental incapacity." As Sunstein (2017) notes in his recent treatise on impeachment in the United States, there may be some very good reasons to leave the conditions for removal vague in constitutions, but doing so means that the door is almost always open to political manipulation.

In sum, because of the limits of information available about what a particular president did or did not do (partial observability), we (citizens and

[5] "Brazil Minister Ousted after Secret Tape Reveals Plot to Topple President Rousseff," *Guardian*, May 23, 2016. Operation Car Wash began I, 2014 and includes the Odebrecht scandal that is currently enveloping much of Latin America's political and business class.

[6] "Brazil Ex-speaker Eduardo Cunha Jailed for 15 years," *BBC*, March 30, 2017.

[7] Initial attempts to impeach Peruvian president Pablo Kuczynski were also extremely rushed: Kuczynski was given just two days to respond to changes of graft ("Bid to Oust Peru's President Falls Short in Congress," *New York Times*, December 21, 2017).

scholars alike) can never fully know the underlying distribution of impeach-able offenses.[8] And, because of the vagueness and flexibility of the law itself, we can never be completely sure whether in any given instance the impeach-ment mechanism (and the like) is being underused (cell C vs. D) or over-used (cell A vs. B). Nevertheless, if political factors systematically map onto presidential exits, then we have good reason to suspect that the rule of law is underperforming in both directions. The next section elaborates just such a theory and links it explicitly to the problem of selective compliance outlined by the editors.

THE POLITICAL LOGIC OF PRESIDENTIAL EXITS

In Chapter 1, Brinks et al. offer a succinct theory of institutional weakness that captures the calculus of noncompliance. Framed as a simple inequality, they argue that noncompliance will occur whenever both the costs of violat-ing the institution are less than the costs of obeying it ($V < S$) and the costs of violating the institution are less than the costs of changing it ($V < C$). Such a calculus maps neatly onto the bargaining theory of presidential crisis that I have developed elsewhere (Helmke 2017).

That theory begins with the familiar premise that Latin American presi-dents enjoy two types of powers: de jure powers, such as the president's formal institutional powers specified by the constitution, and de facto powers, such as the president's level of partisan support in congress or their degree of pub-lic support (cf. Mainwaring and Shugart 1997).[9] To represent this logic more formally, consider the bargaining scenario depicted in Figure 4.1, similar to Powell (1999). Here, I use the following notation: E represents the executive branch, L represents the congressional branch, Q represents the status quo distribution of the president's power to shape policies, and X_E represents the president's offer. Note that unlike standard spatial models, where each actor's utility improves as policy moves closer to his or her ideal point, the figure requires a different interpretation. Think of the distance between, say, the executive branch, E, and the status quo, Q, as the extent to which the presi-dent controls policy-making. Moving Q to the left expands the president's power; moving it to the right contracts it.[10]

---

[8] For a game-theoretic model of the dynamics of scandal, see Dziuda and Howell (2019); see also Nalepa, Vanberg, and Chiopris (2018).

[9] This section draws on chapter 3 of Helmke (2017).

[10] The model is depicted in terms of the legislature's pie, whereby 1 implies that the legislature has total control over policy and 0 represents complete executive control over policy. For the ease of interpretation, the reversionary point for the legislature in the static model is 0.

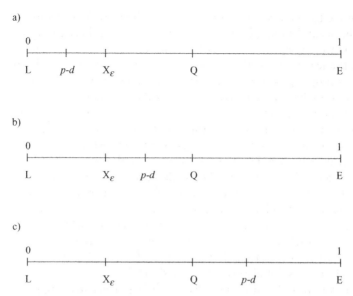

FIGURE 4.1. Bargaining in the shadow of a presidential crisis.

Consistent with Cox and Morgenstern (2002), the size of the gap between the president's partisan support (represented in the model below by the term p) and constitutional powers (represented by the term Q) increases the president's incentives to reign rather than rule. But, crucially, it also increases the opposition's incentives to get rid of the rogue president. In this institutional context, the public also plays a role: public support of the president raises the costs to the legislature for seeking to oust the president; popular disapprobation lowers the costs to the legislature (as represented by d in the model).

The legislature's best response is derived by comparing its utilities over the various outcomes. Thus, imagine that the legislature is choosing between accepting the president's use of her extensive legislative powers versus getting rid of the president. If the legislature accepts the president's proposal, then effectively it receives Q up until its acceptance of the president's proposal and X_E thereafter. Conversely, if the legislature decides to attempt to get rid of the president, its payoffs reflect both the probability that it may win, p (which is a function of the opposition's seat share), minus the costs of carrying out such an attack, d, plus the probability that it may fail, $1 - p$, minus the costs of carrying out such an attack, d. Intuitively, the legislature faces an incentive to attack whenever $p - d > Q$.

As such, the legislature's incentives for getting rid of the president depend on the relationship between these costs and benefits relative to the current distribution of policy-making power, or Q. To clarify this, consider the first figure above, in which the legislature's payoff to attacking is still relatively small and X_E (and by extension Q) remains to the right of $p - d$. Here, the legislature has no incentive to challenge the president, and the president can move policy to X_E. In the second figure, however, $p - d$ now falls in between Q and X_E, but as long as the president sticks with the status quo level of his policy-making powers, the legislature still does not have an incentive to attack. In the third scenario, though, $p - d$ instead falls to the right of both X_E and Q, and the legislature now has an incentive to go after the president.[11]

Several points directly related to Brinks et al.'s hypotheses about institutional noncompliance flow from this. First, the stakes of the presidency (Q), which can be interpreted as the costs of the opposition fulfilling the presidential term (S for Brinks et al.), clearly affect the threshold for interbranch conflict. Specifically, the more policy-making control the executive has (i.e., the further Q is to the left), the lower the legislature's probability of success needs to be in order for it to face an incentive to attack. In the extreme, the strongest presidents imply that Q is pushed to a point where the legislature will face incentives to attack, even if the prospects for success are quite low.

Second, by incorporating both the president's legislative (p) and public support (d), the model also speaks directly to V, or the costs associated with legislators violating fixed terms. Clearly, the less legislative support the president enjoys, the easier it is to facilitate the president's removal. And in line with many of the familiar proximal cause arguments of presidential crises (Hochstetler 2006; Pérez-Liñán 2007; Kim and Bahry 2008; Hochstetler and Edwards 2009) the core model presented here subsumes the basic idea that the lower the public trust is in the president (captured by d in the above model) – the lower the costs are to the opposition for ousting the president prematurely.

Third, the model also provides a converse political logic for the sort of undue forbearance described in the previous section (i.e., cell C in Table 4.1). Trivially, when the president has a legislative majority, the probability of a successful removal is low (witness the debate over whether U.S. Republican senators could ever be persuaded to impeach President Trump). Here, p remains to the left of Q. More counterintuitively, however, the model also suggests that institutionally weak presidents should be secure in office, even if they lack partisan support. At the same time, the model easily incorporates the familiar insight that presidential popularity can also function as the president's shield. Thus, the d term can explain why legislators may still be inhibited from pursuing an impeachment that would be in the public interest whenever the president enjoys wide popular support – think of Fujimori in the lead-up to the 1992 self-coup.

Finally, assuming that the thresholds for removal remain lower than the thresholds for changing the constitution (V < C), we can also extend the logic of the model to understand why the legislature opts for ousting presidents,

---

[11] As I explain in Helmke (2017), the interbranch bargaining problem only emerges in the absence of complete information. In other words, if a president does not know precisely where p – d falls, then she cannot be sure how much she needs to adjust her behavior to avoid a crisis.

rather than stripping them of their formal powers. As such, institutional weakness takes the form of political, not institutional, instability, at least in the sense defined by Brinks et al.[12]

In sum, because the ability to remove presidents early is inherently flexible, it is always in danger of devolving into a partisan tool. This section supplies a logic that explains misuse in *both* directions. In the case of overuse, noncompliance with the basic institution of electing a president for a fixed term is associated with the bargaining failures induced by the gap between the president's de jure and de facto powers as described above. Likewise, in the case of underuse (selective noncompliance or forbearance against using impeachment), the same model allows us to grasp why a president who is violating the rule of law might nevertheless be allowed to remain.

PATTERNS OF PRESIDENTIAL CRISES

Let me now turn to empirics. Here, I draw on the Inter-branch Crises in Latin America Dataset (ICLAD) that I have constructed in order to measure systematically cases where presidential crises occur and where they do not.[13] The unit of analysis is the administration year for eighteen Latin American countries between 1985 and 2008, which yields a total of 474 observations. A complete description of the coding rules is contained in Helmke (2017), but for our purposes here let me underscore the two main criteria that I use to identify a presidential crisis.

First, because my research focus is on separation of powers crises, ICLAD only includes presidential crises where congress plays a discernible role. This effectively means that a handful of the early presidential exits coded by other scholars are not treated as crises in my analysis. For example, Argentine president Raúl Alfonsín left office several months early in the midst of a severe economic crisis, but the Argentine Congress played little role in his exit. Likewise, former Bolivian president Carlos Mesa had to submit his resignation to Congress twice before they accepted it, and there is little evidence that he did so to forestall a congressional threat. Thus, even though these individuals left office early, these cases are coded as "0" from the standpoint of inter-branch crises.[14]

Second, because I am interested in the dynamics underlying the onset of separation of powers crises, congressional attempts that succeed in removing presidents as well as those that fail to remove them are included. This allows

---

[12] See Helmke (2017) for a somewhat different definition of institutional instability.

[13] Data and code are available for download at www.gretchenhelmke.com/data.html

[14] The unit of analysis in the ICLAD dataset is administration-country-year. For every year that the country experienced a presidential crisis, as defined above, the case is coded as a "1." For every observation in which the country did not experience such a crisis, the observation is coded as a "0." See Helmke (2017) for additional details on coding. Note that all of the statistical results described here are robust to a variety of measures of presidential powers, opposition control of congress, and the public cost of launching a presidential crisis (Helmke 2017).

me to incorporate such well-known cases as the failed attempt made by the Colombian Congress to impeach President Samper in 1995–1996 for allegedly accepting drug money during his electoral campaign, as well as the two separate unsuccessful attempts to get rid of Paraguayan president González Macchi in 2001 and again in 2002. By including all such attempts at removal, we also pick up several other lesser-known incidents, such as the foiled attempts to impeach former Ecuadorian president Sixto Durán-Ballén in 1995 following the ouster of his vice president, Alberto Dahik, or threats the same year by the congressional opposition to impeach Nicaraguan president Violeta Chamorro for refusing to promulgate the legislature's constitutional reforms.

These basic coding rules yield a total of thirty-six presidential crises in Latin America between 1985 and 2008. This translates into 8 percent of all administration years, or roughly a third (32 percent) of all administrations in Latin America experiencing a presidential crisis during these three and a half decades.

Underscoring the validity of my coding protocol, the table in the appendix to this chapter shows that nearly all of the presidential crises identified by other scholars of the region (Valenzuela 2004; Pérez-Liñán 2007; Kim and Bahry 2008; Llanos and Marsteintredet 2010; Mustapic 2010) are contained in ICLAD.[15] Likewise, with the single exception of Paraguay 1994,[16] I include all of the cases between 1985 and 2005 that are listed by Hochstetler (2006) as either challenges to the president launched by the legislature or jointly by the legislature and the "street." I also include three additional cases that are classified by Hochstetler as only involving the street: Ecuador (1999), Argentina (2001), and Bolivia (2003). As mentioned above, protests arguably played the most important role in these presidential ousters, but in each of these cases the legislature also mattered.

---

[15] Note that the two major exceptions are Haiti and Argentina. First, because I limit my focus to Spanish- and Portuguese-speaking countries, I do not include Haiti in the dataset (cf. Valenzuela 2004). The only other meaningful difference between my cases and the cases covered in the extant literature involves how the interim Argentine presidents post 2001 are treated. For instance, both Pérez-Liñán (2007) and Mustapic (2010) list Rodríguez Saá but not the other two short-lived presidents. All administrations that last less than six months are excluded from my dataset. Finally, Mustapic also includes both Alfonsín and Duhalde (2002–2003) as examples of ousted presidents, but because Congress was not involved in their resignations, by Rule 1 I do not treat these as interbranch crises.

[16] Under my selection rules, there was no interbranch crisis in Paraguay in 1994. To be sure, there were protests by peasants over agricultural reforms, as well as calls for General Oviedo to step down from the armed forces. Also, at certain points the government pact with the opposition in Congress broke down, but there were no concrete threats or actions taken by the legislature to remove the president. The only potentially qualifying incident was an investigation into President Wasmosy's election as president of the Colorados, but there is no evidence that the investigation called for his removal or was followed up in a way that threatened to foreshorten his tenure (see *Latin American Weekly Report*, June 16, 1994; June 30, 1994; December 1, 1994; December 29, 1994).

Presidential Crises

MAP 4.1. A map of presidential crises in Latin America, 1985–2008.

In Ecuador, there were calls within Congress to impeach Mahuad in March 1999.[17] In Argentina, the legislature's calls for impeachment were arguably the last straw in getting de la Rúa to step down early (Pérez-Liñán 2007: 180). Following the violence associated with the protests in Bolivia, Congress played a similar role in getting Sánchez de Lozada to abandon his post.[18] The rest of the cases included in my dataset stem either from threats or failed attempts to remove presidents that had not been previously uncovered by the literature, or through my inclusion of more recent cases (Map 4.1).

[17] *Latin American Weekly Report*, March 16, 1999.
[18] *Latin American Weekly Report*, February 25, 2003.

TABLE 4.2. *Illustrative cases of the power gap*

	Strong de Jure Powers	Weak de Jure Powers
Unified Government	Chile (1990–2010)	Mexico (pre-1997)
Divided Government	Ecuador (pre-2006)	Mexico (1997–present)

Notice the enormous variation across the region in terms of which countries experience presidential crises and which do not. At one end, there are several countries in which no presidential crises occurred during this period (Chile, Costa Rica, El Salvador, Mexico, Panama, Honduras, and Uruguay). At the other end, there are a total of seven countries that have experienced executive ousters or congressional attempts at ousters multiple times: presidential crises have occurred twice in Colombia, Peru, and Venezuela; three times in Bolivia; four times in Brazil; five in Nicaragua and Paraguay; and a staggering eight times in Ecuador. In the middle, we have just a handful of countries that have only experienced one such crisis (Argentina,[19] Dominican Republic, and Guatemala).

Statistical evidence presented in related work (Helmke 2017) suggests that this empirical pattern covaries precisely with the argument outlined in the previous section about the importance of a gap between the president's partisan and constitutional powers. Specifically, the likelihood of a presidential crisis increases significantly among minority presidents, but only if presidents have substantial formal constitutional powers.[20] To see this conditional effect at work in specific institutional contexts, compare Mexico under unified and divided government to Chile and Ecuador (Table 4.2).

In contrast to many South American presidents, the Mexican president is notoriously weak in terms of constitutional power. Throughout most of the twentieth century, of course, the Institutional Revolutionary Party (PRI) was hegemonic, and precisely because Mexican presidents enjoyed enormous partisan powers, they were able to utterly dominate policy-making (Weldon 1997; Magaloni 2003). And, indeed, during that period in Mexican history, executive–legislative relations were nothing if not stable. Yet even with the collapse of single-party rule at the end of the 1990s and the onset of enormous

---

[19] See footnote 12.

[20] Using the ICLAD data to construct a dummy variable for presidential crises for each administration year, I estimated a series of logit models with numerous measures for the president's partisan powers, the president's constitutional powers, the interaction between these two types of power, and various measures for public support, such as the number of protests, trust in government, etc. Regardless of the measures used, the story is the same: public support consistently shields the president, while the effect of partisan support is entirely conditional on the degree of a formal presidential power.

social violence with the Drug War beginning in the mid-2000s, presidents have been unpopular and lost elections, but they have not been threatened with early exit.

If we switch to contexts in which the president holds far more de jure powers, the effects of divided government become much more noticeable. Specifically, consider Chile and Ecuador. Both countries are in the ninetieth percentile in terms of formal presidential powers, but the distribution of partisan support for the president varies dramatically from one country to the other. In Chile from 1990 until 2010, presidents came from the center-left coalition, Concertación, and essentially controlled the majority of the lower house seats. Since the coup that toppled Salvador Allende in 1973, not a single democratically elected president has been ousted.

Now, take Ecuador. With the exception of President Correa, over the last few decades no Ecuadorian president has even come close to controlling a majority of seats in the legislature. As a result, presidents in the 1980s and early 1990s were often forced to rely on so-called ghost coalitions in order to govern (Mejía Acosta and Polga-Hecimovich 2010). Unlike Chile, such postelectoral coalitions proved fleeting and unstable, as the defection of the Social Christian Party (PSC) from Durán-Ballén's government and the subsequent ouster of his vice president, Alberto Dahik, in 1996 illustrated. Meanwhile, the very institutional reforms that further increased presidential powers in the late 1990s severely undermined the president's ability to sustain such coalitions (Mejía Acosta and Polga-Hecimovich 2010). Given this fateful combination, the massive wave of institutional instability that swept over Ecuador's minority presidents from 1997 until 2006 is entirely in keeping with the political logic advanced in the previous section.

Finally, and entirely consistent with a story rooted in political manipulation and selective noncompliance, it is important to underscore that the vast majority of interim presidential successors have not belonged to the same political party as the failed predecessor. Here, because only cases of actual removal are relevant, it is easy to update the data to 2018. Of the seventeen failed leaders in the region during the last three decades, fully two-thirds of their successors were not from the same political party (Table 4.3).[21]

---

[21] Given the split-ticket rules that operate in many of these countries, in many of the cases the vice president was not from the same party as the president (Collor 1992; Mahuad 2002; Sánchez de Lozada 2003; Gutiérrez 2005; Lugo 2012; Pérez Molina 2015). In other instances, there simply was no vice president waiting in the wings. Between 1858 and 1999, for instance, the Venezuelan constitution had no provision for a vice president. When Carlos Andrés Pérez was suspended in 1993, therefore, the head of Congress temporarily took power until Congress could designate a successor. In Argentina, Carlos "Chacho" Álvarez had already resigned from Argentina's first coalition government in protest over a bribery scandal a little more than a year before de la Rúa was forced from power. In the space of few weeks, Congress designated no fewer than four interim presidents; each was from the Peronist opposition. And in Paraguay, where President Cubas was impeached for allegedly having had his own vice president, Luis Argaña, assassinated, Congress stepped in to designate someone from the rival Colorado faction.

TABLE 4.3. *Presidential crises and succession, 1985–2018*

Country	President/Party	Year of Exit	Replaced by VP	Successor/Party Affiliation
Argentina	de la Rúa/UCR	2001	No	Duhalde/PJ
Bolivia	Siles Zuazo/MNR	1985	No	Paz Estensorro/ MNR
Bolivia	Sánchez de Lozada/MNR	2003	Yes	Mesa/Independent
Brazil	Collor/PRN	1992	Yes	Franco/PRN
Brazil	Sarney/PMDP	1990	No	Collor/PRN
Dominican Republic	Balaguer/SCR	1996	No	Fernández/DLP
Ecuador	Bucaram/PRE	1997	No	Alarcón/ARF
Ecuador	Mahuad/DP	2002	Yes	Noboa/DP
Ecuador	Gutiérrez/PSP	2005	Yes	Palacio/Independent
Guatemala	Serrano/MAS	1993	No	de León Carpio/ Independent
Guatemala	Pérez Molina/PP	2015	Yes	Maldonado/ Independent
Honduras	Manuel Zelaya/ Liberal	2009	No	Micheletti/Liberal
Paraguay	Cubas/Colorado	1999	No	González Macchi/ Colorado
Paraguay	Lugo/FG	2012	Yes	Franco/ARLP
Peru	Fujimori/Peru2000	2000	No	Paniagua/AP
Peru	Kuczynski/PPK	2018	Yes	Vizcarra/ Independent
Venezuela	Pérez/AD	1993	No	Velásquez/ Independent

INSTABILITY TRAPS AND INSTITUTIONAL SPILLOVER

Taken together, the evidence from contemporary Latin America points away from a rule-of-law account of presidential exits and toward a political account of presidential crises driven by gaps between de facto and de jure institutional powers. Whereas the correlates of crises referred to in the previous section treat each presidential crisis essentially as an independent observation, the fact that presidential crises tend to repeat in the same countries also suggests a more dynamic story in which the crises themselves might alter the conditions that produce them. This not only has important implications for drawing conclusions about institutional weakness qua noncompliance at a particular point in time, but also about the possibility for path dependence, or so-called traps of such institutional weakness.

One obvious extension of my main argument is that presidential crises that occur at time t can potentially alter endogenously the salient conditions that confront actors at time $t + 1$. Importantly, such shifts can either reinforce the tendency toward repeating presidential crises or undermine it. Extending the argument in this way recalls the approach to endogenous institutional change described by Greif and Laitin (2004). In their language, we might think of public opinion, or d in the model; partisan opposition, or p in the model; and the allocation of formal powers, or Q, as "quasi-parameters" that shift in the wake of a given crisis, thus making subsequent crises more or less likely.

Consider the following two statements by commentators on recent events in Brazil and Guatemala, respectively:

"This is a coup, a traumatic injury to Brazil's presidential system," said Pedro Arruda, a political analyst at the Pontifical Catholic University in São Paulo. "This is just pre-text to take down a president who was elected by 54 million people. She doesn't have foreign bank accounts, and she hasn't been accused of corruption, unlike those who are trying to impeach her.... It's putting a very large bullet in Brazilian democracy," said Lincoln Secco, a professor of history at the University of São Paulo. "This will set a very dangerous precedent for democracy in Brazil, because from now on, any moment that we have a highly unpopular president, there will be pressure to start an impeachment process.[22]

Mr. Pérez Molina, 64, is the first president in Guatemalan history to resign over a corruption scandal, experts said, a striking rarity in a country long known for the impunity of its political establishment. And though the economy in Guatemala has lagged compared with those of other countries in Latin America, Mr. Pérez Molina's sudden reversal of fortune put it firmly within a wave of efforts elsewhere in the region to make political systems more accountable.[23]

Clearly, the views expressed above about the longer-term effects of presidential crises could not be more different. The first narrative, captured in the quote on the impeachment debacle in Brazil, forebodes a very dark future. In this view, not only is the act of impeachment seen as unjust and undemocratic – overturning the votes of 54 million Brazilians – but the long-term consequences are feared to be even more problematic. Politicians and citizens indeed learn from institutional crises, but they absorb a very different lesson. Thus the implication here is that instability becomes a trap. The latter quote on Guatemala, by contrast, is quite optimistic. Interbranch crises are salutary; they not only cleanse the system of corruption, but they set the country on a new path in which horizontal accountability can finally emerge. Political insta-bility, in a word, inoculates. Hochstetler and Samuels's (2011) analysis of the

---

[22] Andrew Jacobs, "Vote to Impeach Brazil's Leader Passes Strongly," *New York Times*, April 18, 2016.

[23] Asam Ahmed and Elisabeth Malkin, "Otto Perez Molina of Guatemala Is Jailed Hours after Resigning Presidency," *New York Times*, September 3, 2015.

consequences of presidential crises hardly supports such a sanguine picture, but contrary to the most pessimistic warnings, they find that presidential ousters appear to have little effect on broader indicators of political risk, including socioeconomic risks and a range of quality-of-governance measures, such as internal conflict, corruption, law and order, or bureaucratic quality. Likewise, they find little support for the concern that early ousters neces- sarily undermine public support for democracy. However, as they note, their analysis only represents a first cut at adjudicating the negative effects of crises.

Consider, for example, how such crises may affect institutional reforms. If our theory about the institutional stakes of the presidency is right, then one of the most disheartening facts about a country like Ecuador is that, in the wake of such instability, incoming presidents have falsely inferred that strengthening the president's constitutional powers will help them overcome any weaknesses associated with being in the minority. Instead, the model tells us that reforms that push Q to the left will only exacerbate interbranch bar- gaining failures. Along these very lines, Mejía Acosta and Polga-Hecimovich (2010) highlight the perverse consequences of granting the president more unilateral powers in periods following Durán-Ballén's troubled administra- tion. In particular, they describe how such reforms increased the president's incentives to go it alone and reduced the president's capacity to forge lasting coalitions, resulting in the wave of repeated presidential ousters post 1996. Thus, for scholars already concerned about the general tendency in the region to increase presidential powers (e.g., Negretto 2015), this analysis highlights the paradox of how such reforms themselves may directly contribute to fur- ther presidential instability, leading to yet a further concentration of power in the executive, and so on.

Presidential crises may beget additional instability through shifting the other parameters identified in the model as well. For example, even if a previous crisis potentially teaches future leaders how to rein in their power (although see below for a very different possibility), it also potentially teaches opposition politicians how to coordinate to effectively remove presi- dents. More systematic research should be done to assess precisely how these risks shift, but even a cursory glance at the incidence of presidential crises suggests that these are usually not one-off occurrences. With a handful of exceptions, such as the Dominican Republic post Balaguer or Colombia in the wake of the scandal that nearly resulted in the impeachment of President Samper, most countries have experienced either no presidential crisis or mul- tiple presidential crises.[24] Such bimodality in the distribution of crises, of

---

[24] Note that my conclusions about the repetition of presidential crises likely differ from Hochstetler and Samuels (2011) because my data consist of both successful and unsuccessful attempts by legislatures to remove presidents.

course, is consistent with multiple explanations (including that the baseline conditions identified in the previous section are operative); however, if such crises recur under otherwise less propitious circumstances (i.e., the opposition holds fewer seats, the executive is more popular), it suggests that previous crises may be serving to embolden opponents in ways that endogenously shift p.[25]

If crises help lower trust in the institution of the presidency, rather than a specific leader (or, as Hochstetler and Samuels [2011] find, in democracy as a regime writ large), then this should also lower the opposition's threshold for launching presidential crises going forward. Preliminary analysis of Latinobarómetro survey data (Helmke 2017) suggests that presidential crises have a systematically negative effect on the public's trust in the executive branch, at least in the short run. Controlling for levels of public trust in both the executive and the legislature during the year in which the crisis occurred, public trust in both branches suffers in the year immediately following the crisis, declining by twenty-four percentage points for the legislative and approximately thirty-eight percentage points for the executive. Just how long it might take public trust to recover, and whether or not it ever reaches levels that would be sufficient to insulate presidents, we obviously cannot say without further analysis.

Finally, and perhaps most importantly, presidential crises may turn out to have even more pernicious consequences for other branches. To the extent that presidents at risk seek to mitigate threats to their removal, they often target other institutional actors preemptively. By exploiting whatever political capital they have at the beginning of their term, such presidents seek to take over or to disband the other branches of government in order to foreclose the possibility that conditions will shift against them down the road. Thus, presidents operating in contexts where past presidential instability has occurred have been significantly more likely to try to target legislatures and courts than have presidents who do not confront such a legacy (Helmke 2017).

Consider President Correa, who was the first Ecuadorian leader to complete his term in office in more than a decade. Although Correa won the presidency in 2006 with 57 percent of the vote, his grip on the office was far from guaranteed. The headline of the *Andean Group Report* at the time read: "Correa Wins But How Long Will He Last?" Having made the decision not to allow any members of his political movement, Movimiento Patria Altiva y Soberana (MPAIS), to run in the legislative elections, Correa began

---

[25] The other side of coin is that if an earlier attempt to remove the president backfires, then elites might update in the opposite direction and conclude that impeachment hurts, rather than helps, their side. Democrats who were wary of impeaching Trump in 2019, for example, frequently cited the political fallout that the Republicans incurred following Clinton's impeachment in 1998.

his term with no legislative support. As Catherine Conaghan explains, "With this one bold stroke, Correa both unequivocally identified his candidacy with the voters' deeply anti-political mood and accepted the risk that if elected, he would assume office with zero assurance of legislative support and far greater assurance that legislators might move to oust him at any time" (2008: 50).

Instead, as soon as he took office, Correa began to rally public support for a constituent assembly that could potentially be used to dissolve Congress altogether. With his party then winning the majority of seats in the following October elections for the constituent assembly, Correa did not hesitate to act. Within hours of its first meeting, the constituent assembly dissolved the opposition-led legislature. In an interview I conducted with the leader of the opposition party Democracia Popular and its former deputy, Diego Ordóñez, I asked explicitly, "Do you think that Correa had some sort of fear that Congress would [treat] him the way that they did his predecessors?" to which he emphatically responded:

Yes, when the new Congress was established, I said to tell them, "The first day you have to say this: 'President, our hand is stretched out in order to realize the changes this country needs.'" They didn't do that. Instead, they put on gloves and said, "let's fight." Correa, being the biggest contender here, they were killed ... they should have taken a wiser position.[26]

Although such overarching attacks on legislatures are relatively rare in contemporary Latin America, Correa is hardly an isolated case. Although the modalities differ across leaders, wholesale attacks against opposition-led legislatures have arguably been driven by similar motives in Peru and Guatemala during the 1990s and in Venezuela under both Chávez and Maduro. In each of these cases, presidents made the decision to dissolve Congress not merely to expand their policy-making powers, but to avoid being ousted from power. In Fujimori's and Serrano's administrations, Congress had already opened investigations into the president or his inner circle, and had explicitly raised the prospect of impeachment before the president launched a self-coup. In Venezuela, Chávez, as Correa had done, convened a constituent assembly that served to make Congress obsolete. In Maduro's case, as noted in Chapter 1, the president relied on his court to do the dirty work. In both of these administrations, getting rid of the legislature was part of a broader attempt to strengthen the president's grip on power.

If disbanding the legislature in order to mitigate the risk of removal amounts to taking a wrecking ball to democracy and the rule of law, manipulating courts – either through selective removals or packing – often constitutes a

---

[26] Author interview, Quito, Ecuador, July 2008.

more pinpointed method for achieving the same goal. Although judges cannot unilaterally threaten to oust the president, recent events in Venezuela highlight the fact that presidents clearly rely on courts to attempt to alter the threat they face. And because judicial manipulation can be carried out in a multitude of ways, ranging from impeachment and forced resignations to court packing and jurisdiction stripping, focusing on controlling courts is often a much easier strategy for presidents than launching a full-blown constitutional coup or overhaul. This helps make sense of the fact that while legislative instability rarely occurs without judicial instability – in the cases of legislative instability described above, courts were also simultaneously targeted – the reverse is not true (Helmke 2017, 2018).

CONCLUSION

Strong presidents beget weak institutions. This chapter provides a fresh take on this familiar paradox. The more formal constitutional powers are allocated to the president, the more incentives legislative opponents face to ignore fixed terms and to deploy constitutional mechanisms for a president's early removal. At the most basic level, the fact that impeachment in contemporary Latin America has been at least seriously attempted in about a third of all administrations suggests that, if impeachment is intended to operate as a deterrent or remedy of last resort, then the rule of law is not operating optimally. The political logic of selective noncompliance explored in this essay bolsters our ability to understand why, when, and where fixed presidential terms fail.

More generally, the dynamics of institutional instability traps triggered by such crises here are not dissimilar from the negative feedback loops identified by Calvo and Negretto in this volume. Whether by responding to crises by adopting constitutional reforms that further increase presidential powers, or by changing the public's willingness to come to the defense of institutional actors that maintain the status quo distribution of political power, presidential crises have the potential both to breed future presidential crises and to destabilize the other two main branches of government. As in Calvo and Negretto's chapter, this chapter suggests that political entrepreneurs may respond to past presidential crises by launching reforms as a way to hedge their bets against further losses. This chapter extends this sort of defensive logic, however, beyond explaining changes to the electoral rules of the game, and by instead delineating the conditions under which presidents react to past crises by undermining and destabilizing the very institutional checks that could put their own administration at risk.

APPENDIX

Presidential crises in Latin America, 1985–2008

Administration	Country	Crisis Onset	Sources
Siles Zuazo	Bolivia	1985	*Latin American Weekly Report*; Valenzuela (2004); Pérez-Liñán (2007); Kim and Bahry (2008); Hochstetler and Edwards (2009); Mustapic (2010); Buitrago (2010)
Sarney	Brazil	1987	*Latin American Weekly Report*; Mainwaring (1997)
Febres Cordero	Ecuador	1987	*Latin American Weekly Report*; Hochstetler (2006); Pérez-Liñán (2007); Hochstetler and Edwards (2009)
Borja	Ecuador	1990	Pérez-Liñán (2007); Mustapic (2010)
Paz Zamora	Bolivia	1991	Pérez-Liñán (2007)
Borja	Ecuador	1992	*Latin American Weekly Report*; Mustapic (2010)
Fujimori	Peru	1991	Valenzuela (2004); Hochstetler (2006); Pérez-Liñán (2007); Marsteintredet and Berntzun (2008)
Collor	Brazil	1992	Valenzuela (2004); Hochstetler (2006); Pérez-Liñán (2007); Kim and Bahry (2008); Marsteintredet and Berntzun (2008); Mustapic (2010)
Pérez	Venezuela	1992	Valenzuela (2004); Hochstetler (2006); Hochstetler and Edwards (2009); Mustapic (2010)
Serrano	Guatemala	1993	Valenzuela (2004); Pérez-Liñán (2007); Kim and Bahry (2008); Hochstetler and Edwards (2009); Marsteintredet and Berntzun (2008); Mustapic (2010)
Balaguer	Dominican Republic	1994	Valenzuela (2004); Pérez-Liñán (2007); Kim and Bahry (2008); Mustapic (2010)
Durán-Ballén	Ecuador	1995	*Latin American Weekly Report*
Chamorro	Nicaragua	1995	*Latin American Weekly Report*
Samper	Colombia	1996	Hochstetler (2006); Pérez-Liñán (2007); Marsteintredet and Berntzun (2008); Hochstetler and Edwards (2009)
Wasmosy	Paraguay	1996	*Latin American Weekly Report*; Hochstetler (2006); Marsteintredet and Berntzun (2008)

Administration	Country	Crisis Onset	Sources
Alemán	Nicaragua	1997	*Latin American Weekly Report*
Bucaram	Ecuador	1997	Valenzuela (2004); Hochstetler (2006); Pérez-Liñán (2007); Kim and Bahry (2008); Marsteintredet and Berntzun (2008); Hochstetler and Edwards (2009); Mustapic (2010)
Cubas	Paraguay	1998	Valenzuela (2004); Hochstetler (2006); Pérez-Liñán (2007); Kim and Bahry (2008); Marsteintredet and Berntzun (2008); Hochstetler and Edwards (2009); Mustapic (2010)
Cardoso	Brazil	1999	*Latin American Weekly Report*
Mahuad	Ecuador	1999	Valenzuela (2004); Hochstetler (2006); Pérez-Liñán (2007); Kim and Bahry (2008); Marsteintredet and Berntzun (2008); Hochstetler and Edwards (2009); Mustapic (2010)
Pastrana	Colombia	2000	*Latin American Weekly Report*
Fujimori	Peru	2000	Valenzuela (2004); Hochstetler (2006); Pérez-Liñán (2007); Marsteintredet and Berntzun (2008); Hochstetler and Edwards (2009)
de la Rúa	Argentina	2001	Valenzuela (2004); Hochstetler (2006); Pérez-Liñán (2007); Kim and Bahry (2008); Marsteintredet and Berntzun (2008); Hochstetler and Edwards (2009); Mustapic (2010)
González Macchi	Paraguay	2001	Pérez-Liñán (2007)
González Macchi	Paraguay	2002	Marsteintredet and Berntzun (2008); Pérez-Liñán (2007)
Chávez	Venezuela	2002	Hochstetler (2006); Hochstetler and Edwards (2009)
Sánchez de Lozada	Bolivia	2003	Valenzuela (2004); Hochstetler (2006); Pérez-Liñán (2007); Kim and Bahry (2008); Marsteintredet and Berntzun (2008); Hochstetler and Edwards (2009); Mustapic (2010)
Bolaños	Nicaragua	2004	Pérez-Liñán (2007)
Bolaños	Nicaragua	2005	*Latin American Weekly Report*; Hochstetler and Edwards (2009)

(continued)

Administration	Country	Crisis Onset	Sources
Duarte	Paraguay	2005	*Latin American Weekly Report*
Gutiérrez	Ecuador	2004	Mejía Acosta and Polga-Hecimovich (2010); Marsteintredet and Berntzun (2008); Hochstetler and Edwards (2009); Mustapic (2010)
Gutiérrez	Ecuador	2005	Mejía Acosta and Polga-Hecimovich (2010); Marsteintredet and Berntzun (2008); Hochstetler and Edwards (2009); Mustapic (2010)
Lula	Brazil	2005	*Latin American Weekly Report*
Palacio	Ecuador	2005	*Latin American Weekly Report*
Correa	Ecuador	2007	*Latin American Weekly Report*
Ortega	Nicaragua	2007	*Latin American Weekly Report*

5

Coercion Gaps

Alisha C. Holland

Institutions that require the use of coercion to enforce create political headaches. In these settings, enforcement involves fines, jail sentences, and asset seizures that are unpopular with those affected. This chapter highlights how coercive sanctions can generate social and electoral reactions against institutions, even when there is broad support for the underlying institutional aims. Intentional decisions not to enforce the law, or what I call *forbearance* (Holland 2016, 2017), is an important source of the institutional weakness studied in this volume.

Applying coercive sanctions is a challenge in any democracy. But in highly unequal societies, such as those in Latin America, enforcement challenges are compounded by both the power and poverty of those affected by institutional rules. On the one hand, the wealthy often stand above the law, using their money and connections to bend formal rules in their favor and forgo sanctions. For scholars like O'Donnell (2004b), the need for the powerful to receive equal treatment, and thus legal sanctions, is the essence of the rule of the law (see also Méndez, O'Donnell, and Pinheiro 1999). Across a wide range of policies, the wealthy continue to tip institutional design and enforcement in their favor. Firms and wealthy individuals gut environmental protections (Fernández Milmanda and Garay, this volume) and manipulate the interpretation of property rights in their favor (Saffón and González Bertomeu, this volume).

On the other hand, poverty can bring its own, and often less recognized, institutional challenges. Squatters invade land to build housing. Immigrants cross borders in search of economic opportunities and safer lives. Individuals in rural areas grow illicit crops and engage in illegal mining to earn a living. Enforcement in these settings can change lives and plunge vulnerable individuals into deeper poverty. Those who stand below, rather than above, the law are the focus of this chapter.

Institutions that regulate the behavior of the poor often are weakened
by what I call a *coercion gap*. Coercion gaps open due to the divergent
electoral pressures and interest groups present across stages of the policy
process. At the legislative stage, political actors think in terms of abstract
institutional goals. Legislators often increase sanctions in attempts to signal their condemnation of certain behaviors. They also may privilege organized interest groups capable of lobbying for certain provisions. The poor
tend to be poorly represented in the legislative process. Institutional rules
therefore tend to become more punitive as noncompliance grows in society. Meanwhile, at the enforcement stage, political actors confront real lives
being disrupted by sanctions. The distributive impacts of enforcement on
individual lives – rather than the broad institutional aims – become visible.
Territorially organized local interest groups have greater leverage to bargain with politicians. As noncompliance increases, the number of local constituents affected by regulations or sympathetic to their interests can create
electoral pressure to forgo sanctions. Local politicians choose forbearance.
They may select bureaucrats who share these preferences, or use their ability
to hire and transfer bureaucrats, to reduce enforcement and thereby weaken
institutions.

This framework makes two main contributions to our understanding of
institutional weakness. First, I highlight that preferences over institutions do
not necessarily diverge in cases of institutional noncompliance. Instead, actors
disagree with the enforcement measures required to strengthen an institution
(in other words, the public may agree with *io'* but disagree with the measures required to move society from *po* to *io*, to use the framework given in
Chapter 1). Second, this chapter reinforces the importance of thinking about
politics across levels and branches of government. Fernández Milmanda and
Garay (this volume) demonstrate the tension in federal systems where legislators and governors have divergent views on deforestation. I emphasize that,
even in unitary political systems, the disjuncture between those who set the
law and those who must enforce it can create coercion gaps. Because the poor
have less power to pressure politicians to change the sanctions on paper, they
often exert their influence and generate popular sympathy at the enforcement
stage.

I illustrate the coercion gap through a study of how laws against squatting
are set and enforced in Colombia and Peru. In the context of Latin America,
"squatting" refers to the occupation and construction of housing on land
belonging to a private or public owner. Squatting is one of the most frequent
legal violations by the poor in Latin America, and thus an important behavior to study. I review the legislative history of antisquatting laws, showing
how property law violations gradually have been criminalized. I then draw on
interviews with local politicians and bureaucrats in charge of enforcing laws
locally in Lima and Bogotá to underscore their simultaneous desire to end
squatting and opposition to coercive enforcement.

Although my discussion is focused on squatting, coercion gaps emerge for a range of institutional rules that prohibit behaviors by ordinary individuals, or what Ellermann (2009) calls "social regulations." Classic works on regulation like Wilson (1980) recognize that a challenge for democracies is to defend the diffuse benefits of regulatory rules against the concentrated costs of their enforcement. Immigration law follows a parallel split between legislation and enforcement, with heightened tensions due to the relative sympathy of undocumented immigrants. Although legislators (and voters) support strict immigration restrictions when writing legislation and thinking in the abstract, many local politicians, bureaucrats, and nearby voters are less willing to enforce these restrictions when faced with coercive sanctions like deportations, family separations, or worksite raids (Ellermann 2005, 2009). Coercion gaps also open when laws are passed to avoid conflict with powerful interest groups, such as abortion laws maintained to appease the Catholic Church (Htun 2003). Societal opposition can mount once governments try to punish specific violations, as has happened around a woman sentenced to prison for forty years in El Salvador.[1] Locally powerful interest groups also can generate coercion gaps. Faced with widespread illegal gold mining, Bolivia banned and punished its practice in 2014. But pressure from gold mining cooperatives blocked enforcement in practice (Amengual and Dargent, this volume). I now elaborate on the theoretical idea of a coercion gap that unites these diverse circumstances.

THE COERCION GAP

My central argument is that weak institutions can result from the uneven political incentives across the legislative and enforcement process.[2] First, legislators often increase punitive sanctions when confronted with enforcement failures. Criminalizing the behavior of poor individuals is typically driven by popular pressure to appear "tough" on issues of law and order and by interest group pressure at the national level. Second, the imposition of high and concentrated costs on poor individuals makes it difficult for local politicians to enforce the law as written. As institutions move from legislation to enforcement, public attention moves away from the institutional benefits to the personal costs. Elected officials prefer not to enforce punitive laws, and they win supporters by defending those affected by sanctions. Third, politicians must

---

[1] "Juez anula condena contra mujer por muerte de su hijo," *La prensa gráfica*, May 21, 2016.
[2] At a broad level, separating an institutional rule from its enforcement requires a move away from game-theoretic traditions (e.g., North 1990; Levi 1998) that embed enforcement into the definition of an institution. (For a discussion of these issues, see Holland [2017]: 41 and Brinks, Levitsky, and Murillo, this volume.) I follow the institutionalist approach of treating decisions about formal institutions (set through legislation) as separate from decisions about its enforcement (affected by bureaucrats, politicians, and agency heads).

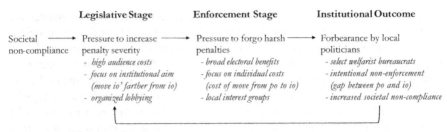

FIGURE 5.1. The coercion gap.

translate their enforcement preferences into bureaucratic behavior that shapes the effective institutional outcome. Depending on the civil service protections, they can use mechanisms of selection, sanction, and transfer to shape the extrinsic and intrinsic motivations of bureaucrats. Figure 5.1 lays out the logic of the argument.

The first step is to consider a legislature confronted with societal noncompliance with an institution. Becker (1968) famously argued that there are two ways to induce compliance: increase the severity of sanctions or increase the frequency. For a rational agent deciding whether to violate the law, these two options have equivalent deterrent effects: the costs of a legal violation increase. Yet increasing the severity of a sanction and increasing the frequency make different demands on state bureaucracies and respond to different pressures. A light penalty requires a bureaucracy capable of monitoring and sanctioning a large volume of violations. A severe sanction requires fewer bureaucrats but greater political and agency commitments to impose concentrated costs on select actors.

Legislators often focus on increasing the severity of sanctions because it is cheaper and easier to dictate severity. Increasing the frequency of sanctions requires new expenditures on the bureaucracy. Punitive laws seem easier to enforce because they only require occasional action, or "raid-like" enforcement behaviors (Dimitrov 2009; Eeckhout, Persico, and Todd 2010). Even if legislators are willing to fund enforcement bureaucracies, they may not have the choice. In politically decentralized countries, national legislators often cannot control how much funding or staff a local government allocates to a particular enforcement task.

Additionally, legislation often responds to general support for an institution's abstract aims and frustration with noncompliance. In the abstract, the public often agrees with the general benefits of an institution and wants to see politicians take a firm stance to ensure compliance. As we will see below, most citizens support the protection of property rights and condemn squatting. There also may be audience costs that lead legislators to write punitive laws to signal the seriousness of an offense to domestic or international publics. An example of this comes from Htun and Jensenius (this volume). Legislators may want to pass severe penalties for violence against women to signal to external donors or domestic advocacy groups their condemnation of such actions. Women suffering from domestic violence want the violence to stop, but do not necessarily support punitive sanctions that would break up families and imprison their abusers.

Punitive lawmaking is less likely – and therefore coercive gaps are smaller – when those exposed to possible sanctions can push back at the legislative stage. Most notably, firms try to affect the policy process through lobbyists and campaign donations, reducing the sanctions for labor and environmental infractions. They can change the law and sanctions involved to move formal institutional rules away from the public interest (on capture, see Carpenter 2014). Fernández Milmanda and Garay (this volume) highlight that wealthy actors can dilute institutional rules against deforestation by making sanctions irrelevant.

Second, once executives start to enforce punitive sanctions, the public sees the harsh consequences of punitive institutional designs. Enforcement brings public attention to the specific individuals affected by coercive measures. When those affected are ordinary individuals, and especially individuals in need of basic goods, the local public may be sympathetic to arguments against the imposition of sanctions.

Forbearance can emerge from the electoral calculations of politicians. Politicians choose forbearance because they perceive heavy electoral costs to enforcement both from those directly affected and from those sympathetic to their situation. As I detail elsewhere (Holland 2016, 2017), a number of empirical observations are consistent with an electoral model of forbearance: forbearance is more likely as elections approach, when larger numbers of voters violate the law in question, and when politicians incorporate those voters affected by sanctions into their core constituency. Electorally motivated forbearance is quite different from the standoffish behavior detailed by Amengual and Dargent (this volume) and Slater and Kim (2015) in that politicians often publicly proclaim their enforcement positions. Politicians campaign and engage directly with the communities affected by enforcement, rather than ignoring their situation.

Forbearance also can emerge from a more empathetic calculation. Some populations affected by regulations are not important voters, such as immigrants and children, or are unlikely to turn out at elections, such as the homeless or sex workers. Yet enforcing laws that regulate the behavior of these groups still can generate shock from the public and empathetic pressure for forbearance. The key point is that citizens and lawmakers often think in terms of avoiding harms when they write legislation. For instance, laws that prevent camping in public areas or prohibit prostitution may seem like valuable ways to defend public interests in the abstract. But their enforcement often requires jailing the homeless or imposing hefty fines on women soliciting clients. Once the public and media focus on the human costs of these actions, popular support may wane for sanctions, even when people understand the underlying aim of the institution.

This dynamic departs from societal coproduction of enforcement in which politicians and bureaucratic agencies gain support from local societal actors to increase state capacity and expand enforcement (Amengual 2015; Amengual and Dargent, this volume). Coproduction hinges on the idea that bureaucracies have local partners who support enforcement. This does not hold for many laws and regulations where sanctions potentially fall on low-income individuals. Groups that oppose enforcement can be organized and sympathetic at the local level, whereas those who stand to benefit are either unorganized (i.e., the general public) or community outsiders (i.e., proregulation interest groups that influence the legislative process).

Third, even if politicians and parts of the public prefer forbearance, they still need coercive bureaucracies to change their enforcement behaviors. This may seem like a trivial task, given that rational-choice models of bureaucracy generally see the problem as one of getting bureaucrats to exert effort (Weingast and Moran 1983; McCubbins, Noll, and Weingast 1987). Forbearance asks bureaucrats to stop doing their enforcement jobs. But bureaucrats have extrinsic and intrinsic reasons to enforce written laws. On the extrinsic side, horizontal accountability agencies have gained power in Latin America. Most Latin American countries have comptrollers or audit courts that can sanction civil servants for inappropriate actions, as well as inaction. Penalties can be quite severe, including suspension from the public sector (*inhabilitación* or *muerte civil*). On the intrinsic side, bureaucrats may have ideological reasons to support enforcement. The challenge for rational-choice accounts of bureaucracy is to explain why bureaucrats often "work" more than shirk (Brehm and Gates 1997) or why "principled agents" exist (Dilulio 1994: 316).

Many bureaucrats hold what I call *legalist* views. Legalists embody the Weberian model in which apolitical agents implement state mandates. They see their job as applying the law as written, believe that the state loses legitimacy if laws go unenforced, and differentiate enforcement from the provision of social welfare. For instance, legalists in the realm of property laws do not question statutes against squatting: "If the people in Congress want to change the law, then I'll do my job differently."[3] Or as another bureaucrat put it, "I'm a municipal inspector; I'm not supposed to go changing the law."[4] Sociologists and historical-institutionalists explain the "working" or legalist tendencies of bureaucrats by the organizational cultures that develop within state agencies. Yet these views do not necessarily come from a strong internal organizational culture due to short tenure in most regulatory agencies and elected governments in Latin America. Instead, legalist views may develop by profession; many bureaucrats charged with enforcement are lawyers or urban planners

---

[3] Author interview with housing director, District of Chapinero, Bogotá, Colombia, July 6, 2010.

[4] Author interview with head of inspections, District of La Florida, Santiago, Chile, June 20, 2012.

who understand the value of regulations as part of their professional training. Legalist views also may stem from individual understandings of the broader legislative process. Those who believe that the government is legitimate and follows procedural norms overall may grant it deference even when they disagree with particular institutions (Tyler 2006).

While many bureaucrats hold legalist positions, some bureaucrats have a contending perspective on the law, which I call a *welfarist* view. These bureaucrats are concerned with what is just and moral in the local community where they work, rather than what legislators write on paper.[5] They believe that enforcement at times undermines the state's authority by demonstrating ignorance of local conditions and perpetuating social inequalities. For example, welfarist bureaucrats enforcing squatting regulations have concluded that it is "socially impossible" to evict the poor,[6] and question whether it would be "good" to impose sanctions.[7] Welfarist bureaucrats think of themselves as what Mahoney and Thelen (2010: 24) describe as "mutualistic symbionts," or actors who disregard "the letter of the law to support and sustain its spirit." Their actions, however, weaken formal institutional rules by allowing legal violations to persist. These individuals are less likely to defer to the government's legitimacy to set the rules.

Many politicians in Latin America have tools – including selection, sanctioning, and transfers – to shape the behavior of their bureaucrats. Which strategy they employ depends on the civil service protections in a country. In some countries, politicians control the hiring of local bureaucrats. They can select bureaucrats who share their views on enforcement, either through direct ideological screenings or using heuristics that correlate with certain positions. In other countries, bureaucrats are hired through competitive exams or enjoy labor protections, but politicians make decisions about retention and assignment. They can sanction bureaucrats who enforce by canceling their contracts or transferring bureaucrats away from enforcement tasks if they disagree with forbearance.

In contrast to the claims of principal-agent scholars and institutionalists who work in advanced democracies, I argue that politicians often exert pressure on bureaucrats to refrain from enforcement. Rather than shirking, bureaucrats often want higher levels of enforcement than politicians. They restrain their behavior when confronted with mechanisms of bureaucratic control. This outcome also differs from institutional conversion (Mahoney and Thelen 2010), which considers how bureaucrats independently leverage

---

[5] Tyler (2006: 4) captured similar distinctions between state legitimacy and personal morality in his classic study of why individuals follow the law. As he puts it, "Normative commitment through personal morality means obeying laws because one feels the law is just; normative commitment through legitimacy means obeying a law because one feels that the authority enforcing the law has the right to dictate behavior."
[6] Author interview with housing inspector, District of Engativá, Bogotá, Colombia, July 13, 2010.
[7] Author interview with housing inspector, District of Santa Fe, Bogotá, Colombia, July 8, 2010.

ambiguities and gaps in the written law to change the institutional outcome. In the case of coercion gaps, the law is often very clear and even draconian. Bureaucrats do not act independently to change its meaning. Instead, politicians intentionally forgo enforcement and pressure bureaucrats to do so for electoral and social ends.

Three key empirical predictions support this coercion gap model: First, legislators tend to increase the punitive nature of the law when confronted with societal noncompliance. Second, local politicians and citizens oppose the enforcement of the law locally, even when supporting it in the abstract. Third, bureaucrats often risk their jobs to uphold the written institution, only to be fired, transferred, or reprimanded by politicians. Over time, bureaucrats learn to anticipate what kinds of decisions are likely to trigger electoral costs and try to preempt political interference by steering clear of controversial enforcement decisions in the first place.

SETTING THE LAW

Laws against squatting in Peru and Colombia went through similar reform processes after democratic openings. Both countries increased the criminal penalties against squatting, informal land sales, and traffickers who promote these acts under pressure from business chambers, construction companies, housing ministries, and urban planning authorities. Increased sanctions came at times of rampant societal noncompliance. Informal construction had expanded over the course of the late twentieth century, to the chagrin of many middle-class groups. Legislators therefore moved to condemn these acts through harsher sanctions, but paid limited attention to how they would be implemented locally.

Peru

The quantity of land settled through squatting in Peru is staggering. Although land invasions tend to be associated with Peru's rapid urban migration in the mid-twentieth century or the debt crisis of the 1980s, squatting continued apace throughout the 1990s and 2000s. Nationwide, the government identified 3,003 informal settlements in 1993, 7,419 in 2002, and more than 10,000 by 2012 (Calderón Cockburn 2013: 46–47; Holland 2017: chapter 6). About half of Lima's population lives on land originally settled through illegal land occupation (Calderón Cockburn 2006: 75). Roughly a third of all state land, or about twenty-six square miles of land, is invaded.[8]

The gap between the written law and actual behavior is enormous. Since 1924, land invasions have been treated as criminal actions that carry a one-to-three year prison sentence for "usurpation."[9] Land invasions also can be prosecuted

[8] "Identifican más de 6,000 hectáreas de terrenos invadidos," *Andina*, November 24, 2014.
[9] Código Penal de 1991, Decreto Legislativo 635, *usurpación*, Art. 202.

in the civil system to restore taken property. Yet the prosecution and restoration of property has been mired in obstacles. Beginning with General Manuel Odría (1948–1950) who took a tolerant approach toward land invasions – with nine in ten squatter invasions succeeding (Collier 1976) – jurists took a narrow read of usurpations. State prosecutors required violence to have been committed against other individuals to constitute a criminal usurpation, while courts previously understood unauthorized entry ("violence against goods," such as breaking a lock or trespassing) to be an act of usurpation. Parallel developments occurred in the police code, limiting police evictions to cases where they caught squatters in the act (*en flagrante,* interpreted as within forty-eight hours). In practice, these changes eliminated criminal prosecutions against squatters and greatly complicated evictions.

Although Peru long had experienced land invasions, frustration with the informal housing model grew with the return to full democracy and the election of Alejandro Toledo in 2001. Toledo reinstated a housing ministry (Ministerio de Vivienda, Construcción y Saneamiento, MVCS) and appointed technocratic urban planners who pushed to stop land invasions. Changes in the types of land invasions also prompted condemnation. Squatters built on increasingly precarious and marginal land, such as environmental risk zones, archeological reserves, and conservation areas (Ramírez Corzo and Riofrío 2006). Organizers of land invasions also became increasingly professionalized (Dosh 2010).

Rising real estate prices in the context of a commodities boom in the mid-2000s also made peripheral land more valuable and led to rapid growth in Peru's secondary cities. Much as Saffón and González Bertomeu (this volume) emphasize, the mining boom created new pressure to define property rights to promote new commercial and infrastructure projects. It also brought migrants to mining cities in large numbers. Secondary cities, such as Arequipa, became the epicenter of squatting activity. For instance, roughly forty thousand new illegal lots arranged in four hundred squatter settlements, or enough to house approximately a fifth of the city's residents, were built between 2004 and 2009 in Arequipa.[10]

Against this backdrop, there was substantial regional and national pressure to increase the penalties for land invasions. Legal reforms were proposed by the Office for the Prevention of Conflicts in the Regional Government of Arequipa, an internationally funded institution created to manage conflicts around the mining industry.[11] The proposal garnered support from the national housing ministry, which was attempting to increase investments in

[10] COFOPRI, "COFOPRI no titular más invasiones en Arequipa," press release, April 13, 2009; "Informe sobre la problemática de las invasiones de terrenos en la región Arequipa," Sesión Descentralizada de Coordinación de la Función Congresal entre Congresistas de la República por Arequipa y el Consejo Regional, February 17, 2014 and April 21, 2014.

[11] Author interview with César Angel Huamantuma Alarcón, director, Office for the Prevention of Conflicts in the Regional Government of Arequipa, October 13, 2015.

social-interest housing programs. Peru's Congress has limited capacity, so the housing ministry and regional government drafted the legal reforms, which were passed under Law 30076 of 2013 (*Ley sobre el delito de usurpación*). In explaining the law's rationale, legislators emphasized the need to break with past practices: "Invasions form part of a social stage that has concluded" and reflect a "communitarian philosophy incommensurate with free markets." The legislative record justifies stronger criminal sanctions because "a wide variety of investments in housing programs mean that the State no longer can continue to be permissive and tolerant of land invasions."[12]

The new legislation strengthened laws against squatting in three ways: First, it extended the time period in which the police can evict squatters without a court order. Second, it introduced a new type of "simple" land invasion punishable with three-five years in jail for individuals who clandestinely enter a property, regardless of whether they employ violence. It also clarified that aggravated usurpations (punishable with up to eight years in prison) include physical destruction of property (like locks or barriers) and the installation of new construction materials. Those who organize, facilitate, or promote land invasions on public or private land ("traffickers") also can receive eight years in prison. Finally, the law established that land intended for public works, such as highways or housing projects, could be restored at any point, regardless of how much time passed since the initial invasion. Meanwhile, private owners have fifteen days after learning of an invasion to begin to recover their land through direct police action (otherwise, they must initiate a judicial action).

Although no public opinion polls exist, there appears to have been broad public support for the measures. Even in the mid-1990s, when Peru had not fully recovered from its economic crisis, the limited public opinion data available from Peru suggests that 21 percent of poor respondents approved of land invasions, compared to 5 percent of nonpoor respondents (AmericasBarometer 1997). No interest groups lobbied to speak out against the criminal code reforms. Most of the media coverage suggests broad condemnation of land invasions, and in particular of those who organize land invasions.[13]

In short, national legislators in Peru have increased penalties against land invasions and land traffickers in response to widespread noncompliance. However, although these legal reforms made it easier for the police to act without judicial authorization, they paid little attention to the agencies or resources necessary to enforce the law.

[12] Exposición de motivos, Oficio no. 009-2013-PR, Proyecto de Ley No. 1898 (Que modifica artículos del código penal y código procesal penal; e, incorpora medidas de lucha para proteger la propiedad pública y privada de las usurpaciones).

[13] "Trujillo: traficantes invaden terreno destinado a escuela de talentos," RPP, August 13, 2014; "Denuncian invasión de traficantes de terreno en zona de Cieneguilla," *El comercio*, January 18, 2011; "Traficantes se aprovechan de la inocencia de incautos pobladores," *Diario voces*, June 13, 2016.

Colombia

Strictly speaking, squatting refers to the illegal occupation of land. Land invasions have been considered a criminal offense with prison sentences in the Colombian Penal Code since the 1930s (Article 261, *usurpación de terrenos*). Yet while land invasions were criminalized, no criminal sanctions existed for the more frequent form of informal construction in major Colombian cities: "pirate urbanizations." Land traffickers captured the policy-making process until the 1990s, preventing more concerted action against trafficking.

In Bogotá, very few land invasions occurred because relatively little land was state-owned. Instead, landowners sold "defective" land (often rural or conservation land), on which urban construction could not occur, to households. Occupants then built their own houses and petitioned the city to change the zoning (Doebele 1977; Gilbert and Ward 1985). Some informal occupations bordered on land invasions, given that traffickers sold land without the permission or payment of private owners. The process imposed large costs on city governments and undercut planning regulations. Developers were supposed to provide basic services to new settlements, but they routinely failed to provide any infrastructure to pirate urbanizations. Those who trafficked or built on nonurban land only could be sanctioned with a modest administrative fine.

Land traffickers were extremely powerful politically and prevented legislative attempts to extend squatting laws to pirate urbanizations. Important land traffickers in the city built political careers by offering squatters access to land in exchange for their electoral support. They also could make squatters' lives quite difficult by demanding loan payments or, in cases where squatters failed to support traffickers politically, reselling their houses to other parties. Most famously, former city councilor and senator Alfonso Guerrero Estrada sold nineteen thousand land plots in more than twenty settlements in Bogotá. Guerrero called himself a "revolutionary" who "solved" the housing needs of poor communities and negotiated land in his informal settlements in exchange for votes. Informal settlements turned out in large numbers to vote for Guerrero's "Bread and Roof" party (Pan y Techo).

Another notorious land trafficker was Rafael Forero Fetecua, who won seats on the city council and then Congress with the Popular Integration (Integración Popular) movement. He promised the incorporation of informal settlements into public investment plans and exchanged land for votes prior to the elections. Guerrero Estrada and Forero opposed any attempts to punish their activity, which they saw as "development in the service of the poor."[14]

---

[14] See "Los dueños del sur," *El Tiempo*, November 4, 1999; "A Guerrero Estrada le premiaron," *El Tiempo*, February 20, 1999; "Cuando la Cruz decidieron vender Bosa," *El Tiempo*, November 5, 1999.

Given that administrative sanctions were written by the city council, land traffickers easily could prevent serious fines being levied against or investigations conducted into informal developments.

By the 1990s, however, the negative externalities from informal developments became increasingly clear. By 1994, 546 neighborhoods in Bogotá, with 800,510 residents, awaited legalization by city planning authorities. By the 2010s, more than 2.1 million people, or about a quarter of Bogotá's population, had acquired their houses through illegal land occupations and pirate developments (SDP 2011). For every hectare legally developed in Bogotá, roughly four were developed illegally (Torres Tovar 2009: 108). The figures were even more extreme nationally. Nationwide, for every four houses promoted by land traffickers, the official construction sector only built one.[15] Over time, the land used also became increasingly precarious; substantial construction occurred in the eastern hillsides intended for environmental conservation or on city land where construction was prohibited due to environmental risks (Torres Tovar 2009; Camargo and Hurtado 2011).

In 1996, Congress retook the issue of squatting and informal land occupations on the initiative of Liberal Party senator Juan Martín Caicedo. Caicedo was the former mayor of Bogotá (1990–1992) and president of the country's largest business association (Federación Nacional de Comerciantes, FENALCO). Caicedo wanted national legislators to stiffen penalties against land traffickers due to his frustration with their capture of the city council.[16] More generally, Caicedo – and the commercial and real estate chambers of the city – were frustrated with the informal growth of the city, which raised land prices and attracted displaced populations and rural migrants.

The new legislation (Law 308 of 1996) increased the sanctions against land invasions, informal sales, and those who promote them. Individuals who occupy land without property authorization can be sentenced to two to five years in prison, with an increased sentence of up to half the imposed time warranted for those who settle on land intended for public works, environmental conservation, or high-risk protection areas. Those who traffic land to resell to individuals – i.e., "pirate" urbanizers – can be subject to three to seven years in prison, with increased penalties in high-risk, ecological, or rural zones. Senators who spoke in favor of the bill, such as future housing minister and vice president Germán Vargas, stressed that the law should

---

[15] "Ley ordena demoler a constructores piratas," *El Tiempo*, August 6, 1996.

[16] Caicedo also seems to have had a personal feud with Forero, and particularly with his membership in the Liberal Party. Forero was elected senator on the Liberal Party ticket in 1990. Caicedo ultimately brought Forero down from political power by prosecuting him for the fact that he included subsidies for city councilors within the budget (against the 1991 Constitution). "Rafael Forero Fetecua: el que peca y reza empata," *Directo Bogotá*, no. 42, September 2013, 5–12.

be applied to white-collar urbanizers who violated urban planning laws, as well as to those who promoted land invasions.[17] There was no discussion of increasing the enforcement capacity necessary to make the sanctions effective, however.

During the drafting, the legislation faced no public challenges from municipal officials. Land invasions, and even informal settlements, were widely condemned. As I detail elsewhere (Holland 2017: chapter 2), three-quarters of respondents in a public opinion poll in Bogotá did not support unauthorized land occupations. However, more than half of this group also saw evictions as too harsh. Citizens supported a position of social regulation in which they both agreed with the institutional rules and disagreed with their enforcement. It therefore seems unlikely that society broadly supported the tolerance of land invasions, informal settlements, or traffickers. Quite the opposite, they may have rewarded legislators who took strong positions in favor of orderly urban development.

Importantly, the legislation passed during a period of expansion in social-interest housing programs. President César Gaviria had promised to revamp social-interest housing programs. The 1991 constitution also recognized a right to housing. The Gaviria government created a new social-interest housing authority (Instituto de Nacional de Vivienda de Interés Social y Reforma Urbana, INURBE) and required that part of payroll taxes on formal-sector workers be earmarked for housing projects for lower-income groups. Much of the discussion therefore centered on the need to replace informal housing development models with state-subsidized alternatives. Interest groups in the construction sector hoped that criminal sanctions against squatters and developers, combined with new demand-side subsidies to allow the poor to purchase formal properties, would shift the balance to formal housing alternatives.[18]

Given that housing programs failed to meet demand, the criminal penalties for land invasions and traffickers generated constitutional challenges. In 1997, the law faced a constitutional challenge for violating the right to housing and the social use of property protected by the 1991 constitution. However, the Constitutional Court upheld the penal code revisions as consistent with the state's need to control the invasion of property and protect collective rights to the environment.[19] Through the 1990s and 2000s, the Constitutional Court reiterated that housing is a progressive right, and that the state could act to guarantee conflicting collective rights, such as the right to the environment.

To summarize, legislative reforms to increase penalties against land invasions and trafficking reflected frustration with local capture by land traffickers and, as in Peru, a national commitment to move to a formal housing model.

---

[17] "10 años de carcel a urbanizadores piratas." *El Tiempo*, June 7, 1995.
[18] "Ley ordena demoler a constructores piratas," *El Tiempo*, August 6, 1996.
[19] Constitutional Court, Sentencia C-157/97.

Construction, commercial, and real estate interest groups supported the legislation as a way to increase formal-sector construction and avoid rising land
prices. Yet little attention was paid to the actual enforcement mechanisms.
Those affected by the penalties, particularly low-income groups and those displaced by the civil war, had little voice in the legislative debates, although their
concerns would come to the fore in the law's implementation.

ENFORCING THE LAW

I now turn to why local political actors oppose enforcement and how they
control bureaucratic behavior. While national legislators increased the penalties and coverage of laws against land invasions, local politicians experienced
the consequences. Especially in low-income communities, politicians might
face social protests or risk losing votes if they enforced the law as written.
They therefore turned to forbearance. To impose their preferences, they hired
bureaucrats with welfarist views, or sanctioned and transferred those who
attempted to enforce existing legislation.

Local Forbearance

In the context of squatting, local politicians in low-income districts see electoral benefits from forbearance. These benefits include both obtaining the
direct votes at stake and developing a reputation for assisting low-income
residents. Politicians risk losing the votes of those affected when they enforce
and acquiring an antipoor reputation. Crucially, most politicians support the
goals of antisquatting laws, but they find their penalties disproportionate in the
absence of housing alternatives for their constituents. Here, I briefly summarize
qualitative evidence suggesting that local politicians favor forbearance toward
squatters (a more detailed account can be found in Holland 2017: chapter 3).

In Lima, politicians emphasized that working with new land invasions
improved their electoral chances. Almost half of the politicians that I interviewed in Lima stressed that evictions were impossible because of the impression they created in the community. One politician was indignant when
I asked about reporting on squatter settlements: "How can I say that I support the poor and then go behind their back to try to get people who need
housing taken off their land?"[20] Beyond simply avoiding political costs, politicians stressed that working with new invasions won votes from those affected
and from broader community members: "People look for politicians who can
empathize with their problems, and when you work for communities that are
just getting off the ground it shows that you understand how hard things are

---

[20] Author interview with Ivan Coronado, local councilor, District of Comas, Lima, Peru,
   November 25, 2011.

and what people need to do to find housing."[21] Similarly, another politician emphasized the importance of visiting land invasions to build goodwill in the community:

My support comes from the poor, so when there is a land invasion, I visit to *show my sympathy*. If you bring in the police, then it's clear to everyone that *the mayor does not really fight for the social needs of people* and isn't really looking for ways to help.[22]

Importantly, local politicians stressed that they would prefer to control land invasions, but that they saw enforcement as politically impossible in the absence of housing alternatives. One mayor, who has been elected multiple times in a poor district, complained about rampant squatting and supported efforts to criminalize squatting. Nevertheless, he concluded, "We can't stop land invasions when there is no policy from the central government to offer housing to people."[23] Another politician expressed a common view that local enforcement decisions hinge on national housing policy investments, explaining, "We're not isolated in how we deal with these themes, because even though there are clear legal norms that people can't invade the land and that the government should act, there's no clear option for what to do with people."[24] These statements were more than cheap talk. As I show elsewhere (Holland 2017: chapter 3), in poor districts, 40 percent of all platforms explicitly proposed some form of forbearance toward squatter settlements.

Similar dynamics can be seen in Bogotá. Colombian law is complex in that the Constitution both recognizes a right to housing and protects private property. As I detail elsewhere(Holland 2017: 111–113), court decisions have struggled to balance housing rights with requirements to protect private property and, increasingly, conservation land. Evictions still are possible in a more limited set of circumstances. Some politicians view their position of forbearance as favoring housing rights over competing rights to private property and environmental protection. Nevertheless, consistent with an electorally motivated model of forbearance, politicians risk a substantial electoral backlash if they evict squatters due to the structure of popular demands. A typical sentiment in Bogotá was, "Any politician who dares to [conduct evictions] dies politically."[25] Even politicians with ideological commitments to enforcement have recognized the electoral costs of their choices. For instance, Antanas Mockus, a former university

[21] Author interview with César Augusto Lerzundi, local councilor, District of Villa El Salvador, Lima, Peru, November 4, 2011.
[22] Author interview with Erasmo Segundo Cardenas Obregon, local councilor, District of Ate, Lima, Peru, November 23, 2011. Emphasis added.
[23] Author interview with Washington Ipenza, mayor, District of Villa María del Triunfo, Lima, Peru (1984–1986, 1999–2006), June 18, 2011.
[24] Author interview with local councilor, District of San Agustino, Lima, Peru, November 18, 2011.
[25] Author interview with judicial advisor, District of Rafael Uribe Uribe, Bogotá, Colombia, July 7, 2010.

rector and philosopher, strongly believes that the tolerance of squatting was part of a "shortcut" culture in which the long-term consequences for quality of life, shared citizenship rights, and urban planning were discounted (Mockus 2012). When in office, Mockus ordered one of the largest housing evictions in Bogotá's history, removing seven thousand people from a newly formed settlement.[26] But he recognized the high reputational costs of his choices. As Mockus explained his reaction to one land invasion that occurred early in his term, "I didn't have any interest in my second day as mayor beginning with an eviction and all the media attention that it generated about not caring about the poor."[27]

Enforcement actions are easier in Bogotá when they involve constructions by the upper class or sanctions against land traffickers. The hills surrounding Bogotá are beautiful spots for the wealthy to build weekend homes. Demolitions of these luxury houses are surprising under capacity-based theories because it is cheaper to demolish the homes of the poor (due to the size of the construction) and less complicated administratively (due to the poor's inferior access to lawyers and bribes). Yet mayors were willing to evict the wealthy due to the lower social and political costs. The political logic of targeting the nonpoor comes out in the comments of bureaucrats:

The city mayor doesn't want to disrupt things. Where are you going to move all these poor people to? What good would it serve to take away their homes? There is no other place for them to go, so you just can't do it ... It's different when wealthy people decide to build weekend chalets in the forest preserve. We took down sixteen elegant homes last year because there is no reason that they should be there.[28]

In addition to evictions of upper-income groups, there is strong support for criminal prosecutions of land traffickers, who tend to be better off than those who live in squatter settlements. Following criminal code reforms, for example, Mayor Gustavo Petro (2011–2015) took a strong stance against the city's main land trafficking organization, known as Los Tierreros. The mayor built popular support for the legal case, as well as an eviction from land that the traffickers had developed, by emphasizing how their actions harmed low-income groups in search of housing. As Petro put it, "They use people's need for housing, invade environmental protection lands, and charge a lot of money."[29] The city compensated individuals who had bought into the illegal development, while targeting the land traffickers. High-level attorneys

---

[26] Statistics come from the 2008 locality reports to the district planning secretary, but only are available for Mockus's second term and exclude the District of Santa Fe due to differences in reporting over time.

[27] Author interview with Antanas Mockus, Bogotá, Colombia, July 29, 2013.

[28] Author interview with construction and housing director, District of Santa Fe, Bogotá, Colombia, September 7, 2011, emphasis added.

[29] "Petro denuncia banda de urbanizadores piratas llamada 'Los Tierreros,'" *El espectador*, January 20, 2012; "Petro anuncia que desmantelará la banda 'Los Tierreros' en Bogotá," *El Tiempo*, January 20, 2012.

managed the investigations against traffickers, which reduced local pressure to maintain the settlements and capture of investigating institutions.

Societal coproduction occurs in a relatively small set of cases around squatting. Landowners tend to hire private guards to protect their own property. When squatters invade private land, there is some evidence that landowners provide cars and additional guards to help bureaucrats expedite their work, close to the societal collaboration dynamics detailed by Dargent and Amengual (this volume). However, these tend to be the efforts of individual landowners to protect their personal land. No organized interest groups operate at the local level to provide more consistent support to state operations. Quite the opposite, individuals opposed to enforcement tend to be better organized at the local level, resulting in forbearance rather than coproduction.

Selecting and Sanctioning Bureaucrats

Even if local politicians prefer forbearance, they need bureaucrats to follow their orders. In cases where local politicians control hiring, as in Lima, they do so by selecting bureaucrats with compatible enforcement positions. Politicians directly screen for positions on enforcement, differentiating loosely between legalist and welfarist views. Welfarist bureaucrats are relatively easy to identify through their concern with enforcement's effects on local communities. They also tend to question the legitimacy of national legislators to set appropriate regulations. Welfarists made comments like, "The law is marvelous, but on the ground, the reality looks nothing like it;"[30] or "People in Congress wouldn't want us to apply the law if they knew what it was like in [this district]."[31]

Conflict between politicians and bureaucrats is rare in Lima because politicians shape the bureaucracy to match their preferences. A minority of bureaucrats (six of sixty-eight) reported disputes with mayors and local councilors, suggesting that preferences were aligned. Bureaucrats understand that their job depends on the mayor, and therefore they did not ruffle feathers and enforce unless with explicit approval. One explained that enforcement creates "an image problem"[32] for the mayor, with another remarking, "This is the most scrutinized area because we impose sanctions...politicians are always asking for the head of this office."[33] Another bureaucrat emphasized that "[t]he Office knows not to do anything that would have a political cost."[34]

[30] Author interview with subdirector of licenses and consumer defense, District of Villa El Salvador, Lima, Peru, May 23, 2011.

[31] Author interview with housing inspector, District of Comas, Lima, Peru, May 16, 2011.

[32] Author interview with subdirector of inspections, District of Villa El Salvador, Lima, Peru, November 21, 2011.

[33] Author interview with subdirector of control and inspections, District of San Juan de Lurigancho, Lima, Peru, October 20, 2011.

[34] Author interview with subdirector of Planning and Cadaster, District of Comas, Lima, Peru, June 14, 2011.

Although bureaucrats did not always agree with the violation of the law, they understood mayors' decisions not to enforce in the absence of social alternatives. A typical remark justified mayors' positions by referencing the needs of the population for housing:

The municipality can control the expansion of the district and evict squatters, but…housing programs are created elsewhere. How are we supposed to stop the expansion of the district and sanction people if there are no social programs in place? It's our job to enforce the law, but on the other hand, it can't really be our job.[35]

It is possible that mayors simply select compliant bureaucrats willing to go along with any executive decision, rather than welfarist bureaucrats. These hiring strategies are difficult to distinguish empirically. Many mayors, however, stress that it is more efficient to choose bureaucrats with shared ideological views on enforcement. For instance, one mayor said, "I choose bureaucrats who come from the local community and understand the housing needs, because I'm not always there when they need to make fast decisions."[36] If we assume that most bureaucrats attempt to do their jobs, then it is easier for politicians to select bureaucrats who define their job as maximizing local social welfare, rather than applying the law as written.

The off-the-line cases of legalist bureaucrats working in low-income districts underscore how selecting bureaucrats with compatible ideological views strengthens the mayor's forbearance position. One legalist bureaucrat, for instance, explained her resistance to tolerate the formation of new squatter settlements. She faced intense local political pressure to stop enforcement because the mayor received substantial electoral support in squatter settlements. She refused to act in ways that conflicted with her legalist views:

It's my job to control these invasions so in the end if politics wins, then fine. But I will not ignore the norms for a group of votes…Local politicians complain that I don't understand, that I'm incompetent, and that I'm bad, and they want to throw me out of my job.[37]

The bureaucrat eventually sought the backing of city and national institutions to combat the mayor's threats, so she retained her job. But she still was not able to enforce against squatter settlements because mayors withheld necessary police support to conduct operations.

A second mechanism through which politicians influence the actions of bureaucrats is sanctioning. Sanctioning includes both the dismissal and transfer

---

[35] Author interview with head of Inspections and Control, District of Ventanilla, Lima, Peru, May 30, 2011.
[36] Author interview with Paulo Hinostroza, mayor (2003–2006), District of San Juan de Miraflores, Lima, Peru, June 24, 2011.
[37] Author interview with director of Planning and Cadastre, District of Comas, Lima, Peru, June 9, 2011.

of bureaucrats in response to their enforcement actions. Local bureaucrats in Bogotá are selected for fixed-term contracts through a competitive exam. Mayors, therefore, are unable to screen bureaucrats based on their enforcement views. However, they have substantial power over bureaucrats because they can choose whether to renew a contract and also can transfer bureaucrats away from enforcement tasks.

The inability to control hiring results in substantial conflict between bureaucrats and mayors in Bogotá. Almost a third of bureaucrats (sixteen of fifty-three) described having their contracts not renewed due to their enforcement efforts. Many bureaucrats do learn to anticipate the political costs of their actions, and refrain from enforcement likely to upset politicians. However, unlike their counterparts in Lima, bureaucrats also must navigate a stringent system of external oversight and therefore learn to go through the motions of doing their job, threading the needle of pleasing politicians and avoiding oversight agencies.

The case of one bureaucrat who reported having his contract canceled in four different districts provides a vivid example. The bureaucrat tried to enforce the law as written on paper, but clashed with the mayor, who favored forbearance. Colombia recognizes a social right to housing in its constitution, but courts still authorize evictions once due process is properly provided and local governments make efforts to protect those affected. In this case, the bureaucrat describes his attempts to enforce:

One of the hardest cases was when I demolished an informal settlement, including a house where a pregnant woman was living. I had gone to the judicial authorities and ombudsman [personería] and got the order to proceed. But then the mayor threw me out for the case because even though I followed all the legal requirements, it looked bad in the community.

Over time, the bureaucrat moderated his enforcement positions and focused on operations approved by the mayor and outside of the campaign season. For instance, he worked for a left-wing mayor who wanted to redistribute resources to the poor. As noted above, some illegal land occupations consist of summer homes of the wealthy. The mayor and bureaucrat therefore focused on demolishing "huge mansions, even though…they hit against powerful interests." The bureaucrat also learned when to conduct enforcement operations. As he describes it, "I stop all operations during the campaign season. Politicians don't even need to call me because I know that it's better not to stir things up or I'll be thrown out of my job."[38]

Stepping back, particularly in developing countries, policy makers and researchers attribute weak enforcement to bureaucrats being lazy, corrupt, or both. Bureaucrats only enforce the law when monitored and held accountable

---

[38] Author interview with judicial coordinator, District of Suba, Bogotá, Colombia, June 16, 2011.

by their political principals. Quite the opposite, the empirical evidence in Lima and Bogotá suggests that bureaucrats often try to enforce the law much more strongly than their political principals want. Bureaucrats often risk their jobs to uphold written institutions, only to be fired, transferred, or reprimanded by politicians. Yet other bureaucrats hold strong beliefs that blind allegiance to written law is misguided. As Lipsky (1980: 15) recognizes, "[T]o a degree society seeks not only impartiality from public agencies but compassion for special circumstances and flexibility for dealing with them." The ability of local politicians to shape hiring and dismissal practices allows them to find bureaucrats whose enforcement views align with their political preferences.

IMPLICATIONS FOR INSTITUTIONAL WEAKNESS

This chapter has traced the politics of squatting as it evolved from the legislative to enforcement process. I have used laws against squatting as an example of an institution that disproportionately affects low-income individuals and prescribes coercive sanctions to effect change in societal behavior. As is the case with many government laws and regulations, affected individuals face powerful interventions to ward off state enforcement. However, unlike firms – which are constrained by economic regulations that they themselves have a hand in drafting – , the poor rarely have the capacity to influence institutional design at the legislative stage. Laws and regulations that affect the poor therefore often have a punitive character on paper. At the enforcement stage, those affected are able to influence the decisions of local politicians and street-level bureaucrats who see the concrete, and harsh, effects of coercive enforcement. Local politicians use forbearance to win votes and signal their commitment to their local communities.

What does this mean for weak institutions? First, this chapter emphasizes that societal preferences over institutions can vary when discussed in terms of abstract desires for compliance and concrete enforcement actions. It is not necessarily the case, then, that institutional weakness arises from disagreement with the ambition of an institution or *io'*, to put it in the terms of this volume's introduction. Instead, political conflict can center over the enforcement measures necessary to achieve a given institutional aim. Compliance with institutional rules sometimes cannot be achieved through paper laws and normative persuasion alone. The politics of enforcement therefore are central to the study of institutional weakness, and often masked in discussions of compliance alone. Compliance, especially when institutions go against individual economic interests, requires hard acts of fines, convictions, and business closures. Such uses of coercive power are challenging in all democracies. They may be especially difficult in unequal ones, where both the rich and the poor have leverage to resist enforcement.

Second, Latin American democracies face different types of institutional challenges when shaping the behavior of the rich and poor. While much scholarship stresses the challenges of using law to constrain the behavior of the wealthy and powerful (O'Donnell 1999b), poverty can create its own obstacles to law enforcement. Legal violations by the rich often are negotiated in private; those about how to treat the poor often are very public. Many local politicians are quite open about their positions toward squatting. Even at the national level, presidents often take stands against law enforcement. For instance, Ecuadoran president Rafael Correa (2012: 96) recently acknowledged in an interview while discussing deforestation, "I can't tell a poor family living next to a forest not to cut down the trees." Discussions about what should be considered as mitigating factors in cases of legal violations reflect judgments about the "deservingness" of individuals. They therefore often center on normative discussions about whether those who violate the law are "truly" poor and include political efforts to mobilize voters in sympathy or rejection of those engaged in legal violations.

A third and related point is that coercion gaps are hard to overcome through processes of societal coproduction because the targets of enforcement are opposed to enforcement efforts. In coproduction scenarios, societal groups can become partners to push for enforcement, often working against recalcitrant subnational politicians (Amengual 2015; Rich 2013). Evans (1995) talks about the possibility for state–society synergy, in which alliances between bureaucrats and civil society organizations result in greater policy implementation. Strengthening civil society thus is an antidote to weak institutions. But, as Migdal (1988) recognizes, strong societies do not always work in the direction of national laws and policies. This chapter has shown that, even when societal actors agree with general institutional goals, they have reasons to oppose coercive enforcement measures. Perversely, strong civil society organizations may make it even harder for state officials to enforce formal institutions. On a more positive note, it is possible that strengthening civil society could make it easier for debates to take place around the law itself, rather than being limited to its enforcement.

More broadly, coercion gaps raise the question of why politicians do not simply change the law. Opposition to enforcement results in forbearance, rather than legal change, under several conditions. First, preferences over enforcement can be heterogeneous. Even if some segment of the public opposes enforcement – such as those affected by coercion or sympathetic to those subject to regulations – other parts of the public can hold divergent views. Debates over immigration in advanced democracies make this quite clear. Polarized views on immigration may result in some more liberal jurisdictions pursuing forbearance, while others exploit the full force of the law. Second, preferences over enforcement can be dynamic and linked to the treatment of other social issues. Although politicians believe that laws should not be enforced in their community or at a particular moment in time, due, say, to the poverty of those involved or high unemployment rates, it does not mean that they never think sanctions should be imposed. In the case of squatting, many politicians are sympathetic to the aims of the law and would support the application of sanctions *if* alternatives like social-interest housing were available for those who need shelter. Local politicians therefore support the law in theory and see little reason to pressure for formal changes; they simply see its application as inappropriate to their constituents and the given political moment. Finally, powerful interest groups may push to keep the law on the books and create costs to changing legislation. Forbearance thus offers a less public path to the same institutional outcome. Construction and business groups in Latin American cities, for instance, push for clear and punitive statutes against squatting. Low-income groups, such as squatters or local politicians from the urban periphery, often have limited ability to pressure for legislative change when confronted with these more powerful interests. What they can change is enforcement.

Whether the use of forbearance is normatively "good" depends. On the one hand, local politicians may act to bring the law closer to their constituents' preferences, or at least their short-term preferences. As this chapter has shown, coercion imposes concentrated costs and thus can be in consistent with some politicians' and constituents' definition of the public interest. There also are cases where the law itself becomes excessively punitive. If legislation is far off the median voters' preferences, then forbearance may be an important corrective to unequal political representation at the highest levels of government. On the other hand, coercion gaps can emerge when minority or myopic interests dominate enforcement politics. In many cases, politicians distort the law to accommodate the preferences of nefarious actors and special interest groups, such as in the case of gold mining in Peru (Amengual and Dargent, this volume) or local landowners in Mexico (Saffón and González Bertomeu, this volume). Local forbearance also tends to privilege immediate over long-run welfare. Many regulations are conceived as representing the public's long-run interest, rather than the near-term economic needs. Most urban planners, for instance, recognize that squatting imposes enormous economic costs on cities, such as sprawl and public service extensions. These are just the types of proregulatory interests that are represented in the formal passage of a law, and absent from local enforcement debates. Long-term planning often requires removing certain issues from immediate political discussion and defending unpopular regulations to defend future interests. Coercion gaps therefore often represent functioning local democracy, but weaken institutions meant to improve long-run welfare.

6

Aspirational Laws as Weak Institutions

Legislation to Combat Violence against Women in Mexico

Mala Htun and Francesca R. Jensenius

In the past four decades, governments around the world have embraced principles of gender equality.[1] Democratic transitions, feminist movements, international norms, lobbying by politicians, partisan competition, technocratic decision-making, regional and global diffusion, and varying combinations of these and other factors have pushed countries to grant women and other marginalized groups equal rights and greater recognition. Governments have reformed laws and adopted policies in many areas, including violence against women, maternity and parental leave, presence in political decision-making, egalitarian family law, abortion, reproductive health, and workplace equality. Still, there is significant cross-national variation in the timing and extent of change (see Htun and Weldon 2018).

One of the areas where the most change has been made *on paper* in Latin America is legislation related to violence against women (VAW), a broad concept that includes rape, intimate partner violence, trafficking, honor killings, stalking, and female genital mutilation. In the 1990s, some fourteen countries adopted legislation on domestic or intrafamily violence. Then, in the early twenty-first century, many Latin American countries adopted "second generation" laws to prevent and punish additional forms of VAW (such as economic violence) and provide services to victims, within the context of addressing women's broader cultural and social subordination.

Feminist and human rights movements have heralded these legal changes as achievements in women's advancement, and a significant amount of research has examined the conditions giving rise to such legal and policy reform (see, e.g., Weldon 2002; Franceschet 2010; Htun and Weldon 2012; Smulovitz

---

[1] The research was conducted with support from the Andrew Carnegie Fellowship and the Research Council of Norway (project number 250753). Replication code and data can be found at www.francesca.no.

2015). At the same time, many provisions of VAW laws are poorly implemented and weakly enforced. The gap between the letter of the law and the actual practices of social actors and state officials raises concerns about whether legislation on VAW is merely another weak institution.

In this chapter, we argue that laws on VAW are part of a broader category of *aspirational* rights, which aim to change society. Aspirational rights project a vision of an ideal and future democratic, inclusive, and egalitarian social order. Laws on VAW are aspirational in that they attempt to change status hierarchies that privilege men and masculinity and subordinate women and femininity (Weldon 2002; Htun and Weldon 2012). In so doing, these rights confront deeply entrenched social norms guiding the behavior of citizens as well as state officials. Aspirational rights can therefore not be expected to have immediate effects, nor will it be possible to activate them overnight.

We explore the ways in which VAW legislation in Latin America, as well as aspirational rights more broadly, can be characterized as weak institutions. In Chapter 1, Brinks, Levitsky, and Murillo argue that some laws and regulations remain weak because they maintain the status quo (insignificance), keep changing to conform to the interests of powerful actors (instability), or are the result of different forms of noncompliance (when people ignore the institution). They distinguish between noncompliance *from above*, including weak state capacity and deliberate choices by state officials not to enforce the institution, and noncompliance *from below*, which involves societal resistance to, or noncooperation with, the institution.

Based on evidence from Mexico, this chapter argues the institutional weakness of VAW legislation is attributable to a combination of deliberate official choices (noncompliance from above) and societal resistance (noncompliance from below). In spite of two decades of institutional development to combat VAW, perpetrators of violence keep violating, few victims of violence report abuse, and many state officials, who are also embedded in society, resist implementation of the law. Unlike other cases studied in this volume, however, patterns of societal resistance are not just a matter of strategic decisions or principled disobedience. Rather, people fail to comply because the laws confront internalized behavioral patterns and social practices. Noncompliance is the product of sticky social norms. Many people tacitly accept the social hierarchies conductive to violence and believe that intimate partner violence is primarily a private matter that should not be discussed publicly.

In this chapter, we develop the idea of VAW as an aspirational right by drawing on data from the Mexican National Survey on the Dynamics of Household Relations (ENDIREH) from 2011. This survey of more than 150,000 women across the country probes respondents' experiences of different forms of violence; their reactions to, and views about, violence; and their experiences with actions taken by state institutions such as the courts, police, health services, and municipal governments. We use the survey responses to evaluate the degree of compliance with the 2007 General Law on Women's Access to a Life Free of Violence, and complementary state-level legislation, on the part of violators, victims, and state officials. Since the survey respondents are all women, we present data on the experiences of violence and reactions as reported by victims of violence – indirectly also getting information about the actions of violators and state officials.[2]

Our analysis demonstrates that noncompliance is pervasive: a striking number of women report different forms of violence originating from their intimate partners, including physical abuse. Though most women know about their legal rights to a life without violence, many of them are unable or unwilling to step forward to claim their rights when such rights have been violated. Significant numbers of women seem to excuse and normalize intimate partner violence. Even among women who say that they consider violence to be wrong, many believe it is a matter that should stay in and be resolved by the family. This noncompliance may also be strategic, since denouncing an intimate partner carries significant emotional, financial, and personal risk. We see evidence of noncompliance with the law by state authorities too. Among those women who do report physical abuse to the authorities, a large minority say that the state authorities they approached did nothing about their complaint, and a few say that the state authorities humiliated them.

Our analysis also shows that the likelihood of being a victim of violence, of reporting violence, and of knowing about the law varies significantly across social groups. In other words, VAW legislation is de facto a weaker institution for some women than for others. Different groups of women are more and less knowledgeable about their rights, and have different access to resources that allow them to claim their rights. This intersectional perspective serves as a reminder of the importance of considering heterogeneity in the analysis of institutional weakness, and allowing for the possibility that institutions can be weak for some people in some contexts and strong for others in other contexts.

A LIFE FREE FROM VIOLENCE AS AN "ASPIRATIONAL RIGHT"

Our objective in this chapter is to explore challenges to the enforcement of aspirational rights, with a focus on VAW legislation. We understand institutions as "humanly devised constraints that structure political, economic, and social interaction" (North 1990), and institutionalization as the process by which these constraints take hold in society. As Brinks, Levitsky, and Murillo discuss in Chapter 1, institutions can also be thought of as "a set of . . . rules that structures human behavior and expectations around a particular activity or goal," and the strength of institutions can be evaluated by their ability to change societal outcomes.

---

[2] In this way we treat the surveyed women both as respondents and as *observers* of the behavior of their violators and state officials (cf. Levitsky and Murillo 2009: 129, fn. 6; Calvo and Murillo 2012: 856).

VAW laws are institutions inspired by feminist analyses attributing sexual and gender violence not just to individual-level factors like aggression or alcoholism but to cultural patterns and values that subordinate women as a status group. Status hierarchies, which elevate men and masculinity and degrade women and femininity, are the enabling condition for VAW in the home and in the street, by intimate partners, family members, bosses, coworkers, and strangers (MacKinnon 1991; Heise 1998; Ridgeway 2001; Weldon 2002; Fraser 2003; Garcia-Moreno et al. 2006; Htun and Weldon 2012; True 2012;). VAW laws aim to prevent violence by changing the social norms that uphold status hierarchies, to facilitate swifter punishment of perpetrators, and to improve protective and support services for victims.

The enactment of VAW legislation signals the achievement of a normative and discursive consensus among diverse sectors of society that violence should be eradicated, that ending VAW requires recognition of women as equals, and that women's bodies, ideas, names, and practices should be included in notions of the "universal," the "nation," and "humanity." These ideas about VAW and women's status are socially desirable for elites: they are well established in international human rights law and the discourse of democratic legitimacy. Civilized states, and state actors that want to participate in the global community, need to uphold them, at least rhetorically (Keck and Sikkink 1998; Towns 2010).

We characterize the right to a life free of violence upheld in laws on VAW as an *aspirational* right.[3] Aspirational rights project a vision for social change. As a form of "expressive" law, aspirational rights communicate new norms – standards of desirable and appropriate conduct – and may therefore help motivate people to act in some ways and not others (McAdams 1997, 2015). In addition, aspirational rights supply cultural categories that potentially lay the cognitive foundations for new preferences and behaviors (Hoff and Walsh 2019). Aspirational VAW legislation thus aims to push society in the direction of greater justice, and add legitimacy to ongoing struggles for social change.

Our concept of aspirational rights differs from some previous usage. Many scholars distinguish between "aspirational" rights, which are not enforceable, and "justiciable" rights, which can be claimed in court. (On the distinction between aspirational rights and justiciable rights, with coding criteria, see Jung, Hirschl, and Rosevear 2014: 5.) Historically, social and economic rights (such as the right to education, health care, housing, water, food, and so forth) have been categorized as aspirational, while civil and political rights (such as freedom of speech and religion, the right to due process, the right to vote, etc.) were seen as justiciable. For example, countries that ratify the International Covenant

---

[3] A "right," here, is defined as a "legitimate claim." This definition contrasts with the Weberian one used by, among others, Brinks (2008: 19), who defines a right as "an increase of the probability that a certain expectation of the one to whom the law grants that right will not be disappointed."

on Civil and Political Rights must enforce such rights immediately, whereas those that ratify the International Covenant on Economic, Social, and Cultural Rights must commit themselves only to *work toward* their realization (Harvey 2004; Wiles 2006: 109). This historical distinction is less relevant today. Over the course of the twentieth century, not only have social (and economic and cultural) rights become increasingly common in national constitutions, but they are also more likely to have justiciable status (Jung, Hirschl, and Rosevear 2014).[4]

Nor does our understanding of aspirational rights map onto the distinction between "negative" and "positive" rights or liberties. In Berlin's classic distinction, negative rights protect individuals from constraints or obstacles on autonomous action (like "hedges" or "shields"), while positive rights refer to the possibility or opportunity to realize a certain purpose, usually made possible through entitlements or expenditures. Holmes and Sunstein (2000) criticize the negative–positive distinction as incoherent, and conclude that, since all rights require resources to be realized, all rights are positive. Rights pertaining to VAW are a good example of their argument since – though the right to be free from violence amounts to a "shield" against assault and abuse – most countries seek to realize this right through proactive measures such as training for law enforcement, support for victims, and public education.

We do not consider aspirational rights to lack enforceability. They can be enforced, at least in theory. Rather, the key characteristic of aspirational rights is their depiction of a reality with a different set of social norms and practices. Such rights are goalposts, stakes in future developments, and guides to the process of social change. They intervene in existing distribution of social power on the side of marginalized and vulnerable citizens (cf. Brinks 2008).

The aspirational quality of VAW legislation does not characterize all rights won by women as part of the "rights revolution." Unlike other women's rights issues, changing laws on VAW did not require defeating an entrenched opposition, as it was not perceived directly to contradict the tenets of religious doctrine. Reform on other issues that involved conflicts between the government and religious institutions, such as divorce and abortion, were possible only when governments were willing to confront ecclesiastical authorities (Htun 2003). Nor did change regarding VAW policies require state-sponsored socioeconomic redistribution. Unlike publicly funded parental leave and childcare, which involve state action to shift the respective roles of state, market, and family for social provision, reform of VAW legislation did not involve the mobilization of Left parties against business opposition (Htun and Weldon 2018). In these other cases, legal change took a while to accomplish, and, by the time it was achieved, the law caught up with social practices that had already been established. VAW laws are aspirational in that legal change *precedes* hoped-for social change.

---

[4] The mechanism of the *tutela*, for example, enables individuals to demand in court that the government protect their rights.

Aspirational Rights as Weak Institutions

Open to popular participation and keen to cultivate legitimacy, many new democracies enacted aspirational rights and other legal norms that were far more egalitarian and progressive than actual social norms and practices (Brinks and Botero 2014; Frías 2014; Levitsky and Slater 2011). Though aspirational rights usually reflect a broad consensus about values and principles appropriate to a democratic society, they have "ideational rather than material roots," and they may therefore "rest very lightly and uneasily on the surface of society" (Brinks 2008: 4). Often, rights that aim to combat inequality, reduce marginalization, and promote inclusion were introduced in response to international norms and pressures. They responded more to moral appeals than to the actual power of subordinate groups (Levitsky and Murillo 2009; Frías 2010, 2013; Towns 2010; Brinks and Botero 2014). Aspirational rights have therefore been referred to as weak or "window dressing institutions" that "power holders have an interesting in keeping [...] on the books but no interest in enforcing" (Levitsky and Murillo 2009: 120).

In their contributions to this volume, Amengual and Dargant (Chapter 7) and Holland (Chapter 5) suggest that weakness of institutions – including laws on VAW as well as provisions against child labor, pollution, regulations of worker health and safety, protection of public spaces from squatting and invasion, etc. – stems primarily from strategic calculations. State actors choose to avoid the costs associated with enforcement. Amengual and Dargent, for example, argue that "standoffish" states may be deliberately indifferent to social problems and the laws intended to solve them, particularly when enforcement brings little political gain. In a context of competing demands on resources, state actors elect to avoid the costs of reallocating resources and alienating groups that benefit from nonenforcement. Under such conditions social pressures are needed to overcome the indifference of the state and impose costs for nonenforcement (Amengual and Dargent, this volume).

Holland's analysis of coercion gaps describes the ways that state officials collude not to enforce the law, particularly when the poor bear the brunt of enforcement. Even when politicians and citizens generally agree that a particular law serves the public interest, they may oppose the application of sanctions against violators. For example, laws against squatting promote rational, longer-term urban planning and may thus improve service delivery to the poor. But in the short term, enforcing the law by evicting squatters inflicts visible misery on poor families, and looks bad to voters. Holland notes that three-quarters of Bogotá residents surveyed condemned squatting, while one-half of these found evictions to be too harsh. She concludes that there may not be a coherent or stable societal preference against which to judge the efficacy of institutions (see Holland, this volume).

As this suggests, weak institutions are not just a matter of weak state capacity or ineffectively formulated legislation. Noncompliance with institutions involves resistance on the part of state and societal actors. Amengual and Dargent suggest that resistance involves a strategic response to power asymmetries: state officials choose to enforce when actors are powerful enough to impose costs for nonenforcement. Holland shows that people may not want, or at least be ambivalent about, the enforcement of punitive laws.

In this chapter, we show that societal resistance may involve another dimension: sticky social norms. People's habituated behavior is a major reason for noncompliance with VAW legislation. Sticky norms produce contradictory perceptions of violence: people condemn violence while simultaneously normalizing and excusing it. This fraught normative terrain informs women's beliefs about experiences of violence, their decisions to make reports to state authorities, and the ways that police officers, social workers, prosecutors, and medical personnel treat victims.

One objective of aspirational rights is to fashion new norms. Aspirational rights are therefore by construction weak institutions, and characterized by a large gap between the law and social practices. In the case of legislation intended to prevent, punish, and eradicate violence against women, institutional weakness may manifest itself in at least five ways. First, noncompliance with the spirit of the law may be pervasive. Though the law condemns and stipulates punishments for violence, specifies that survivors are to be treated a certain way, and mandates the creation of systems of prevention and treatment, women may continue to experience violence in both the public and private sphere.

Second, there may be a discrepancy between what the law considers "violence" to be and the concept of violence according to social norms. Hardly anybody believes that "intimate partner violence" is a good thing. However, people may not consider forced sexual encounters to be "violence" because they consider it the obligation of a woman to sexually satisfy her partner. They may also perceive mistreatment to be justified if a woman talks back to her partner and fails to do what he says, since men are supposed to be in charge. For example, Mexican civil laws on marriage historically upheld both of these aspects of marital power (Htun 2003; Frías 2013).

Third, even when a woman is deeply concerned with the violence she experiences, she may have been socialized to believe that violence is a normal part of intimate relationships. The idea that intimate partner violence is a family or private matter, and not a public concern, has deep historical roots in many parts of the world. In Latin America, criminal codes had historically privatized and condoned violence against women (Barsted 1994). The persistence of beliefs that VAW is a matter of private shame and not a public violation imposes an enormous hurdle to reporting, which many people – especially women in a sexist society – are too ashamed or unwilling to bear.

Fourth, women may opt to stay silent about violent incidents because they fear the consequences of reporting. Penalties imposed on perpetrators may threaten the financial well-being of their families and put their relationships with other family members and neighbors at risk. The costs of enforcement are borne not only by the aggressor who gets thrown in jail. The woman who reports also incurs costs, as she risks disbelief and demeaning treatment by the authorities, retaliation, and getting ostracized by her family and community (Frías 2010: 546). Many people judge that it is in their interest not to report and tend to minimize the importance of violence that they experience. For them, complying with the law is worse than contributing to its violation.

Finally, when women do come forward to report, they may be met with either no action or ridicule by legal and social service authorities, which results in their revictimization. Law enforcement authorities often fail to take claims of partner violence seriously, and have even advised women to have sex with their violent partners in order to resolve the conflict. Most of the dozens of practitioners interviewed by Frías (2010: 546), for example, reported that intimate partner violence is reduced to a matter of sex. These responses show that local-level state officials themselves are embedded in a culture condoning violence against women.

In other cases, nonresponse may be attributable to "standoffish" state officials that acknowledge VAW as a problem, but fail to take action because they see little to be gained by doing so. Women victims of violence have not been an organized constituency able to deliver rewards on Election Day. Only when the media, feminist movements, and human rights groups raise the cost of nonenforcement by helping voters to see the extent of unsolved crimes, state coddling of violators, poor treatment of victims, and so forth, will they make moves toward enforcement. This dynamic seems to describe the history of state action against *femicídios* (homicides committed against women) in Chihuahua, when massive civic mobilization raised the cost of doing nothing, as well as state action against violence in Veracruz (see more below). The "standoffish" perspective also explains why the contemporary #metoo movement compelled many prominent men in the public and private sectors to resign their positions in the face of allegations of sexual harassment and rape. In the context of high public attention and the mobilization of women as voters, consumers, and investors, doing nothing became too costly.

In any given context we may observe one or several of these manifestations of VAW legislation as a weak institution. What is more, though aspirational rights might be weak institutions overall, they may not be *equally* weak for all social groups. The efficacy of rights typically varies according to the resources of claimants and the extent of state investment (Brinks 2008; Levitsky and Murillo 2009; Brinks and Botero 2014), as well as perceptions of their legitimacy, as Falleti emphasizes in her chapter in this volume. People who claim their rights typically need to have resources that enable them to engage the legal system, hire lawyers, produce legally relevant facts, travel to court, take time off of work, and so forth (Galanter 1974; Brinks 2008;

Brinks and Botero 2014). Marginalized citizens, who by definition lack power and resources, require networks of support to compel state actors to enforce their rights. Over time, gaps among women may even grow, as women with more resources are in a better position to take advantage of changes in the law and access to social services than their more disadvantaged counterparts (cf. Galanter 1974). We should therefore expect to observe that women with more education and resources will be both less likely to be victims of violence and more willing to report violations.

By conceptualizing VAW legislation as an aspirational right, we have suggested that it is weak by construction. But after a while, even if aspirational rights have succeeded in bending social norms, they may still be perceived as weak if they achieve the type of "taken-for-granted" status that sometimes happens to rules and regulations that change social norms (see Chapter 1 on this point). In thinking about the institutional strength or weakness of such legislation, it is therefore crucial to evaluate them from a long-term perspective.

LAW AND POLICY TO COMBAT VAW IN MEXICO

The institution of VAW legislation originated with a social movement, like the case of *consulta previa* in Bolivia analyzed by Falleti in this volume. Global feminist networks began to raise awareness about VAW in the 1970s, around the time of International Women's Year and the global women's conference held in Mexico City in 1975. In Mexico, feminists demanded the first legal reforms in 1978, which would have redefined rape and provided targeted services to victims (Stevenson 1999). Beginning in the 1980s, some states established centers to receive victims of violence. Following a scandal of over a dozen rapes perpetrated by bodyguards working in the Mexico City attorney general's office, a coalition of feminist nongovernmental organizations (NGOs) pushed for more services and for changes in legislation. During the presidency of Carlos Salinas (1988–1994), the government began to take action on rape. Under existing legislation, the maximum penalty for rape was five years, and a rapist could pay a fine to avoid going to prison (Beer 2016). Pushed by a coalition of women federal deputies allied with the feminist movement, Congress reformed the criminal code to increase penalties for rape, to broaden its definition, and to reform archaic components of the law such as the requirement that a woman be "chaste" in order to be raped (Lang 2003: 75).

The same alliance between feminist groups and women in Congress pushed for another series of reforms later in the 1990s at the federal level and in Mexico City, including the criminalization of marital rape, affirmation of women's right to be free from violence, and the inclusion of violence as a ground for divorce (Beer 2017). The criminalization of marital rape marked a major normative victory, for previously, many groups assumed that sexual relations constituted a woman's marital obligation. Following the example set by the Federal District, between 1996 and 2006 twenty-nine of thirty-two states adopted legislation to combat intrafamily violence.[5]

This "first generation" of laws were focused almost exclusively on domestic or intrafamily violence, not on the range of phenomena we today think of as "violence against women" (cf. Weldon 2002). And they were contradictory, aiming on the one hand to protect the sanctity of the family (a nod to conservatives) and on the other to apply state power to protect vulnerable family members from abuse (Frías 2010). Their goal was not a normative shift so much as an effort to help victims, adopt prevention programs, and to channel conflict resolution through administrative procedures rather than the criminal justice system, and therefore further the goal of family unity. Indeed, the need to protect the family as the "origin of the social community" was the declared objective of the law in some states (Frías 2010: 543– 545). In practice, state officials from the Department of Family Development charged with implementing violence prevention programs viewed their mandate in similar terms: rather than viewing violence as a crime, they saw it as a conflict they needed to overcome by reconciling the partners (Lang 2003; Frías 2010).

As movement toward interparty competition, civic participation, and public dissent accelerated over the course of the 1990s, the state's approach to VAW (and other issues emphasized by feminists) changed. Under the influence of the feminist movement and feminist legislators primarily from Left parties, state discourse on the family became less centered on the conservative discourse of family unity. It emphasized the plurality of types of Mexican families, the need to recognize the individual rights of family members, and a more egalitarian division of domestic responsibilities (Lang 2003: 81–82). In the Federal District, ruled by the opposition leftist Party of the Democratic Revolution (PRD) after 1997, official discourse on VAW shifted: no longer were women referred to as "victims," but rather as "women who experience situations of violence," in order to preclude social stigmatization and to emphasize their capacity for autonomous choices (Lang 2003: 83).

Starting in the 1990s, the northern city of Ciudad Juárez suffered a wave of *femicídios* (femicides, or murders of hundreds of women), which brought worldwide attention to the problem of VAW in Mexico. Human rights organizations widely condemned the state's failure to properly investigate the crimes, its tendency to blame murder victims for their plight, its lack of transparency and accountability, and the poor treatment of victims' families (Amnesty International 2003). Families of victims appealed to the Inter-American

---

[5] This legislation involved the administration of social assistance, not modifications to civil or criminal codes. The new laws regulated the actions of state agencies with regard to the prevention of family violence and assistance to victims (Frías 2010: 544).

Commission on Human Rights, and then the Inter-American Court of Human Rights, which found that the government's negligence contributed to a climate of impunity that encouraged more violence (Beer 2016).

In the early 2000s, regional and international intervention, feminist activism, and public outrage spurred additional governmental actions. In 2003, the Federal Congress adopted a law to prevent and eliminate discrimination, and in 2006, it passed a law on the equality between men and women. Then, in 2007, three women legislators from the leftist PRD and the centrist Institutional Revolutionary Party (PRI) authored and proposed comprehensive legislation on VAW. The General Law on Women's Access to a Life Free of Violence was then approved under a presidential administration governed by the rightist National Action Party (PAN).

Unlike the first-generation laws on violence, second-generation legislation recognized multiple forms of violence in public and private spheres including physical, psychological, sexual, economic, institutional, community, and femicide, as well as family violence. The law was meant to coordinate and support, across different states and local governments, efforts to prevent, punish, and eradicate VAW. It required states to revise their legislation on VAW to conform to federal standards within a six-month window and established a system to monitor their progress.

By 2010, all of Mexico's federal units had issued some form of new legislation, though with varying levels of enthusiasm (Ramírez and Echarri 2010: 30). Beer's case studies (Beer 2017: 522–524) show that in most cases, alliances of feminist groups and women politicians from center and Left parties constituted the impetus behind the legislation, with some exceptions. In Chihuahua, site of the horrific episodes of femicides, a woman politician from the rightist PAN promoted VAW legislation, which was adopted the year before the federal law. Guanajuato, which was also governed by the PAN, was the last state to adopt VAW legislation (in 2010). Women from the PAN were divided: some sponsored VAW legislation, while others led the opposition to it (Beer 2017: 523). Beer's quantitative analysis across states reveals that neither the partisan composition of the legislature nor the share of seats held by women was associated with more and less comprehensive legal approaches. However, the strength of the feminist movement was significantly correlated with the comprehensiveness of state-level legislation and its implementation (Beer 2017: 529, table 3), conforming to Htun and Weldon's (2012, 2018) and Weldon's (2002) crossnational findings about the correlates of VAW legislation across countries.

The new legislation contains mechanisms to raise the costs of nonenforcement. The system of *alertas de violencia de género* (gender-violence alerts) was designed to put local and state authorities on notice by publicly announcing episodes of nonenforcement. Either they take action to protect women and punish aggressors, or risk further public shaming, which could carry an electoral cost. In the state of Veracruz, for example, public outrage and media attention put pressure on the state government to change its approach from actively ignoring numerous episodes of rape to attempting to enforce the law (Krauze 2016). At the same time, feminist movements successfully compelled the federal government to issue a gender violence alert, in which the Interior Ministry (Secretaría de Gobernación) commanded the state authorities to take various measures to prevent more violence, including increased security patrols in public spaces and public transport, video surveillance, and better lighting, as well as services to victims and longer-term strategies to promote cultural change (Secretaría de Gobernación 2016).

SURVEY DATA ON COMPLIANCE WITH VAW LAWS

To evaluate the degree of compliance with, and enforcement of, the 2007 General Law on Women's Access to a Life Free of Violence and similar state-level legislation, we look at data from the Mexican National Survey on the Dynamics of Household Relations (ENDIREH) from 2011. This survey was designed and implemented by National Institute of Statistics and Geography (INEGI) in collaboration with the National Women's Institute (INMUJERES), with the purpose of learning more about the prevalence and forms of violence against women in the home and at their work place. The survey asked questions meant to capture various forms of violence, including physical, psychological, sexual, and economic abuse. The forms of violence covered in the survey correspond to the different types of violence contemplated by the 2007 federal law.

For this survey, some 128,000 households were sampled from across Mexico, 4,000 in each of the country's 32 states. The sample was chosen to be representative of each state, and also to be representative of urban and rural areas across the country.[6] In each of the sampled households, one key person was asked to respond to questions about all the individuals living in the household. This was done to identify all women aged fifteen or older, and all of these women were then interviewed individually. The final sample interviewed individually consists of 152,636 women, of whom 87,169 were in a relationship, 27,203 had previously been in a relationship, and 38,264 were single. These women responded to a range of questions about their work, living conditions, and personal lives, with an emphasis on their experiences of discrimination and violence.

While previous papers using these data have focused on the overall prevalence of violence against women in Mexico (Villarreal 2007; INEGI 2013), our main concern was to use the survey responses to get a sense of variation in noncompliance with the 2007 gender violence law among perpetrators, victims, and state officials.

---

[6] For further information about the survey methodology, see www.inegi.org.

Physical Domestic Abuse in Mexico

All the women surveyed for the ENDIREH who were in a relationship, or who had been in a relationship at some point, were asked a series of questions about treatment by their intimate partner. Of these women, 49 percent (56,035) responded affirmatively to having experienced at least one of the 30 forms of violence, harassment, or poor treatment included in the questionnaire.[7] Strikingly, 19 percent of women (21,450) report having been victims of *physical domestic abuse* – including being kicked, hit, shot at, or forced into sexual relations.[8] When the survey asked women whether they had experienced physical abuse at the hand of their partner *in the previous year* (2010–2011), some 7 percent responded affirmatively.

There is geographic variation in the prevalence of women who reported experiencing violence. Figure 6.1 shows the share of women reporting experiences of physical domestic abuse during the previous year across the different Mexican states in 2011. As we can see, the state-level values range from about 5 percent in Baja California and Baja California Sur to more than 8.6 percent in the states of Mexico, Zacatecas, and Guanajuato.

The share of women reporting physical domestic abuse also varies by groups of women. Figure 6.2 shows the percentage of women who say they experienced physical domestic abuse in the previous year, subdivided by the education level of the women and whether they lived in an urban or rural area. The figure shows clear differences, although perhaps not as large as we might expect. Whereas between 6 and 8 percent of women with little education say they have experienced physical domestic abuse in the previous year, the number is about 3 percent among women with a graduate degree living in an urban area.

Attitudes toward Physical Intimate Partner Abuse

The survey allows us to explore social norms through responses to questions probing attitudes about violence. As expected, almost all (98.6 percent) the respondents in the survey agree that women have the right to a life without violence and that women have the right to defend themselves if they are subjected to violence (99.2 percent). But the responses diverge more when the questions become more specific, as shown in Figure 6.3. Only 2.3 percent of the women responded affirmatively to the statement that a man has the right to hit his wife. However, more than 20 percent of the surveyed women say they think that a wife should obey her partner in anything he wants, and 17.6 percent responded affirmatively to the statement that a woman is obliged to have sex with her partner.

---

[7] All 30 subquestions of question 6.1 in the survey for women in a relationship.
[8] Subquestions 20–30 under question 6.1 in the survey of women in a relationship.

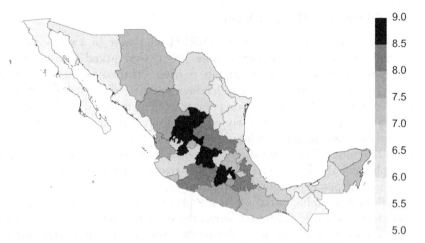

FIGURE 6.1. Percentage of women interviewed for the ENDIREH 2011 reporting physical abuse at the hand of their husband or partner in the previous year.

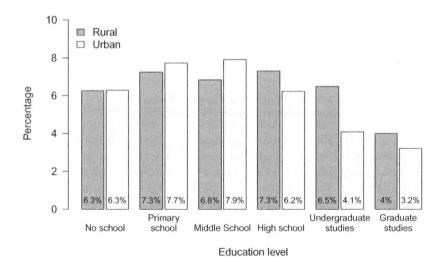

FIGURE 6.2. Percentage of women interviewed for the ENDIREH 2011 reporting physical domestic abuse, by education level and place of residence.

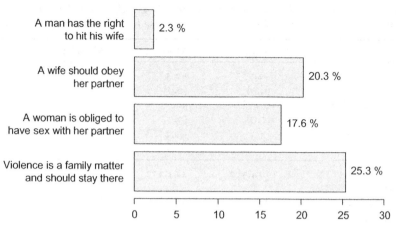

FIGURE 6.3. Social norms and attitudes toward violence among women interviewed for the ENDIREH 2011 (percentages of women responding affirmatively to the statements).

These findings are consistent with our theoretical discussion of how "violence" may mean different things for different people. The 2007 VAW law classifies many types of aggressive and demeaning behavior as violence, including the multiple ways that a man may command his partner to obey his will and chastise her for failing to do so. The fact that many women simultaneously condemn violence while endorsing women's subservience shows that social norms surrounding VAW are far from straightforward.

These responses also provide supportive evidence that the notion of domestic abuse as a private matter is still strong. More than a quarter of the surveyed women say that if there is an incidence of violence in the family, it is a family matter and it should stay that way.[9]

To what extent are attitudes about violence as a family matter associated with women experiencing abuse? Table 6.1 shows the output from regression models of experiences of violence on attitudes toward violence as a family matter. The models are multilevel logistic regression models with individual respondents nested in federal states and in rural/urban areas (and in the primary sampling unit in Model 4). The outcome variable is a dichotomous indicator for whether or not the respondent had experienced physical domestic abuse in the previous year.

In Model 1 we include only the response to the question about domestic abuse as a family matter as an explanatory variable. We see that responding

---

[9] The question is worded as follows: "*¿Si hay golpes o maltrato en la casa es un asunto de familia y ahí debe quedar?*"

TABLE 6.1. *Multilevel logistic regression models of individual characteristics of women who experienced physical domestic abuse by their partner, 2010–2011*

	Model 1	Model 2	Model 3	Model 4
(Intercept)	−2.7***	−2.5***	−0.9***	−1.0***
	(0.0)	(0.0)	(0.1)	(0.1)
Violence Is a Family	0.2***	0.2***	0.2***	0.2***
Matter	(0.0)	(0.0)	(0.0)	(0.0)
Knowledge of Law		−0.2***	−0.3***	−0.3***
		(0.0)	(0.0)	(0.0)
N	114,372	114,372	113,998	113,998
Controls			Y	Y
State and R/U	Y	Y	Y	Y
Random Effects				
PSU Random Effects				Y

Note: *$p < 0.05$; **$p < 0.01$; ***$p < 0.001$.

affirmatively to this question is strongly positively associated with being a victim of violence. Model 2 also includes a dichotomous indicator of familiarity with the 2007 gender violence law, since knowledge of the law may be considered a necessary condition for claiming one's rights according to the law. As expected, people familiar with the law are less likely to be victims of violence. Models 3 and 4 also include some additional control variables: an ordinal indicator for the education level of the woman (the levels are provided in Figure 6.2), a dichotomous indicator for whether the woman had worked in the previous year, her age, and a dichotomous indicator for whether she or her partner (for those with a partner) speak an indigenous language. The indicator for perceiving violence as a family matter remains a significant predictor of violence even when these other variables are included.

Reporting Physical Intimate Partner Abuse

Many victims of abuse – in Mexico and elsewhere – fail to report their experiences to the authorities. Reporting involves significant social, economic, and emotional risk, and historically has led to few positive outcomes for victims. Few complaints of domestic and sexual violence, as well as sexual harassment, in Latin America have actually ended up in formal prosecutions, let alone in sentences for the aggressors (Lang 2003: 77). The Inter-American Commission on Human Rights reports that half of all verdicts in VAW cases end in acquittals, and the Latin American and Caribbean Committee for the

Defense of Women's Rights (CLADEM) claims that 92 percent of femicides go unpunished in the region. Amnesty International calculates that of the approximately 74,000 sexual assaults in Mexico, prosecutors receive only about 15,000 complaints, and, out of the cases brought to court in 2009, only 2,795 resulted in a conviction. Most VAW cases are concluded through out-of-court settlement practices such as conciliation or mediation, in violation of the spirit of the Inter-American Convention on the Prevention, Punishment, and Eradication of Violence Against Women, which stipulates that VAW is a human rights violation. When cases do go to court, judges and prosecutors often question victims about their morality and sexual practices (Htun, O'Brien, and Weldon 2014). Women also often end up dropping charges. As mentioned earlier, women who are financially dependent on their partners may desist due to fear for their livelihood, were their family breadwinners to end up in jail. When police officers have had past experiences with women claimants who have dropped charges, they are less likely to take other women seriously (Frías 2010: 546).

In order to facilitate reporting and reduce its costs, Mexico's 2007 federal gender violence law and its counterparts in the states attempted to make it easier to report abuse and to increase the quantity of services available to victims. The more places that a victim can seek assistance and make claims, for example, the more likely it is that her or his rights will be protected (Smulovitz 2015). As the result of governmental and nongovernmental actions in Mexico, the number of sites has grown dramatically. In Mexico City (D.F.) for example, there are more than a dozen *types* of places where women can go to seek recourse after experiencing gender violence, and most of these agencies and organizations have multiple sites across the city (see Ramírez and Echarri 2010: 80–81).

The ENDIREH 2011 survey does not allow us to look at conviction rates, but it does allow us to look at how many women claim to have reported the violence they experience to state authorities. As reported above, about 7 percent (7,877) of the surveyed women say that they experienced physical domestic abuse in the previous year. As shown in Figure 6.4, 15.3 percent (1,203) of these women say they reported this incident to some authority (of a list including the police, Family Welfare office [DIF], women's agency, and so on).

Figure 6.4 provides an overview of women's reasons for not reporting episodes of violence and abuse. Out of the 7,877 women who experienced physical domestic abuse in the previous year, a substantial number say they did not report this incident out of fear (15 percent), for the sake of their children (16 percent), shame (13 percent), or because they wanted to keep it quiet (9 percent). A striking number of women (19 percent) say they did not report because the incident was "not important," a response indicative of the cultural normalization of violence. The responses also reveal that lack of knowledge of

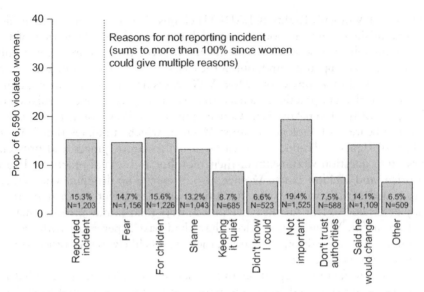

FIGURE 6.4. Reasons for not reporting physical domestic abuse to the authorities.

the law (7 percent saying "Didn't know I could") and a distrust of the authorities (8 percent) contribute to underreporting.

The stories of a lack of action on the part of state authorities discussed above are also reflected in the survey responses. Of the 1,203 women who say they have reported an incident of physical domestic abuse to some authority in the previous year, 79 percent say the authorities had treated them well, 5 percent say they had been treated badly or ridiculed, the rest, some 17 percent, say the authorities had done nothing. The fact that close to one-fourth of women feel the state treated them badly or did nothing about their claims of violence contributes to climate of impunity that discourages reporting.

The patterns in Figures 6.3 and 6.4 suggest that perceptions of what constitutes violence, a normalization of violence, and the idea that domestic abuse is a private rather than a public matter constitute important sources of resistance to laws on VAW on the part of the public and by state officials.

Social norms, knowledge of legal rights, and personal characteristics can explain variation in reporting rates too. Table 6.2 shows multivariate patterns of the characteristics of the women who say they reported incidents of physical domestic abuse in the previous year. The model specifications are the same as the ones reported in Table 6.1, but here the outcome variable is a dichotomous indicator for whether or not a woman reported an incident of

TABLE 6.2. *Multilevel logistic regression models of individual characteristics of women who said they had reported violence they experienced, 2010–2011*

	Model 1	Model 2	Model 3	Model 4
(Intercept)	-1.7^{***}	-1.9^{***}	-1.0^{***}	-1.0^{***}
	(0.1)	(0.1)	(0.2)	(0.2)
Violence Is a	-0.4^{***}	-0.4^{***}	-0.3^{***}	-0.3^{***}
Family Matter	(0.1)	(0.1)	(0.1)	(0.1)
Knowledge of		0.2^{**}	0.2^{*}	0.2^{*}
Law		(0.1)	(0.1)	(0.1)
N	7877	7877	7854	7854
Controls			Y	Y
State and R/U	Y	Y	Y	Y
Random Effects				
PSU Random				Y
Effects				

Note: $^{*}p < .05$; $^{**}p < .01$; $^{***}p < .001$.

physical domestic abuse by her partner. The sample is the subset of women who had experienced physical domestic abuse in the previous year. Here we can see how women who say they consider intimate partner violence to be a family matter are considerably less likely to report the violence they experience. Women knowledgeable about the 2007 gender violence law are more likely to report the violence.

CONCLUSIONS

Our analysis of national survey data from Mexico shows that sticky norms, not just low state capacity or standoffishness, pose an obstacle to more widespread compliance with the country's 2007 gender violence law. In contrast to the law's messages about equality and human rights, striking shares of women continue to believe that men should dominate in a partnership, that women have a duty to obey their husbands, and that violence should remain a private matter. As a result, though most women are opposed in principle to violence, many also justify it under some circumstances, minimize its importance, and feel afraid of reporting the violence they suffer – which is understandable since state authorities in many cases treat victims poorly. However, we also see that among individuals whose beliefs align more with the letter of the law, gender violence is less frequent.

The right to be free from VAW is an aspirational right aiming to transform centuries-old norms and practices that endorse and privatize violence against women. By construction, such rights are weak institutions. The large gap between social practices and legal provisions exists at their origin. VAW laws aim to provide activists with tools and resources to change society. They legitimize the demands of social movements and broadcast messages about appropriate forms of behavior. As Lisa Baldez argues, the global Convention on the Elimination of All Forms of Discrimination against Women (CEDAW) is a *process*, not a policy (Baldez 2014). The same can be true of aspirational rights. They are institutions that exist to push processes of change in slow-moving social norms. To see their effects, we may need to wait a few decades.

7

The Social Determinants of Enforcement

Integrating Politics with Limited State Capacity

Matthew Amengual and Eduardo Dargent

The weak or selective enforcement of parchment rules is a widely recognized problem in Latin American and developing states. In Chapter 1, Brinks, Levitsky, and Murillo theorize institutional weakness as the gap between the way social interactions should be structured by institutions and the actual way social interactions occur. We define enforcement as the set of actions that the state takes to reduce the size of that gap.[1] Our point of departure is that enforcement is often uneven and therefore constitutes a key element of the politics of institutional weakness; when rules are enforced is equally, if not more, important than the content of the rules themselves.

In this chapter, we build an account of the political and societal determinants of enforcement to elucidate why and how weak institutions gain relevance and how strong institutions might, or might not, emerge from state action. By far, dominant approaches to explaining the lack of enforcement in countries with weak institutions point to deficits in state capacity as the key explanatory factor. Strong states have the necessary financial and human resources to pursue their policies, are less prone to corruption or illegal conduct, and have extensive reach in their territory to make laws effective. Many authors have pointed out how Latin American states cannot enforce their laws due to state weakness (O'Donnell 1993; Grindle 2009). The positive relation between state capacity and enforcement leads some authors to regard bureaucratic and state reforms as the cornerstone for building up strong institutions (Echebarría and Cortázar 2006; Rose-Ackerman 2007).

Although state capacity is certainly quite relevant to explain enforcement, focusing solely on this explanatory variable limits our understanding of enforcement and consequently ignores key aspects of the politics of

---

[1] We focus on what happens after formal rules are adopted, rather than design of the rules.

institutional weakness. As studies have shown, lack of enforcement is not always caused solely by the lack of state capacity. Instead, nonenforcement can reflect a political decision (taken by bureaucratic actors or politicians) not to enforce the law (Tendler 2002a; Holland 2017; Holland, this volume; Fernández and Garay, this volume). These studies show that variation in enforcement is caused, at least in part, by variables that are not reducible to state capacity. Political explanations tend to highlight what we call diffuse pressures for or against enforcement generally in a territory or toward a class of social actors.

While these approaches helpfully bring politics back in, we do not want to be too quick to dismiss the barriers within states to enforcement. Where states widely depart from the strong-state ideal, the principal–agent relationship between bureaucrats and political officials is imperfect (Huber and McCarty 2004). With limited capacity, states that have competing priorities may simply ignore noncompliance and allocate resources elsewhere, resulting in non-enforcement even absent political pressure against enforcement. Moreover, societal organizations can directly intervene in the enforcement process. The actions of societal organizations can block states with limited capacity, even if there is political will for enforcement as traditionally understood (Eaton 2012; Dargent, Feldmann, and Luna 2017). Conversely, social groups can support the state operationally, enabling states to overcome limitations in capacity and enforce rules effectively even in contexts where bureaucracies are not strong (Amengual 2016). Thus, limitations in state capacity influence the dynamic elements of enforcement politics; we cannot completely separate capabilities of the state to respond to institutional weakness and immediate political considerations of key actors.

Building on this insight, we explore political and societal pressures to trigger or block enforcement, ultimately resulting in variation in how and when gaps between rules and practice are reduced. We contend that there are two analytically distinct types of political pressure – diffuse and proximate – that affect how and when enforcement responds to institutional weaknesses, especially in contexts of constrained state capacity. Diffuse societal pressure for or against enforcement promotes the enforcement of rules (or their lack of enforcement) in a general way – that is, it aims at a broad class of breakdowns in institutional order. These types of societal pressures are usually directed toward politicians or senior bureaucrats at the central state or subnational governments who oversee the posture of the state toward enforcement. Diffuse pressures for enforcement may lead to what we call a proactive state, institutional action toward making the law effective. On the contrary, diffuse pressures against enforcement may lead to the opposite phenomenon: forbearance, or the intentional tolerance of the violation of the law (Holland 2017). Finally, a lack of diffuse pressure against enforcement does not necessarily mean state action but may lead to what we believe is a more frequent outcome: standoff, or state inaction due to risk aversion or lack of interest (Slater and Kim 2015).

However, politics does not end with such diffuse pressure. Instead, societal support and opposition proximate to the point of enforcement – on the particular actors and instances in which enforcement takes place – also influence enforcement without affecting the overall posture of the state. Social groups acting proximate to the act of enforcement can amplify diffuse support or enable specific enforcement action when diffuse support is absent. Proximate pressures are not, naturally, always conducive to enforcement, and social opposition proximate to the point of enforcement can limit or even block it when states are not omnipotent. Based on this argument, we generate predictions regarding how interactions between interest groups and the state at distinct points in the enforcement process influence enforcement in contexts of widespread weak institutions.

We illustrate the explanatory value of our argument with cases from Argentina, Bolivia, and Peru. We analyze diverse social settings – mining, construction, agroindustry – where there were pervasive institutional weaknesses (e.g., the actual practices depart substantially from those prescribed by formal institutions). Our unit of analysis is a specific set of institutional rules, in a defined geographic area, at a particular time. By focusing on particular rules of the game, we gain analytical clarity and avoid treating states as unitary, homogenous actors. In all cases, state capacity to respond was not strong, but neither was it completely absent. Nonetheless, the states responded quite differently to these challenges, and this variation in enforcement outcomes cannot be explained by state capacity or by the political concerns of elected leaders alone. Instead, these differences can be explained by the interaction of diffuse pressures by social actors (business interests, unions) and proximate ones brought to bear by organized social actors (mining cooperatives, unions, environmental groups, among others) at the point of enforcement. The cases clearly show how interactions between, on the one hand, social actors and, on the other hand, politicians and bureaucrats produce enforcement outcomes that depend not only on state capacity or political will, but also crucially on the configuration of social actors and the resources they can muster. In the conclusion we discuss the implications of these findings for institutional strength and weakness.

THE POLITICS OF ENFORCEMENT

Effective enforcement is usually associated with high levels of state capacity. Diverse definitions of state capacity point to the ability of states to implement their policies (Skocpol 1985; Fukuyama 2004). Skocpol (1985: 9) defines state capacity as the ability "to implement official goals" and Centeno, Kohli, and Yashar (2017) define it as "the organizational and bureaucratic ability to implement governing projects." State capacity is usually operationalized through what Soifer (2008) calls a "national capabilities approach," an approach used in diverse comparative works that analyze variation in state capacity between states or within states (Kurtz 2013; Soifer 2015). This approach assesses the financial and institutional resources mustered by the state as a proxy of state capacity. Strong, professional, and well-equipped bureaucracies are assumed to be capable of implementing the law. Using this lens, nonresponse of the state to the gap between formal laws and effective enforcement is explained by the lack of capacity of the state. Conversely, states should routinely take actions to close the gap when they have capacity, allocating enforcement in a programmatic fashion.

State capacity is, however, a structural variable, and enforcement often changes rapidly and varies within particular jurisdictions, making state capacity an incomplete explanation for enforcement. Indeed, a large literature seeks to explain variation in enforcement while holding state capacity constant, largely by looking to the interests of elected officials. Even under conditions of state strength, elected officials can oppose enforcement and block actions to reduce gaps between formal rules and behaviors. Such a view is a staple of research on countries that are often assumed to have relatively strong states; for instance, studies show that elected officials influence the enforcement of rules governing taxes (Scholz and Wood 1998) and deporting migrants (Ellermann 2009) in the United States.

While the state capacity approach is somewhat more common in developing countries, researchers have also highlighted the role of elected officials apart from any constraints on state capacity. Tendler (2002a) shows how politicians can enter into arrangements with groups, specifically informal firms violating labor and environmental regulations, to exchange lax enforcement for votes. Similarly, Fernández and Garay (this volume) argue that enforcement of forest conservation institutions in Argentina is shaped by politicians' use of a "conflict avoidance" strategy. They develop a theory of variation in enforcement that hinges on the balance of power between large firms that exploit resources, and thus benefit from institutional weakness, and "conservationist coalitions" that support institutional strength. They model subnational politicians as seeking to avoid costly conflict by selectively enforcing, or not enforcing, institutional mandates created by the national government. Congruently, Holland (2017, this volume) presents the concept of forbearance, defined as the "intentional and revocable government leniency toward the violations of the law." She argues that, in many circumstances, nonenforcement is so politically expedient for politicians that even if the state gains more resources (or fewer competing obligations), enforcement will not increase. Also highlighting the political costs of enforcement, Slater and Kim (2015) argue that some states choose not to render societies legible and instead choose "standoffish" strategies. They do so when there are political costs to state engagement that derive from limited (but not absent) capacity. Instead of exercising control over society, these states opt for other, less costly ways of remaining in power. This concept of standoffish states refers not only to risk-averse states trying to prevent the political costs of certain actions, but also to states making de facto decisions to ignore violations of the law out of lack of interest given their limited resources. Standoffish conduct also describes well how Latin American states frequently face social problems – states tend to ignore them.

These theoretical lenses productively bring politics back in; failures of the state to respond to the distance between institutional rules and practices can often be explained by coalitions in favor of broad institutional weakness that create incentives for politicians who have much to gain from nonenforcement (and a lot to lose from enforcement). Most of the literature summarized above focuses on what we call diffuse pressure. Pressures are diffuse when they influence the political payoffs (or costs) to enforcement in general, as enforcement relates to institutional breakdowns involving a broad class of actors (or a geographic area). For example, diffuse pressures are at work when politicians seek to gain votes from classes of individuals by increasing or reducing enforcement in an entire jurisdiction.

In addition, in contexts of limited state capacity, absence of diffuse opposition to enforcement will not result in enforcement but to what we call, building on Slater and Kim, standoffish outcomes. It is often assumed in the work on politicized enforcement that politicians either gain or lose from enforcement. Yet enforcement is often not salient. There is little notice one way or another, at a general level, of politicians' positions toward enforcing particular regulations, especially in contexts where people who suffer from violations are marginalized. In such circumstances, strong states with unlimited capacity may enforce anyway, even without a political upside, because autonomous bureaucracies will seek to impose institutional order. However, where resources are limited, the absence of broad opposition for enforcement may be insufficient for enforcement to occur, as bureaucrats have constrained resources and many violations to address. Classic research on street-level bureaucrats takes as a given that officials face many demands and limited resources, forcing them to make trade-offs and to ration or triage (Lipsky 1983). O'Brien and Li (1999) build on this insight and describe selective policy implementation in China, arguing that local state officials in China decide not to apply law due to competing priorities, especially the need to respond to the bureaucratic goals set by the central state.[2] Indeed, we believe that selective enforcement is a modal form of nonenforcement in Latin America; there are many points of institutional breakdown where there are simply no strong political or societal interests pushing the state to take action and allocate limited resources that could be spent elsewhere. In these instances, bureaucracies can enforce certain regulations or adopt the kind of standoff conduct mentioned above. Building on these insights, we illustrate in our cases how the presence or

[2] In Holland's conceptualization, such selective policy implementation is distinct from forbearance (2017: 16).

absence of social forces exercising diffuse pressure for or against enforcement results in three distinct state stances toward enforcement: proactive, standoffish, and forbearing.[3]

We illustrate the first stance, proactive, in two of our cases: illegal gold extraction in Peru and construction in Peru. In both of these cases, illegal conduct was initially ignored by the central state but eventually diffuse societal pressures led politicians and bureaucrats to be proactive in attempting to enforce regulations. The second stance (standoffishness) is exemplified by the cases of brickmakers in Córdoba, Argentina, and environmental regulations in Santa Fe where the absence of strong diffuse societal pressure for or against enforcement led the state to avoid, when possible, engaging in regulation of these industries. Finally, the case of gold extraction in Bolivia is an example of forbearance, an instance in which the political gains of the party in power, the Movement for Socialism (*Movimiento al Socialismo*, MAS), allows cooperative gold miners to violate the law.

But this is just the first stage of enforcement politics; we need to look deeper than diffuse pressures to understand actual enforcement outcomes in our five cases. In a second stage we go further to examine political pressures highly proximate to the point of enforcement and that involve pressure around a single instance of enforcement. These are pressures created by actors that either resist enforcement at the point of the behavior, or support it in particular instances. For example, a firm that violates environmental regulations may take actions to avoid enforcement on that firm, without taking actions that alter the political costs or benefits of enforcement overall in the firm's industry (e.g., advocating against enforcement on the firms' competitors). Such proximate politics of enforcement are particularly important when states are limited in their capacity to carry out the will of politicians (or act autonomously). Under such conditions, resistance by actors at the point of the behavior, or support by other actors, can be decisive for rules to be or not be enforced.[4] Pressure proximate to the point of enforcement is particularly important in contexts of limited state capacity because states with limited capacity cannot easily respond to diffuse pressure and overwhelm resistance proximate to enforcement, and because limited states may benefit from support at the point of enforcement. We address both of these possibilities in turn.

To begin with, when there is diffuse pressure for enforcement, but at the point proximate to enforcement there are dominant groups with considerable resources that oppose it, the state is likely to be blocked – even if elected officials have an incentive to enforce. Eaton (2012: 647) defines such state

---

[3] For a more detailed discussion of diffuse pressures over the Peruvian and Bolivian states to enforce and not enforce laws against illegal gold mining, see Baraybar and Dargent (2019).

[4] Naturally, reality can be more complex: there can be more than one societal actor exercising diffuse or proximate pressure for or against enforcement. Our cases focus on instances where there is one dominant actor at both levels.

challengers as those actors who "contest [the state's] monopoly on the legitimate use of violence or seek to prevent or escape the implementation of its laws and policies." Challengers are not only violent actors such as guerrillas or criminal groups; they can also be actors not complying with laws and regulations and opposing enforcement. Thus, where state capacity is limited, diffuse support for enforcement is insufficient, as the state may not be able to overcome strong opposition to enforcement that is proximate. If this strong social opposition is found at each instance that the state attempts enforcement, then the enforcement of rules becomes ineffective. If this resistance varies in strength, then we should find some instances where the institution is enforced and others in which it is not. We illustrate this dynamic of strong social actors opposing the state proximate to the point of enforcement through the case of enforcement on informal gold mining in Peru, what we call blocked enforcement.

But social forces can contribute to enforcement. As pointed out by works on state-in-society, social actors can become crucial allies to achieve the state's goals (Migdal, Kohli, and Shue 1994; Boone 2003). Building on this literature, Amengual (2016) shows how states with medium levels of state capacity are able to enforce labor and environmental regulations thanks to their linkages with proenforcement social actors. When diffuse support for enforcement combines with proximate support, we expect that the state will allocate resources and societal groups will join them. This creates "coproduced enforcement," in which better-resourced states with strong linkages to social groups receive informational and operational support from these groups to enforce the law. In such circumstances, social actors report violations to state agencies and even lend some support to carry out enforcement. For instance, as we will show in the case of construction in Peru, triggering enforcement required a coalition to push the central state, but it did not require that the particular firms that benefitted from enforcement were more powerful than those groups that were interested in weak institutions. However, firms did place pressure proximate to enforcement, amplifying the action of the state.

When there is no strong coalition against or for enforcement at the diffuse level (standoff), social pressure proximate to the point of enforcement by mobilized groups can create a cost for nonenforcement to elected officials or bureaucrats and trigger state action in particular places. Here we build on the concept of "society-dependent enforcement," in which whether enforcement takes place depends on the interests and resources of societal actors that have ties to the state (Amengual 2016). These groups can provide pressure highly proximate to the point of enforcement and in-kind resources to relieve constraints on state capacity. Due to its dependence on proximate pressures, this type of enforcement will be more uneven than in instances where diffuse pressure activates a more general institutional enforcement. Our case in Santa Fe Argentina, where local environmental groups are able to activate the enforcement of national regulations, illustrates well this dynamic.

Although more conflictive than the previous outcome, we may also find uneven forms of enforcement if there is diffuse pressure against enforcement and societal pressure for enforcement at a proximate level. The presence of dominant social actors exercising pressure for enforcement at a proximate level may lead politicians and bureaucrats to enforce regulations that authorities at the diffuse level have decided to forbear. In these cases, the proximate pressures have to be more considerable than in the previous one to surmount diffuse pressure to forbear. Although we do not have a case to illustrate this outcome, we can identify it in the literature. For example, Brinks (2008: 34) argues that, in the case of judicial responses to police killings, where there is a "non-supportive political environment" for punishing police, "private resources" from society can be used to trigger enforcement in particular instances. In these cases, inequalities in the resources that groups have to push for enforcement lead to sharp inequalities in enforcement. In the following sections, we analyze our five cases, identifying the breakdowns in institutional order, the state responses to them, and the politics that underlie these responses.

NONENFORCEMENT BY FORBEARANCE: GOLD MINING COOPERATIVES IN BOLIVIA

In the early 2000s, mineral prices exploded. Gold was no exception; the price of gold increased by 360 percent from 2004 to 2012 to reach US$1,669 an ounce (Poveda 2015). Even after prices dropped following their peak, they remained high by historical standards. In many Latin American countries, high prices led to an explosion of small-scale mining conducted in ways that violated basic laws and regulations: uncontrolled pollution, child labor, mercury poisoning, conflicts between miners and peasant communities, tax evasion, and transnational export mafias (Devisscher 2008: 20–24; Amazon Conservation Association 2014; SPDA 2015; Córdova (CEDLA) 2015;).

In Bolivia, the increase of small-scale gold mining resulted in intense pressures on institutions that regulate mining. Gold was not extensively exploited by the state or large firms. Instead, gold mining was dominated by small-scale cooperatives (Interviews with Córdova 2016 and Oporto 2016).[5] Mining cooperatives have a long legacy in Bolivia. Many were established in the 1960s and grew dramatically with the collapse of the state-run mining firm, Corporación Mineral de Bolivia (COMIBOL), in the 1980s. Legally, cooperatives are meant to be nonprofit associations that are internally democratic. Due to their social purpose, cooperatives receive favorable treatment in the mining law: a minimal 2.5 percent royalty and no taxes. However, many cooperatives have never remotely approximated the legal ideal. Many are profit-seeking firms that are

---

[5] Author interviews with Héctor Cordova, La Paz, March 1, 2016, and Henry Oporto, Expert in Bolivian mining and researcher in Fundación Pazos Kanki, La Paz, March 4, 2016.

hierarchically controlled by a few individuals (Francescone 2015: 747). Gold mining cooperatives have broken institutional rules in the extreme and not only fail to meet basic definitions of cooperatives but also violate environmental and criminal laws, evade paying royalties, operate without proper authorization, and exploit dependent workers.

The gap between institutional rules and social practices may lead an observer to conclude that the Bolivian state lacks the capacity to enforce. This conclusion is supported when examining failed state actions to curb violations. Efforts to formalize gold-related activities, such as the creation of the Bolivian Gold Company, a national organization in charge of buying gold production, failed to take root. This organization had only fourteen officials and lacked the basic resources necessary to accomplish its mandate (SPDA 2015: 31–32). In 2007, the Servicio Nacional de Registro y Control de la Comercialización de Minerales y Metales (SENARECOM) was created and put in charge of gold trade and of collecting cooperative contributions, but it has ended up being more an ally than an effective regulator. For example, SENARECOM collects cooperative fees for national and regional associations (SPDA 2015: 40). The mining law reform in 2014 created the Autoridad Judicial Administrativa Minera (AJAM), which centralized a series of competences related to gold extraction. Its work has been focused on recognizing mining rights, not enforcement of laws against illegal operations (interviews with Pantoja 2016 and Ríos 2016).[6] In general, the image of the Bolivian state is one of a weak state being overrun by social actors.

However, a close look into the political dynamics surrounding gold extraction suggests there is more than limited state capacity holding back enforcement. Indeed, the Bolivian state has shown the capacity to take highly costly actions against multinational firms in both mining and natural gas industries when it is politically convenient – thus, the state has, at least in some circumstances, enforced its will against powerful actors. Thus, state inaction is not due to limits in capacity alone; rather, the political benefits gained by the ruling party, MAS, from its linkages with cooperatives explain the lack of enforcement. State capacity in these areas is not low merely because the Bolivian state is weak: keeping low capabilities responds to political decisions determined by the diffuse pressure of cooperatives not to enforce the law.

The political importance of mining cooperatives for the MAS is clear. Close observers of Bolivian mining politics describe cooperative actors as cogoverning with President Evo Morales (Anria 2013, 2016; Salman, Carrillo, and Soruco 2015: 363; Interview with Oporto 2016).[7] Cooperatives also have multiple representatives in the Bolivian state that are aligned with the ruling party. Gold cooperatives are active and crucial supporters of the MAS, as was seen in Evo Morales's campaign to run for a third term. Regional and

---

[6] Author interviews with Gabriela Pantoja and Nestor Ríos, La Paz, March 9, 2016.
[7] Author interview with Henry Oporto, La Paz, March 4, 2016.

national members are included in the MAS's party lists for parliamentary elections, and they run for local office under the MAS banner. There is a group of congressmen acting on behalf of mining cooperatives. In addition, the Vice Ministry of Cooperatives and the Vice Ministry of Mining Development are run by individuals with close ties to the cooperatives, such as former leaders of key cooperatives. Furthermore, cooperatives are awarded seats in COMIBOL, the Bolivian state mining enterprise.

At the same time, cooperatives are not mere subordinates. They are autonomous from the government and are able to take action against the MAS when it meets their interests. For example, cooperatives mobilized against a proposal to allow unions to form in cooperatives. The cooperatives confronted the government, eventually leading to the murder of Vice Minister of the Interior Rodolfo Illanes. Cooperatives have also placed pressure on the MAS by entering into conflicts with other actors (salaried miners, peasant communities) that form the MAS's base (Anria 2013: 37; Francescone 2015; Salman, Carrillo, and Soruco 2015; Amengual 2018).

The central benefit the government delivers in exchange for the support of the cooperatives is forbearance: letting them operate without enforcing regulations. Cooperatives do not receive other types of benefits from the state that one would expect in a classic corporatist agreement. While the government created a program to provide cooperatives with machinery and credit to enhance their operations (SPDA 2015: 30–32), it only provided thirty-four loans between when it was established in 2009 and 2015 (Interview LP07). A report on gold mining and cooperatives argues that the greatest benefits to gold cooperatives are found in the lack of control – the cooperatives' illegal access to extract valuable minerals is worth much more than the value of subsidies or credit (Gandarillas, Jiménez, and Campanini 2013).

There is a clear pattern of "undoing with one hand what you do with the other" that further demonstrates the government's decision not to enforce the law. For example, the government struggled to gain cooperative support for the mining legislation enacted in 2014, eventually leading to a law that forbids and punishes illegal mining and at the same law authorizes illegal miners to continue their activities while they seek proper formalization. Similarly, repressive actions carried out by parts of the state against illegal mining are limited by other actors within the state. Héctor Córdova, former vice minister of Mining Development and later president of COMIBOL, recounted how when he was vice minister in 2010 the state launched an enforcement campaign against tax evasion by illegal miners in border areas. Five seemingly successful operations ended up failing because other areas of the state eventually recognized these associations as cooperatives (Interview with Córdova 2016).[8]

---

[8] Author interview with Héctor Córdova, La Paz, March 1, 2016.

In conclusion, this case shows how societal pressures at a diffuse level lead to nonenforcement. In contrast to the case of Peru discussed below, it is not that the Bolivian government is attempting to enforce generally and being stopped in contexts where there is political resistance proximate to the point of enforcement. Instead, there is a clear message that there is a purposive choice to not enforce the law due to diffuse pressure from social actors that support the government. This state of affairs brings more predictability to social actors violating laws and regulations. This alliance evidently constitutes a source of institutional weakness.

NONENFORCEMENT BY STANDOFF: BRICKMAKERS IN ARGENTINA

The case of the brickmakers in Córdoba, Argentina, represents a distinct dynamic of the lack of enforcement: there was no explicit arrangement of forbearance, but rather the state ignoring a problem and prioritizing other areas for enforcement.[9] Bricks are a key element of the Argentine construction industry that grew during the commodity boom. They are manufactured under precarious conditions using rudimentary technology. In this industry, violations of basic labor laws – especially regarding child labor and health and safety – have been pervasive and persistent. A survey of workers conducted in 2006 in the sector found that 96 percent were denied legally mandated benefits, such as social security (Pizaro 2008). Many of the workers are migrants, often from Bolivia, who are subject to abuse by human traffickers. Wages in the industry were illegally low, often not in compliance with collective bargaining agreements for the sector. For instance, on some worksites, laborers were paid three dollars for each thousand bricks, instead of the twenty dollars mandated by the collective bargaining agreement. Health and safety conditions on the worksites have been well below standards. Workers live in encampments on the worksites in substandard conditions, often lacking basic services such as potable water, sewage, and electricity.

All of these practices are violations of institutional rules in which the owners of the small brickmaking sites are failing to respect basic rights and exploiting their workers. These violations have persisted for decades. During the boom years that followed the financial crisis, violations became especially evident as demand for bricks picked up. In 2006, the Cordobés newspaper *La voz del interior* ran a series of investigative articles about migrant Bolivian workers in the brick-making sector, bringing widespread awareness of the issue. At the same time, the Center for Bolivian Residents of Córdoba (Centro de Residentes Bolivianos en Córdoba) took the plight of the brick makers to a variety of government agencies seeking assistance. Media reports indicated that between 2008 and 2017 eleven children have died in brick-making sites.

[9] This case draws from Amengual (2016).

Notwithstanding the violations, enforcement has largely not occurred. The problem was not that the violations were unknown to leaders of the main government agency responsible for enforcing labor laws, the Labor Secretariat of Córdoba (STC). Senior officials from various administrations recalled being aware of problems in the sector. All suggested that "more needed to be done" to reduce violations in the brick-making industry (Interview C04). Even after the problems became salient, there was only a modest increase in enforcement efforts for a short time. When in 2008 two children died on worksites, the STC began sending inspectors to conduct operations in brick-making sites once again.[10] For the first time, an inspection resulted in the closing of a worksite with child laborers and atrocious conditions. However, the inspectors never closed more than a handful of sites, and inspection operations quickly came to an end.

Why such a tepid response to a clear breakdown in institutional order? Nonenforcement in the brick-making industry cannot be explained by state capacity alone. Quite simply, Córdoba's labor regulators have demonstrated the capabilities to enforce regulations in other sectors when they are politically motivated. For instance, in the construction sector, regulators engaged in a sustained campaign of enforcement, suspending work in unsafe workplaces. It would be difficult to describe this as forbearance as a political strategy – no politician wanted to be associated with child labor. Moreover, there was no organization of employers or owners for brick-making sites that lobbied the governor or regulators. One would be hard-pressed to find the political advantage of nonenforcement for elected officials, or a coalition that was truly interested in maintaining such weak institutions. Yet there was little pressure for enforcement either. The organizations that represented the workers were weak, and many workers were not Argentine citizens who could vote.

The allocation of resources to enforce labor regulations in Córdoba was structured around a political exchange between the Peronist governor and labor unions. Nearly all senior officials appointed by Peronist governors had substantial ties to unions. They established routinized processes that facilitated tight coordination and collaboration between inspectors and powerful unions. These linkages resulted in enforcement being allocated to industries with powerful unions. For example, the metal workers' union, Sindicato de Mecánicos y Afines del Transporte Automotor de la Republica Argentina (SMATA), constantly placed pressure for enforcement in particular on workplaces that the union selected. In response, in 2008 there were twenty-eight inspections per month in the metal industry, which accounted for 10 percent of inspections, even though only 2 percent of workers in the province worked in this industry. By comparison, after a series of reports about violations in the brick-making industry, there were an average of 1.8 inspections a month in the brick-making industry, which constituted only 0.2 percent of all inspections

---

[10] "Intensificarán controles en los cortaderos," *La voz del interior*, November 8, 2008.

conducted by the STC. Quite simply, state resources for enforcement were allocated where there was proximate pressure and societal groups that could enable the state to enforce, leaving the brick makers out.

The Cordoba brick-making industry illustrates a case where practices radically depart from institutional rules, but there is no sustained enforcement. Yet the explanation of nonenforcement is quite different from that in the Bolivian cooperatives case because there was no diffuse pressure to continue institutional weakness. Instead, limited available state resources were directed to sectors where there were powerful supporters of enforcement. Without proximate pressure for enforcement, officials had little choice but to ignore (i.e., stand off from) the plight of the brick makers, even if there was little political upside to doing so.

BLOCKED ENFORCEMENT: ILLEGAL AND INFORMAL MINING IN PERU

The gold rush in Peru brought about similar problems to the ones seen in Bolivia. Along with the economic expansion, the increase in gold mining activity gave rise to a social grassroots base consisting mainly of artisanal workers. The number of illegal miners sharply increased from approximately fifty thousand in 2009 to over three hundred thousand in 2014.[11] Illegal and informal mining became a powerful challenge to state regulation.[12] In clear contrast to Bolivia, though, in an overwhelming majority of cases these actors lacked the recognition and authorizations that cooperatives enjoyed in Bolivia. Artisanal mining and mining unions were not as extended and powerful in Peru as they were in Bolivia, so the workers who joined the sector did not join the ranks of these organizations. Also in contrast to Bolivia, artisanal mining activities were (and currently remain) either criminalized or under state pressure to become formal.

Pressure on artisanal mining to follow institutional rules did not closely follow the growth of the sector. From 2004 to 2008 there was an initial stage of inaction similar to the previous case discussed (standoffishness), in which the state turned a blind eye to the problem (Valencia Arroyo 2014; Dargent and Urteaga 2017). Eventually, diverse processes led to the state's decision to face the problem and enforce its environmental and criminal laws, first weakly (2008–2009) and then in a more comprehensive manner (2011 to the present).

---

[11] Damonte Valencia (2013). Fernando Rospigliosi, "Mineros traicionados," *El comercio*, October 28, 2014.

[12] *Illegal mining* refers to mining activities in protected areas of the territory, and thus that are impossible to formalize. *Informal mining* refers to activities that could be formalized but currently have not been authorized by the state. In reality, both forms of mining are illegal, and informal activities are in many instances virtually impossible to formalize.

There were a series of interrelated political processes that brought about this change. Two initial changes stand out as being particularly important. First, the Peruvian state needed to uphold environmental commitments included in its free trade agreement with the United States. This process led to the creation of the Ministry of the Environment in 2009, which took initial actions against gold mining in the Amazon basin (Ruíz Muller 2011). Second, the state faced growing pressure from transnational networks of environmental organizations and their domestic allies that criticized the lack of enforcement in the media (Swenson et al. 2011). In response, starting in 2008–2009, the state adopted a weak policy of formalization of informal mining and one of proscription of illegal mining.

A third source of societal diffuse pressure emerged in 2009 and contributed to a more comprehensive response. Powerful mining companies demanded that the state respond to the challenge (interviews with Abanto 2014 and Galliani 2014).[13] Formal miners, under pressure from repeated accusations of environmental and social damage, launched a strong public campaign to reduce these pressures. They sought to show that formal mining complied with environmental rules and that the "real" polluters were illegal miners. As part of this effort, they supported strong state enforcement on illegal mining. A series of public statements by business associations shows the width and relevance of this campaign (Dargent and Urteaga 2017). The contrast to Bolivian is striking – the Morales government would not protect private mining firms even when they were actively invaded by cooperatives (Amengual 2018), let alone because cooperatives were tarnishing the image of the private miners.

It was in 2011, with the inauguration of Ollanta Humala's government (2011–2016), when the state launched an ambitious and comprehensive plan of formalization and interdictions. The former aimed to authorize gold exploitation concessions only for miners that met technical and environmental standards. The latter tried to eradicate illegal mining from restricted areas by destroying machinery, chemicals used in production, and settlements. In addition, other measures were taken to deal with the stage of commercialization of the mineral, such as the enhancement of customs control and investment in intelligence and raids for tracking the routes of illegal gold. Furthermore, the state controlled the inputs supply, such as fuel and chemicals used in illegal mining. In 2013, the government created a special office to coordinate these activities.

Therefore, the Peruvian state had embraced a comprehensive policy aimed at curbing illegal and informal mining. According to Salomón Lerner, former prime minister (2011), illegal mining became a priority for the president, who understood it as a matter of national security (Interview with Lerner 2015).[14] The growing awareness of the problem, and the demands toward the

---

[13] Author interviews with Alicia Abanto, Lima, January 15, 2014, and Luis Galliani, February 15, 2014.
[14] Author interview with Salomon Lerner, Lima, February 25, 2015.

executive, were undoubtedly increased by the abovementioned diffuse societal pressure. Considerable resources were invested in enhancing the areas of the state in charge of dealing with the problem, especially the ones tasked with formalization and implementation of coercive measures. According to budget information from the Economics and Finance Ministry (MEF), the budget of these areas rose from five million soles in 2014 to forty million in 2019.

Nonetheless, as shown by diverse independent reports, the state failed to enforce its policies and to reduce significantly the negative impact of illegal gold mining (OEFA 2013; Defensoría del Pueblo 2014; SPDA 2015). It can be argued, reasonably, that this was the expected outcome of a state that has historically been weak. Most reports point to the difficulties of carrying out formalization processes due to the state lacking bureaucratic resources necessary for such an immense challenge. Interdiction requires continuous presence in the territory, which was difficult for the Peruvian state to maintain.

While this outcome can be partly explained by the lack of state capacity, solely focusing on capacity would miss half of the picture. Strong societal and territorial bases of resistance from below blocked the enforcement efforts even after the state was considerably strengthened. Miners organized in a number of mining associations that, although dispersed, were able to resist the state. The countervailing pressure miners could put on the state was augmented by their large numbers in some territories and their ties with subnational political elites, including members of Congress, who advocated their demands.

In the past few years, each time the state has attempted to enforce its authority, there has been a confrontational response from the mining associations. Their most common strategies are public demonstrations, strikes, that have a great appeal among miners and that sometimes are openly supported by local authorities.[15] While the executive branch has been strong in its position, it often has had to give in to pressures by, for example, extending deadlines for formalization.[16] These and other actors also oppose enforcement through corruption.

Ultimately, the results of the enforcement push against illegal and informal mining in Peru have been far from encouraging. Formalization and interdiction have had contradictory effects. While the latter was supposed to induce illegal and informal miners to become formal ones, until now it has rather had the effect of alienating them. Most artisanal miners still work informally or illegally (Defensoría del Pueblo 2014). The actions of social actors help to

---

[15] See, for instance, some news headlines from the newspaper *El Comercio*: "Puerto Maldonado está paralizada con protestas por combustible," April 9, 2014; "Mineros ilegales en Lima: 'Vamos a hacer correr sangre,'" March 26, 2014; "Mineros de Nasca levantaron bloqueos tras una semana," March 27, 2014; "Mineros ilegales también dejan aislada a Juliaca," March 25, 2014.

[16] "Gobierno y dirigentes mineros siguen sin lograr acuerdo," *El comercio*, March 25, 2014; "Mineros de 5 regiones y Ejecutivo llegaron a acuerdo," *El comercio*, March 26, 2014.

explain both the decision to enforce regulations and enhance state capacity, as well as the limited effect of enforcement. The Peruvian state's failure to enforce regulations to address informal and illegal gold mining can be attributed not only to its state capacity, but also to the societal resistance the state faces while trying to deploy its authority.

SELECTIVE ENFORCEMENT: ENVIRONMENTAL REGULATION IN SANTA FE, ARGENTINA

Environmental regulation in Santa Fe, Argentina, illustrates a distinct dynamic.[17] Santa Fe is the host to major industries that feed off the province's agricultural production. Major sectors, such as those that process grains to make vegetable oil, put pressure on environmental quality. Pollution from these industries accelerated during the commodity boom.

Yet before the onset of the commodity boom, Santa Fe had adopted a set of environmental laws that created institutional structures to prevent such contamination. As the former head of the provincial regulatory agency noted, "What has happened in Argentina … is that it is really easy to pass a law … and copy whatever are the best laws from the United States … or the European Union" (Interview B12). Potential opponents of environmental regulations did not even bother to mobilize at the time of legal adoption of many laws; an environmental activist explained this behavior, stating that firms "didn't care much because they [could] neutralize [regulations] at the point of application" (Interview B2).

Indeed, in Santa Fe, enforcement of basic environmental regulations was extremely weak. Officials from the regulatory agency, the Santa Fe Secretaría de Medio Ambiente (SFSMA), estimated that half the firms that should have been in the regulatory system were "not totally identified" and operated without control (Interview S01). In 2008, when economic growth was strong, officials inspected only approximately 3 percent of industrial facilities, and when officials found violations, only 5 percent of firms were actually fined (Interview S49). By all accounts, basic restrictions on pollution and mandates for pollution prevention technology were routinely ignored by industry.

There was no diffuse support for enforcement of environmental regulations generally. The enforcement apparatus was formally controlled by the governor of the province. Governors neither made enforcement a priority, nor sought to block it by allowing allies of industry to run the agency. There were no strong signals from politicians that they were taking a forbearance approach to environmental protection in order to gain political support. Yet focusing on diffuse political support or opposition alone misses much of the politics of enforcement. When there was proximate pressure for enforcement

---

[17] This case draws from Amengual (2016).

in specific firms, regulators did take action. One such occasion of sustained enforcement occurred in the Santa Clara plant, located in the city of Rosario. The Santa Clara plant was owned by Molinos Río de la Plata, an Argentine agroindustrial firm that produces vegetable oils and a variety of processed food products. This industrial process results in a variety of pollutants that are legally required to be treated before they are released to the air and the water. According to inspectors, the Santa Clara plant was violating a range of environmental laws with impunity. The former secretary of the environment, who was leading the agency at this time, recounted: "The state...was not complying with its own rules to apply sanctions and implement legislation" (Interview B12). Thus, institutions were weak, in that actual practices departed from the formal rules of the game and the state did little to enforce.

Yet in 2004, enforcement shifted, even without any change in diffuse pressure for or against enforcement. Community organizations mobilized to demand enforcement in response to a series of fires and explosions in the silos that held sunflower seeds (Interview S36). One neighborhood group was the Vecinal Santa Teresita, which mobilized and sought out allies in the municipal government, then controlled by the Socialist Party, to place pressure on provincial regulators, who operated under a Peronist governor. Soon after the fire, officials published information highlighting public health problems linked to the plant. Local leaders also engaged a law firm that began to file civil suits on behalf of the individuals against the owner of the plant (Interview S25). As the conflict escalated, the managers began to feel threatened and feared the community would demand that the plant be closed down or relocated (Interview S36). According to regulators, "the pressure of the neighbors was so strong that the firm had to solve the problems, or the plant could not keep working" (Interview S13).

In response, provincial and municipal governments took steps to resolve their conflicts and address the problem by conducting joint inspections. One key element of the change in enforcement came when neighborhood activists and city councilors started a monitoring committee to bring together all the actors involved in the conflict (Interview S25). The monitoring committee, which met at a local office of the SFSMA, included representatives from the neighborhood, the SFSMA, health professionals, city council members, and eventually plant managers. The state became "a mediator, demanding actions from the plant and...monitoring the plant to make sure the changes were adequate" (Interview S13). Regulators from the SFSMA worked directly with the Vecinal Santa Teresita and conducted a series of inspections (Interview S47). The SFSMA kept monitoring the plant, pushing it along and evaluating the technical aspects of the improvements it was making, while the community organization served as local observers and, in combination with the municipal government, kept political pressure on the regulators and the firms. By 2006, the firm had invested over two million dollars in updating the plant, and completed the projects necessary to bring it into compliance.

The Santa Clara case was an example of how a standoffish state was pushed to enforce by social mobilization proximate to the place of enforcement. Santa Clara was not unique, but rather indicative of the logic of enforcement that occurs when social conflict activates institutions in particular instances.[18] Whenever enforcement occurred, it involved some sort of community mobilization and conflict, followed by actions of the SFSMA to take steps to enforce environmental regulations. What explains enforcement in this case? To begin, there was little interest in elected officials proactively pushing for enforcement, but when there was proximate pressure, there was a political incentive to act. As an official noted, "When there was a high-conflict issue, it was necessary to give a response because of two interests. First, to defend the government so it isn't criticized. Second, so they don't fire me" (Interview B12). Quite simply, proximate political pressure created a downside to ignoring institutional weakness in a particular case. Moreover, neighborhood groups were able expand the operational capabilities of the state, making up for the lack of capacity. Therefore, while the lack of resources within the state constrained it and prevented widespread systematic enforcement, there was sufficient capacity for targeted firefighting. Enforcement happened when there was highly proximate pressure, resulting in unevenness and inequality. What separated Santa Clara from other nearby plants was not an electoral district or a risk of violations, but rather the existence of social organizations that could mount pressure proximate to the particular institutional breakdown.

COPRODUCED ENFORCEMENT: BUSINESS AND THE STATE
AGAINST CONSTRUCTION RACKETEERING IN PERU

In recent years, there has been an explosion of construction in Peru. The sector grew impressively between 2002 and 2008, an average of 6.8 percent annually, and grew at an even higher level of 10 percent from 2009 to 2013 (Saravia and Wiesse 2014). The sharp rise was spurred by an increasing and widespread demand on private and public infrastructure for new housing, commercial sites, and leisure-related activities. Simultaneously, this construction boom gave rise to extortion in the construction sector. The number of construction unions in the sector grew impressively, from eighteen in 2005 to 115 in 2012. Most of them were shelters for criminal mafias who used the unions as a way of "legally" infiltrating the sector and therefore making it easier to operate from inside (Arias 2010; Saravia and Wiesse 2014).

Initially, the Peruvian state did not tackle the problem, once again adopting a standoffish approach to the problem. The significant delay empowered criminal unions engaged in blackmail, invasions of worksites, destruction of machinery, and murder of union leaders (García Ayala and Valle-Riestra 2015). The first attempt to curb the problem was the Plan Ladrillo, launched by the Toledo administration in 2005. However, it was unsuccessful. The lack

---

[18] There was a similar case in the northern city of Rafaela.

of capacity of state agencies, mainly the police, to deal with the problem, along with police corruption, hindered the enforcement. Eventually, the plan was dismantled in 2007, to be relaunched in 2009 with similarly limited results.

This chaotic situation became unsustainable for construction business groups, mainly the business association Cámara Peruana de la Construcción (CAPECO), and the Federación de Trabajadores en Construcción Civil (FTCCP), which demanded immediate state action. Especially relevant were the demands placed by CAPECO, a traditionally influential organization that had amassed further power due to the construction boom. Business groups threatened a massive stoppage of ongoing construction projects. That same year, the Ministry of the Interior announced a more ambitious plan, mainly focused on institutional redesign and intelligence actions, to tackle the problem.

García and Valle Riestra (2015) show in a case study how these linkages with business actors were decisive for the plan's adoption and success. A new specialized agency was created, the Dirección de Protección de Obras Civiles (DIPROVC), whose main function was to protect construction works in the Lima region. The agency was reinforced with four hundred agents, most of them experienced personnel in addressing organized crime and extortion. In addition, the government adopted tighter legal requirements for union operation and for creating new unions. The new measures showed positive results. According to observers and business associations, extortion has considerably reduced in private construction. At least nineteen criminal gangs were dismantled and more than five hundred individuals arrested in 2010. Also, the number of unions decreased by almost 50 percent from more than one hundred unions in 2012 to seventy-five in 2014 (Saravia and Wiesse 2014; García and Valle Riestra 2015).

In this case, social actors' relevance did not end with diffuse pressure to enforce the law. CAPECO *coproduced* the enforcement of criminal regulations. This association lent its strength to the state from below. To begin with, it became a source of much-needed material resources for DIPROVC (electronic devices, transport vehicles, furniture, etc.), which recognized that it could afford by itself. This initial support amounted to approximately US$150,000, which was crucial to starting up operations in an underfinanced state area. This link became formalized with an agreement between CAPECO and the Ministry of the Interior.

Construction firms also provided valuable information for a state effort that needed accurate information for its deployment. They were key allies for enforcement, providing resources and information to the state. Undercover agents worked in construction sites, providing information that allowed for preventive actions. These actions curbed violence to a considerable degree in Lima. Due to this success, private construction firms in the city of Chiclayo, in the northern region of Lambayeque, asked DIVPROC to ignore its jurisdictional limits and intervene against a powerful criminal organization

(La Gran Familia), in order to control extortion and land trafficking in the region. The enforcement campaign was successful. In order to respond to this national demand and due to its success in Lima and Chiclayo, in July 2014 DIVPROC became a national agency, Dirección Nacional de Protección de Obras Civiles (DIRPROC). In strong contrast to the previous case, where social groups pressured the state at the more proximate level of enforcement but not in a diffuse way, in this case enforcement went beyond particular instances and became more general. Thus, instead of being confined only to the locations where there were groups that could support the state, there was enforcement in the entire sector, albeit with an emphasis on large firms as a class of actors.

Nevertheless, there are limits to this pattern of enforcement. Police actions have focused more on big business construction that on extortion in general. The phenomenon could only be relatively curbed in Lima and some nearby areas, where the police benefited from its links with CAPECO. Smaller construction firms and other sectors experiencing extortion have not seen similar solutions. In other areas of Peru, especially northern regions, construction mafias continue to flourish. In these parts of the territory, the subnational police offices lack the resources as well as the links with powerful business groups that could provide it with the pressure and staff to operate. Also in contrast with the purely political approach, the limitations in state capacity remain important. It is not the case that as soon as there was political pressure from above that the state could unilaterally augment enforcement – there were constraints that needed to be overcome by social group subsidies and pressure from below. Although extortion still harms activities such as commerce, transportation, and private schools, nonetheless the case of DIVPROC shows a successful state–society collaboration in regard to enforcement. And this form of diffuse pressure ends up producing a more programmatic and general enforcement that increases institutional strength.

CONCLUSION

This chapter illuminates the complex politics that surround enforcement that have been obscured by dominant theories. Enforcement is a key element of institutional weakness because by failing to enforce, states allow departures between rules and practices to continue. State capacity, however, cannot fully account for much of the variation in enforcement that we observe, and important recent contributions to comparative politics have shown how electoral politics can create incentives for nonenforcement. Yet we cannot ignore state capacity entirely – the limitations in capacity condition the politics of enforcement. Specifically, we show how standoffish states frequently fail to enforce the law out of indifference rather than political intention; states could enforce in any particular instance, but they opt not to do it because there are no political upsides to enforcement and often constrained resources. We suggest that this enforcement outcome may be more pervasive than current theories about state capacity or politicized enforcement recognize. We propose that social actors exercise diffuse pressure to enforce, triggering state action, or not to enforce. In doing so, we show that social actors are crucial determinants of enforcement in developing countries.

In addition, we show how social actors can exercise pressure proximate to the point of enforcement, helping states to enforce the law or preventing them from doing so. By blocking or supporting the state, these actors and the resources they muster are also relevant to understand the persistence and distribution of enforcement. Looking in detail at these interactions, only discernible by careful observation, allows us to better understand the effects of these types of enforcement or nonenforcement on institutions. However, our focus at the micro level leaves open questions about how enforcement politics aggregate across sectors and lead to structural change in societies.

We highlight five implications of our analysis for the understanding of institutional strength. First, institutions are more likely to gain strength in instances of standoff than forbearance. As discussed, politically motivated nonenforcement can be caused by multiple variables, and this equifinality obscures distinct dynamics with varying institutional consequences. While forbearance sends a strong signal to social actors letting them know that institutions are really only parchment rules and unlikely to be activated if political conditions remain unchanged (even punishing those trying to activate them), standoffish states are not committed to enforce the law, but neither are they committed not to do so by way of an alliance with a coalition in favor of institutional weakness. Thus, triggering enforcement in standoffish states may require less strength in actors in favor of institutional strength than we might expect if these actors need to overcome an existing political alliance.

Second, our findings reaffirm that state capacity is key to overcoming institutional weakness and cannot be ignored even when we bring politics back in. As states increase in capacity, standoffish behavior may also decrease and bureaucracies may become less selective in their implementation efforts, as there are more resources to allocate to various areas of enforcement and the state is less dependent on societal groups for subsidies. Bureaucracies may become stronger and more autonomous in their decisions to enforce rules.

Third, when enforcement is coproduced, there is more likelihood that institutions will gain relevance, especially if social support is sustained in time, than when enforcement occurs only by diffuse or proximate pressures alone. At the same time, this enforcement will not necessarily lead to stronger institutions in the long run as enforcement depends not on state capacity, but on social actors' preferences and resources. Therefore, when power distributions change, enforcement may change as well if state capacity is not developed.

Fourth, and related to the previous point, even though enforcement is a response to weak institutions, there are at times institutions that structure the politics of enforcement itself. When diffuse pressure triggers enforcement, it does so through electoral institutions and bureaucratic control institutions, which mediate between pressure for enforcement and where enforcement occurs. However, when pressure is proximate to the point of enforcement, successful cases of enforcement will only occur where *those in favor of enforcement* are locally powerful and their political actions are largely unmediated by institutions. As a result, pressure from below is unlikely to lead to a generalized enforcement that can respond to and reduce institutional weakness broadly in society.

Finally, instances of blocked enforcement may be a blessing in disguise by helping to strengthen state capacity. Enforcement in these cases may look ineffective, but it may be producing an increase in more independent state capacity that, under a change of circumstances (a reduction in the price of gold in our Peruvian case), can lead to enforcement that is more effective.

8

A Multilevel Approach to Enforcement

Forest Protection in the Argentine Chaco

Belén Fernández Milmanda and Candelaria Garay

This book is based on the premise that formal institutions in several Latin American democracies are weak; they are unstable and their capacity to shape actors' behavior is limited. Institutional strength not only varies across countries, but also at the subnational level, as many institutions are unevenly enforced within countries (Bergman 2009; Amengual 2013, 2016; Holland 2017, this volume). Focusing on why some institutions take root in some places and not in others, we address the enforcement of forest protection legislation, a domain of environmental rules that has experienced important innovations in Latin America since the early 2000s.

As it boosted economic growth across the region, the commodity boom of the 2000s also intensified environmental degradation and sparked conflicts over the regulation of mining (see Amengual and Dargent, this volume) and the protection of forestlands jeopardized by the expansion of the agricultural frontier. Environmental damage and related conflict drove governments throughout the region to adopt new environmental institutions, including forest protection laws. Since the early 2000s, eleven countries in the region passed forest protection legislation, including some of the largest deforesters in the world, such as Argentina, Brazil, Bolivia, and Paraguay. While these institutions might be seen as "window dressing" (see Chapter 1, this volume), enacted to show concern for environmental damage while maintaining the status quo at a time of booming commodity prices, a key question concerns whether and under what conditions these institutions achieved higher levels of enforcement.

To address this question and contribute to our understanding of the sources of institutional strength, we focus on the implementation of national forest protection legislation in the Argentine Chaco, one of the world's deforestation hotspots. The Argentine Chaco represents 60 percent of the Chaco Americano, the second-largest forest in the Americas, and is primarily located within four core provinces: Chaco, Formosa, Salta, and Santiago del Estero.[1] During the commodity boom, deforestation accelerated in the Argentine Chaco. From 2006 to 2016, these provinces lost 2.8 million hectares of forestland, propelled largely by the expansion of soybean cultivation. Forest loss in the Chaco explains why Argentina became one of the top-ten deforesters in the world.[2]

The adoption and implementation of a native forest protection regime (NFPR), approved by the Argentine Congress in 2007,[3] during the heyday of the commodity boom, provides an excellent case for investigating enforcement and institutional weakness more generally. The federal law mandated provinces to classify forestlands according to their conservation value and establish agencies to enforce forest regulations. Although the core Chaco provinces share many characteristics – they are forest-rich and economically poor, they have similarly low state capacity, and incumbents have comparable electoral power – they display significant variation in the enforcement of the NPFR.

In this chapter, we propose a multilevel approach to understand the politics of enforcement. Unlike much of the literature, which focuses on state capacity and the electoral incentives of local authorities in charge of rule enforcement, we argue that institutional weakness in decentralized federal systems can be better understood by focusing on the factors that affect the enforcement of a given law at different levels of government (national and subnational) and at different stages of the policy-making process (policy design and implementation). In the case of forest protection legislation, those bearing the costs of enforcement – i.e., subnational authorities and large agricultural producers – mobilized to dilute the national law's impact by introducing ambiguities or opportunities for discretion in the law itself, which has allowed provincial governments in charge of implementation to significantly relax its enforcement without necessarily contradicting it.

Cross-provincial variation in enforcement among the forest-rich provinces of the Chaco resulted not from differences in state capacity but rather from governors' incentives to enforce the NFPR. We find cases of open nonenforcement and of moderate enforcement depending on whether governors faced powerful large producers, who strove for lax provincial regulations and minimal enforcement of the forest protection regime, and/or a conservationist coalition formed by those affected by agricultural expansion, who mobilized for provincial regulations to be designed and enforced in accordance with the conservationist spirit of the NFPR. Governors primarily sought to *avoid*

---

[1] Forestlands represent at least 50 percent of the provincial surface area.

[2] Argentina ranks ninth and the other Chaco Americano countries rank as follows: Brazil, second; Paraguay, tenth; and Bolivia, eleventh. See Global Forest Watch, www.globalforest-watch.org/countries/overview.

[3] Ley 26331. Presupuestos Mínimos Ambientales para la Protección de los Bosques Nativos. El Senado y Cámara de Diputados de la Nación Argentina.

conflict among competing interests, and they used specific tools in the law (e.g., zoning maps and sanctions) to respond to pressures, resulting in varying types of regulations and levels of enforcement.

In the following section, we discuss our multilevel approach to enforcement in federal systems. The third section then analyzes the design and implementation of the NFPR. We identify and account for the weaknesses in the national law that generated opportunities for variable levels of enforcement, and we assess the extent to which governors exploited these weaknesses and enforced the NFPR across the core Chaco provinces. The third section explains governors' choices in the implementation of the NFPR. We develop an original empirical strategy to measure institutional weakness that looks both at the stages of *rule writing* and *enforcement*. Finally, we illustrate the dynamics of enforcement in multilevel systems with the case of Salta, where a dramatic increase in deforestation originally drove large environmental nongovernmental organizations (NGOs) to lobby Argentina's national Congress for a forest protection regime. Implementation of the NFPR in Salta resulted in weak enforcement, as flawed provincial regulations allowed for "legal" noncompliance, as well as "nonpunitive enforcement," by which very low sanctions were imposed on infractions. The governor's choice to weaken the enforcement of the NFPR resulted from pressure from powerful large producers and the absence of a conservationist coalition that could counterbalance their power.

ENFORCEMENT IN MULTILEVEL SYSTEMS

Scholars argue that in weakly institutionalized environments, existing formal institutions fail to generate the shared expectations that shape behavior. In this context, formal institutions, rather than taking root, are frequently changed and/or weakly enforced, if at all (Levitsky and Murillo 2013). Lack of enforcement is facilitated by low state capacity or by the purposive action of those in charge of enforcing formal rules to do so selectively (see Ronconi 2010; Levitsky and Murillo 2013; Amengual 2016; Holland 2017). Weak enforcement of formal rules therefore results from politicians being either unable to mobilize state infrastructure to achieve implementation, or from their inability to coproduce enforcement with societal actors (see chapters by Schrank and by Amengual and Dargent, this volume), or from subnational authorities being unwilling to enforce existing regulations. Intentionally weak enforcement has been explained by politicians' incentives to enforce regulations in the presence of potential electoral gains (Ronconi 2010) as well as by their electoral incentives not to enforce when their constituencies would bear the costs (Holland 2017).

Building on this literature, we propose a multilevel approach that highlights the complex political dynamics involved in the enforcement of national legislation by subnational actors in decentralized systems, an aspect of the politics of enforcement in weakly institutionalized environments that deserves further attention. Although it is not always stated explicitly, studies of enforcement tend to view the politics of designing formal rules and the process of the rules' implementation as separate from each other (see Mahoney and Thelen 2015: 195). One arena, usually the executive or congress, writes a law that another arena, usually the bureaucracy or subnational entities, has to implement. The motivations and incentives of the actors involved in the formulation of the law are generally not analyzed in connection with the interests and incentives of the actors or agents in charge of implementation. We argue that this separation across arenas is either attenuated or nonexistent in multilevel systems. This is especially the case in decentralized federal polities, where subnational authorities have important policy-making responsibilities.

In federal systems, subnational units have constitutionally based powers that restrict the scope of national authority over specific issues, and subnational units participate, sometimes actively, in the design of national legislation that affects provincial interests (Stepan 1999; Gibson 2004, 2005). In the senate or territorial chamber, where malapportionment is common across Latin America and particularly acute in Argentina (Samuels and Snyder 2001), subnational organized interests seeking to block legislation or undermine its enforcement may have greater chances of influencing the content of the law. Rule makers in the territorial chamber may be strongly influenced or even directly represent those who resist a given law, and thereby strive to minimize its impact.

We propose a multilevel approach that establishes a stronger connection between the stages of policy design and implementation, of which enforcement is a key component. Our approach identifies (1) the domains of the policy-making process that shape the conditions for enforcement, and (2) the actors operating in these different domains who seek to influence both the law's design and its enforcement mechanisms. In this approach, the factors shaping the enforcement are therefore not circumscribed to the implementation stage. The enforcement of a given law may be deliberately limited by institutional features inserted during the design of the law by those who will bear the cost of enforcement. These actors may introduce ambiguities or inconsistencies between the national law and the implementation rules, allowing for what Thelen (2004: 36) calls "institutional conversion" – or the deployment of institutions toward new purposes without altering the letter of the national law. During implementation, and depending on subnational power configurations or "institutional environments" (see Pierson 2004: 138), these inconsistencies provide room for subnational variation in the enforcement of the law.

We propose three mechanisms through which enforcement may be shaped by legislative design. First, formal rules themselves may limit the power of the national agencies in charge of monitoring compliance and sanctioning noncompliance at the subnational level. Even if this does not override the possibility of attaining compliance in other ways, it makes enforcement more difficult.

This is especially problematic in the case of the forest protection regulations created during the heyday of the commodity boom, when compliance with anti-deforestation rules was hard to attain in the absence of decisive enforcement of the law.

Second, opportunities for discretion and ambiguity in the law may allow for variable levels of enforcement to take place (see; North 1990: 59; Thelen 2004; Brinks, Levitsky, and Murillo, Chapter 1, this volume). This is in line with the literature on bureaucratic delegation in wealthier democracies (Huber and Shipan 2002), which relates variable levels of ambiguity in the law to politicians' calculations of who has control over implementation. Our framework speaks to this scholarship as it connects aspects of enforcement with strategic decisions by policy makers at different levels of government, yet it applies to contexts of weak institutions, such as those characterizing the Chaco provinces (see Amengual 2013; Ardanaz, Leiras, and Tommasi 2014).

Finally, when subnational governments are responsible for establishing the exact procedures for implementation within their jurisdictions (e.g., the design of forest zoning maps, setting the rates of fines), the enforcement of the national law may be undermined at this second, provincial-level *design* stage. This is even more likely if the national law leaves some room for discretion or is ambiguous on important matters affecting enforcement, thus allowing provincial governments to establish regulations that deviate from the law's statutory goals.

The following examples illustrate these mechanisms. Representatives from the Chaco provinces in Congress vehemently argued that the provincial ownership of natural resources established in the constitution barred a national-level agency from overseeing the enforcement of the NFPR. As a result, the NFPR awarded limited powers to the federal environmental agency to fix misclassifications of forest areas (i.e., zoning maps) and to sanction infractions. At the same time, senators fought against the establishment of standardized fines and eventually compromised on a broad range of rates that have allowed provincial governments to set exceedingly low fines, which producers easily internalize as production costs. With respect to land use, legislators from forest-rich provinces opposed an exhaustive definition of activities permitted in areas suitable for sustainable management in which clearings are forbidden. Provincial governments often exploited this ambiguity by permitting economic activities that involve some level of deforestation.

In sum, our multilevel approach advances three main points concerning the politics of enforcement in decentralized systems. First, we emphasize the importance of not only paying attention to the politics of enforcement of a given policy or law by analyzing its implementation, as much of the literature on Latin America has done, but also of investigating the stage of policy design. Second, we argue that it is crucial to consider whether specific mechanisms contained in the letter of the law limit its enforcement, such as ambiguity that may result in implementation rules or behavior that undermine the law's statutory goals without necessarily violating it. Finally, analyzing how national-level actors affect implementation and how subnational actors affect the design of a national law are important aspects of the study of enforcement. Just as power struggles and political conflict shape the inception of institutions (Knight 1992; Thelen 2004), they also affect implementation, as subnational actors, sometimes represented in the design of the national law, struggle to further adapt subnational rules to their interests.

THE NATIONAL FOREST PROTECTION REGIME:
NATIONAL DESIGN AND SUBNATIONAL IMPLEMENTATION
IN THE CORE CHACO PROVINCES

In this section, we analyze the design of the NFPR and measure its implementation across the core Chaco provinces. When analyzing the national law, we identify critical weaknesses – e.g., ambiguities – that could undermine its statutory goals and that resulted from concessions to opponents of forest protection in the Chaco region. When measuring the implementation of the NFPR across the Chaco provinces we gauge the extent to which the content of provincial-level regulations is consistent with the NFPR and assess the enforcement of the law.

Designing the NFPR

High commodity prices drove soybean cultivation and cattle ranching into the Chaco Forest, increasing clearings and triggering social conflict. As deforestation accelerated, national environmental NGOs mobilized for the adoption of a forest protection regime to regulate land use. As a result of intense societal pressure, Congress approved the NFPR in 2007. The new legislation substantially altered the status quo in the Chaco. It required provincial legislatures to enact a territorial classification of native forests (OTBN) in accordance with the NFPR. The OTBN would include land-use regulations and a zoning map classifying forests according to their conservation value into three categories allowing for different levels of economic transformation – no transformation in high-conservation (red) areas, sustainable management in medium-conservation (yellow) areas, and agriculture in low-conservation (green) areas. The NFPR also required that the design of the OTBNs be subject to social participatory processes and that prior to an OTBN's approval, provincial authorities could not issue deforestation permits.

The original NFPR bill was submitted to Congress by center-left legislators from Buenos Aires in 2006 and met vigorous opposition from representatives of the Chaco provinces. These legislators raised two fundamental critiques to the bill. First, they argued that the bill was an attempt by the wealthier provinces that had exhausted their forests to curtail unprecedented economic opportunities benefiting the less developed forest-rich provinces.[4] Second, they posited that by imposing federal rules on land use, deforestation permits,[5] and sanctions for noncompliance, the law would truncate their constitutional right to administer natural resources in their territories.[6]

The bill was approved unchanged in the lower chamber, where its proponents were allied to the governing Front for Victory-Peronist Party (FPV-PJ). In the Senate, where Chaco provinces had greater weight due to overrepresentation, two crucial concessions to forest-rich provinces ultimately enabled the passage of the law. First, senators agreed to create a compensatory fund to pay producers for their environmental services and to build provincial enforcement capacity.[7] This fund would receive at least 0.3 percent of the national annual budget plus 2 percent of the revenue collected from duties on agricultural, forestry, and livestock exports, which represented a huge positive incentive for the Chaco provinces to implement the law. Second, having blocked a unified sanctions regime, which could be a formidable negative incentive for compliance, the Senate bill established a wide-ranging – and far lower – scale of fines,[8] allowing governors to impose more modest penalties for infractions. Compromises across opposing interests resulted in an NFPR that both preserved the conservationist spirit of the bill and contained ambiguities regarding sustainable management and sanctions that could undermine its enforcement.

Subnational Implementation of the NFPR

Provinces in charge of establishing implementation regulations and zoning maps defined these rules more or less consistently with the NFPR. Below we measure the consistency of provincial implementation regulations with the NFPR and assess its enforcement.

---

[4] Cámara de Diputados (2006); Cámara de Senadores (2007); authors interview with Marta Maffei, Legislator for the province of Buenos Aires (2004–2007), Vice-president of the Natural Resources and Environment Committee, Buenos Aires, July 1, 2015; authors interview with Juan Carlos Díaz Roig, Legislator for Formosa (2005–2017), Buenos Aires, July 1, 2015; Comisión de Recursos Naturales y Conservación del Ambiente Humano y de Población y Desarrollo Humano, Honorable Cámara de Diputados. 2006. Orden del Día 1479.

[5] Whereas the bill as a whole was approved with 156 votes in favor and only two opposed, the article forbidding the extension of clearing permits until after the OTBN's approval received eighty positive and sixty negative votes.

[6] The national government establishes environmental standards that provinces have to follow.

[7] Salta PJ senator Sonia Escudero, who proposed the fund, noted: "[I]t was a very tough fight within the PJ caucus where we, the senators from the northern provinces [...] stood firm and, without the fund, it was impossible to have the necessary votes to pass the bill. So [the fund] was an imposition from the legislators of the provinces with forests" (authors interview with Sonia Escudero, Senator for Salta (2001–2013), Salta, July 10, 2015).

[8] Fines range from three hundred to ten thousand times the lowest national public-sector salary. In the original bill, the highest fine was thirty thousand times that salary.

Consistency of Provincial Rules with the NFPR

To measure NFPR–OTBN consistency in the classification of forestlands, we focus on three indicators. First, we assess the level of conservationism of provincial zoning maps. Toward this end, we compare whether provinces attributed similar conservation values to forests that cut across provincial borders. A study by García Collazo, Panizza, and Paruelo (2013) systematically selects points on provincial borders to evaluate whether zoning maps of adjacent provinces categorize their share of the same forestland equally. The study reveals low levels of agreement across core Chaco provinces. The highest comparability is found on the Santiago del Estero–Chaco border, where forest areas are defined similarly at 58 percent of the selected locations. The study concludes that Santiago del Estero attributed higher conservation values to forest areas than did Chaco, Salta, and Formosa, in that order (Table 8.1).

Second, we measure NFPR–OTBN consistency in land-use regulations focusing on yellow areas. These areas constitute the most challenging aspect of the NFPR, as sustainable management allows for economic activities but not for changes to land use (i.e., forest clearings). With the exception of Formosa, which classified 74 percent of its forest area as green, most of the forestland of the remaining core Chaco provinces is classified as yellow.[9] The NFPR provides no guidelines as to what sustainable management entails. OTBNs allow for two types of activities: forest grazing – selectively clearing undergrowth to breed cattle – and controlled timber extraction, both of which draw a thin line between legal and illegal forest management. Governors often also issued resolutions and decrees allowing for clearings in yellow areas for pasture. In some provinces, these clearing allowances are significant (up to 20 percent), with Formosa, Salta, Santiago, and Chaco, in that order, being the most flexible with regard to clearings in yellow areas (Table 8.1).

Finally, we assess whether OTBNs allow for the recategorization of individual farms to lower conservation levels, which Formosa, Salta, and Santiago del Estero all do. Salta even defined its zoning map as "guidelines,"[10] and unlike Santiago del Estero, which established a plural council to determine recategorizations, it gave its environmental agency – which is politically dependent on the governor – the power to evaluate requests. Salta's governor eventually repealed this provision in 2014 in response to dubious recategorizations denounced by national NGOs.[11] In Formosa, where most forestlands were classified as low conservation value (green), indigenous communities, which control most yellow areas, can request the recategorization of their lands.

---

[9] Between 63 and 74 percent.

[10] Law 7543 Ordenamiento territorial de bosques nativos de la Provincia de Salta defines the OTBN as *orientativo*.

[11] Authors interview with Juan Manuel Urtubey, Governor of Salta (2007–2019), Salta, July 8, 2015.

TABLE 8.1. *Implementation of the NFPR: Consistency of design and enforcement, core Chaco provinces, 2007–2016*

| | Design | | | | Enforcement | | | |
	Conservation Ranking (Zoning Map)	Regulation of Yellow Areas[a]	Discretion to Recategorize Farms?	Consistency Score[b]	Deforestation in Protected Areas (% of Total Deforestation)[c]	Total Deforestation (% of Forest)[d]	Enforcement Score	Implementation Score[e]
Chaco	2	High	No	High	33.3	7.3	Moderate	Moderately high
Formosa	4	Low[f]	Yes: high[f]	Low	N/A[f]	7.6	Low	Low
Salta	3	Low	Yes: high	Low	37.8	9.3	Low	Low
Santiago	1	High	Yes: low	Moderate	71.2	12.9	Low	Moderately low

Notes:

[a] Scores based on percent of farmland that can be (1) cleared, and (2) used for grazing, and the farm size threshold after which an environmental impact evaluation is required for sustainable management projects.

[b] *High:* conservationism and regulation of yellow areas are high, and recategorizations are prohibited. *Moderate:* (1) conservationism and regulation of yellow areas are high and power to recategorize is limited; or (2) conservationism and regulation are both moderate, or one dimension is high and the other is moderate, regardless of whether recategorizations are allowed; or (3) conservationism is high, regulation is low, and recategorizations are prohibited. *Low:* (1) conservationism is high, regulation is low, and power to recategorize is high; or (2) conservationism and regulation are both low, or one dimension is moderate and the other is low.

[c] From the OTBN's enactment through 2016.

[d] From the NFPR's enactment through 2016.

[e] Combined consistency and enforcement score.

[f] The OTBN does not follow the NFPR and assigns low conservation value to three-quarters of its forestlands.

Sources: Elaborated with data from SAyDS, national and provincial legislation, and García Collazo, Panizza, and Paruelo (2013). Adapted from Fernández Milmanda and Garay (2019).

Enforcement of the NFPR

If the NFPR were successfully enforced, there would be no deforestation within red and yellow areas, in which clearings are forbidden. Combining deforestation in both red and yellow areas, Santiago is the worst performer, with 71.3 percent of total deforestation in these areas (Table 8.1). In Formosa, where most forestlands, as noted, have been (mis)classified as low conservation value, deforestation in red and yellow areas represents only 2 percent of the total forest lost.

Our enforcement score also considers total deforestation because provinces (mis)classified some forestlands into lower conservation categories and the NFPR forbade new clearings until the OTBN was approved. Overall scores show that deforestation continued after the enactment of the NFPR (Table 8.1). Yet there is important variation across provinces, with total forest loss ranging from 7.3 percent in Chaco to 12.9 percent in Santiago.

Collectively, these different measures reveal remarkable variation across provinces and dimensions of implementation (i.e., design of provincial regulations and enforcement), which is summarized in Table 8.1. Salta and Santiago designed OTBNs with different levels of consistency with the NFPR – low and moderate, respectively – but both had low enforcement, with high levels of deforestation. Chaco, in turn, displays a high OTBN–NFPR consistency and moderate enforcement. Finally, Formosa displays both low consistency and low enforcement. Together with Salta, this case illustrates how the design of subnational regulations may impede the effective enforcement of the NFPR.

EXPLAINING GOVERNORS' IMPLEMENTATION CHOICES

To understand variation in the implementation of the NFPR, we focus on governors' incentives to favor or dilute its conservationist spirit in the design and enforcement of the OTBNs. Governors are fundamental actors because they have the formal power to draft regulations, push them through local legislatures, and use veto and decree powers to modify them. They also establish – fund, staff, and locate – the agencies in charge of enforcing these regulations. Scholarship on Argentina's federal system has generally emphasized the limited division of powers at the subnational level, which allows governors to control institutional resources and amass power (see Gibson 2005; Ardanaz, Leiras, and Tommasi 2014).

In line with studies of decentralized forestry management (Andersson et al. 2005), we assume that subnational executives have no inherent preferences regarding forest protection. We argue that governors choose to exploit opportunities for discretion in the NFPR depending on two factors: (1) the power of large producers seeking to expand production into forestlands and (2) the existence of groups resisting the expansion of the agricultural frontier, what we here call a *conservationist coalition*.

Large Producers

Large producers are understood as landowners and investors with parcels of at least 2500 hectares.[12] During the commodity boom, large producers drove soybean cultivation into previously unexploited areas. The expansion of the agricultural frontier favored real estate speculation, incentivizing forest clearings as land prices climbed. Producers were lured by the relatively lower land prices in the Chaco, the availability of large farms – which allowed them to increase production and maximize profit margins – and the absence of actual restrictions on forest clearing before the sanctioning of the NFPR.

Large producers have sought to avoid regulations that would curtail massive expected profits. They have preferred OTBNs with lax regulations and light enforcement and have lobbied, both collectively and individually, provincial governments to minimize the conservationist aspects of the OTBNs.

The comparative literature distinguishes between two sources of power, political (or instrumental) and economic (or structural) (Lindblom 1977; Hacker and Pierson 2002; Fairfield 2015). Given the importance of agriculture and cattle ranching for provincial economies, both sources of power are intertwined in the core Chaco provinces: large producers have political power because of their economic weight. Large producers channel their political power in different ways – lobbying the executive and/or the legislature, financing political campaigns, running for office, occupying state positions, or through informal and personal contacts with policy makers.

Given the intertwined nature of large producers' instrumental and structural power, we assume that large landowners have greater capacity to influence policy-making in provinces in which they control a larger share of productive land. Specifically, we consider large producers to be powerful if they concentrate at least 50 percent of a province's total farmland, and they thus constitute the main rural economic actor. Table 8.2 displays the share of provincial land in large farms at the beginning of the commodity boom. In Salta, large producers are especially powerful, as they control 75 percent of total farmland. At the other extreme, Chaco has a relatively small share of land in large farms (31 percent), comparable to its share in small farms (29 percent); thus, large producers are not dominant actors in rural politics as they are in Salta.

Conservationist Coalitions

Conservationist coalitions are organized societal and economic interests opposing the expansion of the agricultural frontier over forests.[13] In the core Chaco provinces, conservationist interests primarily consist of sectors concerned about the negative effects of soy expansion on their own economic

---

[12] About five times the size of the average farm in Argentina (588 hectares).
[13] For a similar use of the term *coalition*, see Murillo (2001).

TABLE 8.2. *Large producers, core Chaco provinces, 2002*

	% Productive Land in Small Farms	% Productive Land in Large Farms	Average Farm
	(<=500 ha)	(>2500 ha)	(ha)
Chaco	29	31.7	375.8
Formosa	11.1	46.2	575.7
Santiago del Estero	14.1	58.1	498
Salta	6.1	75.1	765.8

Source: Based on Barsky and Fernández (2008) and INDEC (2002).

activity and livelihoods, i.e., timber producers, peasants, and indigenous communities. These groups constitute a conservationist coalition when they press for the strict implementation of the NFPR, which they perceive as a critical tool for protecting themselves from agricultural expansion.

These organized interests do not necessarily act together in favor of forest protection, but each group's collective action – even if not concerted – puts pressure on governors to design and enforce the conservationist aspects of the NFPR. Conservationist groups have connected forest protection to property rights, the recognition of indigenous communities, and the preservation of indigenous cultures and livelihoods – forming what scholars have called the "environmentalism of the poor."[14] Despite the common challenges that conservationists face across the Chaco, these groups share with other environmental groups the local nature of their demands (Svampa 2015), the absence of cross-provincial solidarity with actors affected by similar processes, and the difficulty of scaling up and connecting in a sustained way with national and transnational movements (Anguelovski and Martinez-Alier 2014).

Conservationist coalitions are present in Chaco and Santiago but have not formed in Formosa and Salta. In Chaco, the conservationists include the timber industry and indigenous communities. The timber industry – which represents 6.6 percent of private formal employment in the industrial sector, 10.3 percent of the province's industrial gross product, and 20 percent of its exports – has opposed the expansion of soybean cultivation into forestlands.[15] Its associations are well connected to the government and to the forest agency through formal and informal ties. Indigenous communities, which are numerous and well organized, have also pressed for

[14] See Martínez-Alier (2013).
[15] Ministerio de Economía y Finanzas Públicas (2015).

a conservationist OTBN, especially through the Chaco Indigenous Institute (IDACh) (Fernández Milmanda and Garay 2019). In Santiago del Estero, the absence of property titles among small peasants has led to the emergence of the Santiago del Estero Peasant Movement (MOCASE), whose mobilization capacity grew during the commodity boom (De Salvo 2014). This movement has forcefully pressed for conservationism in the design and enforcement of the NFPR (Fernández Milmanda and Garay 2019).

Conservationist coalitions have not formed in Formosa and Salta. In Salta, NGOs working with indigenous communities, universities, and national environmental groups have tried to influence the design and enforcement of the NFPR, but their ability to sustain collective action and pressure the provincial government has been limited, as we show below. In Formosa, our fieldwork showed that the timber industry and the peasant movement are small and co-opted.[16]

Governors' Choices: Implementation as Conflict Avoidance

Why did some governors choose to design their OTBNs in accordance with the NFPR while others did not? Why do some governors enforce the NFPR more strictly than others? We argue that the power of large provincial producers and the presence or absence of a conservationist coalition shaped governors' choices to exploit ambiguities in the law for or against conservation. While the NFPR affects relevant economic interests, it also provides governors with distributive tools (e.g., regulations, sanctions) that can be used to appease conflict. Governors have used critical *design features* (e.g., zoning maps, land-use regulations) as well as *positive incentives* (e.g., subsidies) and *negative incentives* (e.g., sanctions) to induce compliance, not simply as tools to advance forest protection but primarily to ensure their own continuity in power by reducing potential instability and discontent among contradictory interests. Therefore, the design and enforcement of these tools is not guided by environmentalism but rather by power dynamics, resulting in variable levels of deforestation.

Governors deploy a *conflict avoidance* strategy in implementing the NFPR, granting concessions to competing conservationists and agricultural interests in the design of provincial regulations and enforcement of the national law. Schematically, when governors face large producers with formidable vested interests in the expansion of agriculture, they have strong incentives against conservationism. With the tools available in the NFPR, governors are likely to design an OTBN that includes a lax definition of land use in yellow areas, low penalties for infractions, and zoning that allows for significant expansion

---

[16] On the peasant movement, see Lapegna (2016).

TABLE 8.3. *Governors' choices: Design of provincial regulations and NFPR enforcement*

		Conservationist Coalition	
		Yes	No
Powerful Large Producers	Yes	Moderate consistency; low enforcement *Santiago del Estero*	Low consistency; low enforcement *Salta; Formosa*
	No	High consistency and enforcement *Chaco*	

Source: Adapted from Fernández Milmanda and Garay (2019).

of agriculture and ranching. Governors may relax enforcement by failing to build adequate monitoring capacity and apply sanctions. By contrast, when governors face a conservationist coalition, they are motivated to design a stricter OTBN, consistent with the conservationist spirit of the NFPR, and to develop monitoring capacity and impose sanctions on illegal clearings.

These two factors combine as displayed in Table 8.3, resulting in the following incentive structure and outcomes across provinces. When they face powerful large producers and no conservationist coalition (top, right), governors are pressured to dilute the conservationist spirit of the NFPR in response to producers' demands and/or their perceived preferences (i.e., structural power) out of fear that they might lose investments and public support if opposing such powerful interests. In these cases, governors are likely to exploit ambiguities in the NFPR by assigning to forest areas lower conservation value, allowing for recategorizations of individual farms – something producers demand as a way to avoid the strictures of the law – and/or approving land-use regulations that are in violation of the NFPR. They are also likely to establish minimal sanctions. In the context of weak institutions, the absence of a strong conservationist coalition reduces the incentives to abide by the NFPR, and executive agencies in charge of enforcement are likely not empowered to monitor and sanction forest clearings. The cases of Salta and Formosa exemplify this dynamic.

Where governors face a powerful conservationist coalition in a context in which large producers do not control a substantial share of the province's productive land, they are motivated toward conservationism (bottom, left). In these cases, governors are likely to design an OTBN that is more consistent with the NFPR and that incorporates the demands of conservationist groups. They are also more likely to invest in capacity building to enforce the law by monitoring forest clearings and imposing sanctions, as the conservationist coalition is more or less actively involved in denouncing illegal forest clearings and producers are not sufficiently powerful to undermine enforcement. This is the case of Chaco, where a conservationist coalition of forestry producers, local environmental groups, indigenous communities, and small-scale producers influenced the OTBN and pressed for the law's enforcement.

Governors may also face both powerful large producers and a conservationist coalition (top, left). In these cases, they are likely to cater to both sectors, as conflict and the threat of instability emerge forcefully in the context of the rapid expansion of the agricultural frontier. Facing a conservationist coalition, governors likely design an OTBN consistent with the NFPR as watchful conservationist interests make it difficult for the government to relax its design. However, governors respond to producers by relaxing enforcement, which satisfies producers and is harder for conservationists to control, even if they actively denounce clearings. This is the case of Santiago del Estero, which approved an OTBN that was moderately consistent with the NFPR, including exceedingly high penalties, yet failed to enforce it, as producers were lightly monitored and sanctioned.

Overall, implementation resulted in cross-provincial variation in both the design of subnational regulations and the enforcement of the NFPR. In some cases, governors catered to powerful producers by designing subnational OTBNs that even allowed them to violate the NFPR without breaking the law (Salta, Formosa). Governors would then lightly enforce these flawed regulations, resulting in widespread (and often legal) deforestation. In other cases, governors were not only confronted by large producers but also by a powerful conservationist coalition, which prompted them to design an OTBN consistent with the NFPR (Santiago). In order to cater to powerful producers, governors relaxed enforcement. Finally, where governors faced a powerful conservationist coalition but weak producers, they designed subnational regulations consistent with the NFPR and expanded the territorial reach of the forestry agency to monitor its effective enforcement (Chaco). In all four cases, governors prioritized their political goals of stability and continuity over environmental concerns.

No case among those studied here features the absence of both a conservationist coalition and large-scale producers. Forest-rich provinces in the context of a commodity boom are likely to see both or either pressure from investors to open up land and/or from a conservationist coalition seeking to protect the forest from the threat of clearing.

MULTILEVEL DYNAMICS IN SALTA

We apply our multilevel approach to enforcement to the case of Salta, a province with large forestland areas and high rates of deforestation propelled by the expansion of agriculture and cattle ranching. We show how Salta's powerful large producers strove to influence the design of the NFPR, and how Salta's governor exploited the resulting ambiguities and opportunities for discretion in the NFPR to shape provincial regulations to the advantage of extremely powerful producers in order to avoid conflict. Among other institutional mechanisms, the governor engaged in what the editors of this volume call "nonpunitive enforcement" by applying light sanctions on infractions. Based on interviews with key informants, document analysis, and deforestation data, we show how the governor's strategy resulted in the weak enforcement of the NFPR.

Salta's Organized Interests and the Design of the NFPR

One of the central claims of this chapter is that in federal systems, subnational organized actors seeking to undermine the enforcement of national regulations that affect their interests do so by engaging in the legislative design process through their representatives in congress. Instead of circumscribing their influence to the subnational implementation of the NFPR, Salta's large producers sought to influence the NFPR bill in the Senate, where, as previously discussed, their chances of blocking or modifying it were higher.[17]

Salta's large producers commissioned the Fundación para el Desarrollo Sostenible del Noroeste Argentino (FUNDESNOA), a local think tank with strong ties to grain producers,[18] and whose director was Romero's former secretary of environment, to draft an alternative bill to the NFPR. Senator Sonia Escudero, an ally of Romero's, introduced FUNDESNOA's bill in the Senate.[19] This bill departed from the one that had been approved in the lower chamber. It granted more autonomy to the provinces to define native forests and did not identify any criteria for determining levels of conservation value, thus allowing provinces to define their zoning maps unconstrained. Critically, unlike the NFPR, it did not suspend the extension of deforestation permits until the OTBNs had been approved, a particularly sensitive issue in Salta. The only innovation proposed by FUNDESNOA that made it into the NFPR, however, was the compensatory fund to pay for environmental services. The elements that producers could not introduce in the text of the NFPR – the classification of forestlands, regulation of land use in protected areas, and the suspension of clearing permits – were fought for during the law's implementation at the provincial level.

---

[17] In the lower chamber, where the NFPR's passage was secured by the governing coalition, however, the only two representatives to vote against it were aligned with Salta's PJ governor Juan Carlos Romero (1995–2007), a politician with strong ties to rural elites.

[18] Some of the largest agricultural producers in the province (e.g., CRESUD, Desde el Sur) sponsored FUNDESNOA.

[19] Senado, Diario de Asuntos Entrados Expediente 0716-S-2007; authors interview with former president of PROGRANO, Salta, July 8, 2015.

Designing Salta's OTBN

Large producers put pressure on Salta's governor to dilute the impact of the NFPR. When the NFPR's approval was imminent, Governor Romero quickly issued clearing permits that covered close to 435,000 hectares, equivalent to 5 percent of Salta's forestlands and comparable to the total area authorized for clearing in the previous three years.[20] Acknowledging that clearing authorizations would be harder to obtain under the NFPR and that this would negatively affect land prices, Romero sought to protect large producers' property rights and their expected profits. In November 2007 alone, there were public hearings to clear 130,000 hectares under the regulations established by the preexisting provincial environmental law (Leake and de Ecónomo 2008; Schmidt 2010b: 8), which was lenient toward deforestation.

The October 2007 gubernatorial election pitted Romero's favored candidate (his vice governor) against his former secretary of state, Juan Manuel Urtubey, who sought to differentiate himself from Romero by criticizing his environmental policy.[21] Although Urtubey's victory might have increased producers' uncertainty, contributing in some way to the spike in clearing permits triggered by the approval of the NFPR, Urtubey, like Romero, belonged to a traditional family of landowners and PJ politicians, and his administration did not significantly threaten producers' interests.

Once he was in office, Urtubey set out to design the OTBN. The governor faced intense pressure from producers to reduce legal uncertainty over their investments and properties, as well as to end the temporary ban on clearings that the NFPR had established. Salta's landowners are mainly local, and during the design of the OTBN they advanced their demands through direct legislative representation, positions in government, and powerful lobbies such as PROGRANO and Sociedad Rural.[22] National environmental organizations, alerted by Romero's clearing permits, put additional pressure on the government to abide by the NFPR. However, in the absence of a well-organized conservationist coalition in Salta, their power to influence provincial-level politics was significantly more limited than their ability to mobilize public opinion nationally.

Partly in observance of the participatory requirement in the NFPR, Urtubey held public forums to discuss the OTBN in early 2008. However, he held separate meetings for each sector involved in the process (e.g., indigenous communities, peasants and small producers, and large producers), and the plural

---

[20] "La cicatriz que Juan Carlos Romero dejó en la Provincia de Salta," *El intransigente*, May 8, 2013.

[21] Authors interview with Juan Manuel Urtubey, Governor of Salta (2007–2019), Salta, July 8, 2015.

[22] According to a key informant, "producers finance political parties … politicians' campaigns" and "with the exception of the *Partido Obrero* [a minority left party] no politician here would oppose producers." Authors interview with anonymous informant, Salta, July 10, 2015.

debate prescribed by the NFPR did not take place. Because disagreements among these actors as well as resistance to the NFPR from sectors of large producers were especially strong, the OTBN bill sent by the executive to the legislature in November 2008 lacked a critical component: a zoning map. The bill was indisputably favorable toward large producers, as it established that the zoning map would be "for guidance" only and allowed for the recategorization of individual landholdings, which was forbidden in the NFPR.

Even so, Urtubey's bill met fierce resistance from large producers led by Senator Alfredo Olmedo, the son of Salta's "soy king," who had benefited from Romero's scandalous concession of massive amounts of provincial land during his tenure as governor. Olmedo submitted an alternative bill that was based on existing provincial legislation and classified 5.8 million hectares or 63 percent of Salta's forestlands as green (Redaf 2008; Schmidt 2010a, 260–264). Although Olmedo's proposal was not endorsed by the main producers' organizations, it did signal the preferences of a sector of large producers and pressured Urtubey to compromise on a watered-down zoning map. A former head of PROGRANO, the main provincial producers' organization, noted that he opposed Olmedo's bill because it completely disregarded environmental criteria and was politically unfeasible.[23]

Salta's OTBN bill was passed in December 2008, incorporating features from Olmedo's proposal. The OTBN established that 19 percent of Salta's forests would be classified as green, 65 percent yellow, and 16 percent red. This distribution of conservation areas was closer to Urtubey's proposal, but far from the benchmark of 10 percent green areas that experts advising the provincial secretary of environment had proposed to the governor (see Luft 2013: 191). The OTBN further allowed for a broad range of activities in yellow areas, which cattle ranchers demanded and which constituted a potential source of clearings that the NFPR banned.

Most crucially, Salta's OTBN had two unique features: First, it was approved without a zoning map, which the governor was supposed to produce within two months after the law's enactment; and second, and most important, it stipulated that this map would be "for guidance," and that the reclassification of individual farms to lower conservation values (e.g., from red to green) would be allowed.[24] The OTBN, which was approved with almost unanimous support, was therefore fundamentally flawed. Because the bill lacked a zoning map, the classification of forestlands within each conservation category became a matter upon which the governor would decide with "discretion,"[25] behind closed doors, withdrawing zoning decisions "from the public debate...to keep them as private as possible."[26] This map, moreover, would have little strength, as it

---

[23] Authors interview with former president of PROGRANO, Salta, July 8, 2015.
[24] Concretely, the zoning map would be "orientativo."
[25] Authors interview with Claudio Del Plá, Provincial legislator (2003–), Salta, July 7, 2015.
[26] Authors interview with Sonia Escudero, Senator for Salta (2001–2013), Salta, July 10, 2015.

constituted "guidelines" only and would be subject to case-by-case amendments, via recategorizations. Senator Escudero, who had played a critical role in the approval of the NFPR, understood that Salta's producers only accepted the OTBN because of the possibility to recategorize individual farms. In her words, "That was the key ... Producers wanted to decide how their farms would be classified. Think: forty, fifty thousand hectares ...".[27] The weakness of the OTBN was noted by the former head of PROGRANO: "Legally speaking, there are no hectares of forest that are red, no hectares of forest that are yellow, no hectares of forest that are green. The map is for guidance. So if you want to sue the province for classifying your farm red, then [they say] 'no, there is no red forest, where did you get that your land is classified red? ... the map is for guidance' ... this is a mess without a solution."[28]

Urtubey's strategy can be viewed as one of *conflict avoidance*. Facing intense pressure from powerful producers, some of whom adopted radical positions regarding the OTBN, he created a legal mechanism that allowed him to decide which forestlands would be affected by environmental restrictions on a case-by-case basis, thereby defusing producers' pressures with discretion. By doing so away from the public eye, he sought to avoid reactions from national level NGOs in the face of concessions. In reference to the OTBN, Urtubey asserted, "Is this a great law? No. It is what was possible to accomplish ... the maximum level of consensus we could reach." Regarding the role of the executive in its implementation, he noted: "The executive ended up being a player in this game when this should not be so. The state has to structure the game ... But [instead] they [large producers] put you in the game because of the level of intransigence that they have."[29]

Soon after the approval of the law, and while the executive appeased producers' demands through the design of the zoning map behind closed doors, the Supreme Court agreed to rule on a lawsuit (*amparo*) from indigenous and peasant communities – which had been marginalized from the debates over the OTBN – against the provincial and national governments. With the backing of religious organizations, these groups challenged the clearings authorized at the end of the Romero administration on the grounds that they would have cumulative deleterious environmental and social consequences. The Supreme Court temporarily stopped the clearings in the four departments where the holdings affected by the permits in question were located.[30]

---

[27] Authors interview with Sonia Escudero, Senator for Salta (2001–2013), Salta, July 10, 2015.
[28] Authors interview with former president of PROGRANO, Salta, July 8, 2015.
[29] Authors interview with Juan Manuel Urtubey, Governor of Salta (2007–2019), Salta, July 8, 2015.
[30] Salas, Dino y otros c/ Salta, Provincia de y Estado Nacional s/ amparo; CSJN, "Derecho Ambiental," November 2012.

Although large producers were by far the most influential sector on Urtubey's decisions, and despite their efforts to establish a law that legalized violations to the NFPR, the judicial activism of indigenous and peasant communities, which brought the question of deforestation to the national media, generated some concern. A mudslide that ravaged the northern department of Tartagal in February 2009 further attracted national-level media attention to Salta. This event, which was immediately connected by public opinion and environmental NGOs to deforestation, built up pressure on the provincial government.

In June 2009, after the Supreme Court's decision to suspend clearing permits in affected areas, Urtubey promulgated Salta's OTBN and the zoning map was made public. The map classified as yellow all of the holdings that were disputed by the indigenous communities in the Supreme Court case, and the clearing permits affecting those areas were reversed. The governor further issued a decree temporarily banning clearings in forestlands claimed by indigenous or peasant communities until both a survey of indigenous communities and negotiations with those making claims on the land had been carried out. This measure sought to avoid conflict with indigenous communities and prevent the emergence of more powerful organizations out of their reaction to clearings, as had happened with the peasant movement in neighboring Santiago. These areas came to be labeled by government officials as "social yellow," and the ban continued to be extended beyond the initial period of three years, given that neither the survey nor the negotiations were carried out.

Although it may seem at first sight that the groups that spearheaded legal action nationally constituted a *conservationist coalition* capable of imposing higher consistency with the NFPR, this was not the case. These interests had little influence on provincial politics, and precisely for that reason, they operated at the national level in order to pressure the governor by making their case visible and engaging national authorities. Moreover, the effect of their pressure was geographically circumscribed to the disputed areas. After their case was decided by the court, the coalition's power diluted. Furthermore, as discussed below, these groups had no impact on enforcement. While the Supreme Court's suspension was in effect, 53,202 hectares affected by the ruling were deforested (AGN 2014: 113; Defensoría del Pueblo 2014: 4).

These measures, which aimed at fixing some of the abuses in the OTBN, generated vigorous opposition from producers led by Olmedo and FUNDESNOA.[31] In response, Urtubey set up an advisory council for the implementation of the OTBN that was entirely made up of representatives of large producer groups. Indigenous communities, small-scale producers, and environmental NGOs were not included. One of the advisory council's critical tasks was to issue

[31] Authors interview with Gustavo Paul, Salta's Secretary of Environment, Salta, July 8, 2015; authors interview with former president of PROGRANO, Salta, July 8, 2015.

monthly recommendations on recategorizations.[32] In 2010, moreover, Urtubey issued another decree that further specified the conditions under which recategorizations would be done. This decree was eventually repealed by the governor in 2014 – and recategorizations were suspended – in response to accusations by environmental NGOs pointing out that decisions benefited producers with political connections.[33]

Overall, Salta's OTBN radically departed from the NFPR and undermined its statutory goals. In designing the bill, the governor pursued a conflict-avoidance strategy to accommodate pressures from extremely powerful producers who controlled over 70 percent of provincial land, and whose power was not counterbalanced by a conservationist coalition capable of pushing for regulations that would be consistent with the NFPR. As a result, the OTBN allowed for "legal" violations to the spirit and the letter of the NFPR, which, together with lax "nonpunitive enforcement" – analyzed below – resulted in wide deforestation.

Enforcing the NFPR in Salta

Due to producers' pressures, and to the absence of a conservationist coalition capable of counterbalancing those pressures, the enforcement of the NFPR in Salta has been weak. As noted above in the subsection entitled "Enforcement of the NFPR," the most direct indicator of NFPR enforcement is the extent to which the law is able to prevent deforestation in what the OTBN defines as protected areas (yellow and red areas). Salta was the second-worst performer in the Chaco provinces, with 37.8 percent of its total forest loss between 2009 and 2016 occurring in protected areas. Another measure of enforcement is the share of land deforested without clearing permits. According to the provincial ministry of environment, between 2008 and 2014, Salta lost 465,406 hectares of forest, 55.4 percent of which was cleared without permits (SAS 2015: 149–151). Data on authorized and nonauthorized deforestation in Figure 8.1 indicate that the implementation of the NFPR had no significant impact on reducing nonauthorized clearings until 2014, when they dropped considerably. However, total deforestation did not drop, as authorized clearings spiked that year.

Because enforcement of the NFPR in Salta was weakened by design features that "legalized" irregular clearings, focusing only on deforestation in protected areas or on nonauthorized clearings may provide an incomplete measure of enforcement. Deforestation in areas recategorized to low conservation value, for example, is another indicator of weak enforcement. Data are only available for 2014, when recategorized forestlands represented 25,442 hectares, a

---

[32] Decree # 2211, 2010.
[33] Authors interview with Claudio Del Plá, Provincial legislator (2003–), Salta, July 7, 2015; authors interview with Juan Manuel Urtubey, Governor of Salta (2007–2019), Salta, July 8, 2015.

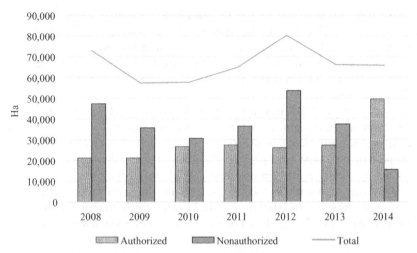

FIGURE 8.1. Authorized, nonauthorized, and total deforestation, Salta, 2008–2014 (hectares).
Source: Authors' elaboration, based on SAS (2015).

significant amount, equivalent to 37 percent of the total forest loss that year, and 1.6 times the area cleared without permits.

Finally, total deforestation rates provide an indirect measure of enforcement. Figure 8.2 shows that the implementation of the NFPR did not deter deforestation in Salta. It was only in 2015, six years after the enactment of the OTBN, that deforestation dropped to pre-commodity boom levels. The data clearly show exceptionally high levels of deforestation in 2008, between the sanction of the NFPR and its implementation in the province, when several of the fraudulent clearing permits awarded by the Romero administration in anticipation of more stringent regulations were executed.

As proposed in our framework, the governor used design features to respond to producers' pressures and passed an OTBN that was tailored to their demands. The governor further weakened enforcement of the NFPR, and thus lightened its impact on producers, both by failing to build capacity to monitor and sanction noncompliance and by unevenly applying low fines. Despite the fact that Salta received the second-largest share of the compensatory fund, 30 percent of which was supposed to fund NFPR enforcement (MAyDS 2016: 16–17),[34] there is no evidence of improvement in state capacity. According to the secretary and experts at the provincial ministry of environment, the fund has been primarily used for salaries and equipment at the ministry headquarters in the capital city. The province built no new facilities to monitor forestlands in the interior,

---

[34] This amounted to 152.4 million pesos between 2010 and 2015.

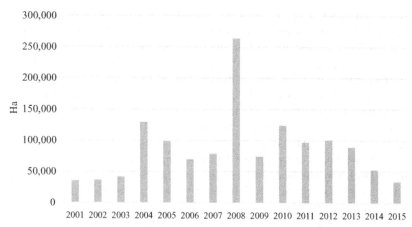

FIGURE 8.2. Annual deforestation, Salta, 2001–2015 (hectares).
Source: Authors' own calculations, with data from Global Forest Watch.

especially in forest-rich departments.[35] A report by the national ombudsman further indicates that in 2012, only one team monitored deforestation on the ground (Defensoría del Pueblo 2014). Convergent with the chapters by Schrank and by Amengual and Dargent (this volume), the case of Salta shows how low state capacity is a product rather than a cause of nonenforcement. Not building monitoring capacity is part of the enforcer's strategy to ameliorate the costs of noncompliance for large producers.

Sanctions are a crucial tool for enforcement. When the cost of violation (V) offsets the cost of compliance (S), fines create powerful negative incentives to obey the law. As we discussed above in the section "Designing the NFPR," the NFPR was weakened on this aspect by producers' resistance to a nationally standardized sanctions regime, which they voiced through their representatives in Congress and lobbied against at the provincial level. Key informants, including producers and public officials, acknowledged that sanctions were extremely low.[36] In the words of the governor:

[In Argentina, fines], not only environmental ones, are almost symbolic. Well, I do not want them to be symbolic, I want fines to "break your head." Then you will say "well, if it costs me two or three harvests to pay a fine, then I won't do it." But if you can pay for it with 20 or 10 percent of your yield then, what's the problem? You'll pay for it.[37]

---

[35] Authors interview with Gustavo Paul, Salta's Secretary of Environment, Salta, July 8, 2015.
[36] The president of Salta's rural producers' federation, Carlos Segón, recognized that illegal clearings continued in Salta because fines were ridiculously low and recategorizations were discretionary (Carlos Segón, "En Salta hay desmontes ilegales y multas irrisorias," *El tribuno*, September 1, 2014).
[37] Authors interview with Juan Manuel Urtubey, Governor of Salta (2007–2019), Salta, July 8, 2015.

Between 2013 and 2015, the province issued ninety-six infractions on 88,900 hectares, which represented on average a penalty of fifty-nine liters of gas per cleared hectare, for nonauthorized clearings identified between 2006 and 2014 (SAS 2014: 43–47; SAS 2015: 49–52). These fines are not only small in number given the high rate of deforestation; they are also extremely low. Consider the following example. An illegal clearing of 715 hectares of high and medium conservation value forests in the department of Anta in 2014 was fined with 35,000 liters of gas, or approximately US$50,000 at the time. The value of a cleared hectare in Anta can sell for as high as US$7,000, whereas a hectare of forest sells for at most US$1,800. If the landowner were to illegally clear the land, pay the fine, and sell the farm, she could still make a profit of approximately US$3.7 million.[38] In other words, violators can easily absorb the costs of noncompliance.

In sum, in the face of massive pressure from large producers to undermine the enforcement of the law, Salta's governor pursued a strategy of conflict avoidance. He did not simply accept the most radical positions of large producers seeking to attribute low conservation value to most forestlands because of fear of exposure and denunciation by environmental NGOs. However, the effect of the NFPR on deforestation until 2014 was limited. In the absence of a conservationist coalition that could effectively influence policy design and vigorously denounce weak enforcement, producers' preferences prevailed. The rates of deforestation grew in 2008 in anticipation of constraints on land use owing to the passage of the NFPR and the expected concomitant effect on land prices. Lack of resources does not explain this outcome, as Salta had significant funds for monitoring compliance and did a worse job than other provinces in the region, such as Chaco, which expanded and strengthened monitoring capacity and infrastructure throughout its forest areas despite having received fewer funds.[39]

CONCLUSION

This chapter has used the case of the implementation of the NFPR in the Argentine Chaco to contribute to our understanding of the sources of institutional weakness. We contend that to account for the politics of enforcement in multilevel systems, we should consider not only whether and why sanctions are applied by subnational authorities, which is the focus of a broad literature, but also analyze the different arenas – national and subnational – in which a law's enforcement may be shaped.

---

[38] Authors' estimates with data from Compañía Argentina de Tierras. Land prices correspond to August 2012.
[39] Authors' assessment based on provincial documents and fieldwork. See Fernández Milmanda and Garay (2019).

The design and content of national and subnational implementation regulations is critical to the politics of enforcement. Ambiguities and opportunities for discretion embedded in the national law – lobbied by the actors that would pay the cost of enforcement – allowed subnational authorities in the Argentine Chaco to design provincial regulations that undermined the enforcement of the NFPR. Thus, weak enforcement may result not only from whether and how sanctions are applied, but also from how implementation regulations are designed. These regulations may allow for "legal" violations of the law (e.g., permitting clearings in yellow areas) or for "nonpunitive enforcement" (e.g., setting extremely low fines).

The case of Salta illustrates how violations of the NFPR were legalized in provincial regulations, resulting in both "legal" noncompliance and "nonpunitive" enforcement. The governor exploited ambiguities in the national law and embedded discretionary provisions in provincial regulations to respond to extremely powerful producers seeking to dilute the NFPR's impact. Conservationist interests were poorly organized on the ground and thus unable to counterbalance the influence of producers. When conflict with indigenous communities emerged, localized exceptions rather than systematic decisions to protect these communities were made in order to avoid conflict.

9

What/Whose Property Rights?

The Selective Enforcement of Land Rights under Mexican Liberalism[1]

María Paula Saffon and Juan F. González Bertomeu

[Some seek] to interpret the disentailment law in such an expansive way that many...plan to denounce the ranchos the indigenous people have called a community...to dispossess them with all their fruits. Is it fair that [the dispossessor] sits down to eat with his mouth full at the table that for several centuries these Indians have prepared and covered with delicacies, whose elders have cultivated?

Amparo petitioner's brief (1862)[2]

Strong property rights[3] tend to be considered a crucial condition for almost all that is good, including economic growth, peace, state capacity, even democracy. However, not all types of property rights institutions are considered capable of achieving these purposes. It is often assumed or argued that property rights – or at least the *right kind* of property rights – are liberal ownership rights,[4] which can only be held by individuals, are transferable and allocable only through market forces, and are secure from state expropriation or intervention.

[1] We thank Miriam Hernández-Delgado, Inés O'Farrell, Julián Salazar-Gallego, Georgina Timossi, and Esteban Villa-Turek for their invaluable assistance selecting and coding judicial cases. We also thank the detailed and pertinent comments made by Mike Albertus, Alisha Holland, Andrew Schrank, Catalina Smulovitz, Hillel Soifer, the anonymous reviewers and editors of this volume, as well as the comments of participants at the conferences associated with this book and at the Red de Economía Política de América Latina (2016), Latin American Studies Association (2017), and American Political Science Association (2016, 2017) annual conferences at which we presented earlier drafts. All errors are ours.
[2] Supreme Court of Justice of Mexico, March 18, 1872 (San Lorenzo Ixtacoyotla).
[3] Following Chapter 1 (this volume), we define *property rights* as an institution composed of bundles of rules. There are different types of property rights institutions, such as liberal and nonliberal ones.
[4] See, for instance, North and Weingast (1989); North (1990); Olson (2000); Acemoglu et al. (2001, 2002).

In this chapter, we chronicle the "activation" (Levitsky and Murillo 2014) of individual property rights in Mexico, driven by liberal ideology and enabled by increased state capacity, with indigenous groups resisting the elimination of their collective rights and wealthy landowners (*hacendados*) pushing to turn the process to their advantage through biased enforcement. The first period after enactment of these laws is marked by selective enforcement against the church, with forbearance toward indigenous groups who were allies of the government. This is followed by the fuller activation of the individual property rights institution, with the consequent weakening of public and collective land rights.

The latter, of course, have been preeminent in the history of land politics in Latin America, and their holders have tended, disproportionately, to belong to marginalized sectors – notably ethnic groups and poor peasants (Saffon Forthcoming). Public and collective property rights can also achieve important goals. Public rights can ensure the state's control of certain goods for the purposes of their conservation, regulated exploitation or conditional allocation, which can favor the poor if progressive criteria are used. Collective property rights can foster the empowerment of disadvantaged groups, their ability to access state institutions and participate in politics, and even their household investments and income.[5] However, under a liberal perspective, public and collective property rights are generally considered "dead hand assets," obsolete and inefficient institutions that thwart investment, since they set the grounds for the tragedy of the commons (Aristotle 1946: 1261b; Hardin 1968) and often restrict alienation.

These competing perspectives explain why, though liberal and nonliberal property rights can and often do coexist, measures to expand the former at the expense of the latter are likely to be enacted when liberal governments ascend to power. In the case of land, such measures have consisted in laws ordering the enclosure (i.e., survey and transfer to private hands) of public lands and the disentailment (i.e., fragmentation and declaration of alienability) of communal lands (Saffon 2015, n.d.). The main stated aim of such laws is economic growth, believed to stem from the revenues generated by land transfers, the increased productivity resulting from private investments, and the expansion of the rural-owning class.

Of course, the mere appearance of a government with a liberal ideology might not be enough for land laws to be complied with in practice. The enclosure and disentailment of lands are complex processes. They require state capacities – including land surveyors, notaries and public registries, and administrative or judicial authorities in charge of monitoring processes and

---

[5] On the positive effects of collective land titling, see Grueso et al. (1998) (social safety nets); Deininger and Hans Binswager (1999) (resource pooling); N'gweno (2000) (participation and resource management); Peña et al. (2017) (housing investments, household income, and school attendance); Alfonso (2018) (social welfare).

resolving disputes – which can exhibit divergent levels of independence or proximity to social actors. As Amengual and Dargent and also Fernández Milmanda and Garay argue in this book, the constraints imposed by state capacities and multilevel politics might not lead to full noncompliance, but rather to selective enforcement, driven by social resistance and elites' interests. An important part of the story we will tell relates to the ability of the state to create less biased enforcement for poor individuals (though not for groups), against local interests, through centralizing mechanisms like judicial oversight.

In this chapter we examine how liberal ideology, social resistance, and elites' interests shaped the politics of compliance with land laws under Mexico's liberal era (1855–1910). During that period, several liberal governments held power, all recognizing the enclosure of public lands and the disentailment of collective lands as key endeavors. However, the content and enforcement of land laws varied significantly across governments. The administrations of the 1850s and 1860s – the most renowned of which was Benito Juárez's (1858–1872) – enacted the liberal Reform laws ordering collective land disentailment and fomenting enclosures. But such laws and ensuing regulations preserved (admittedly restricted) room for the collective rights of indigenous *pueblos*, which had held corporate land titles since colonial times; they also foresaw the distribution of collective lands among *pueblo* members. Further, the laws regarding indigenous groups were largely underenforced by state authorities, something that clearly changed during the 1876–1910 government of Porfirio Díaz.

At first sight, this difference could be explained as the outcome of divergent levels of state capacity. In the 1850s and 1860s, international and factional wars submerged Mexico into deep instability and economic stagnation, while Díaz's semiauthoritarian government accomplished the "miracle" of establishing the monopoly of political power while achieving economic growth (Knight 1986: 35; Haber, Razo, and Maurer 2003: 42–44). Nevertheless, state capacity was only part of the story. Weak capacity was not an impediment to the enforcement of land laws against church corporate landholdings during the 1850s and 1860s, despite the immense power of ecclesiastical authorities (Bazant 1971; Knowlton 1976). Moreover, strengthened state capacity did not prevent the selective enforcement of liberal land laws under the Porfiriato. The alignment of economic and political interests led state authorities to apply liberal laws against indigenous lands that were coveted by neighboring estate owners (*hacendados*) – which led to the enclosing and disentailing of lands meant to be excluded from the scope of the laws and to the exclusion of indigenous individuals from the laws' protections.[6]

---

[6] Orozco (1898); González-Roa (1919); McBride (1923); Tannenbaum (1930); Simpson (1937); Silva-Herzog (1959); Reina (1980); Coatsworth (1981); González-Navarro (1985); Knight (1986); Hernández (1993).

We argue that variation in compliance with Mexican liberal land laws was the result of elites' political motivations.[7] As Amengual and Dargent argue, in contexts of limited state capacity, such motivations can lead governments to focus enforcement on certain priorities while exhibiting a "standoffish behavior" with regard to other issues. Liberal governments of the 1850s and 1860s focused on enforcing land laws against their main target – the church – while underenforcing them when lands were held by indigenous groups. In contrast, under the Porfiriato, increased state capacity enabled the expansion of law enforcement against indigenous groups, but elite alignment motivated an abusive enforcement of the laws to satisfy *hacendados'* interest in indigenous lands.

We identify two additional factors that influenced the selective politics of enforcement, which can be relevant to the discussion of the sources of institutional weakness/strength. First, the anticipation of indigenous resistance likely led the makers of liberal land legislation to restrict but not altogether eliminate their collective land rights, as well as to recognize indigenous individuals as beneficiaries of the distribution of fragmented lands. Consequently, legal or interpretative conflicts concerning the enforcement of disentailment laws were likely to emerge not only between indigenous groups and *hacendados* but also within those groups.

Second, liberal land laws involved different levels and types of enforcement.[8] While the laws and regulations regarding church and public landholdings were enforced by federal administrative authorities, those concerning indigenous lands enlisted state-level authorities to further enact regulations – a first-order stage of enforcement – and local-level authorities to apply them – a second-order stage. Since enforcement could generate interpretative conflicts, courts were likely to intervene to resolve conflicts between parties and to check upon the actions of enforcers (by resolving *amparo* writs of rights protection), thus becoming third-order enforcers. Courts were also located at different levels, with local ones resolving private conflicts, federal courts at the district level resolving rights-related conflicts, and the Supreme Court reviewing both.

We study the Supreme Court's *amparo* decisions reviewing claims of land rights violations to capture how authorities of diverse types and levels contributed to the strong or weak enforcement of different actors' rights, as well as to tell apart the potentially different motivations at play. We theorize, first, that both interest-based motivations and liberal-ideological motivations could lead to the enforcement or overenforcement of individual private

---

[7] Brinks (2008); Levitsky and Murillo (2009); Holland (2015, 2016, 2017). On property rights, see Haber, Razo, and Maurer (2003); Onoma (2010).

[8] By *levels* of enforcement we refer to national versus state versus local levels (as in Fernández Milmanda and Garay). By *types* of enforcement we refer to the different authorities or branches concerned (judicial versus administrative) at those levels.

property rights to the detriment of collective property rights. But only interest-based motivations could lead to the weak enforcement of property rights of indigenous or poor individuals. Liberal ideology should make authorities equally protect the individual rights of rich and poor, indigenous and nonindigenous alike.

Second, we conjecture that, because local authorities were closer to, and hence more subject to influence from, local economic elites, they were more likely to decide based on interest, and consequently be biased against poor indigenous individuals. In contrast, central-level authorities – especially those with the reputation of being more independent, like the Supreme Court – were more likely to decide cases based on ideology.

We constructed a novel dataset of all land conflict cases published by the Mexican Supreme Court between 1871 and 1910. Although (old) judicial cases bring up methodological challenges and shortcomings, they are a rich source for understanding enforcement. Combining basic descriptive statistics with qualitative analysis, we show that local-level authorities were the most frequent alleged perpetrators of land rights violations against indigenous people, and that indigenous groups' access to justice was severely restricted by the judiciary. However, we also find that individual indigenous peasants were not less likely to succeed in court than other individual petitioners.

THE POLITICS OF ENACTING AND ENFORCING LIBERAL LAND LAWS

The Reform Period (1855–1875)

Mexican liberals rose to power in the mid-nineteenth century. Through the 1854 Ayutla Revolution, they forced into exile President Santa Anna, a conservative who held power several times between the 1830s and 1850s and who declared himself perpetual dictator in 1853. Liberal rule was unstable given the challenges to power coming from both conservatives and foreign invaders, as well as internal splits. However, liberals had a clear-cut political and economic reformist agenda, which they began to promote as soon as they reached power. It entailed secularization, the elimination of corporate privileges in favor of formal equality before the law, and economic progress (Hale 1968). Land rights reform was considered crucial.

Disentailment of Corporate Lands

The central piece of legislation concerning land was the Lerdo Law of June 25, 1856. The law ordered the "disentailment" – i.e., fragmentation and alienation – of landholdings held by corporations, except for those devoted to corporations' immediate service or object. The law provided that disentailed lands should be allocated by local authorities to their renters or beneficiaries, who would pay a price or acquire a mortgage. If a plot was not so allocated within three months, anyone could request its allocation, or else authorities would auction it. From then on, corporations would cease to have the legal capacity to hold or administer property other than that exempted. Conflicts should be heard by first instance judges in an oral procedure. While the immediate aim of the law appeared to be the disentailment of church lands (Kourí, n.d.: 5), "civil" corporations were also object of the law. These evidently included indigenous corporations, the main type of which were *pueblos* (Tanck 2005; Saffon 2015).

Indigenous groups resisted the application of the law since its enactment (Fraser 1972: 639; Powell 1972: 659–662). The law allowed them to retain some of their communal lands,[9] to receive the price of disentailed lands, and to demand initiation of disentailment processes for unrented lands to be allocated to their members. However, indigenous groups either desired to retain *all* their lands in common or agreed with the goals of disentailment but feared detrimental applications of the law – which could target excluded communal lands or allow outsiders to obtain fragmented lands.

In response to indigenous resistance, the government quickly issued notices (*circulares*) to governors and local authorities, which interpreted the law to their benefit. Perhaps most important was the October 9, 1856, *circular*, in which Lerdo – author of the law and minister of treasury – denounced abusive interpretations that presented the law "to the poor, and especially to the indigenous, as opposed to their interests, when its main objective was…to favor the most defenseless classes."[10] Understanding that the law's reference to renters as the main beneficiaries of disentailment could exclude indigenous individuals cultivating *pueblos'* terrains, the notice clarified that the latter could also claim allocations. Anticipating that claims might not be made by the poor due to lack of resources, the notice established that, when lands cost less than 200 pesos, taxes and procedural costs would be exempted. It further declared the law's deadline to claim lands was not applicable to the poor and indigenous.[11]

But the central government also insisted on the importance of disentailing indigenous lands, and often promoted restrictive interpretations of the

---

[9] *Fundos legales* (population centers) and perhaps *ejidos* (communal lands), but not *propios* (lands rented to outsiders) or *terrenos de repartimiento* (individual parcels held by village members under usufruct). See Knowlton (1998); Kourí (n.d.: ch. 2).

[10] Ministry of Treasury, *Circular* of October 9, 1856, "On the objects of the disentailment law," available in Dublán and Lozano (2004: Tome VIII, pp. 264–265).

[11] This rule was later expanded to exempt indigenous individuals from paying for nonrented lands, which should be divided up among villages' neighbors [see Presidential Decree of February 5, 1861, regulating Nationalization Laws and referring to cofradías, available in Dublán and Lozano (2004: Tome 9, pp. 54–62); and Presidential Regulatory Decree of April 20, 1878, referring to the allocation of communal lands in general, available in Dublán and Lozano (2004: Tome 13, pp. 501–503)].

type of land to be excluded from disentailment. Early *circulares* established that only the lands serving the common good were exempted, and that local authorities were the best judges to make those decisions (Fraser 1972: 641–642, 4). While it was clear that population centers (*fundos*) where public buildings resided complied with the condition, doubts remained concerning communal lands (*ejidos*). Section 27 of the 1857 constitution raised the Lerdo Law to constitutional level but did not dissipate doubts (Fraser 1972: 627, 345; Marino 2016: 303).

Still, attempts to enforce the law encouraged indigenous mobilization. In September 1856, indigenous protests in central Mexico had become so frequent that the minister of government urged governors to take a more decisive attitude against protests (Powell 1972: 662). According to Reina's (1980) data, the largest number of protests in the nineteenth century can be found during the Reform period (1855–1861), and most occurred in the first two years after the Lerdo Law passed. Most protests complained against the effects of disentailment.

At first, the government combined its propoor but proenforcement interpretations of the law with punctual repression (Powell 1972: 661; Reina 1980). However, its attitude rapidly changed to a "standoffish"[12] tolerance toward prevailing nonenforcement. Though individuals could request the initiation of disentailment processes with respect to specific plots, state-level laws were required for local authorities to promote disentailment across the board (Kourí n.d.: 7). Most of these laws only began to be enacted after 1868 (Marino 2001: 41) and actively enforced after 1880 (Ducey 1997). From 1858 on, few regulations and notices were issued by the central government concerning indigenous land disentailment (Fraser 1972: 646–677), and systematic attempts to enforce the law were halted (Kourí n.d.: 6).

The explanation has partly to do with the War of Reform (1858–1860) and the French intervention (1863–1867), which limited liberals' capacity to use state institutions. In both periods, Juárez was forced to run a parallel government while waging war. Though they prevailed, liberals' capacity to rule in the aftermath of conflict was hampered by profound financial problems (Centeno 2002: 60–61). Yet liberals' enforcement capacity was not null, as their attitude toward church lands illustrates.

The War of Reform was initiated by conservatives largely against the enforcement of laws affecting the church. By 1857, massive amounts of lands had been disentailed,[13] and quite strong measures had been used to ensure enforcement, such as publishing lists of church assets and forcing loans (Bazant 1971: chs. 2–3). Rather than thwarting their enforcement will, the war led liberals

---

[12] We use the concept as proposed by Amengual and Dargent (this volume).

[13] Analyzing transfers of church assets in six states, which concentrated two-thirds of ecclesiastical wealth, Bazant (1971) showed that, by 1857, disentailment was almost complete in Veracruz, Michoacán, and Jalisco, quite profound in Puebla and Mexico City, and restricted in San Luis Potosí.

to radicalize measures against church lands, and the constraints imposed by the war effort did not hinder their implementation. On July 12, 1859, Juárez enacted the Ley de Nacionalización de Bienes Eclesiásticos, which implied that confiscation without compensation would replace sales to renters. The law widened the scope of potential targets by referring to both ecclesiastical corporations and individuals, and to the assets they administered – not just owned. Regulation foresaw that big properties would be divided up and that everything would be auctioned and sold. Special administrative authorities – *jefaturas de hacienda* – were created to enforce the law.

Upon the liberals' victory, the decree of February 5, 1861, was enacted to revert the effects of conservatives' laws annulling disentailment and encourage nationalization. The latter was actively pursued until the French intervention and the subsequent war against Maximilian's imposed empire (1863–1867), which suspended confiscation in practice but did not abrogate its effects. After 1867, Juárez's triumphant but deeply indebted government saw in vigorous nationalization a crucial way to increase revenue while weakening church power. Given the destruction of documents resulting from the war, the government developed a strategy of denouncing "hidden" church assets, which could be in the hands of frontmen. Though this generated legal insecurity and a depreciation of values, it increased the scope of nationalization (Knowlton 1976: ch. 7).

All in all, on the grounds of the disentailment and nationalization laws, a vast amount of property exited the clergy's hands between 1857 and 1876.[14] Liberals' fierce targeting of church assets contrasts with their passivity toward indigenous lands. Though the rationale for turning those lands into private property was the same, indigenous lands ceased to be a priority after 1859 (Fraser 1972: 647). Given the constraints imposed by weak state capacity, the aim of seizing church assets clearly prevailed. Indigenous groups were both a less attractive source of revenue and a potential source of support during conflicts. This explains not only the nonenforcement of disentailment laws against indigenous lands, but also important concessions made to indigenous groups. For instance, *cofradía* lands (which were ecclesiastical but held by indigenous groups) were exempted from nationalization, and several plots of vacant lands (*baldíos*) were allocated to *pueblos* to be distributed among their neighbors (Fraser 1972: 647–650).

The Enclosure of Public Lands

As Juárez gave closure to civil conflicts and to the nationalization of church lands, he began to promote the expansion of private property rights on public lands. The first important law was enacted on July 20, 1863. It established

---

[14] However, against the spirit of the laws, the assets were mainly bought by big landowners (*hacendados*) and merchants (Bazant 1971; Knowlton 1976).

that the allocation of up to 2,500 hectares of public lands could be claimed if the prices established by decree were paid and surveying costs covered. Renters, usufruct holders, and occupants were preferred claimants for a short period. After that, third-party claimants would receive the lands in preference. If claimed lands were not vacant, possessors could claim compensation. All claims had to be made before federal district judges.

The law generated incentives for powerful actors to denounce occupied lands without clear boundaries as public, either by claiming to be possessors or by presenting claims before occupants did. *Pueblos'* lands were easy prey, since they were based on colonial titles whose demarcations were often imprecise or unregistered (Tannenbaum 1930; Womack 1968: 46; Knight 1986: 92; Hernández 1993; Falcón 2015: 262). In 1867, recognizing that the law could affect indigenous peasants, Juárez ordered district-level *jefes políticos* to clarify that public land allocations should respect possessors' rights, to encourage indigenous possessors to request titles, and to issue them without cost, "so as to avoid controversies" (Wilkie 1998: 146).

Liberals also began to promote colonization, which they considered an avenue to increase private property and foster immigration. On May 31, 1875, now president Lerdo enacted a provisional decree authorizing the executive to survey and value public lands, promote their occupation by settlers, and give private surveyors one-third of the lands for free. Though the incentives for privatizing public lands were strong, the law's enforcement was limited before the late 1870s (Holden 1994: 9).[15]

To recapitulate, the politics of land law enforcement from the 1850s to the early 1870s illustrate Amengual and Dargent (this volume)'s notion that limited state capacity constrains but does not block enforcement. Weak capacity forced liberals to set priorities and focus on the nationalization of church lands, leaving indigenous and public lands largely untouched. But why would liberal laws cover indigenous lands at all if their authors could anticipate strong resistance from what was an important basis of support? The response seems to be that liberals believed that disentailment would not only contribute to economic progress but also benefit indigenous people by turning them into a middle class of yeomen. Yet indigenous groups did not think likewise, and their resistance held back enforcement and led politicians to ignore it – especially when their need to obtain military support became urgent. However, indigenous resistance was not strong enough to push for the abrogation of liberal land laws, which remained susceptible of being enforced when economic incentives or the political balance of power changed. Such a change took place under Porfirio Díaz.

[15] As Holden shows, of the 45.7 million hectares of public land transferred to private hands in 1867–1905, only 1.6 were transferred before 1877.

The Porfiriato (1876–1910)

Though Díaz had been a prominent liberal leader in the War of Reform and the French intervention, he revolted against Juárez's and Lerdo's attempts at reelection in 1871 and 1876, respectively.[16] While his first revolt failed, the second was successful. It forced Lerdo to step down and push for a special election in 1877, with Díaz as the sole candidate. Although he obtained and retained power through elections and with functioning legislative and judicial powers (Kuntz 2010b: 5), Díaz's government is often classified as authoritarian because elections were rigged, and the opposition silenced (Guerra 1985: 97–106; Knight 1986: 20–21). Still, the government was quite popular, since it managed to deliver political order and economic development (Knight 1986: 35; Haber, Razo, and Maurer 2003: 44).

After more than half a century of wars and frequent alternation, Díaz managed to monopolize power and established the so-called Pax Porfiriana. He further replaced economic stagnation and deficits with sustained growth (Coatsworth 1981: 4; Haber, Razo, and Maurer 2003: 43; Kuntz 2010a: 329–331). Because of the international demand for crops, Mexico experienced an export boom (Kuntz 2010a: 329–331). Production was facilitated by the development of transport infrastructure and the promotion of investment-friendly policies (Coatsworth 1981: 4).

Díaz's government invested heavily in strengthening the state's capacity to protect property rights, though this did not translate into universal enforcement. The government aligned its goals and preferences with those of economic elites (Haber, Razo, and Maurer 2003). In the rural world, this meant promoting the interests of *hacendados*, who sought to seize valuable lands and devote them to commercial agriculture (Saffon 2015 ch. 3, n.d. ch. 4). Such lands did not only include still-existing public, vacant lands but also indigenous collective lands. Seizing indigenous lands could engross *hacendados*' properties as well as ensure labor supply (Tannenbaum 1930; Womack 1968; Knight 1986).

Now, Díaz did not serve *hacendados*' interests by repealing liberal laws' recognition of (limited) indigenous rights. In the discourse, there is more continuity than rupture between prior liberal governments and Díaz's. However, there is consensus among analysts that, by the end of the Porfiriato, indigenous groups had lost almost all their lands to *haciendas*.[17] The government encouraged enforcement of liberal laws in a context in which economic interests were extremely strong and, as a result, biased interpretation by local and state-level authorities was almost inevitable. Like his predecessors, Díaz addressed abuses through punctual intervention, but he generally let disputes be solved at the subnational level, turning a blind eye to bias.

[16] This section is based on Saffon (n.d.: ch. 4).
[17] Even revisionists of the "black legend" of the Porfiriato agree (Marino 2001: 40).

Disentailment of Corporate Lands

The enactment of state-level legislation in the 1870s finally regulated the disentailment of indigenous lands at the local level (Kourí n.d.: 7). The central government further pushed enforcement by issuing guidelines that simplified rules, clarified matters, and promoted the intervention of federal authorities – all to the detriment of corporate lands but not of indigenous individuals.

To ensure benefits to "the helpless indigenous class," the regulation of April 20, 1878[18] asserted that any poor individual possessing lands worth less than 200 pesos could claim their free allocation. In turn, the notice of October 28, 1889,[19] established that the Constitution's prohibition of corporate property included *ejidos*, but it stated that disentailment should benefit all *pueblos'* members by ensuring the free, "proportionate[] and equitabl[e]" allocation of land to them. To avoid abuses deriving from "arbitrary preferences and even unjustifiable speculation," political authorities and district judges (or local ones they entrusted) should be present in disentailment processes and title deliveries.

Finally, the notice of May 12, 1890[20] urged governors to promote the conversion of all corporate lands (except population centers and those necessary for public services) into private property as soon as possible, partly on the grounds of "the high sentiments of the suffering and hard-working indigenous class."

Enclosures of Public Lands

Díaz's government strongly pushed for prompt privatization of public lands. On December 15, 1883, it enacted the Law of Colonization, which endorsed the government's authority to establish contracts with private companies for the surveying and valuing of public lands, as well as for the transportation of settlers. Companies would obtain one-third of the lands but could only sell up to 2,500 hectares. Fragmented lands would be sold or freely allocated to settlers by the state. Survey operations had to be authorized by federal district judges, and local judges would adjudicate controversies.

Public land privatization skyrocketed thereafter (Holden 1994: 9). Though the law allowed for the suspension of surveying procedures pending a challenge before courts, it did not clarify the conditions under which an opponent could

---

[18] Presidential Regulatory Decree of April 20, 1878, "For the allocation of coounity terrains," available in Dublán and Lozano (2004: Tome 13, pp. 501–503).

[19] *Secretaría de Fomento, Circular* of October 28, 1889, "On the intervention of district judges in the delivery of titles in the fractionalization of ejidos," available in Dublán and Lozano (2004: Tome 19, p. 761).

[20] *Secretaría de Gobernación, Circular* of May 12, 1890, addressed to state governors "so that ejidos and *terrenos de común repartimiento* of *pueblos* are reduced to individual property," available in Dublán y Lozano (2004: Tome 20, p. 107).

prevail. Hence, the question of whether possessed lands could be surveyed – which had been solved under Juárez – seemed again open to interpretation. A 1778 order of the Secretaría de Fomento addressed to the Governor of Chiapas and grounded on several files concerning non-disentailed *ejidos* lands that were being denounced stated that the latter should be fragmented and divided up among villagers if they had already been surveyed, or otherwise first surveyed and then fragmented and divided.[21] That seemed to resolve the long-lasting doubt about whether *ejidos* should be fragmented (Knowlton 1998: 84) before the above cited general notice of 1889, but it also allowed survey procedures to take place in occupied lands, with uncertain results for disputed lands. In the notice of October 28, 1889, the *Secretaría de Fomento* established that the Ministry of Treasury should initiate disentailment processes against *ejidos* and other still-entailed lands before local authorities, making sure that public vacant lands were not unduly occupied or distributed among villagers.

Thus, while the central government showed some concern for the situation of indigenous people, it promoted disentailment as the main solution, and it clarified that occupied lands with unclear titles should be considered public and hence not distributed among indigenous occupants. The government also drastically expanded privatization incentives. The law of March 26, 1894,[22] lifted size limitations to land allocations and to sales by survey companies, and it waived the duty to cultivate allocated lands. The law further stated that prior violations to these conditions would no longer be penalized. Ill-acquired lands and titles could not be reclaimed or revised. They could actually be legalized by their recording in the Registry of Property, also created by the law.

Still, the law recognized some limited space for the protection of indigenous lands. Though it endorsed corporations' incapacity to hold property and prompted state authorities to continue disentailment, it recognized *pueblos'* right to request the allocation of possessed lands and their authorities' legal capacity to defend communal terrains from illegal claims and to carry out disentailment. But the government kept enforcement in the hands of local authorities, and claims of abuses kept rising.

As opposition to his regime increased, Díaz attempted more energetic measures to address abuses. In 1901, he promoted an amendment to Section 27 of the Constitution to attenuate the prohibition of corporate property, which exempted the lands necessary for the sustenance of corporations. In 1909, he even ordered the suspension of public land sales and the revision of delimitations made so far (Wilkie 1998).

---

[21] Supreme order of the *Secretaría de Fomento* to the Governor of Chiapas of March 26, 1878, available in Government of Mexico (1885: 32–34). Knowlton (1998: 87–88) also refers to three similarly aimed orders of the *Secretaría de Fomento* to the Governor of Sonora of November 16, 1880, January 7, 1882, and November 17, 1885.

[22] Law on the Occupation and Alienation of Public Vacant Lands of the United States of Mexico, available in Dublán and Lozano (2004, Tome 24: 36–45).

Thus, Díaz's attitude toward indigenous lands was different from that of prior governments, since he strongly promoted the enforcement of disentailment and privatization laws, despite the increased abuses they produced. However, Díaz also insisted that the laws were supposed to benefit indigenous people, and hence left some room for protections, which he tried to expand as abuses became too evident. These attempts were belated, since the Mexican Revolution erupted in 1910, strongly supported by peasants aggrieved by land dispossessions (Saffon 2015, n.d.).

Before that, however, indigenous protests were scarce under the Porfiriato.[23] This was likely the result of higher fear of repression but also of the belief that the laws still left a space for indigenous people to claim the protection of their rights. As Saffon (2015, n.d.) shows, this belief is illustrated by the more than one thousand requests for land titles copies that indigenous groups made before the National General Archive with the purpose of using them in court.[24]

JUDICIAL CASES AND THE MOTIVATIONS FOR SELECTIVE ENFORCEMENT

As the previous discussion shows, liberal governments (especially Díaz's) favored economic elites interested in accumulating lands by adopting and pushing the enforcement of laws ordering the disentailment of indigenous lands and the privatization of public ones. However, they neither explicitly abrogate nor violate indigenous land rights, insistent as they were on the benefits the laws would have for the poor. Abuses, hence, likely came mainly from local political elites, who were in charge of solving many land disputes and possibly influenced by local economic elites. Of course, national elites were responsible by omission, insofar as they did not consistently control abuses. Such responsibility accrued as the standoffish attitude of the first liberal governments vis-à-vis indigenous lands was replaced by the active encouragement of enforcement under the Porfiriato despite increasing abuses.

What role did judges play in this scenario? Mexico's writ of *amparo*[25] provides a unique opportunity to study judicial enforcement, since claims of rights violations could be brought before federal district courts and were revised ex officio by the Supreme Court, which published most decisions.[26] But *amparos* are also

[23] Reina (1980) identified only nine protests in the more than thirty years of Porfirian rule, and most occurred in the first two years.

[24] Many such claims explicitly stated the purpose of initiating legal action. On the use of courts by indigenous people, see also Knight (1986); Knowlton (1990); Escobar-Ohmstede (1993); Marino (2006, 2016); Ávila-Espinosa (2010).

[25] The *amparo* is a special writ for the protection of rights that originated in Mexico and is now prevalent throughout Latin America (Brewer-Carías 2009). It featured in the short-lived Constitutive and Reform Act of 1847 and was reintroduced in the 1857 liberal constitution.

[26] For prior studies of *amparo* cases on property, see, among others, Knowlton (1990, 1998); James (2013); Marino (2016). We benefitted from these studies.

a rich source through which to examine the politics of institutional enforcement by other authorities, given that claims could be made against state authorities of any type and level – administrative and judicial, local, state, and federal – and entailed the interpretation of regulations by courts.

In what follows we offer a preliminary and exploratory study of all *amparos* concerning land conflict cases published by the Supreme Court of Justice between 1870 and 1910. The study can help understand both the interaction between the different enforcers of liberal land laws and the motivations behind enforcement.

As noted, the federal government enacted a bundle of legal rules ordering the disentailment of some types of corporate property and the privatization of public lands. While some of these rules were constitutional and statutory, others were administrative (like *circulares*). The latter can be considered a first stage of enforcement. However, all these rules left important gaps to be interpreted, which were so at a second-order stage of enforcement carried out by local administrative and judicial authorities when implementing land disentailment and privatization procedures. At a third-order stage of enforcement, if an *amparo* was filed, procedures were reviewed by the federal judiciary, which at once determined whether rights violations had occurred and offered authoritative interpretations of the laws involved.

At each of these levels, we can try to capture selective enforcement and unravel its political motivations by examining the type of right holders that were privileged and affected. Access to federal courts was formally open to petitioners throughout the country, though important material barriers existed. Petitioners could file *amparo* writs in the nearest federal district court, each state having at least one. In urgent cases, litigants were authorized to file by telegraph and to appoint informal counsel. As Map 9.1 shows, our land-related cases are spread out across states and districts, suggesting that state capacity was above a minimum both for local authorities – who were sued, and hence acted, in diverse localities – and for federal district judges – who decided cases even in remote areas of the territory.

Albeit imperfect, judicial cases provide interesting indicators of enforcement bias, such as the type of petitioner and rate of judicial success. Within the scope of this study, the former may signal bias in access to judicial institutions if some petitioners (such as indigenous groups or individuals) bring very few suits. We divide petitioners of land conflict cases into five main types: ecclesiastical corporations, indigenous corporations (whose main type are *pueblos*), indigenous individuals (which we take to be synonymous with villagers or peasants[27]), *rancheros* or middle-income landowners, and *hacendados* or large landowners. The rate of

---

[27] By the mid-nineteenth century, in many places indigenous villages did not have a homogenous ethnic composition because of interethnic relations and conversion to Catholicism. The terms *indio*, *vecino de pueblo*, and *campesino* were often used interchangeably.

judicial success is an additional indicator of bias if certain types of petitioners are systematically more likely to win a case than other types who also access justice.

Judicial cases further allow us to inquire about the motivations of biased enforcement. We propose two basic types of motivation driving the enforcement of land laws: *interest* and *ideology*. Interest would lead enforcing authorities to favor economic elites, because by doing so they could gain material wealth or social prestige, regardless of the goals or letter of the laws. Liberal ideology, in turn, would lead enforcers to privilege individual property over corporate property, but to afford equal protection regardless of petitioners' ethnicity or class.

Disentangling the two motivations is not straightforward concerning corporate property. Perhaps ideology may lead to a zealous enforcement of land laws against both church and indigenous corporations, while interest might lead to higher enforcement against indigenous groups than the church, since the latter was a more powerful actor. Also, one can suspect interest is a motivation when the laws are overzealously enforced against indigenous corporations, as when interpretations arguably overreach the laws' scope. However, ideology, as we know, generates fervor, so those interpretations might also be ideologically-driven. Now, strictly ideological interpretations can favor powerful economic interests, and their continuous alignment to the latter makes it hard to still call them ideological.

In contrast, when we examine individual land rights, interest and ideology can be more neatly distinguished, since liberalism sought to protect *equally* the rights of rich and poor, indigenous and nonindigenous. We posit that a systematic imbalance in terms of the absence of indigenous individuals as claimants may signal bias due to interest. Similarly, a systematic refusal by local authorities to enforce the rights of individual *indigenous* petitioners could have the same motivation, and judicial decisions that endorsed those second-order decisions perhaps did so as well – even if judges were not direct beneficiaries, they could entrench the interests of the powerful.

Since local authorities were closer to, and hence more subject to influence from, local economic elites, we argue they were more likely to decide cases based on interest, i.e., with bias against poor indigenous individuals, because of the potential for obtaining economic benefits or social prestige. In contrast, federal authorities – especially those with the reputation of being more independent like the Supreme Court – were more likely to decide cases based on their members' ideology.

It is important to note that most of the cases under analysis were produced by a new Supreme Court under Díaz. In the 1877 election in which he was popularly confirmed as president, eight new justices were appointed[28] to join

---

[28] Based on the 1857 constitution, citizens voted electors who in turn chose delegates to select the court's justices.

the three who had vowed allegiance to the "plan" to depose former president Lerdo. Chief Justice Vallarta was the commanding voice of the court during this period and would have a lasting influence in ensuing decades. The ideology of justices of this court was in tune with that of previous ones. Most were part of the so-called "brilliant" liberal generation and had occupied positions in the local and federal governments (Bravo-Rodríguez 1990: 1115). They were also close to the new administration, often recurring to the then common revolving-doors practice of taking temporary leave to join executive posts. However, commentators note that at least some justices remained fairly independent from both the administration (Lara et al. 1990: 984) and state and local interests (Marino 2016: 307).

General Trends in Judicial Cases on Land Conflicts

We collected around 3,700 decisions involving land conflicts[29] that the Supreme Court issued and published in *Semanario Judicial*[30] between 1870, when this report was first published, and 1910, when Díaz was ousted by the revolution. Land conflict cases account for roughly one-quarter of the approximately sixteen thousand court decisions published in the period. Though the court heard different types of cases involving land,[31] roughly 95 percent are writs of *amparo*. Given the mandatory review of these writs by the court in this period, our dataset comprises all published decisions on them. Map 9.1 georeferences the distribution of cases – dark dots show *amparo* cases, white ones all other types. Cases were spread out across the country, and many came from regions quite distant from the capital city. However, as Figure 9.1 shows, a clear correlation exists between number of *amparo* petitions and state population.

Furthermore, we constructed a subset of decisions from four states – Michoacán, Veracruz, Estado de México, and Oaxaca – for which we gathered more fine-grained information. These states have a high rural population density, as well as a strong tradition of legal land disputes.[32]

---

[29] Our basic criterion of inclusion was that a case involved a piece of nonurban land.

[30] The *Semanario* published most Supreme Court decisions, in many cases preceded by the first-instance court decision. Due to alleged "administrative and financial reasons" that coincided with Díaz's ascension to power, the *Semanario* went out of publication from 1877 to 1880. Still, *amparo* decisions rendered during these years appeared in such specialized magazines as *El foro* and *El derecho* (Martínez-Godínez 2009: 7) and were commented on by some authors. We resort to those sources for the period.

[31] E.g., decisions on allocation of public lands made by federal district courts in first instance and reviewed by the Supreme Court and *casación* appeals decisions on ordinary civil and criminal cases.

[32] See Knowlton (1990) for Michoacán; Kourí (2004) for Veracruz; Marino (2006) and Falcón (2015) for Estado de México; Mendoza-García (2011); Reina (2013) for Oaxaca.

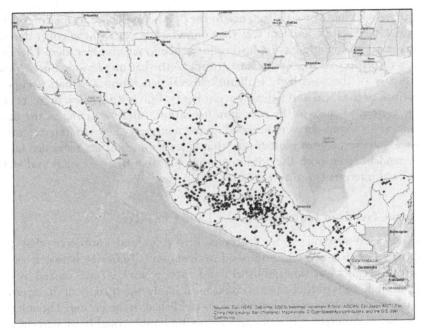

MAP 9.1. Judicial cases on land conflicts by type of case (1871–1877, 1881–1910).
Note: Georeferenced using data coded from *Semanario Judicial*.

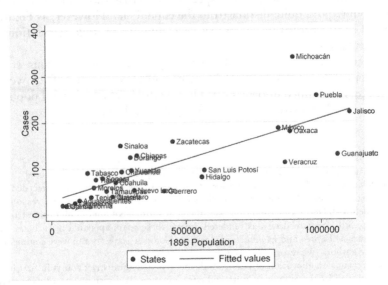

FIGURE 9.1. *Amparo* petitions (1871–1877, 1881–1910) and population (1895).

TABLE 9.1. *Writs of* amparo *concerning land rights conflicts (type 1) per decade by type of conflict and petitioner*

Period	Type of Case			Type of Petitioner		
	Dispossession	Other Property Cases	Total	*Pueblos*	*Haciendas*	Total
1871–1877	50 (86%)	8 (14%)	58	2 (17%)	10 (83%)	12
1881–1890	195 (75%)	65 (25%)	260	3 (25%)	9 (75%)	12
1891–1900	292 (64%)	166 (36%)	458	6 (8%)	67 (92%)	73
1901–1910	694 (42%)	952 (58%)	1646	14 (6%)	214 (94%)	228
TOTAL	1,231 (51%)	1,191 (49%)	2422	25 (8%)	300 (92%)	325

We classified land *amparo* cases into two main types: (1) cases in which the conflict was mainly about the ownership, possession, or use of land; and (2) cases in which land rights were secondary in the dispute (e.g., inheritances and mortgages). Type 1 cases correspond to around 70 percent of *amparo* cases. As Table 9.1 (first column) shows, half involved an alleged land dispossession – i.e., a claim that the land occupied by the petitioner was illegally or wrongfully seized by another.

Type of Petitioners and Rate of Success

Most *amparo* petitioners in the large dataset (65 percent) were individuals or groups with respect to whom we cannot tell whether they were rich or poor or whether they belonged to a *pueblo*. Focusing on the subset of cases from Michoacán, Veracruz, Estado de México, and Oaxaca allows us to reduce unidentified petitioners to around 30 percent, so results concern them. *Pueblos* are rare petitioners – 4 percent of total petitions. We do not find cases concerning ecclesiastical corporations. The remaining petitioners are members of indigenous villages who file individually or in a small group of aggrieved persons (12 percent), *hacendados* (6 percent), and, in the largest category, *rancheros* and other owners or possessors of small or medium plots of land (46 percent).

In terms of success rate, all petitioners seem to prevail in a relatively similar proportion, except perhaps for individual members of *pueblos*, who win a bit more often – though the difference is not significant. Table 9.2 summarizes this.

Collective Petitioners

Even though they do not seem to fare worse in trial than others, the extremely small percentage of *pueblos* who accessed justice is a pretty clear evidence of bias.[33] It stands in sharp contrast to the large number of grievances villages

---

[33] Our discussion of the court's cases greatly benefitted from Knowlton (1990, 1996); Cabrera Acevedo (1990); González-Navarro (1990); James (2013).

TABLE 9.2. Amparo *petitioners from four states at the Supreme Court*

Petitioner	Cases	% Wins
Pueblos/Indigenous Collectively	27 (4%)	48
Indigenous Individuals	74 (12%)	66
Haciendas	36 (6%)	44
Rancheros	294 (46%)	55
Unidentified Individual Possessors	193 (30%)	49
Other	15 (2%)	

had and their expressed interest in bringing them to justice. This is not just the result of state capacity, organizational weakness, or lack of entitlement, given that members of *pueblos* did reach courts and that *pueblos* showed a strong collective action capacity since colonial times not only by protesting (Reina 1980), but also by frequently petitioning state authorities (Ruiz 2010; Saffon 2015, n.d.; Franco-Vivanco 2018). Liberal land laws, regulations, and interpretations reserved a space for indigenous collective land rights to continue being protected, so it was quite plausible for villages to believe they could have their day in court.

Villages' restricted access to courts seems to have been the result of the Supreme Court's far-reaching interpretations against corporate ownership, establishing not only that indigenous groups could not hold property, but also that they had ceased to exist as legal entities and were thus forbidden to even petition in court. Though the court's stance had a firm grounding in liberal ideology, it could be suspected to favor the interests of the rich, since it was not indisputably based on legal text, it was only consolidated under the export boom, and it was maintained even after its negative effects on indigenous individuals were acknowledged.

Before the Díaz administration, petitions involving the protection of collective land had received a mixed reaction by courts, but *pueblos* were surely authorized to litigate as corporations. In 1872, the Supreme Court granted a petition by the representative of all the dwellers of the *pueblo* of San Lorenzo Ixtacoyotla (in Hidalgo), who claimed the state had ordered the transfer of vast tracts of land they had bought in 1713 to a single person.[34] Both the district court and the court found the dwellers deeds' valid and sided with petitioners, saying that the state had wrongly reallocated the lands.

In contrast, in a case from 1875, a representative of most villagers of Charo (in Michoacán) claimed that the villagers had bought their lands in 1705 from

[34] Supreme Court of Justice of Mexico (hereafter SCJM), March 18, 1872.

Spanish royalty, and that their common lands had been duly disentailed, but a *jefe político* had given the land not subject to disentailment to other people. The court tersely denied the petition, claiming, as it had done in a few other cases,[35] that the Constitution's Section 27 banned corporations from holding property. The court ignored the petitioners' argument that the lands were not subject to disentailment.[36]

The faint hope *pueblos* could have in courts evaporated after Díaz reached power. The court adopted a stance against indigenous corporations that was *more royalist than the king's*. Its anticollective decisions became both more uniform and far reaching. They were often accompanied by an explicitly individualistic rationale that seemed largely absent before. And the court began to systematically deny *pueblos'* legal standing, closing most if not all available legal avenues for collective property to be defended.

The first relevant case (*Servín de Capetillo*) was decided in January 1879. It revolved around a decision from a local authority in Estado de México to grant a *pueblo*'s petition to demarcate the land it had been granted in 1680, with notice to external neighbors.[37] A neighbor protested the demarcation and the court sided with her, saying that the demarcation was not "innocent," since its aim was to extend the *pueblo*'s lands. The court noted that both the Constitution and the legislation prohibited corporations from holding property beyond their *fundo legal*, and that the land had to be transferred to village neighbors. A year later, however, in a case involving the *pueblo* of Tiripetío (in Michoacán), the court treated petitioners complaining about a dispossession as commoners under the law, showing that the court's criteria were not yet fully settled.[38]

Two years later, the court announced a string of decisions deepening the individualistic foundation of *Servín*. In January 1882, Chief Justice Vallarta wrote a long opinion joining the court's decision to deny a petition filed by the villagers of Chicontepec (in Veracruz) against a *jefe político*'s alleged dispossession of the land they had recently bought under the legal form of a "cattlemen's association" (*asociación de ganaderos*), a form they claimed was not prohibited by the Constitution.[39] Vallarta decried the fact that "perpetual" corporations could exist, regardless of their name. He was baffled that indigenous people attempted to circumvent the rules by resorting to other legal forms. He remarked that, far from depriving indigenous members of their land, the disentailment rules both preserved and ensured that the land would become fruitful to exploit "under the tutelage of individual interest." For the justice, the elimination of indigenous corporations and entailed lands

[35] SCJM, December 5, 1871.
[36] SCJM, June 1, 1875.
[37] SCJM, January 9, 1879, cited in Marino (2016: 294).
[38] SCJM, January 14, 1880, cited in Cabrera Acevedo (1990: 145).
[39] SCJM, January 9, 1882.

could only "favor the most underprivileged classes" – i.e., the indigenous, "an unfortunate race worthy of better luck" – even if they had not asked for the parceling of the land. The court applied a similar rationale in other cases, including a decision from 1883 involving an "agricultural association" in Totoltepec (Estado de México).[40]

However, the most striking disavowal of collective property resulted from the court's decisions concerning corporations' standing to litigate. *Pueblos'* ability to grieve their concerns through the filing of *amparos* and other actions was a basic element of their capacity both to defend themselves and to protect villagers' *individual* property from external encroachments, which might result from the disentailment process or the application of public land laws. Preventing *pueblos* from appearing before a judge would have enormous social and political repercussions.

In an 1882 decision involving the Techuchulco community (in Estado de México),[41] a set of villagers petitioned that a legal action initiated against them by a neighboring *pueblo* be deemed void because the *pueblo* should not be authorized to litigate. By unanimity, the court denied the petition, saying that the legal action had been initiated thirty years earlier, before the enactment of the disentailment law. But, two months later, the court announced a firmer criterion against standing. Several villagers of Santiago Mitlatongo (in Oaxaca) filed an *amparo* in their individual capacity complaining about an authorization given to a neighboring *pueblo* to demarcate the land it possessed.[42] In his concurring opinion, Chief Justice Vallarta reiterated the liberal mantra that corporations could not hold property, and further argued that individual petitioners were authorized to litigate. It was the authorization to the *pueblo* seeking to demarcate the land that was legally wanting. Vallarta claimed that indigenous communities could not appear before a judge to defend the individual property rights of their members or even to promote the disentailment of their lands, which would eventually lead to their disappearance. Corporations could not do on behalf of others what they could not do on their behalf. It was up to individual villagers to exercise their rights, including the right to ask for the parceling and allotment of village lands. While he acknowledged both that there were conflicting views on the matter and the serious collective action problems this might entail, Vallarta insisted that the spirit of the Reform demanded the immediate disappearance of corporations. And, contrary to critics who said the Constitution only prohibited certain forms of collective property but did not prevent *pueblos* from resorting to courts, Vallarta replied that corporations had the absolute civil incapacity death produces.

[40] SCJM, August 16, 1883.
[41] SCJM, January 11, 1882.
[42] SCJM, March 18, 1882, cited in González-Navarro (1990: 1080) and Cabrera Acevedo (1990: 581).

A wrong way to interpret this judgment would be to claim that, by making it more difficult to divide land, the court was defending the persistence of collective property. The push for disentailment was already strong, so if *pueblos* as collectives did not promote it, someone within or outside the community would – possibly with interests at odds with those of the community. The decision put *pueblos* at the mercy of strong *hacendados* and unscrupulous local authorities, and Vallarta himself partly recognized it.

Later in 1882, the court decided a writ filed by the villages of San Bartolomé Tepetitlán and San Francisco Sayula (in Hidalgo) against a decision by a local judge in an action petitioners had brought against an *hacienda* alleging dispossession.[43] Petitioners attempted to show that they were not one of the corporations the Constitution forbade to hold property. The court denied the petition, again with a long opinion by Vallarta. The opinion argued, first, that the *pueblos* had not complied with state legislation requiring authorization from the executive to litigate, and that this authorization could never have been given anyway, since *pueblos* did not have legal standing. While Vallarta recognized the "countless abuses" committed against the "unfortunate race" of indigenous people, such abuses did not allow communities to preserve stagnant property or "resuscitate the dead person" of the community. It was up to each member of the former community to bring action.

The court's case law was so pernicious for indigenous corporations that, as we saw, it led Díaz himself to promote a law in 1894, which, despite legalizing irregular land transfer operations, authorized corporations to litigate. Possibly as a result, cases involving *pueblos* and *ayuntamientos* (locality governments) increased (see Table 9.1). But there were still few of them, and they were confined to the discussion of relatively marginal issues regarding *fundos legales*. For most intents and purposes, the court's case law had fulfilled its own prophecy that *pueblos* were dead, or at least seriously ill.

Individual Petitioners

The court's restrictive stance in cases of indigenous groups was not mirrored in cases of individual indigenous petitioners. From the numbers above, it is not possible to know whether these petitioners suffered from bias in access. Though only 12 percent of petitioners in our subsample were recognized as indigenous villagers, it is possible that some of the owners or possessors of individual terrains (*rancheros*) and of unidentified petitioners also were. Indigenous individual petitioners received considerably better treatment in *amparo* cases than *pueblos*. Compatible with the winning rates depicted above, the court's case law was quite protective of their interests. By underscoring due process and legality

[43] SCJM, November 9, 1882, cited in Cabrera Acevedo (1990: 582).

constraints and the prohibition of land seizures without compensation,[44] the court time and again brought to a halt the actions of local authorities that resulted in dispossession of individual units of land.

While the types of cases the court dealt with were manifold, there were trends. Many challenged a local or state authority's decision to allocate a petitioner's possessed land to a third person under the justification that the authority was distributing a village's disentailed land, that the land was public and could be privatized, or that levied taxes on the land had been left unpaid.[45] In most cases, the court ruled that, given the petitioner's opposition, the administrative authority lacked jurisdiction to decide on the issue, which had to be adjudicated by an ordinary judge. Other cases involved complaints of dispossession resulting from a civil court's proceeding entailing a land allocation that did not name the petitioner as party and hence deprived her from exercising opposition. In many occasions, the court concluded that such proceedings had been irregular, halting the allocation.

While it is unlikely that all decisions by state and local authorities were a function of their direct interest or alliances with local elites, many probably were. Some decisions offer stark examples. In an 1898 case from Oaxaca, a series of municipal officials petitioned a court for their release from jail. They claimed they had been thrown in there because of their opposition to a local judge's decision to illegally adjudicate a plot of land to...himself. The court sided with the petitioners.[46] In a case from Campeche decided in 1908, a peasant claimed that a local judge, who was his neighbor, ordered him to destroy a fence protecting his cultivated land. The court also sided with the petitioner.[47] In a case from 1906, a peasant claimed that a neighbor, who was a relative of the municipality's mayor, had built a well in the petitioner's property. The Supreme Court again sided with the petitioner.[48]

The court's active protection of individual villagers' rights was likely a corollary of its displayed hostility toward corporate property and legal standing.

[44] These rights were enshrined in Sections 14, 16, and 27 of the 1857 constitution. According to James (2013: xvi), the first two were the most often litigated rights in *amparos* before the revolution.

[45] SCJM decision dates include the following: March 25, 1872; June 11, 1884; December 17, 1885; June 6, 1887; February 2, 1889; November 12, 1890; December 11, 1893; June 23, 1894; February 8, 1895; June 27, 1896; November 23, 1898; March 4, 1899; March 15, 1900; July 15, 1901; March 12, 1902; May 29, 1903; September 17, 1903; May 10, 1904; March 23, 1905; January 13, 1906; February 3, 1906; November 20, 1906; December 1, 1906; May 16, 1907; June 12, 1907; July 17, 1907; April 20, 1908; July 13, 1908; August 29, 1908; September 10, 1908; October 28, 1908; November 14, 1908; November 20, 1908; December 2, 1908; October 2, 1909; November 24, 1909.

[46] SCJM, Aust 11, 1896.

[47] SCJM, July 1, 1908.

[48] SCJM, February 3, 1906.

In several cases, villagers claimed the individual ownership or possession of small tracts of land inside *pueblos,* implicitly challenging the power of *pueblos* or higher-level municipal authorities to maintain the integrity of collective lands or to regulate their distribution. When the court ruled in their favor, it weakened corporations' power to impose internal restrictions on group members, which are vital for collective property protection and group cohesion (Kymlicka 1995).

But not all petitions raised by individual village members against authorities challenged collective ownership. In multiple cases, petitions aimed to defy these authorities' decisions to allocate collective lands to outsiders instead of villagers. They could hence be attempts to protect collective lands, or at least to preserve disentailed lands in villagers' hands, now that *pueblos* could no longer act collectively to do so. In those cases, the court's decisions might have had the unintended effect of protecting the cohesion of indigenous communities and their lands, although *pueblos'* incapacity to defend themselves left them vulnerable to subsequent dispossession.

In short, it is clear that throughout this period individual property rights were strengthening. Individual claimants appear to have prevailed, at least in court, even in the face of class and ethnic differences. When local administrators introduced selective enforcement, or outright violations of the institutional requirements, the federal courts stepped in to correct the outcome. Meanwhile, collective claimants were even denied their day in court. By the end of the period, it appears that individual property rights won out even over venal, self-interested judges and powerful local interests.

Different Types and Levels of Enforcement

Challenged Authorities

Petitioners challenged different types of authorities located at different levels through their *amparo* submissions. As Table 9.3 shows, about 55 percent of petitions targeted a state or local judge's decision (mostly in a civil action that led to what petitioner saw as dispossession), and 6 percent dealt with a nonjudicial state authority. Another 30 percent of cases revolved around decisions from an *ayuntamiento* or *municipio* – that is, the local authorities under whose jurisdiction the smaller *pueblo* existed. Thus, state and (especially) local authorities were responsible for a clear majority of alleged grievances concerning dispossession.

The remaining 9 percent of cases consisted of actions by *jefes políticos*. These were district-level agents of the central and state executives (Mecham 1986: 143), who in several states had substantial powers for making land allocations and solving emerging disputes related to disentailment (Marino 2001: 41; Falcón 2015: 269). *Jefes* were used by Díaz as a power-centralizing tool (Guerra 1985: 110–112; Knight 1986: 24–30; Falcón 2015: 213–214) and were

TABLE 9.3. *Authorities challenged by* amparo *petitions, by courts' outcomes*

Authority Responsible for Alleged Dispossession	Cases (%)	Petitioner Prevails at Supreme Court (%)	Petitioner Prevails at District Court (%)
Ayuntamiento/ Municipio	30	60	58
State or Local Judge	55	44	41
Nonjudicial State Authorities	6	59	38
Jefe Político	9	70	62

portrayed as the most dreaded authorities under the Porfiriato. Yet *jefes* were not nearly as challenged as local and state authorities were.

Furthermore, the data show that *jefes políticos* were the authorities to whom the court was least deferential. It also showed more deference toward judicial than nonjudicial decisions both at the state and local levels.

The previous findings suggest that, apart from being a potentially useful device citizens could use to ask for prompt redress of rights violations, the *amparo* was a tool for the federal judiciary to check (and moderate the actions of) local authorities, thus contributing to institutional strengthening.[49] It was also a tool for the court to review federal district judges' decisions.

Amparo Judicial Enforcers

District courts performed fairly similarly to the Supreme Court. Of all petitions against alleged dispossession, the court granted around 53 percent, compared to the 48 percent of district courts. The lower courts and the Supreme Court agreed about 80 percent of the time. When they did not agree, the Supreme Court was slightly more protective of petitioners. In 60 percent of nonconvergent cases, the Supreme Court granted a petition a district court had denied, and in the remaining 40 percent the reverse was the case. The difference between these courts is more marked if only considering cases brought by indigenous individuals. In these cases, while both courts still agreed most of the time, when they did not, the Supreme Court was considerably more protective than district courts (the Supreme Court sided with the petitioner in 75 percent of cases of nonconvergence).

---

[49] The members of Congress who submitted the first *amparo* statute of 1861 to the floor (Mariano Riva Palacio Díaz, José Linares, and Ignacio Mariscal Fagoaga) implicitly acknowledged this by saying that the constitution provisions behind the *amparo* "give federal courts a sort of conservative or moderating power over all public authorities," quoted in Márquez (2015: 347).

These subtle but perhaps nonnegligible differences may be explained by the peculiar institutional and political role district courts played vis-à-vis the Supreme Court. District judges became politically salient during the Juárez and Lerdo administrations for their active role as judges in *amparo* proceedings (Cabrera Acevedo 1990: 42). They were likely more susceptible to the influence of local elites and authorities than the court justices were. In the words of the nineteenth-century historian Wistano Orozco, "[I]t is neither the powerful nor the big *hacendados* who have seen millions of hectares of land taken from their hands but the miserable, the ignorant, and the weak...those who cannot call a district judge, a governor or a state minister a pal (*compadre*)" (quoted in Silva-Herzog 1972).

However, district judges were perceived to be less under the sway of elites than local judges and authorities, and they were perhaps closer to the court because of the role the latter had in their appointment.[50] According to a present-day commentator, "[T]he people have had more trust in district judges, who are not subject to the power of local political bosses (*caciques*), and in the Supreme Court, which is far from the influence of local politicians" (Cabrera 1985: 191).

CONCLUSION

This overview demonstrates the process by which the institution of individual property rights strengthened in the late nineteenth and early twentieth centuries in Mexico. Starting even before Díaz came to power, but with a renewed impetus thereafter, the Mexican federal judiciary was strongly hostile to legal defenses of collective ownership, to the point of announcing an outright ban on indigenous corporations appearing before court. The extremely low number of *pueblo* petitions, partly the result of that hostility, is as telling as the Supreme Court's reticence to grant the few claims that were made. In contrast, courts were more receptive to claims involving the defense of *individual* property, which of course benefitted *hacendados* but also the property of less privileged landowners like *rancheros* and even individual members of *pueblos*. The courts, then, were a crucial mechanism for strengthening an institution that was favored by the central government.

There were, of course, pressures that could have weakened the institution through selective enforcement. The enforcement of individual rights by local and state authorities was probably biased toward the rich at the local and state levels. But the federal courts, using the *amparo* mechanism in defense of individual property rights, appear to have reined in the bias by extending to indigenous individuals the protections afforded to the rest. It seems likely that the motivation behind this strengthening was liberal ideology rather than

[50] The court sent short lists of three candidates to the country's president, who selected one.

naked self-interest, since strictly interest-based motivations probably would have led courts to decide against the poor. District courts were slightly more deferential to local authorities than was the Supreme Court in individual cases involving peasants, perhaps suggesting that they were more prone to local capture, although this is speculative, since the difference is small.

Of course, it remains possible that the rights protections afforded by the federal judiciary may not have been strong enough to shield indigenous people from land dispossessions. *Amparo* judges had no jurisdiction to verify the enforcement of their rulings. And they did not solve disputes in a definitive fashion, since rulings could only determine whether cases entailed the violation of a right by a state authority and order its redress. There are many ways, impossible to verify at this point, in which local authorities or powerful landowners could achieve an outcome like the one blocked in the *amparo* proceeding. At the same time, it is remarkable that the federal courts actually protected individual rights to that extent, regardless of class or ethnicity.

The strengthening of individual land rights, of course, came at the expense of collective ones. The end of indigenous corporations' capacity to act collectively in defense of their land made them quite vulnerable to dispossessions by the powerful. As dispossessions became more systematic, their redress became less likely, both because of the court's case law and of dispossessions' legitimation by federal legislation foreclosing judicial review. As many historians have argued, this institutional strengthening may well have been one of the powerful motivators that caused the Mexican Revolution to erupt.

10

Imported Institutions

Boon or Bane in the Developing World?

Andrew Schrank

A substantial body of literature holds that imported institutions are innately inferior to their indigenous counterparts (Evans 2004; Rodrik 2007; Weyland 2009; Stiglitz 2013), and developing country civil service laws have frequently been invoked by way of example. Civil service laws that are adopted at the behest of foreign powers are at best likely to go unenforced, the literature implies, and at worst likely to insulate not the "specially trained officials" (Gerth and Mills 1946: 370) anticipated by Max Weber but their ill-qualified predecessors (Shepherd 2003; Longo 2005; Schuster 2012).

Are imported institutions really likely to bomb or backfire in this way? I address the question by examining data on the recruitment and management of the inspectors responsible for the enforcement of labor and employment law in the Dominican Republic (DR) and find no cause for concern. While the Dominicans responded to foreign pressure by abandoning partisan for merit-based recruitment in the 1990s, and did so under duress, they have nonetheless come to embrace the reforms, and by all accounts boast a model meritocracy today. The Ministry of Labor (Ministerio de Trabajo) has not only been portrayed as the "exception to the rule" (ALEPH SA 2002: 32) in the otherwise patrimonial DR but has been dispatching representatives to neighboring countries that are undertaking reforms of their own.[1] And I therefore conclude by discussing the conditions under which imported institutions are likely to succeed or fail and underscoring the importance of stakeholder influence, agency size, and the status and organization of the civil servants themselves, on the one hand, and the tension between personal loyalties that help "activate"

---

[1] "Rafael Alburquerque dice que sistema inspecciones de Trabajo, evita la corrupción e incompetencia," *Diario dominicano*, March 1, 2008. See also Díaz (2010); Nuñez (2011); Gomera (2012).

(Brinks, Levitsky, and Murillo, Chapter 1, this volume) civil service laws in an unfavorable context and the "impersonal commitments" (Rueschemeyer 2005: 154) that provide their raison d'être, on the other. While personal loyalties are both "in limited supply" and "at odds with the impersonal meritocratic standards" (Rueschemeyer 2005: 145) that underpin the Weberian model of bureaucracy, according to Dietrich Rueschemeyer, they are no less necessary when institutions are homegrown than when they are imported or imposed by foreign powers, and the Dominican experience thus speaks to the vulnerability not of imported institutions but of *all* institutions that tie the hands of the very officials who are – directly or indirectly – responsible for their enforcement. Whether they are imported or indigenous in origin, I argue, institutions that are designed to check the authority of public officials require at least the tacit support of their stakeholders and subjects. Otherwise they will produce little more than a "feedback loop of institutional weakness" (Elkins 2017) marked by replacement and noncompliance.

I have divided the paper into five principal sections. First, in "Intellectual Context," I discuss the debate over imported institutions, in general, and imported civil service laws, in particular. While the international financial institutions (IFIs) echo Weber by portraying civil service reform as a bulwark against corruption and incompetence, their critics worry that – in the absence of local ownership – civil service laws will at best go unenforced and at worst be used to protect unethical or ineffectual officials from discipline or dismissal. Second, in "Case Selection," I treat the Dominican labor inspectorate as a particularly demanding test of institutional importation. After all, the island nation has traditionally been hostile to meritocracy (Lundahl and Vedovato 1989; Longo 2005), and the Dominicans reformed their principal workplace regulatory agency at the behest of the United States in the 1990s – amidst concerns that by doing so prematurely they "could conceivably end up complicating public-sector efficiency, rather than improving it, given the kinds of workers who would be guaranteed security of tenure" (Hartlyn 1998: 207). Third, in "Longitudinal Data Analysis," I highlight the success of the reform and discount the risk of "tenure protections for patronage appointees" (Schuster 2012: 10) by examining longitudinal data on individual inspectors. I find that in the aftermath of civil service reform in the early 1990s, ill-qualified incumbents were decidedly less likely to be promoted, and decidedly more likely to leave the agency, than their professional counterparts. Fourth, in "Discussion," I ask why the "merit trap" (Shepherd 2003; Schuster 2012) failed to take hold in the DR and highlight one proximate and four distal causes. While Labor Minister Rafael Alburquerque initially recruited meritorious applicants who were to some extent familiar to him, and thus combined meritocracy with loyalty, he was able to institutionalize the reforms by taking advantage of: first, the externalization of monitoring by foreign stakeholders; second, the deepening of democracy – and corresponding empowerment of educated workers – at home; third, the small size and limited resources available to the agency itself; and, fourth, the skill and solidarity of the inspectors by whom the agency was staffed. And, finally, in the chapter's conclusion, I place the Dominican inspectors in regional context and discuss the broader implications of my findings.

I want to make my aims and ambitions as clear as possible from the outset: my goal is neither to explain the enforcement model adopted by the Dominican inspectors (see Piore and Schrank 2018) nor to gauge their variable performance, but to account for the efficacy of the civil service laws that protect the inspectors' own jobs from partisan politics, and my findings are therefore of theoretical as well as policy import. They not only call into question the by now hackneyed "celebration of the local" (Herring 1999: 14; Kiely 1999: 30; Tendler 2002a: 3) in development policy making but blur the boundaries between and among the concepts of "political choice," "lack of capacity," and "societal cooperation" that are central to this volume's treatment of nonenforcement (Brinks, Levitsky, and Murillo, Chapter 1, this volume). After all, the apparent *lack of capacity* that ensured the nonenforcement of Dominican *labor law* in the late twentieth century was itself a product of a *political choice* regarding the nonenforcement of *civil service law* in the DR more generally, and when the Dominicans at long last began to apply the civil service law in their labor ministry in the early twenty-first century, they required not only a *choice*, in the conventional sense of the word, but a broader process of *social cooperation* (and conflict) that was itself an unintended consequence of myriad choices made by many actors in distinct ministries (e.g., trade, industry, agriculture, education, etc.), constituencies (e.g., activist groups, political parties), and even countries (e.g., the United States as well as the DR) over many years. What the Dominican story highlights, therefore, is less a one-off lesson in institution building than the innate tension between individual self-interest, on the one hand, and social norms, on the other. "Any institution-building requires orientations which transcend individual rational-instrumental behavior," argued Rueschemeyer (1986: 59). Otherwise, rational principals would be unwilling to tie their hands by delegating their authority to their agents in the bureaucracy, and rational agents would be loath to trust their principals when they promised to reward short-run loyalty with long-run security. The puzzle thereby produced involves complex motivations, as well as collective behaviors and feedback loops, that we can only begin to understand in the abstract – but they are not necessarily more complicated for their importation.

INTELLECTUAL CONTEXT

Institutional importation involves the transfer of a "model or practice" (Badie 2000: 91) from one country to another. It tends to occur at the behest of foreign powers or donors, and observers therefore discuss a continuum from voluntary to coercive transfer (Dolowitz and Marsh 1996; Benson and Jordan 2011; Takao 2014). In theory, of course, a transfer could be *entirely* voluntary or coercive; in practice, however, most cases "fall somewhere in the middle of the spectrum" (Dolowitz 1993: 103).

The administrative reforms championed by the international donor community provide a classic example. They are based on a "Western, Weberian" (Badie 2000: 141) template that offers qualified officials "secure positions of employment" in exchange for dedicated service. They "rationalize" public administration by decoupling official career paths from personal or political affiliations. And they are the price developing countries pay for aid, trade preferences, and legitimacy. "Where instead promotions are personalized or politicized," the World Bank explains, "civil servants worry more about pleasing their superiors or influential politicians, and efforts to build prestige through tough recruitment standards are undercut" (World Bank 1997: 93; see also World Bank 1993: 175).

The merits of meritocracy have nonetheless been questioned by critics who worry that civil service laws that are adopted under duress will at best go unenforced and at worst be used to protect incompetent officials from discipline or dismissal. For instance, Christian Schuster worries that politicians and public officials have an incentive "to hijack civil service reforms – frequently sponsored by donors and civil society actors – to orient them toward enhanced job stability through tenure protections," and goes on to bemoan the risk of a "merit trap" when "reforms designed to enhance bureaucratic capacity end up enhancing bureaucratic autonomy of appointees (from dismissal) only" (Schuster 2012: 10; see also Badie 2000; Shepherd 2003; Klingner and Arellano Gault 2006, esp. pp. 71–72; Parrado and Salvador 2011, esp. p. 707).

Nor is Schuster alone. Others worry not only that merit-based practices will be "circumvented in favor of procedures that allow employment for reasons of patronage or personal trust" (Shepherd and Valencia 1996: 14) but that the most qualified public officials will defect to the private sector in search of better pay and benefits over time (Armstrong and Matsuda 2003: 3; Bertucci 2007: 4). "Pay offered by international organizations may also affect the incentives of public sector officials," explains Marie Chêne, "and contribute to the brain drain of the most competent civil servants" (Chêne 2009: 3).

Concerns about institutional transfer are by no means limited to civil service reform, however, for the scholarly literature is skeptical about the prospects for cross-cultural learning and mimicry more generally. While modernizers like Peter the Great, Kemal Atatürk, and the architects of the Meiji Restoration have been portrayed as inveterate importers of Western models and methods (Lewis 1961; Gerschenkron 1962; Dore 1973; Skocpol 1979; Westney 1987), they have simultaneously been dismissed as exceptions to a rule acknowledged by dozens of historians and social scientists.[2] "Countries are simply too different, economically, legally, politically, and culturally to make fruitful policy borrowing a serious possibility," in the words of Martin De Jong and his colleagues (De Jong et al. 2007: 5). "If they differ too much from one another, even ambitious policy actors in the recipient country who actively attempt such an adoption, will run into incompatibility and incongruence which make the transfer impossible or even deleterious."

The alleged sources of incompatibility and incongruence are cultural as well as material, and Alejandro Portes portrays the long-neglected concept of social roles as the key to their interpretation and analysis.[3] Consider, for example, the differences between formally similar roles in fundamentally different societies. "That of 'policeman' may entail, in less developed societies, the expectation to compensate paltry wages with bribe taking, a legitimate preference for kin and friends over strangers in the discharge of duties, and skills that extend no further than using firearms and readily clubbing civilians at the first sign of trouble" (Portes 2006: 243). When "modernizers" try to professionalize the police officer's role, therefore, they will run into opposition not only from the officers and their kin, who have come to expect and – perhaps depend upon – payoffs and preferential treatment, but from public officials and their allies, who have come to treat the police force less as a public service provider than as their personal militia.

Portes has carried out the bulk of his empirical research in Latin America, and his fears are widely shared in the region. After all, Latin America bears the scars of a number of debatable imports, including French legal codes that by all accounts work better at home than abroad (Merryman 1996; Beck, Dmirgüç-Kunt, and Levine 2003; Berkowitz, Pistor, and Richard, 2003a; LaPorta, Lopez-de-Silanes, and Shleifer 2008; Kogut 2012); presidential regimes that are prone to gridlock in the United States and *golpes* – which were replaced by presidential resignations and impeachments after democratization – south of the border (Loewenstein 1949; Mainwaring 1990; Helmke 2010; Maeda 2010; Helmke, this volume); human rights that are valued on paper and violated in practice (cf. Falleti, this volume; Htun and Jensenius, this volume;

---

[2] For instance, Theda Skocpol and Ellen Kay Trimberger noted that in the run-up to modernization neither Russia, Turkey, nor Japan "had been incorporated into a colonial empire" (Skocpol and Trimberger 1977–78: 107). Cyril Black found that "their capacity to mobilize skills and resources" (Black 1975: 483) was – perhaps for that very reason (Black 1978: 414) – all but unparalleled among non-Western societies. And Samuel Huntington maintained that Peter and Atatürk – if not the Meiji oligarchs – nonetheless "created 'torn countries,' unsure of their cultural identity" (Huntington 1996: 35).

[3] See also Falleti (2018) on the "internalization of routines or practices perceived as legitimate" in this volume.

as well as Rosenberg 1992; Hathaway 2002); and a Washington Consensus – codified by a British expatriate, no less (Edwards 2010: 65) – that has proven disappointing to supporters and critics alike (Kuczynski and Williamson 2003; Serra and Stiglitz 2008; Babb 2013). Experts on the region are therefore beginning to abandon the idea of "blueprints" and "best practices" for aphorisms like "one size doesn't fit all," "there are no silver bullets," and "local solutions to local problems" (Pritchett and Woolcock 2002; Evans 2004; Devlin and Morguillansky 2012; Pritchett et al. 2012; Shearer and Tres 2013).

Indigenous institutions are by no means silver bullets, however, and their proponents have arguably gone too far in their efforts both to distinguish them from their "imported" counterparts and to discredit the latter, for most institutions are – to one degree or another – imported (Mamadouh, De Jong, and Lalenis 2003: 278), and Latin American history is replete with examples of the adaptation of foreign models to local context. Examples would include Saint-Simonian development banks (Glade 1989: 45), German approaches to vocational education and training (Weinstein 1990: 390–391), and arguably liberalism itself (Negretto and Aguilar-Rivera 2000: 366). The question, therefore, is less "to import or not to import" than "what to import, whether and how to adapt, and what explains success and failure?"

CASE SELECTION

The Dominican effort to recruit and retain professional labor inspectors offers an ideal opportunity to address these questions, and to test the merit-trap thesis in particular, for the island nation plays host to a traditionally patrimonial polity (Lundahl and Vedovato 1989; Hartlyn 1998; Iacoviello and Zuvanic 2006); the Dominicans adopted their reforms not of their own accord but at the behest of the United States Trade Representative (USTR) (Méndez 1993; Frundt 1998; Murillo and Schrank 2005; Schrank 2009); and they did so sequentially, and thereby allowed for the direct comparison of professional recruits and partisan incumbents over time. I will introduce the Dominican reforms by elaborating on each of the rationales for their study.

A Demanding Test

John Gerring holds that case studies are most convincing when they take place in demanding environments that make their predictions "risky" (Gerring 2007: 236), or unlikely to occur if their theoretical priors are wrong, and the DR offers proponents of civil service reform a particularly demanding test. After all, the Dominican public sector has been marked by "personalism and patronage" (Franks 1997: 4). Patronage-based parties "have shown little inclination to create permanent public positions" (Sánchez-Ancochea 2005: 715).

And Schuster himself therefore worries that the DR's formal protections will prove substantively meaningless "in a context of weak legal enforcement" (Schuster 2014: 13).

An Exogenous Shock

The merit-trap hypothesis holds that civil service reforms are most likely to backfire when they are imposed by foreign actors (Shepherd 2003; Parrado and Salvador 2011; Schuster 2012), and the Dominicans reformed their labor inspectorate not of their own volition but under the watchful eyes of US officials – who condition preferential access to their domestic market on the protection of labor rights by their trading partners. According to Henry Frundt, the USTR first came to doubt the Dominican commitment to labor rights in the late 1980s, when a series of scandals broke out in the country's export-processing zones (EPZs) and sugar plantations (Frundt 1998: 213–214), and her concerns gradually intensified over the course of the next few years, when the scandals – involving union busting in the EPZs and forced labor by Haitian migrants in the sugar industry – refused to go away. While President Joaquín Balaguer had long been able to appease his North American benefactors (see, e.g., Schrank 2003), and would do his best to allay their latest concerns, his efforts to defend his country's laws and practices would nonetheless fail to impress (Frundt 1998; Murillo and Schrank 2005), and by the early 1990s he therefore had little choice but to respond to the "imminent threat" (Hartlyn 1998: 206) of US trade sanctions by adopting new labor laws and appointing a well-regarded secretary of labor, Rafael Alburquerque, to oversee their enforcement.

Alburquerque would pursue his mandate by drawing upon Spanish, US, and World Bank support to triple the number, decentralize the administration, and rationalize the recruitment of the DR's labor inspectors. He not only adopted new recruitment criteria – including a law degree beginning in 1992 and a competitive exam in addition to a law degree beginning in 1994 (Iacoviello and Zuvanic 2006: 453; RIAL 2009: 9; see also Alburquerque 2005; MAP 2014) – but publicized the new positions, criteria, and exam dates by word of mouth, the local media, and orientation sessions in government offices (SET 2000: 10–14; BID-SET 2002: 479–483). And by the late 1990s, therefore, more than half of the 203 inspectors found in the country's thirty-six regional offices had graduated from law school; more than one-third – including two-thirds of the lawyers – had been recruited by means of a competitive exam; and approximately 85 percent had been incorporated into the country's nascent civil service (Schrank 2009: 95).

Other incorporations would follow (SET 2000: 87–88), and the Ministry of Labor would therefore go on to earn the highest marks in the country on an index of "meritocracy, performance evaluation, and risk in public

TABLE 10.1. *Labor law enforcement resources in the Dominican Republic*

Variable	Prereform (1991)	Postreform (Circa 2011–2012)
Number of Inspectors	70	201
Credentials	NA	Law degree
Recruitment Criteria	Party loyalty	Competitive examination
Mean Salary (Month)	US$75.44	US$1,232.90
Job Security	None	Civil service protection

Note: Credentials and recruitment criteria apply to new inspectors; incumbents (well under 20 percent today; see Cepeda 2008) are grandfathered into the system; attrition had reduced the number of inspectors from 203 to 201 by 2012, but the ministry recently began to fill the vacant positions.
Sources: SET (2000); Banco Central de la República Dominicana (2003); Banco Central de la República Dominicana (2013); Ministerio de Trabajo (2015); unpublished data provided by SET.

employment" (Oviedo et al. 2007: 39) applied to a sample of comparable agencies in the mid-2000s.[4]

Table 10.1 underscores the transformation of the inspectorate between 1991, when Alburquerque took over the Ministry of Labor, and 2012, when core fieldwork came to an end, and suggests that the Dominicans have pursued a textbook model of Weberian administrative reform (Heredia and Schneider 1998; Evans 2005). By offering qualified individuals attractive salaries, secure tenure, and opportunities for advancement, they hoped not only to augment the ministry's human resource base but to raise the costs and risks of misconduct – and to thereby break the vicious circle of private sector mistrust and public sector malfeasance that tends to characterize inspection regimes in patrimonial societies (World Bank 2004; Coolidge 2006). After all, the returns to inspector malfeasance are a known function of short-run bribes and payoffs. The costs of inspector malfeasance are an unknown function of expected lifetime earnings on the job multiplied by the risk of discovery and dismissal discounted by the opportunity cost of current employment. And inspectors who are well paid and confident in their career prospects are therefore likely to find malfeasance less rewarding and appealing in a relative sense than inspectors who are poorly paid and insecure.

---

[4] In an interview conducted in 2005, Alburquerque explained that the inspectors had traditionally been ill-educated political loyalists prone to extortion and fraud, and asserted that they had not imposed a single fine between the adoption of the old labor code in 1951 and the promulgation of the new one four decades later (March 9, 2005). One might wonder whether his assessment of the inspectorate he inherited in the 1990s was self-serving; however, he offered a similar assessment in the early 1980s when serving as a professor at the Autonomous University of Santo Domingo (Alburquerque 1984 [1992]: 65–66). And José Itzigsohn, who carried out a comprehensive study of labor markets in the DR in the early 1990s (Itzigsohn 2000: 21), labeled the country's regulatory institutions "predatory-repressive" at the time.

A STAGED INNOVATION

By the same token, however, the Dominicans allowed incumbent inspectors not only to keep their jobs but to be incorporated into the civil service (SET 2000: 87–88), and thereby opened the door to the merit trap. After all, the merit trap allegedly results from the coordinated machinations of partisan politicians, on the one hand, and the uncoordinated brain drain of skilled professionals, on the other, and the DR would appear to have been vulnerable to both threats, for the island nation has not only been ruled by four different presidents from three different parties since the adoption of reform but has also experienced rapid private sector growth and a corresponding demand for legal services.

Is the merit trap inevitable or avoidable and, if the latter, under what conditions? I address these questions by drawing upon two different sources of data in the next two sections of the paper: first, longitudinal data on the survival and promotion prospects of the partisan incumbents who took office prior to the onset of reform and the professional recruits by whom they were replaced between 2005 – when the reform campaign had gone far enough to protect the former and recruit the latter – and 2016, when the most recent data were made available; and, second, open-ended interviews with eighteen inspectors in eight different offices, as well as private labor lawyers, representatives of donor agencies, officers of two of the DR's three largest union confederations, the first director of the country's reformed labor inspectorate, his immediate successor, ancillary ministry officials and consultants, and former minister of labor Rafael Alburquerque, who introduced the initial reforms.[5] While the longitudinal data suggest that the partisan incumbents are more likely to leave the agency – and less likely to be promoted – than the professional recruits, the interviews illuminate a number of impediments to their survival, including the externalization of monitoring by foreign stakeholders, the deepening of democracy – and corresponding demand for good government – at home, the small size and limited patronage resources available to the agency, and the growing skill and solidarity of the inspectors themselves.

By way of prologue, therefore, I hold that civil service reforms are most likely to be effective in smaller agencies that are responsive to foreign and

---

[5] The interviews occurred in the country's two largest cities, several smaller cities, and a number of distinct agricultural zones between 2004 and 2017. They lasted anywhere from an hour to half a day, included a number of return visits to particularly informative sources, and occurred against the backdrop of interviews with more than 30 different textile and apparel exporters – as well as a number of their import-competing counterparts – that I have been carrying out continuously since 1998, as well as a broader collaborative study of labor inspectors throughout Latin America (Piore and Schrank 2018). I thank Washington González of the SET for making the quantitative data available to me, Enemencio Gomera for his technical and interpretive assistance, and my respondents for their time and insight.

domestic stakeholders, populated by skilled and/or solidary professionals, and resource poor in any event. And I thus conclude that "the development of state-society relations conducive to effective state action is not necessarily a matter of a global change in attitudes, value orientations, and understandings," as Dietrich Rueschemeyer argued, but is instead "likely to be restricted for long times to certain enclaves where groups have interests that can be served by interaction with the state as well as orientations that are compatible with such interaction" (2005: 151).

LONGITUDINAL DATA ANALYSIS

I begin by analyzing the survival prospects of partisan incumbents and professional recruits from March 2005 to February 2016 using individual-level data provided by the Ministry of Labor. Approximately two-thirds of the 203 inspectors working for the ministry in 2005 were lawyers, or "professionals," most of whom had been recruited by means of competitive exams. Almost two-thirds of the 203 inspectors found working for the ministry in 2005 were still working for the ministry in 2016 – almost invariably as inspectors or supervisors. And the professional recruits were decidedly more likely to survive the interval than their partisan predecessors (Figure 10.1).

In fact, the relative odds of *survival* were approximately five times higher for professional recruits than for partisan incumbents (OR = 5.06; p < 0.001). The odds of *promotion* were more than ten times higher for professionals who survived than for their partisan counterparts.[6] And the results would therefore seem to contradict the merit-trap hypothesis and speak to the enforcement of the DR's civil service law.

My point is not, however, to dismiss the *possibility* of a merit trap. "Most administrative reforms fail," explains Gerald Caiden (1991: 151), and they are more likely to fail when they are imported from abroad "without adequate appreciation of supporting infrastructure" (Caiden 1991: 167; see also p. 265). "Laws are changed, structures reorganized, people moved around, manuals altered, and instructions revised, but the same behavior patterns are continued" (p. 151).

The Dominican case would thus seem to constitute an exception to the rule. After all, the Dominicans not only adopted new personnel practices in the 1990s but adhered to them for more than a decade, through four different presidents from three different parties, and apparently reaped a return in terms of official behavior. In 2015, for example, their inspectors carried out 92,687 inspections (Ministerio de Trabajo 2016: 27) – almost double the 46,867 they had carried out in 2005 (SET 2005a: 9) – and the "ratio of preventive to post

---

[6] Graph not shown; analysis and graph available from author on request.

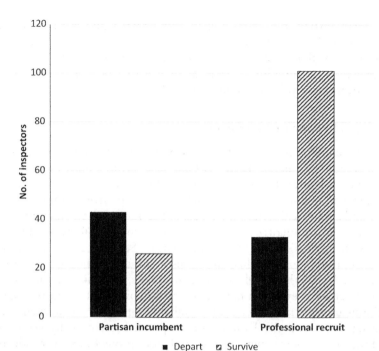

FIGURE 10.1. Inspector survival by origins, 2005–2016.
Sources: SET 2005a; Ministerio de Trabajo (2016).
Note: $X^2 = 27.6$; $p < 0.001$.

hoc (or special) inspections," which serves as an "admittedly crude indicator of the efficacy of the overall enforcement effort" (Schrank 2009: 99), had grown from 1.3 to 5.8 as well.[7]

DISCUSSION

What, then, explains the Dominican success? While the Dominicans adopted their reforms in response to a crisis, i.e., the imposition of trade-related labor standards by the United States, Rueschemeyer holds that crises are at best "triggering and facilitating factors" (Rueschemeyer 2005: 161) that demand ongoing reinforcement, and my interviews in the DR underscore his point by highlighting four additional factors: the externalization of monitoring by

---

[7] Preventive inspections are carried out at the behest of the authorities. They are targeted at high-risk employers of vulnerable workers who would be unlikely to come forward on their own, and are considered "best practices" in the field. Insofar as preventive inspections are designed to render post hoc inspections – which occur in response to complaints from individual workers – unnecessary, the ratio of the former to the latter can serve as a proxy for the success of the overall inspection effort.

stakeholders abroad, the deepening of democracy – and the corresponding empowerment of skilled workers – at home, the small size and limited patronage resources available to the agency, and the skill and solidarity of the inspectors themselves. I will address each factor in turn and, where possible, test their implications with simple quantitative data.

The Externalization of Monitoring

Albert Hirschman portrayed the "disparity of attention" between core powers hoping to impose their will on dependent countries and dependent countries hoping to escape their clutches as a boon to the latter, for the "dependent country is likely to pursue its escape from domination more actively and energetically than the dominant country will work on preventing this escape" (Hirschman1978: 47). While the Dominicans were able to use their "'asymmetrical' desire for independence" (Schrank 2003: 415) to resist US pressure in the 1960s, when the Johnson administration tried to impose an export-led growth model on the country in the wake of the so-called Dominican crisis, they were unable to escape US oversight in the 1990s, when the Clinton administration set out to combat labor repression in their export-processing zones and the Dominicans responded not only by establishing "new laws, new courts, new rights, and new protections" (Frundt 1998: 223; see also Schrank 2009) but by building a more or less model enforcement agency out of whole cloth. By way of illustration, Rafael Alburquerque, who would eventually be elected vice president of the Dominican Republic, described the agency he inherited in 1991 as "deficient, discredited, and permeated by corruption" (Palacio 2008: 6). Approximately seventy inspectors covered more than three million workers in the country as a whole, and few had any qualifications to speak of. By 2016, however, fully 85 percent of the agency's two hundred inspectors were lawyers who had been incorporated into the country's nascent civil service; most had been recruited by means of an exam and held their positions for more than a decade; and thirty-four of their thirty-five supervisors had been promoted on the basis of merit rather than partisan loyalty.

What had changed between the late 1960s, when tens of thousands of US troops were unable to impose their will on the DR, and the 1990s, when the USTR was able to do so with a global staff of approximately 150 professionals (Cohen 2000: 60; Chorev 2007: 131)? My interviews suggest that by giving nongovernmental organizations (NGOs) the right to petition the USTR on behalf of foreign workers, policy makers in Washington had effectively externalized the costs of monitoring the labor standards they had incorporated into their trade agreements and preference schemes. After all, the United States no longer had to make an effort "to counter or effectively rein in" (Hirschman 1978: 48) a potentially recalcitrant country like the DR; labor and human rights groups would simply monitor the EPZs and sugar estates and ask the USTR to remove their preferences in the event of noncompliance with international norms and obligations (Frundt 1998).

North American activists filed several petitions on behalf of Dominican workers and Haitian cane cutters in the DR in the late 1980s and early 1990s (Frundt 1998: 219), and Dominican authorities initially responded to their entreaties by adopting a new labor code (Murillo and Schrank 2005) that allegedly lacked teeth. Women were still being exploited in EPZs, the activists argued, and Haitians were still being exploited in the sugar fields, in large part due to bribery and corruption among the officials responsible for the code's enforcement (see, e.g., AFL-CIO 1993). The problem was not simply the evasion of the code, however, but the nonenforcement of civil service laws that served to bolster the broader enforcement apparatus.

In May 1993, therefore, Alburquerque condemned both public and private authorities for their shortsightedness, noting that their persistent failure to enforce and respect the new code would inevitably bring sanctions upon the country and, in so doing, redound to the detriment of all parties. North American activists immediately seized upon his words in a campaign to deny the DR trade preferences (AFL-CIO 1993). And the Dominicans responded by dedicating more resources to the recruitment and retention of professional inspectors according to more demanding civil service criteria in a variant of the "boomerang pattern" discussed by Margaret Keck and Kathleen Sikkink in their work on "advocacy networks" (Keck and Sikkink 1998: 12–13; see also GAO 1998; Schrank 2009). Over the course of the subsequent decade, moreover, they deployed professionals to the EPZs and sugar plantations monitored by the activists. Data provided by the Ministry of Labor suggest that by 2005, for example, more than two-thirds of the DR's professional inspectors had been assigned to a mere nine of thirty total provinces that invariably played host to large-scale EPZ and/or sugar employment – a difference that is unlikely to have occurred by chance.[8]

The Deepening of Democracy

Much of the literature on state formation portrays the public, in general, and the public's need for employment, in particular, as impediments to administrative rationalization. For instance, Martin Shefter traces the prevalence of political patronage in the contemporary era to the timing of mass mobilization and administrative reform in history, and implies that – once introduced – patronage politics are hard to overcome. While precocious professionalization takes public employment out of political competition, and thereby forces

[8] Analysis based on administrative data kindly provided by Washington González in 2005. The nine provinces were Barahona, El Seibo, La Altagracia, La Romana, Puerto Plata, Santo Domingo, Santiago, San Cristóbal, and San Pedro. See PNUD (2008: 495) and INAZUCAR (2018) for coding sources; statistical analysis available from author upon request.

parties to compete on a programmatic basis when democracy takes hold, premature mobilization places public employment at the heart of partisan competition, and thereby militates against the rationalization of the public sector in the democratic era (Shefter 1977). Nor is Shefter alone. On the contrary, Samuel Huntington notes that "early efforts at republicanism left Latin America with weak governments which until the twentieth century lacked the authority and power to modernize the society" (1966: 410). Göran Therborn holds that "the most basic problems of establishing a *state order* had been solved before the struggle for democracy began" in the currently advanced countries (1979: 96). And Robert Wade maintains that "the stability of a new democracy depends on the development of broad-gauged political institutions prior to the expansion of political participation" (1990: 374) – and invokes the East Asian cases. But the Dominicans not only abandoned patronage for meritocracy in their labor inspectorate but did so in the midst of their own democratic transition, which most observers date to the late twentieth century (see, e.g., Mainwaring, Brinks, and Pérez-Liñán 2001: 49).

How did the Dominicans reconcile bureaucratization and democratization? A more recent literature brings the demand-side back in by focusing less on the supply of pork and patronage than on "the circumstances that make citizens accept or reject clientelism" (Royo 2003: 217) in the first place, including their skill levels and "cognitive capabilities." Some hold that the marginal utilities of immediate, particularistic payoffs are higher for less skilled or educated voters than for their more skilled or educated counterparts (see, e.g., Kitschelt 2000: 857; Calvo and Murillo 2004: 743; Cleary and Stokes 2006: 148; Weitz-Shapiro 2014: 12), and thereby offer a rational choice account of the link between education and meritocracy. Others maintain that middle-class or professional support for merit-based management, and opposition to personalism and pork, derive neither exclusively nor primarily from self-interest but from "middle-class values and identities" (Ozarow 2014: 181) that are at least nominally – and at times sincerely – sympathetic to the ideal of meritocracy and hostile to patronage and personalism (see, e.g., Dick 1985; Owensby 1999; Silva 2009).

Proponents of both the rational choice and cultural accounts posit a link between the supply of education and the demand for improved services, however, and their predictions are borne out in the Dominican case. My interview subjects attributed their decision-making at least in part to the impatience of the increasingly literate and empowered Dominican workforce in the late twentieth century. Survey data from the Latin American Public Opinion Project (LAPOP 2004) reveal that almost 60 percent of Dominican secondary school graduates – as opposed to just over 40 percent of their less educated compatriots – considered corruption a "very grave" problem in 2005.[9] Administrative data imply that educated workers were significantly

---

[9] Data analysis available from author on request.

more likely to petition the Ministry of Labor than their less educated counterparts in the same time period (Schrank 2009: 98). And a survey carried out by Latinobarómetro in 2005 suggests that more than 90 percent of college graduates felt at least a degree of protection from the country's labor laws, with the percentage falling steadily by educational achievement until it reached 77 percent among primary school leavers – and less than three-quarters among the country's many illiterates (OR = 1.23; p < 0.01). The same schools that create the "competent personnel" (Rueschemeyer 1986: 59–60) who staff Weberian bureaucracies therefore foster demand for their services – and in so doing create positive feedback loops that render the foreign boomerang that brought the bureaucracy into being less central over time.

The Size of the Agency

Rueschemeyer expects bureaucratic development to derive less from "a global change in attitudes, value orientations, and understandings" (Rueschemeyer 2005: 151), however, than from incremental adjustments to discrete agencies, and his prediction is for the most part borne out in the Dominican labor ministry. After all, the Dominicans abandoned patronage for merit under pressure from the USTR, but they consolidated their reforms under the watchful eyes of both US NGOs and their own increasingly – but unevenly – educated citizens. When Rueschemeyer adds that adjustments are likely to be confined to "certain enclaves," however, he is adding the question of scale to the mix.

Are smaller agencies more readily reformed than their larger counterparts? And, if so, why? My interview subjects answered in the affirmative, noting that the labor inspectorate had few patronage appointments to offer in the first place, and was therefore more easily sacrificed by machine politicians who allegedly coveted divisible benefits to be traded for political support, and their claims are consistent with statistical data, which suggest that indicators of agency size (i.e., number of personnel) and professionalization (i.e., the percentage incorporated into the country's civil service) were inversely correlated (r = –0.7; p < 0.001) across the population of twenty Dominican ministries in the early 2000s.[10]

The Skill and Solidarity of the State Agents

I have argued that bureaucratic development is most likely to derive not from a crisis or shock alone but from a crisis or shock that occurs to a relatively small agency that is monitored on an ongoing basis by a potentially powerful – if perhaps latent or disjointed – coalition of domestic and international actors,

---

[10] See ONAP (2004) for data on professionalization and STP (2005) for data on agency size.

and that the Dominican labor inspectorate offers an illustrative example. But Rueschemeyer's second concern continues to loom large: "Any institution-building requires orientations which transcend individual rational-instrumental behavior" (Rueschemeyer 1986: 59).

Why did the newly recruited inspectors come to believe the ministry's guarantees and/or adopt the "new orientations" indispensable to the development of rational legal authority? My interviews suggest that the Dominicans relied upon informal as well as formal procedures to get their reforms off the ground, and in so doing pursued a personalistic path to an impersonal bureaucracy. Alburquerque not only established competitive recruitment procedures in the early 1990s, for example, but made an active effort to convince honest lawyers of his own acquaintance to enter the competition, visited their offices to monitor their progress after they had been incorporated, and did everything in his power to build their esprit de corps along the way. And despite his best efforts, the initial recruits were skeptical. When I carried out my initial interviews with Dominican labor inspectors in the mid-2000s, for example, many continued to take private legal cases on the side and viewed their public appointments more as part of an income diversification or hedging strategy than as a lifetime career.[11]

By the end of the decade, however, their salaries had grown, their appointments had survived a partisan shift in government, and their concerns had dissipated – if by no means disappeared. Fewer and fewer preserved their private practices; more and more seemed like career bureaucrats who were committed to their jobs; and several had formed a union to defend their goals and guarantees in light of perceived threats to their autonomy. While their desire to unionize arguably speaks to their persistent insecurity, their willingness and ability to do so both underscore and reinforce their autonomy, and the union itself has proven invaluable when threats to their independence and authority have appeared.[12]

The point is to exaggerate neither the success of the reforms nor the security of the inspectors. The mere fact that their independence and authority have been challenged, on occasion, serves as a useful reminder that state autonomy is not only relative but fragile, especially when used by the "left hand of the state" (Bourdieu 2010: 67) to defend workers and communities from "the most flagrant inadequacies of the logic of the market." But relative autonomy, however fragile, is autonomy nonetheless, and cannot be taken for granted.

[11] Dominican labor inspectors are allowed to pursue private legal practices involving nonlabor-related cases in their free time.
[12] "Piden al ministro de trabajo evitar designaciones sin concurso," *Diario libre*, April 30, 2012. See also Trucchi (2015).

CONCLUSION

The Dominican success story would appear to call the consensus in favor of homegrown institutions and against their imported counterparts into question. After all, the Dominicans not only reformed their labor inspectorate in response to foreign pressure in the 1990s, but did so with donor support, and they have therefore recruited and retained skilled professionals, dispatched their partisan predecessors, and made seemingly significant improvements to both the quality and quantity of their workplace inspections. According to Diego Sánchez-Ancochea, the results have therefore "been instrumental in contributing to a gradual improvement in labor regulation in the Dominican Republic" (Sánchez-Ancochea 2013: 123).

My goal, however, is less to defend institutional importation, in general, than to illuminate the conditions under which imported personnel practices are most likely to take root in the public sector, in particular, and toward that end I have highlighted the roles of foreign and domestic stakeholders, democratic politics, agency size, and the skill and solidarity of the civil servants themselves. While the Dominicans thereby transformed a more or less typical bastion of patronage into a model meritocracy in the 1990s, they did so under extraordinary circumstances and by means of unorthodox practices, including Alburquerque's deliberate efforts to draw professionals into the inspectorate through personal networks. His efforts may have been contrary to Weberian norms, which call for impersonal procedures and practices, but they apparently helped tailor Weberian institutions to the inauspicious Dominican context.

What are the broader lessons of the case? The Dominican experience suggests that institutions are most likely to gain traction when they are compatible with the interests of domestic and foreign stakeholders and embedded in democratic environments, and thus speaks to the importance of both the international pressures and the empowered citizenries discussed in Chapter 1 of this volume. But the interests of domestic stakeholders are themselves endogenous to both international pressures and institutional design. Consider, for example, the traditional opponents of meritocracy in the Dominican labor ministry: rogue employers who feared regulation and incumbent inspectors who feared dismissal. While the former feared trade sanctions more than regulation, and thus had their preferences altered by foreign pressure, the latter feared job loss more than meritocracy per se, and thus welcomed their new colleagues – and concomitant raises – as long as their own positions were equally secure.

In other words, the USTR and Alburquerque turned potential victims of reform into beneficiaries, and in so doing made short-run success that much more likely. Over time, moreover, employers have adjusted (Schrank 2013), incumbents have moved on, professionals have grown in number as well as influence, and Dominicans have come to take an effective labor ministry for granted, making the unraveling of the reforms less likely – if not entirely impossible.

By way of conclusion, therefore, I would simply note that the problem with imported institutions is less that they are imported than that they are institutions, and institutions necessarily have noninstitutional underpinnings that are difficult not only to build *or* import as part of a policy imperative but to explain in terms of self-interested utility maximization. Somewhere in the chain of command there has to be an architect willing to don handcuffs. Somewhere below the architect there have to be people who believe the cuffs will hold. Neither party is easy to come by – let alone to come by and coordinate simultaneously. And in the event that both were found the process would be opaque to social scientists who treat self-interested utility maximization – and corresponding mistrust and myopia – as assumptions rather than variables in any event.

11

Social Origins of Institutional Strength

Prior Consultation over Extraction
of Hydrocarbons in Bolivia

Tulia G. Falleti

INTRODUCTION

Why do some political institutions become strong, while others remain weak?[1] Why do imported international legal norms remain aspirational rights in some countries, but are complied with and enforced in others?[2] Why do institutions born out of similar conditions subsequently diverge in their levels of institutional strength? Social scientists have amply demonstrated that strong institutions are essential to economic and political development. At the dawn of the twentieth century, Max Weber (1978 [1922]) famously argued that capitalist development required the development of a strong, rational, state bureaucracy. More recently, political scientists and economists alike have highlighted the importance of strong political institutions for economic growth and development (Haggard 1990; North 1990). In political science, scholars have developed theories of why and how institutions originate and change (Knight 1992; Steinmo, Thelen, and Longstreth 1992; Thelen 2004).

[1] This chapter draws from my collaborative research with Thea Riofrancos, which appeared in Falleti and Riofrancos (2018). For research assistance, I thank Santiago Cunial, Javier Revelo Rebolledo, and Gabriel Salgado. I am also indebted to Christopher Carter, Belén Fernández Milmanda, Alisha Holland, Ned Littlefield, Victor Hugo Quintinilla Coro, Julia Maria Rubio, María Paula Saffon Sanin, Zachary Smith, Oscar Vega, the three volume editors, the anonymous reviewers, the participants in the 2018 Latin American Studies Association panel, and the participants in seminars at Columbia University, the University of California, Berkeley, the University of Wisconsin–Madison, and the University of Pennsylvania for their very helpful comments.
[2] For a discussion of imported institutions, see Shrank (this volume); and for a definition of "aspirational rights," see Htun and Jensenius (this volume).

However, much less attention has been paid to the questions of why and how institutions strengthen or alternatively remain weak, which are at the center of this edited volume.

In Chapter 1, Brinks, Levitsky, and Murillo, propose a typology of weak institutions and, articulating the costs of institutional compliance with the costs of institutional violation and change, provide examples of institutional creation and design that are connected to different types of weak institutions. In this last empirical chapter of the volume, rather than analyzing a case of institutional weakness, my goal is to offer an explanation and example of institutional strengthening in Latin America. The domain of my argument is the subset of *state-sanctioned institutions that have been adopted due to demand from civil society.* Among these institutions, my main argument is that institutional strengthening not only requires that the costs of violation and change be higher than the cost of compliance for the actors with vested interests in the institution, but it also requires, at least from a sociological standpoint, the political incorporation of the social actors who initially mobilized for the creation or adoption of the institution. I argue that these social actors must be politically incorporated during the phases of regulation and implementation of the institution. Thus, social compliance with the institution is likely to be based on the institution's legitimacy in the eyes, hearts, and minds of the social actors who demanded it. In such cases, the state is more likely to be compelled to enforce the institution due to societal pressure.[3] Moreover, as my case study shows, the state may be compelled to enforce the institution even when its preferences change.

Empirically, my analysis will be based on the study of prior consultation, which is the collective right of indigenous communities to be consulted prior to the realization of megainfrastructure or extractive projects that could affect their environment.[4] This institution originates in the International Labor Organization (ILO) Convention 169 on Indigenous and Tribal Peoples, of 1989. To date, twenty-two countries around the world have ratified the convention; fifteen of them are in Latin America (see Map 11.1), which makes the study of prior consultation very relevant in the region. Moreover, the increase of extractive projects and industries in Latin America during the commodities boom (2000–2014) makes prior consultation not only highly relevant but also a site of conflict with high stakes, as it articulates conflicting (often incompatible) social actors' interests. The institution is applied in what César Rodríguez Garavito (2012) calls

---

[3] As the chapter by Amengual and Dargent (this volume) shows, when there is no societal pressure, state enforcement is weak or nonexistent.

[4] I am indebted to Thea N. Riofrancos for having first called my attention to the institution of prior consultation.

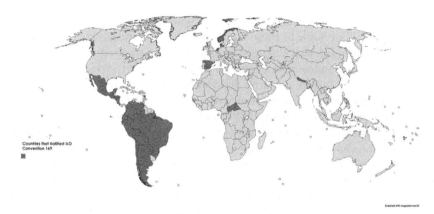

MAP 11.1. Countries that have ratified ILO Convention 169.

"mined social fields": sites where the interests in favor of natural resource extraction of states, which obtain royalties, and corporations that obtain large profits from extraction, are often directly opposed to the interests of indigenous communities that, at least in part, seek to preserve their natural environment and way of life. Moreover, given the asymmetry of power between extractive corporations and indigenous communities, it is hard to think of a harder case for institutional strengthening. In other words, if I can show that the institution of prior consultation has strengthened in mined social fields, with conflicting interests and high asymmetries of power among the actors articulated by the institution, then I would expect the theoretical implications derived from this single-case study to apply to other state-sanctioned and socially demanded institutions. I follow the definition of institution proposed by Brinks, Levitsky, and Murillo (Chapter 1, this volume), i.e., "a set of formal rules structuring human behavior and expectations around a statutory goal by (1) specifying actors and their roles; (2) requiring, permitting, or prohibiting certain behaviors; and (3) defining the consequences of complying or not complying with the remaining rules." Prior consultation is a type of participatory institution, i.e., a *formal, state-sanctioned institution explicitly created to augment citizen (in this case indigenous) involvement in decision-making over public goods or social services* (Davies and Falleti 2017; Falleti and Riofrancos 2018). These institutions provide citizens with a normal-politics means of interacting with the state, and are potentially more substantive than sporadic electoral participation at the ballot box, while at the same time less disruptive than social protest (Fung and Wright 2003; Cameron, Hershberg, and Sharpe 2012).

Latin America is the ideal setting to study participatory institutions, as the region has led the world in their creation and implementation (Souza 2001: 162;

Avritzer 2009: 26; Baiocchi, Heller, and Silva 2011: 43–44; Tranjan 2016).[5] Nonetheless, while some of these institutions have acquired strength, enabling citizens' meaningful participation in the decision-making process over the distribution or management of public goods or social services, others have remained weak – merely window dressing institutions that are not enforced. Why have participatory institutions with very similar institutional designs followed such different trajectories? What are the implications of these differing trajectories for explanations of institutional weakness and for the scholarship on institutional development more broadly?

In the next section, I present alternative explanations of institutional strengthening of participatory institutions and argue for the need to scale up our analysis. In the third section, I articulate my own argument. In doing so, I provide a theoretical and operational conceptualization of institutional strengthening and discuss the concept of political incorporation of indigenous movements. In the fourth section, I justify the selection of the case of Bolivia and its hydrocarbons sector. In the fifth section, I analyze the process of adoption, regulation, and implementation of prior consultation in the extraction of natural gas.[6] This process has two stages. The first stage can be characterized as a reactive type of sequence (from 1990 to 2005) of reactions and counterreaction events between an increasingly organized indigenous movement and the national governments. The second stage conforms to a self-enforcing sequence of events (from 2005 to 2017), where the key reforms and events in the earlier part of this period (most significantly from 2005 to 2011) strengthened indigenous rights and the position of the indigenous movement in Bolivian politics. In the final section, I conclude with the implications of this study for the literature on participatory institutions and institutional strengthening.

ALTERNATIVE ARGUMENTS

The existing literature on participatory institutions in the developing world identifies several local-level variables and conditions to account for their institutional strength, including a developed civil society (Baiocchi, Heller, and Silva 2011), a high degree of fiscal decentralization combined with weak opposition to leftists ruling local governments (Goldfrank 2007), capable local leadership (Grindle 2007; Van Cott 2008), and the technocratic agency of policy makers (McNulty 2011), among other local-level variables. These invaluable studies

---

[5] For a comprehensive survey of the participatory institutions, consult LATINNO, www.latinno.net.

[6] The concepts of institutional adoption, regulation, and implementation aid the analysis of state–society relations in different phases of institutionalization, even if in reality these phases are often intertwined.

provide subnational comparisons of participatory institutions, both within and across countries, to explain their varying degrees of success and institutional strengthening. However, as in previous collaborative research (Falleti and Riofrancos 2018), I propose to scale up the analysis, and study instead the national-level dynamics that lead to the creation and strengthening of participatory institutions. The fate of many of these institutions at the local level is heavily dependent on how they come about in the first place, which often takes place at the national level. Their fate is also dependent on the regulatory and enforcement institutional framework, which again is designed and negotiated at the national level.

Regarding alternative arguments of institutional strengthening at the national level, Levitsky and Murillo (2013: 97–100) point to political regime instability, electoral volatility, social inequality, institutional borrowing, and rapid institutional design as contributing causes to institutional weakness in Latin America. But while all these conditions have historically characterized the case of Bolivia, prior consultation has strengthened. Moreover, whereas Levitsky and Murillo (2009: 122) are most focused on the threat that elite actors – economic, military, or religious – pose to institutional enforcement and stability, I show below that the relations between state and grassroots social movements can account for institutional compliance and enforcement.

INSTITUTIONAL STRENGTH AS SOCIETAL COMPLIANCE AND STATE ENFORCEMENT

In Chapter 1, Brinks, Levitsky, and Murillo conceptualize the strength of an institution as the distance between the outcome we would expect to see in the real world absent the institution (*po*), and the outcome we actually see with the institution (*io*). As that distance between *po* and *io*, labeled *S*, gets larger, the institution gets stronger. If *po* and *io* can indeed be observed and measured, this definition provides an excellent operationalization of institutional strength. However, this conceptualization remains silent about the sources of that strength. Why does the institution in question systematically produce change in individuals' behaviors such that a dramatic change between *po* and *io* ensues? Do individuals' behaviors change due to fear of punishment or to avoid fines, hence weighing the costs of violations versus the cost of compliance, as the editors note? Or have those individuals' underlying preferences with regard to the institution changed, and therefore they now comply with an institution (*io*) they would not have complied with in the past (*po*)? In other words, are individuals complying with the institution due to fear of sanctions or because they now believe "it is the right thing to do"?

In order to dig deeper into what accounts for a larger *S* in any given institutional situation, I define *institutional strength*, my dependent variable of interest, as the degree to which institutions are complied with by society and enforced by the state. Moreover, I claim that for the institution to be strong, civil society compliance must not be solely based on fear of punishment, but instead on legitimacy and efficacy.[7]

Observationally, it can be a thorny endeavor to distinguish between compliance due to fear of punishment and compliance due to legitimacy in any single behavioral case. However, as Weber (1978 [1922]: 214) masterfully wrote: "[T]he legitimacy of a system of domination may be treated sociologically only as the probability that to a relevant degree the appropriate attitudes will exist, and the corresponding practical conduct ensue." In other words, when observing compliance with a new institution (*io*), we cannot fully ascertain whether individuals' change in behavior is due to the legitimacy of the institution, self-interest, imitation, opportunism, or any other possible source of behavioral change. However, when analyzing compliance with an institution over time and as it applies to a social group, it might be possible for the social scientist to attach a probability to the possibility that legitimacy of the institution might be the leading cause of a group of individuals' change in behavior. For example, in her research on local institutions in the context of civil war in Colombia, Arjona (2015, 2016) observed that legitimate institutions are those "that most members of the community believe[d to be] rightful" or fair (2015: 183). In my view, if social actors demand the adoption of a new institution and the state's enforcement of it, such institution should enjoy a high level of legitimacy with that social group. For instance, if an organized indigenous movement demands from its national government the adoption of an international norm such as ILO Convention 169, I expect prior consultation – included in such convention – to enjoy a high level of legitimacy with the mobilized indigenous movement, particularly if subsequent to institutional adoption they continue to mobilize to demand state enforcement of the institution. Similarly, if Brazil's *sanitarista* (sanitarist) movement demands the recognition and enactment of the constitutional right to health care in the courts of Brazil, I expect the constitutional right to health to enjoy a high level of legitimacy among the *sanitarista* movement. Amengual and Dargent (this volume) provide another example of environmental groups and citizens demanding that the municipal and provincial governments enforce environmental laws that only existed on paper (Santa Clara and Santa Fe, Argentina). In all these cases, mobilized social actors are demanding that the state adopt and activate institutions, which I expect enjoy a high level of legitimacy among such social groups.

Legitimacy is an essential component of institutional strength and compliance with the institution, but it is not enough. As Arjona noted, high-quality

---

[7] In fact, it is not only individuals but also the state that must comply with the institution, as noted by Amengual and Dargent (this volume) and Holland (2016). For the purpose of this chapter, and given space constraints, I focus on compliance as it applies to civil society and on enforcement as it applies to the state.

(or strong) institutions must also be "obeyed." For Arjona, the degree to which individuals obey or follow the rules (i.e., comply) is a function of institutional efficacy (2016: 130). In other words, an institution is efficacious when individuals see its value when complied with. Or as Weber (1978 [1922]: 215) puts it, "'Obedience' will be taken to mean that the action of the person obeying follows in essentials such a course that the content of the command may be taken to have become the basis of action for its own sake." This is to say, if the institution is efficacious, individuals will obey or comply with it without doubt or resistance, for its and their own sake.

In the case of prior consultation, *the primary goal of the institution is to negotiate the differences between indigenous communities, corporations, and the state over extraction of natural resources*. Thus, to me, prior consultation will be legitimate when individuals in the indigenous communities, in the extractive corporations, and in the state approve of the rules that prior consultation puts in place to resolve conflicts, without disputing their validity. Moreover, prior consultation will be efficacious when the indigenous communities, the extractive corporations, and the state follow those prior consultation rules to negotiate their differences and resolve conflicts. In other words, where prior consultation is strong we should observe extraction taking place via prior consultation and with comparatively lower levels of social conflict between indigenous communities and extractive corporations than would have been the case had the institution not been in place or only weakly complied with or enforced.

This leads me to the second dimension of institutional strength: enforcement. As Brinks, Levitsky, and Murillo note in Chapter 1, enforcement is related to the likelihood of punishment for not following the rules.[8] Because prior consultation must be implemented by the state (i.e., the state must convene and lead the process of the prior consultation between indigenous communities and extractive corporations, the state must write and validate all the agreements that are signed between the parts, and the state must ensure that all parties follow through with the resulting agreements), I operationalize enforcement as the degree to which the institution is enacted by the state. Enforcement is not solely a function of the state's institutional capacities, but also of its willingness to apply the law and enact the institution.

This definition of institutional strength – entailing high levels of state enforcement and societal compliance, which in turn are rooted in the institution's legitimacy and efficacy – brings together insights from various traditions of institutionalism in sociology, economics, and political science that are seldom combined. From the sociological tradition, I take the idea that individuals' internalization of routines or practices perceived as legitimate are at the core of institutional compliance that is stable in the

---

[8] For a more extensive definition of enforcement, see Levitsky and Murillo (2009: 117), and fn. 1.

long run.⁹ In other words, legitimacy is what keeps an institution in place and complied with once the political interests or coalitions that existed at the moment of its creation are no longer there. From the economics tradition, I borrow the idea that institutions solve conflicts and generate stability by limiting the range of options actors confront (e.g., North 1990). Efficacious institutions are those that are obeyed by social actors, because they provide not only cognitive maps, but also practical shortcuts for social action. As Brinks, Levitsky, and Murillo note (Chapter 1, this volume), rational actors weigh the cost of institutional compliance against the costs of institutional violation or change. Efficacious institutions are those where the cost of compliance is consistently lower than the costs of violation or change, or at least this is the internalized perception of social actors who may not even care to change or violate the institution because it provides them with what appears to be an optimized strategy for individual and collective action. Finally, from political science's historical institutionalist tradition, I borrow the idea that a key source of institutional strength is the alignment between the interests of the political coalitions bringing about the institution, on the one hand, and the institution's goals and distributional effects, on the other (e.g., Pierson 2016). Moreover, due to positive feedback mechanisms, institutions continue to be enforced (and sometimes gradually evolve) after the political coalitions or circumstances in which they originate change. As long as the institution proves legitimate and efficacious, it could continue to be enforced and strengthened even as the originating coalition ages or collapses.

These dimensions of institutional strength are mutually reinforcing: legitimacy facilitates efficacy, both lead to societal compliance, and this in turn eases state enforcement. For social actors, it is easier to obey rules they consider right and fair. If institutional legitimacy and efficacy are high, violations of the institution will be few (high societal compliance) and state enforcement easier (fewer transgressors) and more attainable (the state is more likely to have the will to enforce). As the empirical study of prior consultation in Bolivia's gas sector demonstrates, this multidisciplinary conceptualization of institutional strength provides analytical leverage for the study of institutional genesis and development.

Compliance by society and enforcement by the state may be also conceptualized in terms of a state–society dynamic process. Figures 11.1 and 11.2 schematically represent a series of logical steps expected in the path to institutional strengthening. Figure 11.1 centers on compliance, or the societal side of institutional strengthening. Once an institution is adopted due to demand from civil society, the first question becomes: do the mobilized social actors

---

⁹ E.g., Weber (1978 [1922]); see also Bourdieu (1984, esp. ch. 8), albeit not strictly an institutional approach.

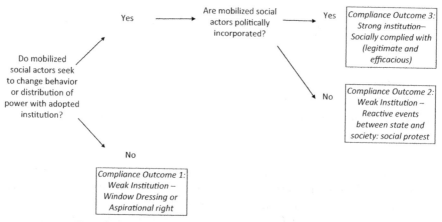

FIGURE 11.1. Compliance: Societal side of institutional strengthening.

involved in the creation of the institution seek to change individuals' behavior or the distribution of power among relevant actors with this institution? If the answer is no, the resulting institution will be a *window dressing* weak institution or an *aspirational right* (see Htun and Jensenius, this volume, for an example) (Compliance Outcome 1). If the answer is yes, as we would expect if the proposed institution enjoys a high level of legitimacy among the social actors proposing it and if they conceive of the institution as highly efficacious in navigating the social order if complied with (i.e., not merely an aspirational right, but one that can be realized), then the question becomes: are the mobilized social actors politically incorporated (either within the state or in other organizations of political or civil society)? If the answer is no, the likely outcome is a weak institution and a reactive sequence of events between state and social actors over the meaning and implementation of the institution, such as *social protests* or *overt conflict* (Compliance Outcome 2).[10] If the answer is yes, if the mobilized social actors have been politically incorporated during the process of institutional regulation and implementation, then we should expect a *strong institution* (Compliance Outcome 3). As shown below, prior consultation in the hydrocarbons sector in Bolivia conformed to Compliance Outcome 2 from 1991 until 2005 and to Compliance Outcome 3 starting in 2007.

On the other hand, we can analyze this process from the standpoint of the state's behavior vis-à-vis the mobilized social actors, in order to assess institutional enforcement, as schematically represented in Figure 11.2. Once an institution is in place due to mobilization from below, the first question

---

[10] For a description of reactive sequences, see Collier and Collier (1991); Mahoney (2000); Falleti and Mahoney (2015).

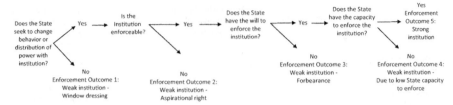

FIGURE 11.2. Enforcement: State side of institutional strengthening.

is: does the state seek to change individuals' behavior or the distribution of power with this institution? If the answer is no, the institution is likely to remain ambiguous, flexible, or intentionally flawed.[11] It will be a *weak institution* (Enforcement Outcome 1). If instead the state is actively seeking to change individuals' behavior or the distribution of power among the affected actors with this institution, then the next question becomes: is the institution enforceable? *Aspirational rights*, for instance, are largely not enforceable by design, at least at the time of their adoption, and thus are conceived as *weak institutions* (Enforcement Outcome 2). If the institution is enforceable, then the question becomes: does the state have the will to enforce the institution? If the answer is no, the outcome is a weak institution due to *forbearance* (Enforcement Outcome 3).[12] If the state has the will to enforce, then the question becomes: does the state have the capacity to enforce the institution? A negative answer will yield a *weak institution* due to lack of state capacity to enforce (Enforcement Outcome 4).[13] If the state has the will and the capacity to enforce, the institution will acquire that important feature of institutional strength (Enforcement Outcome 5). Prior consultation in Bolivia's hydrocarbons sector transitioned from a weak window dressing institution (Enforcement Outcome 1) to a strong institution (Enforcement Outcome 5). This change started in 2005 (with the Hydrocarbons Law) and became self-enforcing once the Movement for Socialism (MAS) politically incorporated the indigenous movement and groups that had fought for the adoption of prior consultation into the institutions of the state. Furthermore, due to such incorporation and the

[11] For an example, see the case of the territorial classification of native forests law in the province of Salta, in Fernández Milmanda and Garay (this volume).
[12] For examples of this outcome, see Holland (2016). The case of lack of state enforcement of labor and environmental violations in the gold mining sector in Bolivia is another example (Amengual and Dargent, this volume).
[13] As Amengual and Dargent show (this volume), coproduction of enforcement with civil society could be an alternative to this outcome. Moreover, as noted by several of the chapters in this volume, state capacity and will to enforce an institution may not be evenly distributed across the territory, or across sectors to which the institution may apply.

increasing compliance with the institution, prior consultation remained strong even after the mid-2010s, when the state's willingness to implement prior consultation decreased.

Political Incorporation of Mobilized Social Actors

Between the stage of adoption of a participatory institution and its institutional strengthening, there is a fundamental intervening process: the political incorporation of the mobilized actors that brought about the institution. In a previous comparative analysis, Thea Riofrancos and I (2018) showed that without the mobilized actors' political incorporation during the stages of regulation and implementation, participatory institutions remain weak. In the case of prior consultation, indigenous movements are the key actors bringing about the demand for its adoption by the state. Beginning in the 1990s, when the corporatist citizenship regime was in crisis in Latin America and, largely due to the implementation of neoliberal reforms, indigenous identities were politicized (Yashar 2005), indigenous movements demanded the ratification of ILO Convention 169.

Ruth Berins Collier and David Collier's (1991) comparative historical analysis of the incorporation of the labor movement in Latin America offers a template to theorize indigenous incorporation in the region. I define *indigenous political incorporation* as the sustained and at least partially *successful attempt by the state to legitimate and shape an institutionalized indigenous movement.*[14] How does indigenous political incorporation take place? Indigenous political incorporation can occur through three main routes. It can occur via the state (as appointments in the bureaucracy, for instance), via the political parties (whether in ruling or opposition parties, with voice and representation in the political institutions of the country, such as in congress or constitutional assemblies), or via parastate institutions such as nongovernmental organizations (NGOs), indigenous unions, or lobbying groups, academics (including expert anthropologists), and activists.

As in the case of labor incorporation, during the process of indigenous political incorporation, the state plays an innovative role in constructing new institutions of state–indigenous relations and new approaches to articulating the indigenous movement with the party system. Although unlike the case of labor, in the case of indigenous incorporation, NGOs (local, national, and international) also play a creative role in the advancement of indigenous demands. Examples of new institutions of state–indigenous relations that evince a process of indigenous political incorporation include

---

[14] Adapting from Collier and Collier (1991: 5, 161–168).

prior consultation, indigenous territorial autonomies, the recognition of indigenous languages, indigenous control of bilingual education and development agencies, legal pluralism that recognizes indigenous justice, the recognition of *ayllu* (in the Andes region of South America) or other forms of indigenous communal governance, and the definition of the state as plurinational so as to include the right of self-determination of originary peoples and tribes. In terms of new approaches to articulating the indigenous movement with the party system, examples of indigenous political incorporation include the principle of descriptive representation in the selection of political party candidates to national-level representative positions, and the creation of legislative seats reserved for representatives of ethnic groups.[15] And lastly, NGOs, experts, and activists can provide community and individual training, lobbying opportunities, and logistic and legal support that can be instrumental in facilitating the political incorporation of indigenous movements, especially through the recognition of indigenous communities and ancestral territories, legal representation, and drafting of legal and regulatory proposals.

METHODOLOGY AND CASE SELECTION

This chapter constitutes a case study of institutional strengthening. I select Bolivia for several reasons: First, it was one of the first countries to ratify ILO Convention 169 (Mexico and Norway ratified it in 1990 and Bolivia and Colombia in 1991). Second, 40 percent of the population self-identify as indigenous (Htun 2016: 26), and the indigenous movement was highly organized by the 1990s (Lucero 2008; Van Cott 2008; Yashar 2005: ch. 5). Third, the state heavily relies in extraction and exports of gas.[16] Combined, these attributes make the institution of prior consultation in hydrocarbons highly relevant. Moreover, Bolivia has historically had low levels of state capacity, making it a hard case for state enforcement.

Why prior consultation in the hydrocarbons sector? According to ILO Convention 169, prior consultation should take place in any instance of megainfrastructure or extraction project that could potentially affect the land and environment of indigenous communities. However, in the mining sector, prior consultation was only legally introduced in 2014 (Law 535 of Mining and Metallurgy, Title VI, Articles 207 to 216) and applied for the

---

[15] This is to say, legally and institutionally, incorporation entails more political transformations than does the process of inclusion understood as "the presence in decision making of members of historically excluded groups" (Htun 2016: 4).

[16] In 2011, commodities represented 86 percent of the total exports of Bolivia, and hydrocarbons over 50 percent of its exports (Campello and Zucco 2014: app. B, 5).

first time in 2015.[17] In infrastructure, prior consultation was amply demanded in 2011 by the indigenous communities who opposed the construction of a major highway programmed to run through the natural reserve territory known as Territorio Indígena y Parque Nacional Isiboro Sécure (TIPNIS), in the lowlands of Bolivia. The Bolivian government delayed the implementation of the prior consultation until 2012 and only rolled it out after high mobilization within the indigenous movement.[18] The indigenous communities of the TIPNIS were split in their approval or rejection of the highway. However, due to the prior consultation process and the controversy over the construction project, the highway was suspended in 2013.

In hydrocarbons, interestingly, the Hydrocarbons Law of 2005 opened the possibility for enforcement with clear rules and mandates on what the state had to do and how. Once the MAS assumed power, the minister of hydrocarbons, Omar Quiroga, had an interest in applying the institution, and started to do so systematically in 2007, thus strengthening it. In the next section, I employ the technique of process tracing to study the adoption, regulation, and implementation of prior consultation in Bolivia's hydrocarbons sectors, aiming to identify the events and evidence that point to different levels of legitimacy, efficacy, and enforcement of prior consultation. I draw on data collected from in-depth interviews conducted with state, sectoral, and social movement actors; archival research on the adoption, regulation, and implementation of prior consultation; and secondary literature on the history of indigenous mobilization, political party incorporation, and constitutional reforms.[19]

---

[17] See "AJAM hace inédita consulta previa minera," *La razón*, July 19, 2015. According to Karina Herrera Miller, national director of the Intercultural Service for Democratic Strengthening (SIFDE) of the Supreme Electoral Tribunal (TSE) of Bolivia, 165 prior consultations in the mining sector had been initiated since 2015, and 84 of them had been concluded by October 2016 (see Herrera Miller, n.d., accessible at www.slideshare.net/TSEBolivia/consulta-previa-67197278, accessed November 21, 2018). See also "En un año, el OEP acompañó 165 procesos de consultas previas en minería," *Fuente directa*, October 13, 2016, http://fuentedirecta.oep.org.bo/, accessed November 21, 2018. I thank Marcela Torres Wong for her related comment about prior consultations in the mining sector.

[18] On September 25, 2011, government security forces heavily repressed an indigenous protest against the construction of the highway in Chaparina, Beni. Members of the indigenous movement and NGOs interpret this event as a critical juncture in the relationship between Evo Morales and the indigenous movement, which the government has sought to divide and control ever since. Author interview with Victor Hugo Quintinilla Coro, Sucre, July 23, 2015; "La crisis con indígenas se inicio en Chaparina." *El tiempo*, September 26, 2017, www.lostiempos.com/actualidad/economia/20170926/crisis-indigenas-se-inicio-chaparina, accessed February 10, 2018.

[19] Fieldwork was conducted in March 2014 and in July 2015.

PROCESS TRACING OF PRIOR CONSULTATION IN BOLIVIA

The Contentious Adoption of Prior Consultation in Bolivia

From 1990 to 2005, the process of adoption of prior consultation in Bolivia was reactive, characterized by reaction/counterreaction dynamics between neoliberal administrations and indigenous organizations. Affected by neoliberal policies, lowlands indigenous groups, which had been excluded from the corporatist pact resulting from the 1952 revolution, demanded the recognition of international-level indigenous rights as well as political and economic inclusion.[20] They were organized in the Confederación Indígena del Oriente, Chaco y Amazonía de Bolivia (CIDOB), and "demanded indigenous territory; organizational autonomy to decide the terms of political participation and development; the right to self-government; recognition of customary law and legal pluralism; and the right to cultural survival and development," among other rights (Yashar 2005: 203). In response to the CIDOB's 1990 March for Territory and Dignity, in 1991 President Jaime Paz Zamora ratified ILO Convention 169.[21] While ratification of this international norm was important for the recognition of indigenous collective rights, Law 1257 of July 11, 1991, consisted merely of 143 words, one paragraph saying that ILO Convention 169 was approved and would have the status of a national law. The ratification did not include any clauses as to how or when the new law was going to be regulated, implemented, or who, when, for how long, and with what resources the consultations were to be conducted. Law 1257 conformed exactly to the definition of a window dressing institution: an institution designed not to be complied with or enforced.

Lacking a regulatory framework, the few consultations that the employees of the Directorate for Environmental Management of the Ministry of Hydrocarbons and Energy carried out in the late 1990s were guided by the ILO convention and Bolivia's 1992 Law 1333 on the environment.[22] Despite being a quite extensive law (7,518 words long, followed by three regulatory norms, amounting to 47,642 words), no article made reference to prior consultation, and only two articles referred to public consultations with affected

---

[20] The corporatist pact following the 1952 social revolution refers to the alliance between the victorious populist leadership of the Nationalist Revolutionary Movement (MNR) and part of the insurgent popular sectors, organized in worker and peasant unions. The post-1952 corporatist regime promoted universal suffrage, greater labor rights, nationalization of industry, and agrarian reform. It incorporated the popular sectors of the Andes and of the valleys of Cochabamba, but largely excluded those of the lowlands, creating the conditions for the resurgence of ethnic grievances (Rivera Cusicanqui 1990: 104, 107–109; 2004: 20).

[21] Author interview with Oscar Vega Camacho, independent researcher and writer, La Paz, Bolivia, March 20, 2014.

[22] Author interview with Monica Castro, former employee of Directorate for Environmental Management of the Ministry of Hydrocarbons and Energy, La Paz, Bolivia, March 21, 2014.

communities. These public consultations, however, had very restrictive features in terms of the procedures available to communities that wanted to raise concerns about projects affecting their environment.[23] During the 1990s, prior consultation remained a weak institution

Further extensions and amendments to prior consultation followed the heightened social mobilization that occurred during the gas wars of October 2003. As a result, President Gonzalo (Goni) Sánchez de Lozada decreed that natural gas would only be exported with "consultations and debates."[24] But protest over Goni's neoliberal policies continued, leading to his resignation soon thereafter. When Vice President Carlos Mesa assumed the presidency, he called a national referendum on hydrocarbons, which contained five questions relating to their exploitation and administration. Overwhelmingly, Bolivians favored state ownership of hydrocarbons (92 percent) and the refounding of the national oil company Yacimientos Petrolíferos Fiscales Bolivianos (YPFB) (87 percent). In 2005, Mesa presented a bill on hydrocarbons to Congress, but the political context was less than conducive to compromise.

The political left, led by Morales and the MAS, with overwhelming support from self-identified indigenous voters and groups, demanded more state participation in the ownership and administration of natural gas (Giusti-Rodríguez 2017). Previously separated indigenous organizations, of which the most salient were the CIDOB and the Consejo Nacional de Ayllus y Markas del Qullasuyu (CONAMAQ), came together in a national indigenous movement that coordinated its political action vis-à-vis the neoliberal state. They formed the Pacto de Unidad (Unity Pact), which brought together the CONAMAQ, CIDOB, the Confederación Nacional de Mujeres Campesinas Indígenas Originarias de Bolivia–Bartolina Sisa (CMCIOB "BS"), the Confederación Sindical de Comunidades Interculturales Originarios de Bolivia (CSCIB), and the Confederación Sindical Única de Trabajadores Campesinos de Bolivia (CSUTCB), representing a wide array of indigenous peoples. Meanwhile, the political right, led by the Comité Cívico de Santa Cruz in the eastern department, demanded more departmental autonomy as a counterbalance to the rising power of the indigenous movement and to safeguard their territorial and economic interests. Amid a new wave of popular protests, Mesa resigned to avoid having to either sign or veto the new Hydrocarbons Law.[25] Days later, the president of Congress, Hormando Vaca Diez, signed the law into effect.

Law 3058 on hydrocarbons was paramount to the institutionalization of prior consultation in Bolivia and the direct result of these reactive/

[23] Bolivia, Ley No. 1.333 Ley de Medio Ambiente, Gaceta Oficial de Bolivia, June 15, 1992, see Articles 162 and 164.

[24] Decree 27,210.

[25] Author interviews with Carlos Mesa, in La Paz, Bolivia, March 21, 2014, and in Philadelphia, September 12, 2014.

counterreactive dynamics between the government and the indigenous movement. As anthropologist Denise Humphreys Bebbington (2012: 59) writes, "This law... represented the culmination of years of mobilization, lobbying and negotiation with executive and legislative officials, bringing indigenous lowland groups closer to their goal of effective control over their territories." One of the law's ten titles was explicitly devoted to "the rights of the peasant indigenous and original peoples" (Title VII). The law directly invoked ILO Convention 169 and legislated that a mandatory process of consultation of indigenous communities must take place prior to the implementation of any hydrocarbons exploitation project. Not only was the process of prior consultation mandatory, but the "decisions resulting from this process of consultation ought to be respected" (Article 115). The law also specified the Ministries of Hydrocarbons, Sustainable Development, and of Indigenous Affairs and Originary Peoples as jointly responsible for implementing the consultation with funding from the presidency (Article 117).[26]

It is noteworthy that neither President Mesa's original bill nor the MAS bill included such a lengthy section on prior consultation. Mesa's proposal mentioned that in indigenous communal lands (Tierras Comunitarias de Origen, TCOs), a process of consultation with indigenous communities would be mandatory prior to the study of environmental impact. It was a short, one-sentence paragraph within the environmental monitoring article, toward the end of the bill.[27] Similarly, the MAS proposal included one sentence indicating that ILO Convention 169 would have to be complied with when hydrocarbons activities involved TCOs.[28]

Instead, a proposal to legislate on the consultation of indigenous communities and peoples was elaborated by the Centro de Estudios Jurídicos e Investigación Social (CEJIS), an NGO that worked closely with the Pacto de Unidad (CEJIS 2014: 189–206), and this proposal was likely the template of Title VII for Law 3058. In fact, ten days after the law was approved, the Pacto de Unidad presented a letter to the president of Congress requesting, among other changes, that the consultation process be "binding."[29] Although no such reform was made, the demands of the organized indigenous movement reflected its degree of political capacity and coordination just before the MAS assumed the presidency and during the legislative sessions and debates that led to the Hydrocarbons Law.

---

[26] This funding scheme changed in 2007.

[27] Presidencia de la República, Proyecto de Ley de Hidrocarburos, Art. 107, 37, September 6, 2004.

[28] Bancada Parlamentaria MAS-IPSP, Proyecto de Ley de Hidrocarburos, Art. 62, transcribed in CEJIS (2014:139).

[29] Pacto de Unidad, Proyecto de Modificatoria a la Ley No. 3058, Ley de Hidrocarburos, La Paz, Bolivia, May 27, 2005. Consulted in the Central Archive of Bolivia's National Congress.

Between 1991 and 2005, prior consultation was a weak institution, practically not enforced by the state, and hence not complied with by either corporations or indigenous communities (despite the fact that it was a highly legitimate institution in the eyes of the Bolivian indigenous movements, who demanded it as one of their indigenous rights). Law 3058 gave teeth to the weak institution. It provided very explicit rules on who ought to be consulted, when, and how in cases of extraction in the hydrocarbons sector. Could this have been enough to strengthen the institution? My contention is that while the Hydrocarbons Law provided the *opportunity* to strengthen prior consultation in the extraction of hydrocarbons, the law was not enough. In order for prior consultation to be implemented, the indigenous movement had to be politically incorporated.

Indigenous Political Incorporation and Institutional Strengthening of Prior Consultation in Bolivia

After the MAS assumed the presidency in 2006 and until 2009, the process of institutionalization of prior consultation became self-enforcing, as the government largely supported the demands of the indigenous movement, which constituted the core of its social base and part of its leadership (Van Cott 2005: ch. 3; Madrid 2012: 50–58; Schavelzon 2012; Anria 2013, 2018). As a movement party, the MAS facilitated indigenous political incorporation in (at least) four ways: "First, the MAS has established close ties with a vast number of indigenous organizations in the country. Second, the MAS has run numerous indigenous candidates, including for high-profile positions. Third, the MAS has made a variety of symbolic appeals to Bolivia's indigenous population. Fourth and finally, the MAS has aggressively promoted traditional indigenous demands" (Madrid 2012: 53). Therefore, after 2006, the indigenous movement had been politically incorporated in the state and in the political party system. As Anria (2018) argues, the indigenous movement was meaningfully represented in state institutions and their policies, such as those of the national ministries, and in the process of candidate selection. Moreover, as Htun (2016: 35) shows, in 2011, 25 percent of Bolivia's deputies and 16 percent of its senators were indigenous.

When the constitutional assembly was in session from 2006 to 2009, 137 of its 255 seats were controlled by the MAS (Madrid 2012: 52). The indigenous sectors of the party successfully pushed for the adoption of radical legal innovations, including the identification of a new social subject, the "indigenous original peasant peoples and nations";[30] the definition of Bolivia as a

---

[30] The introduction of this concept in the constitution of 2009, without commas or hyphens, was a demand of the indigenous movement that took part in the constitutional convention (conversation with Diego Pary Rodríguez, member of the Constituent Assembly and Bolivian ambassador to the Organization of American States, in Philadelphia, March 7, 2018).

plurinational state; the adoption of living well as a constitutional principle;[31] the recognition of Mother Earth's rights; and the right of indigenous peoples to prior consultation with regard to the exploitation of nonrenewable natural resources in their territories.[32] Moreover, the resulting constitution recognizes the collective right of indigenous peoples and nations to self-government, listing their rights and responsibilities alongside those of the national and subnational governments. Because the indigenous movement was included in the Morales government, in the MAS, and represented in the Constitutional Assembly, its demands were largely adopted and prior consultation continued to gain legitimacy among indigenous groups.

Starting in 2007, the Ministry of Hydrocarbons and Energy (MHE) conducted consultations over gas extraction in indigenous territories. The Hydrocarbons Law and three regulatory decrees provided the legal framework for implementation.[33]

Since then, the process of prior consultation occurs in four stages: convocation, planning, execution, and validation. Each of these stages concludes with all parts signing a binding document (*acta*).[34] In this process, the extractive company agrees to pay indigenous communities for any damage that will be caused to their environment. Through secondary sources, I found that between 2007 and 2017 the MHE led fifty-eight consultations prior to the extraction of gas in territories of indigenous original nations and peasant communities. Map 11.2 shows the municipalities where those consultations took place, in some of them more than once.[35]

The available information on these processes is incomplete, but government documents, news media, case studies, and interviews indicate they involved contracts with a handful of large corporations, including the nationalized YPFB and its subsidiaries.[36] In all cases, the communities approved the

[31] The notion of Suma Qamaña, often translated as "buen vivir," or "living well," which emphasizes community and harmony with nature, was incorporated as a guiding principle in the 2009 Bolivian constitution, in response to demands from indigenous groups.

[32] Bolivian Constitution of 2009, Art. 11; Art. 30, II.15; Art. 304, I. 21; Art. 403; see also Schavelzon (2012).

[33] Decrees 29033 and 29124 (2007) and 29574 (2008) establish that hydrocarbon corporations ought to finance consultations (instead of the national executive, as per the Hydrocarbons Law), which cannot last longer than two months (with one extra month for compliance with the terms of the consultation).

[34] Author conversation with Xavier Barriga, director of environmental management, MHE, La Paz, Bolivia, March 20, 2014; see also Fundación TIERRA, www.slideshare.net/FTIERRA2010/omar-quiroga, accessed March 20, 2017.

[35] For the full list of consultations, see Table 1 in supplementary material for Falleti and Riofrancos (2018), doi:10.1017/S004388711700020X.

[36] For excellent case studies of consultation processes in the hydrocarbons sector, see Bascopé Sanjinés (2010); Flemmer and Schilling-Vacaflor (2016) on the limitations of indigenous participation; Humphreys Bebbington (2012); Pellegrini and Ribera Arismendi (2012); Schilling-Vacaflor (2012).

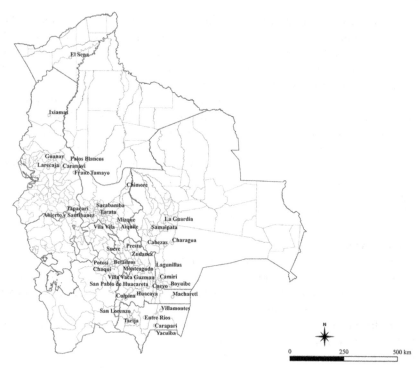

MAP 11.2. Municipalities with prior consultations since 2007, Bolivia.

extraction of natural resources; only one case was brought before the constitutional tribunal.[37] The size of the projects, the amount of compensation that
the communities receive, and the input they have on the extractive project and
required environmental licenses vary from case to case. In some cases, such as
in Charaguá Norte, where the indigenous community was well organized, had
trained environmental observers, and was supported by environmental and
legal NGOs (such as CEJIS), meaningful discussions and input were achieved
through prior consultation (de la Riva Miranda 2011: 40–56). In other cases,
the process consisted of negotiations between the parties to arrive at agreeable
compensations.

Whether the process is truly participatory and meaningful, or whether it
consists of a series of routinized practices to arrive at agreeable compensation, the difference in outcome for the communities the institution makes (*io*),

---

[37] This was the case of the Asamblea del Pueblo Guaraní (APG) of Itika Guasu against the
Argentine company, Repsol, in the fields of Margarita (Tarija), cited in Pérez Castellón
(2013, 15–16).

compared to what their situation would be if the institution were not in place or were not enforced (*po*) is rather large (*S*). If information were available, such distance could be measured in the millions of Bolivian pesos paid by corporations to the indigenous communities as compensation for environmental degradation.[38] Or perhaps more tellingly, if information were available, such distance could be measured in the decline of social conflict surrounding extraction of natural gas in indigenous territories in Bolivia.[39] Despite gaps in information, and despite criticisms of prior consultation as ineffective to stop extraction, prior consultation as an institution is highly legitimate in the eyes of indigenous groups. This is the reason why, in 2011, indigenous communities forcefully pressured the government to call a prior consultation over the construction of the TIPNIS highway – and they continue to do so to this day.[40] High legitimacy of prior consultation in the eyes of the indigenous movement was also the reason why in 2014 the indigenous organizations of the Pacto de Unidad worked on a national framework for a law of prior consultation that would further extend its reach to nonindigenous communities, to sectors other than hydrocarbons, and to stages of extraction as well as exploration. The bill was debated in Congress in 2014, but due largely to opposition from the mining sector, was not approved.

In addition, a significant decline in the price of hydrocarbons led the national government in 2015 to pass four regulatory decrees aimed at circumventing prior consultation. Decrees 2195, 2298, 2368, and 2366 (all from 2015) limit the amount of time for the consultation process, set the maximum compensation for environmental damages (to be between 0.3 and 1.5 percent of total investment), declare hydrocarbon pipes to be of national interest, and allow for extraction in national parks without prior consultation. Indigenous organizations have mobilized against these decrees and demanded prior consultation in nationally protected areas, once again showing the high level of legitimacy that the institution enjoys with the indigenous groups in

---

[38] Despite a formal request for information from the MHE, I did not have access to the signed agreements that result from prior consultations. News coverage of some agreements indicate that the amounts of compensation can be significant, particularly for highly impoverished communities.

[39] Following the news and based on interviews, this seems to be the case, with the exception being the region of the Gran Chaco, where conflicts remain between the Bolivian government and the APG over gas extraction.

[40] Conflicts with the government have run so high over the TIPNIS highway that the two main indigenous organizations, CIDOB and CONAMAQ, have divided. These divisions even transpired at the local level during the 2015 departmental and local elections, when indigenous groups supported or led the local political opposition to the MAS. See "Revolt from Indigenous Base Challenges Bolivia's Morales," Associated Press, May 21, 2015, www.usatoday.com/story/news/world/2015/05/21/indigenous-revolt-bolivia/27699325/.

Bolivia. During these conflicts, President Morales asserted, "We shouldn't be wasting so much time in the so-called consultations. This is the big weakness of our State."[41]

Interestingly, despite the president's reluctance to enforce the institution and the seemingly crippling decrees, despite the political splits within the indigenous organizations – exacerbated since 2014 – and despite the absence of a prior consultation national framework law; prior consultations in the hydrocarbons sectors have been systematically complied with and enforced since 2007, and they continue to be carried out throughout the country. Between 2014 and early 2017, at least fifteen consultations were underway.[42] Furthermore, the compensation that gas corporations pay to communities has been invested in local social development projects, such as schools, health clinics, and infrastructure for the affected communities. Indigenous organizations such as CONAMAQ and the Asamblea del Pueblo Guaraní (APG) continue to press for the enactment of a national prior consultation law. In their eyes, the institution of prior consultation is a legitimate right of indigenous communities and all those whose environments are affected by extractive projects.[43]

Despite the structural asymmetry between corporations and communities, prior consultation has provided indigenous communities in Bolivia with a normal politics means of interacting with the state and the extractive corporations. Even in instances where indigenous communities felt deceived by extractive corporations or the government, their demand to the state has been to properly carry out prior consultations.[44] Prior consultation is therefore an impactful and recurrent institution for the participation of indigenous communities affected by the extraction of gas in Bolivia. It has replaced the contentiousness that characterized the relationship between state and indigenous movements throughout the 1990s and early 2000s. It has become legitimate in the eyes of the indigenous communities that demand its extension to other communities and, after the 2015 decrees and laws, to protected natural areas (including TIPNIS). It is efficacious because the negotiating

---

[41] My translation. Original text reads: "No es posible que en las llamadas consultas se pierda tanto tiempo, esa es la gran debilidad que tiene nuestro Estado." Evo Morales, quoted in "Nueve consultas a pueblos indígenas terminaron con la aprobación de proyectos petroleros," *Página siete* (La Paz), July 26, 2016.

[42] See Table 1 in supplementary material for Falleti and Riofrancos (2018), doi:10.1017/S004388711700020X.

[43] Author interview with Renán Paco Granier, leader of CONAMAQ, La Paz, Bolivia, March 19, 2014.

[44] "Tacanas, el pueblo engañado," *Pagina siete*, October 22, 2017, www.paginasiete.bo/revmiradas/2017/10/22/tacanas-pueblo-enganado-156451.html.

parties follow through on the resulting agreements – or otherwise they make public their grievances. And it is enforced by the state, which, with the reluctant support of high-level officials, does not allow gas extraction without prior consultation.

CONCLUSION

Institutional strengthening is a multiphase, sequential process where the timing of its constitutive events, both in relation to each other and to their relevant political context, is highly consequential. In general, social mobilization in the process of adoption is necessary for an institution to gain strength (Falleti and Riofrancos 2018). But if political contention continues during the regulation and implementation phases of institutionalization, the interactions between social movements and states may significantly undermine institutional strengthening (see, for example, the case of Ecuador in Falleti and Riofrancos 2018). The timing of the political incorporation of social movement actors vis-à-vis the type of state and governmental policies through which they are incorporated is also highly consequential.

Unlike participatory budgeting and other deliberative institutions studied in the participatory democracy literature, prior consultation directly involves the corporate sector. The fact that prior consultation could potentially disrupt strategic extractive projects has important implications for corporate profits, state revenues, and state–society dynamics. This is the reason that the institution has been criticized by Evo Morales since 2015 and why states and corporations are reluctant to adopt it in countries such as Argentina. And yet we see that through political incorporation of the indigenous movement in the context of the progressive state after the ascension of the MAS to power in 2006, prior consultation gained institutional strength in Bolivia.

Against the backdrop of a neoliberal state, the MAS was formed as a social movement organization of peasants and coca growers that later developed a national strategy and forged links with the indigenous movement. When the party won the presidency in 2006, the indigenous movement was incorporated in the national state and participated actively in the process of regulating and implementing prior consultation. In terms of timing, the ascension of the MAS coincided with the crisis of the neoliberal state and the crystallization of the progressive state, which could organically incorporate indigenous movement demands. Thus, the MAS governed over the first sustained and at least partially successful attempt by the state to legitimate and shape an institutionalized indigenous movement. Such political incorporation meant that the indigenous movement had a say over the regulation and implementation of prior consultation. Prior consultation has enjoyed a high level of legitimacy among the indigenous in Bolivia. When applied in the hydrocarbons sector, it has been efficacious and the state is societally pressured to enforce it.

What are the lessons that can be drawn from this chapter, as it relates to the rest of the volume? First, state enforcement of prior consultation did not require a high degree of state capacity. The level of resources and personnel dedicated to prior consultation is relatively low. However, the state's will to roll out the institution was initially (as of 2006 and 2007) very important. Second, it appears that the high degree of legitimacy of prior consultation in the eyes of indigenous communities has kept it a stable institution over time.[45] It is very unlikely that without that constant pressure and demand for the implementation of the institution by the indigenous movement the Bolivian state would continue to enforce it. This leads to the third lesson: in order to stay strong, the institution must be continually enacted and defended. The indigenous movement has demonstrated the capacity to do so in their communities, asking the state to roll out and comply with prior consultation when necessary. But it has also shown the capacity to do so in the legislature, the constituent assembly, and more recently the courts. And if everything else fails, at least some sectors of the indigenous movement are ready to take their demands to the streets or the highways.

This important strengthening of prior consultation notwithstanding, it must be recognized that in Bolivia, as in other Latin American countries, prior consultation is set against the backdrop of the geographic expansion of natural resource extraction and heavily conditioned by it. In the 2000s, the commodity boom deepened economic dependency on the extraction of natural resources. With notable exceptions (such as the case of the Apaporis national park in the Colombian Amazon studied by Rodríguez-Franco 2017), prior consultation has not served as a tool against extraction. On the contrary, as several scholars have shown (Rodríguez Garavito 2012; Torres Wong 2018b), prior consultation is increasingly becoming a vehicle for negotiated extraction.

The theoretical implication of this case study is portable to other contexts. In democratic or political regimes with at least a moderate level of political accountability – an important scope condition of the argument – the expectation is that when the social sectors mobilized for the adoption of an institution are politically incorporated (either via state institutions or through a competitive political party system) in the regulatory process, the institution they help bring about will gain legitimacy and efficacy, and thus will be complied with and enforced. Without political incorporation, participatory institutions, at least, are either likely to die in the letter of the law as a mere window dressing institution or to fuel conflict between state and mobilized social actors for its activation. The strength of prior consultation in the hydrocarbons sector

---

[45] This is unlike other countries, such as Mexico, where indigenous communities are experimenting with *auto-consultas* due to the low legitimacy of prior consultation, particularly as an instrument to reject extraction (see the ongoing research of Marcela Torres Wong on this topic).

in Bolivia has been inextricable from the actions of the mobilized indigenous movement that brought it about in the context of the neoliberal state in the early 1990s, and through political incorporation into the state and the political party system was able activate what until then had been a window dressing institution. After 2007, prior consultation in hydrocarbons in Bolivia has enjoyed high levels of legitimacy with indigenous communities, who comply with the institution, as do corporate actors – some of whom have substantially "upgraded" their social responsibility discourse. And the state, even if begrudgingly as the price of commodities dropped, is being held accountable to enforce the institution.

12

Conclusion

Daniel M. Brinks, Steven Levitsky,
and María Victoria Murillo

We began this book with the premise that what ultimately distinguishes strong institutions from weak ones is that the former matter more than the latter. The same institution, in two different contexts or at two different times, is stronger if it makes more of a behavioral difference in one instance than in the other. As the chapters in this volume make clear, however, it is difficult to evaluate exactly how much an institution "matters." It is relatively simple to say that an institution is strong because, on paper, it possesses features that should make it matter – for example, it commands great things. But it is an altogether different – and, we believe, far more interesting – thing to say that an institution is strong because it actually produces an outcome that is substantially different from what we might have observed in its absence, and that it continues to produce that outcome even in the face of pressures to change it or avoid it altogether.

The chapters in this volume reveal a striking diversity in terms of institutions' effects: strong ones and weak ones, ones that endure and ones that crumble at the first touch of political resistance. The chapters chronicle failures of enforcement and failures of compliance, top-down indifference and bottom-up resistance. They uncover institutions that appear designed to be weak, because the sanctions for noncompliance are patently and predictably inadequate to produce a change in behavior, and institutions that change with alarming frequency even though they seem, on paper, designed to endure. They also find institutions that actually have important effects – the ones, it appears, they were designed to have (albeit sometimes only after a belated activation).

The contributors to this volume provide a more nuanced understanding of the categories of institutional weakness put forth in the introduction. Most of the chapters highlight the conditions that shape variation in compliance, such as limited enforcement, insufficient state capacity, or societal cooperation.

For example, Falleti characterizes Bolivia's prior consultation law as a *window dressing* institution that was subsequently given teeth by the MAS government in a context of social mobilization and changing power distributions. Holland's chapter highlights local government officials' incentive to engage in *forbearance* where the costs of enforcing certain national laws are borne locally, generating what she labels a "coercion gap." Saffón and González Bertomeu describe the *selective enforcement* of Mexican property rights laws during the mid-nineteenth century, as the church's collective properties were targeted for privatization but indigenous community lands were not. (Over time, rising land prices triggered by a late nineteenth-century commodity boom led to the law's activation – mainly via judicial interpretation – and application to indigenous communities as well.) Likewise, Fernández Milmanda and Garay examine how variation in the power of provincial landowners and environmental nongovernmental organizations (NGOs) yields differential enforcement of forest protection regulation and varying degrees of discretion in defining protected areas and applying sanctions. Fernández Milmanda and Garay also show how compliance may be low despite regular enforcement: low sanctions for the violation of forest protection regulation in the Argentine province of Salta are an example of nonpunitive enforcement, or an *unsanctioned institution*.

Two other chapters highlight the role of state capacity. Amengual and Dargent argue that *standoffish* states generally require a mix of societal pressure and cooperation to enforce laws and regulations. Their chapter shows how the presence or absence of societal coproduction – often through monitoring and resource sharing – affects compliance with environmental, mining, and labor regulations. Htun and Jensenius's chapter on Mexico's law on violence against women highlights not only the centrality of societal cooperation (in this case, in the form of reporting) but also the strategic incentives of rule writers who design such laws even when they know that prevailing social norms will limit compliance. Htun and Jensenius describe these as *aspirational laws*.

Two of the volume's chapters examine the roots of institutional instability in Latin America. Calvo and Negretto analyze the instability of electoral laws, which in much of the region may be characterized as *serial replacement*. Helmke shows how institutional instability generated by repeated executive–legislative conflict may result in long-run *instability traps*.

Finally, two of the volume's chapters examine unexpectedly strong institutions in Latin America. In their chapter, Albertus and Menaldo explore the conditions under which authoritarian constitutions endure beyond democratic transitions that remove their designers from power. And Schrank's chapter explores the conditions under which institutions borrowed from abroad may take root in a seemingly unfavorable domestic environment.

Table 12.1 below organizes the chapters according to our typology on institutional weakness.

TABLE 12.1. *Categories of institutional weakness described in chapters*

	Type	Description	Chapters
Insignificance		Institution has zero ambition, in that it does not prescribe a meaningful change in actors' behavior even when fully enforced and complied with.	*Window dressing institutions*: **Falleti** on Bolivia's prior consultation laws before 2005. *Forbearance*: **Holland** on laws against squatting in Lima and Bogotá. *Selective enforcement*: **Fernández Milmanda and Garay** on forest protection laws in Argentine provinces; **Saffon and Gonzalez Bertomeu** on the application of private property laws in Mexico; **Helmke** on the application of impeachment regulations.
Noncompliance	Type I: Nonenforcement	Institution prescribes significant behavioral change, but state officials choose not to enforce it systematically.	
	Type II: Nonpunitive Enforcement	Rule is enforced and sanctions are applied, but the sanctions are too weak to change behavior.	*Unsanctioned institutions*: **Fernandez Milmanda and Garay** on forest protection laws in Salta.
	Type III: Weak State Capacity Relative to Societal Resistance	Government officials seek compliance with the institution but lack sufficient state capacity or societal cooperation to systematically enforce it.	*Standoffish states*: **Amengual and Dargent** on mining, environmental, and construction regulations in Peru and Bolivia. *Aspirational laws*: **Htun and Jensenius** on laws against gender violence in Mexico.
Instability		Rules change at an unusually high rate and in contradictory directions, preventing actors from developing stable expectations around them.	*Serial replacement*: **Calvo and Negretto** on electoral law reforms in Latin America. *Instability trap*: **Helmke** on the instability caused by executive–legislative conflict.

Research on institutional weakness is thus reshaping our understanding of how politics works in Latin America and elsewhere. When actors design or reform institutions, they consider not only the rules' substance but also the likelihood of their compliance and endurance. Some institutions, like window dressing laws, are created precisely because actors do not expect compliance. Others, like the aspirational laws described by Htun and Jensenius, are created with the knowledge that they will not be complied with in the short term, but in the hope that they will reshape norms and behavior in the longer term. Alternatively, actors may create rules that they expect to comply with in the short term but not in the long term (e.g., presidential term limits in twenty-first-century Bolivia and Venezuela). This variation in expected compliance and stability affects political behavior and outcomes in important ways. Indeed, research that takes this variation seriously has led scholars to rethink and revise important institutionalist theories in comparative and Latin American politics.

In the remainder of this concluding chapter, we examine how our contributors addressed the multiple measurement challenges that are inherent in the study of institutional weakness. We also discuss the conditions behind the persistence of institutional weakness in Latin America. Finally, we conclude by focusing on processes of institutional weakening and its possible implications beyond Latin America.

MEASURING INSTITUTIONAL WEAKNESS

Measuring institutional weakness can be extremely difficult. Because non-compliance entails rule breaking, actors often seek to hide or disguise it, leading to underreporting and undercounting. Insignificance poses a very different problem, one of causal identification: because everyone acts in accordance with the rule, insignificant institutions can be easily confused with strong ones. Instability is easier to observe but harder to interpret. How are we to distinguish a pattern of instability from one of normal institutional adaptation or change, which is, rather, a sign of strength? Each of the chapters in this volume grappled with these issues of measurement and developed innovative techniques for capturing institutional noncompliance or instability. The strategies for measuring weakness vary considerably. In this section, we provide a brief – and by no means exhaustive – summary of these efforts, highlighting both the potential advantages and some of the limitations and pitfalls of each.

Measuring Noncompliance

A central challenge in measuring compliance is not only the fact that non-compliance is often hidden, but also that the difficulty of observing non-compliance is at least partially endogenous to the strength of the institution.

Rule violations often result in clear victims (labor law violations, police violence, domestic abuse), but the weaker the institution, the more likely it is that these violations will be underobserved and underreported. Monitoring and reporting are important contributions of societal coproduction, but the more an institution challenges social norms, the less likely we are to find coproduction. As a result, measuring compliance often requires strategies that *indirectly* capture noncompliance by either assessing outcomes or relying on measurement strategies that deal with social desirability bias.

Direct Observation of Violations

The most direct way to measure compliance is, of course, to count the frequency (or, better, the ratio) of violations. As noted above, this is often not a viable strategy for observational reasons. It is, for example, difficult to directly measure levels of bureaucratic corruption, vote buying, tax fraud, or violence against women, because these behaviors are usually hidden. Still, researchers have at times found creative solutions to these problems. In some instances, new technologies allow for direct observation (e.g., satellite pictures may be used to track illegal mining and deforestation). In other cases, experimental techniques such as list experiments may be used to overcome the effects of social desirability bias and assess the prevalence of certain norm-violating behavior (Gingerich 2010; González Ocantos, de Jonge, and Nickerson 2014).

Sometimes, however, the difficulty is interpretive rather than observational. Some behavior that potentially constitutes a violation is highly visible, such as when presidents overstay their terms (Elkins 2017) or are removed early (Helmke, this volume), but it is nevertheless difficult to determine whether the behavior constitutes a violation of the rules. For example, Alberto Fujimori and Evo Morales were each elected under constitutions that prohibited reelection but oversaw the adoption of new constitutions that established US-style two-term limits. Both presidents sought to run for a third term (Fujimori in 2000, Morales in 2014) on the grounds that their first term, under the old constitution, did not count. Whether the two presidents violated the rules was a matter of intense legal and political debate. Likewise, does the impeachment of a president based on a technicality or a pretextual rationale (e.g., the 2012 impeachment of Paraguayan president Fernando Lugo) constitute a violation, and thus evidence of weakness, or is it simply the exercise of institutional prerogatives, and thus a sign of strength (Helmke 2017, this volume)? As Helmke observes in her chapter, it is often difficult to reach agreement on whether an impeachment is rule abiding or rule violating.

When the legal appropriateness of a particular behavior is disputed, it is up to scholars to develop clear criteria to score cases as instances of a violation or not. Scholars have done so using internal analyses – that is, by evaluating the rationale offered for the behavior and deciding, according to the relevant standards of legal or professional analysis, whether it is in conformity with the rules. But this is subjective and difficult, and it often exceeds the expertise of a researcher. Moreover, it can easily be called into question, especially when the behavior is legitimized by, say, the highest court of the country (which is charged precisely with deciding whether the behavior constitutes a rule violation). External analyses based not on the legal bases of each decision, but rather on an examination of whether decisions align more clearly with political or other motives than with legal rationales, can be more objective, even if they are less direct. This is the approach Helmke takes in her recent work on interbranch crises in Latin America (2017: 19–50). To determine whether a legislature's removal of the president constitutes a violation of impeachment rules, for example, Helmke suggests asking whether the president is replaced by a partisan ally or an opponent (2017: 36–38). Where the latter occurs, and the legality of the removal is contested, it seems reasonable to score it as a violation.

In some cases, violations may be assessed by simply looking for the outcomes the institution is designed to prevent. For instance, overall deforestation rates may be used as a proxy for avoiding environmental regulations (see Fernández Milmanda and Garay, this volume). But often the point of the institution is not to eliminate an outcome altogether but rather to subject it to certain conditions. Presidents may be impeached, but only for legitimate reasons, and forests may be cut down, but only certain ones, and only up to a point. Here again, an external analysis can assist with measurement. We can compare outcomes to earlier periods (e.g., before a regulation was established) or to other cases where levels of compliance are known, can be estimated, or can be assumed to vary randomly (e.g., regional or international averages). For instance, Fernández Milmanda and Garay (this volume) compare deforestation rates on either side of provincial lines in the same rain forest to estimate failures of compliance on one side or the other.

A pattern of covariation with political variables is often the clearest indication that an institution is failing to produce the right outcomes. Forests typically do not vary on either side of a purely political boundary, but politics do; and the legitimacy of land claims typically does not vary according to the wealth of the claimant, but power and influence do. Conversely, there are instances in which outcomes more closely match the institutional logic than one of traditional influence. Schrank, in this volume, finds patterns in hiring, assigning, and promoting inspectors that vary according to the logic of a Weberian meritocracy rather than according to a more patrimonial, influence-based logic.

Observation of Sanctions

Although rule violations are often difficult to observe, the sanctioning of violations is often public and thus more easily measured. Assuming we can somehow hold the relative rate of detection constant, we could use the frequency of punitive sanctions as an indirect measure of compliance. For instance, the marked increase in punishments meted out to both doctors and women involved in illegal abortions in El Salvador and Nicaragua has been taken as evidence that antiabortion laws are now being enforced (albeit with class-based disparities), and thus strengthened, in those countries (Viterna 2012; Center for Reproductive Rights 2014).[1] Similarly, Nichter (2011) uses evidence of the increased number of prosecutions for vote buying in Brazil, paired with evidence showing increased public demand for prosecutions, to argue that anti–vote-buying institutions are strengthening. Such claims, of course, hinge on the assumption that the underlying rate of violations remains roughly constant, and that what has changed is the level of enforcement. This is why evidence of increased prosecutions must be paired either with evidence that violations have increased (to show institutional weakening) or with evidence that enforcement effort has increased (to show institutional strengthening) before it can be interpreted.

Even when the levels are more static, the relationship between frequency of sanction and compliance is often far from clear. Infrequent sanctions may be a manifestation of high compliance (e.g., prosecution of Swedish security officials for human rights violations) or low enforcement (e.g., prosecution of Guatemalan security officials for human rights violations). Frequent sanctions may be so mild that their systematic application has little effect on behavior (see Fernández Milmanda and Garay, this volume). Sometimes the enforcement effort and the number of violations are both changing, which makes it nearly impossible to know whether the institution is actually strengthening or not. For example, the number of sanctions against illegal miners in Peru increased markedly in the 2000s, but it almost certainly did not keep pace with the increase in the number of illegal miners (Amengual and Dargent, this volume), which would suggest institutional weakening despite increased enforcement effort.

Even in relatively straightforward cases of increased enforcement, the relationship between reporting or sanctioning and compliance is likely to be nonlinear. As rates of sanctioning increase, we would expect compliance to gradually increase due to the deterrence effect of successful prosecutions; as compliance grows, however, rates of reporting and sanctions should naturally decrease. Increased enforcement effort should thus produce a bell-shaped pattern: an initial surge in both reporting and sanctions, followed by a tailing off as compliance increases. This is not to say that a bell-shaped pattern is always evidence of institutional success. Although such a pattern may be evidence of newfound institutional strength, a lower rate of prosecution could also be caused by a backlash against enforcement. Thus, to determine whether increased enforcement signals an increase in institutional strength, we still need additional information about the underlying rate of violations or the level of enforcement effort.

[1] See "Miscarriage of Justice: Abortion in El Salvador," *Economist*, December 1, 2016.

Measuring Enforcement Effort

Another indirect measure of compliance is the level of state investment in enforcement. Thus, an increase in state investment in bureaucratic capacity – professionalization, resources – can be used as a proxy for increased enforcement. Schrank (2009), for example, uses the number of labor inspectors and investment in training labor inspectors as a proxy for the enforcement of labor regulation in the Dominican Republic. In his chapter for this volume, he points to the increasing professionalization of the labor regulatory bureaucracy as a measure of the strength of civil service regulations.

This proxy measure, however, also has some drawbacks. A small state investment in enforcement does not necessarily imply a weak institution, as there might be other enforcement mechanisms at work. Institutions might depend on "fire alarm" as opposed to "police patrol" enforcement measures, or they may be sustained by self-help measures, political threats, reinforcing social norms, market incentives, and much more. No institution depends solely on state enforcement – indeed, our chapters show that enforcement is often coproduced by the state and societal actors.

Additionally, state investment must be considered in relation to the enforcement challenges. We cannot classify an institution as strong simply because there is a substantial commitment of resources and a great deal of organizational development if it is merely a valiant effort in an otherwise losing battle to change practices. A state's effort may still be insufficient to increase compliance, even when the investment in enforcement is high relative to that in other areas of the state (or in other countries) (Dargent, Feldmann, and Luna 2017). Indeed, the conditions that permit a greater investment in enforcement resources may also be fostering greater societal resistance. For example, rising mineral prices may generate greater state revenue, thereby permitting the government to hire more inspectors, but they also create stronger incentives for illegal mining. In that case, we would want to say that the relevant institution remains weak despite greater investment in enforcement.

Coproduction as an Indirect Measure of Compliance

In cases where "fire alarms" are an important mechanism of monitoring, and where the cost of enforcement is shared with societal actors who benefit from compliance, scholars could use societal coproduction of enforcement as an indirect measure of institutional strength. This potentially enables scholars to capture two different sources of strength. For one, where coproduction is at work, state-based enforcement efforts are supplemented by a nonstate actor with a comparative advantage in monitoring. In addition, the investment in monitoring and other forms of coproduced enforcement is institution-specific, giving participating actors a greater stake in the institution's success (Pierson 2004; Thelen 2004). We thus have good theoretical reasons to believe that coproduction reflects the sort of societal roots that would both deter noncompliance and prevent a dismantling of the institution.

An example of how societal support for compliance may be used as a proxy for compliance is survey evidence of citizens' normative adherence to new parchment rules or "aspirational" rights. This is the strategy Htun and Jensenius employ in their chapter on compliance with violence against women in Mexico. Because enforcement of domestic violence laws requires coproduction, in that citizens must report instances of abuse to state authorities, survey-based evidence of the level of societal commitment (or resistance) to reporting is a potentially useful measure of institutional strength. Likewise, survey experiments using vignettes could be employed to assess whether societal norms lead individuals to view noncompliance as justified – in other words, to gauge the "coercion gap" described by Holland (this volume).

Measuring Insignificance

Distinguishing institutional insignificance from institutional strength is especially challenging. As noted in the introduction, insignificant institutions are those that have no effect because actors would behave in the same way even if the rule did not exist. S is zero. The problem is distinguishing insignificance from an institution so strong that it generates full compliance: when a rule is never violated, p_0, and therefore S, is unobservable. Is full compliance with a low minimum wage evidence of a strong institution that induces firms to pay higher wages than they might otherwise pay? Or is it simply evidence of an insignificant institution that sets a very low minimum wage in a tight labor market?

To complicate measurement even further, some institutions are so effective that, over time, they reshape societal norms in ways that render the formal institutions insignificant. When such laws are first put in place, S may be large, requiring vigorous enforcement efforts. But over time, societal norms may evolve to match the law. As individuals internalize these new norms, compliance becomes taken for granted and enforcement ceases to be necessary. As a result, S shrinks, sometimes to near zero, transforming what had been a strong institution into an insignificant one. Examples might include mandatory seatbelt laws and public smoking bans in the United States.

Of course, whether or not strong institutions have lost relevance – just how much S has shrunk – is difficult to discern and may be the subject of considerable dispute. For example, when the US Supreme Court struck down key provisions of the 1965 Voting Rights Act (VRA) in 2013, the decision was based in part on the claim that S had shrunk – that behavior had changed such that strict oversight and enforcement mechanisms were no longer necessary. In other words, in the view of the Supreme Court, the VRA had drifted into insignificance. Critics of the decision disagreed, viewing high levels of compliance as evidence that the VRA's enforcement mechanisms were effective (and thus necessary) rather than insignificant. As Justice Ruth

Bader Ginsburg wrote in her dissent, doing away with VRA oversight was like "throwing away your umbrella during a rainstorm because you are not getting wet."[2]

Distinguishing insignificant from strong institutions thus requires some understanding of underlying preferences and norms. Survey evidence could be used, for example, to evaluate the degree to which rules have been internalized and taken for granted. Alternatively, we could compare political units (provinces, countries) with similar social norms but contrasting rules to assess the impact of the institution on behavioral outcomes. Finally, we can examine whether behavioral outcomes change in cases where seemingly arcane laws are removed from the books, as when Canada repealed its antidueling legislation in 2017. If behavior changes significantly once the institution is removed (something that, to our knowledge, has not occurred with Canadian dueling!), we might conclude that it was, in fact, still doing important work in constraining behavior.

Measuring Instability

At first blush, measuring institutional instability should be simple. Changes in formal rules are almost always observable. Yet institutional change is not always an indicator of instability. As we argued in the introduction, many instances of institutional change should be understood as normal adaptation, in the sense that they are expected or necessary responses to changes in the external environment. Regulatory reforms in the face of new environmental conditions or technological developments are one example. When environmental conditions change dramatically, altering the effects of existing institutions, institutional change may be necessary to maintain the spirit of the original rules. That is, if the preinstitutional outcome changes or the institution loses potency because of a changing context, adaptation may be necessary to ensure that the institution is really making a difference and has not "drifted" into insignificance. In those cases, we would categorize institutional reform as adaptation rather than instability because it seeks to preserve the spirit of the original rules in the face of environmental change. The challenge, then, is to distinguish adaptation from institutional instability by focusing on whether the changes are meant to produce an altogether different effect, or to preserve the relevance and goals of the original institution.

In some cases, we can use the rate of change relative to a comparative benchmark to measure instability as opposed to adaptation. The implicit assumption is that the benchmark, either established using some theoretical criteria or relying on empirical frequencies to define what is "normal"

---

[2] *Shelby County, Alabama v. Eric Holder, Jr.*, 570 US 529 (2013).

adaptation, reflects a "normal" rate of institutional change. For instance, Elkins, Ginsburg, and Melton (2009) find that since 1789, the average constitution has endured for seventeen years. Bolivia and Ecuador, in contrast, have each changed constitutions about twenty times since independence less than two centuries ago, for an average duration of fewer than ten years. Bolivia had eleven different constitutions in its first fifty-four years of independence, for an average duration of about five years, and it has had seven different ones since 1938 – an average duration of about eleven years. Using the global benchmark, we can say that both Bolivia and Ecuador have experienced a high level of institutional instability – their constitutions have generally been weak institutions. Absent some evidence of special circumstances justifying the high frequency of change in these countries, it seems clear that this instability is not driven by adaptation to changes in background conditions, but rather by low barriers to change, coupled with changing preferences among the actors who effectively controlled the constitution-making process. Calvo and Negretto employ such a strategy in their chapter on the stability of electoral laws in Latin America.

An indirect way to identify when change signals instability rather than adaptation is to find rules that do not survive their rule writers. At least one goal of institutional creation is to decouple the desired outcome from the power relations in place at the time of institutional creation. Stable institutions, therefore, should generally endure despite changes in governing coalitions (Huntington 1968). Thus, when every change in government coalitions is accompanied by rule reforms that push S in different directions, we are more likely to be observing institutional instability than adaptation. One measure of strength, therefore, is when an institution's distributive effects are accepted – or at least are not contested – by all of the principal coalitions competing for power. This was the case with some of the authoritarian constitutions discussed in Albertus and Menaldo's chapter, including Pinochet's 1980 constitution in Chile and Fujimori's 1993 constitution in Peru.[3]

The Counterfactual Benchmark

Our conceptual framework does not eliminate all the methodological difficulties with measuring institutional strength, but it helps to clarify the requisite tasks. Often, measuring institutional strength will depend on carefully constructing a counterfactual from which we can impute either the institutional outcome or the preinstitutional one, and thus derive what S might be, given all the relevant circumstances. For instability, the goal is to understand whether the

---

[3] Even authoritarian constitutions eventually see their supporters literally die out; Albertus and Menaldo find that such constitutions become vulnerable to replacement after the death of the former authoritarian leader.

changes tend to protect or eliminate S, which requires estimating what the social impact of the institution would have been if the institution had not changed. For example, are frequent changes to the minimum wage meant to preserve a wage premium in light of inflation, or do they alternately raise and eliminate the wage premium? For noncompliance, if we observe only the non-institutional outcome, we need to estimate what outcome the institution would have produced in the case of compliance, and vice versa. Would deforestation take place at a lower rate in Salta if the fines were greater and the rules were complied with? A comparison with deforestation in the neighboring province of Chaco suggest that is likely to be the case (Fernández Milmanda and Garay, this volume). In spite of these difficulties in assessing the value of *io* and *po*, we believe the measures used in the chapters of this volume provide examples of how to construct this counterfactual comparison. The problem of what might have happened if not for x is ever present in social science; measuring institutional weakness is just one more instance of that problem.

THE PERSISTENCE OF INSTITUTIONAL WEAKNESS IN LATIN AMERICA

This volume has argued that institutional weakness has deep roots in Latin America. When Latin America joined the club of early decolonizers in the 1820s, many of the region's founding constitution writers were highly ambitious, designing institutions – modeled, to a significant extent, on the United States – aimed at accelerating the transformation of social norms and power structures. Early constitutions were thus characterized by a sharp disjuncture between the ambition of rule makers and reality on the ground, which resulted in widespread noncompliance and institutional instability. Indeed, the political instability that characterized much of twentieth-century Latin America may have been rooted, in part, in an institutional instability trap created by the postcolonial strategy of designing aspirational rules sustained by weak coalitions.

Yet the third wave of democratization marked a dramatic change in Latin America. Nearly every country in the region has held competitive elections since 1990, and many can now boast at least moderately well-functioning democracies, with clean elections, pluralization of power, effective civil and political rights, increasing citizen participation, and reasonably responsive governments.

There are good reasons to expect three decades of democracy to strengthen political institutions. For one, it is now more difficult for rulers to change laws and constitutions unilaterally. Pluralization of power and, in many countries, political fragmentation mean that institutional reform now requires concessions to multiple veto players in exchange for the desired outcome (see, e.g., Brinks and Blass 2018: ch. 6). This should increase the cost of institutional change relative to earlier decades, particularly in democracies with more effective checks and balances.

Democracy has also contributed to the strengthening of enforcement institutions, such as courts and prosecutors (see, e.g., Couso, Huneeus, and Sieder 2010; Brinks and Blass 2017, 2018), as well as the emergence and strengthening of new mechanisms of horizontal accountability (see, e.g., O'Donnell 1998; Mainwaring and Welna 2003). A robust legislative opposition is often crucial to the creation and operation of effective electoral oversight mechanisms (Schedler, Diamond, and Plattner 1999). From central banks (Keefer and Stasavage 2003) to judiciaries (Ginsburg 2003; Bill Chavez 2004; Helmke and Ríos-Figueroa 2011), greater pluralism should enhance horizontal accountability. The increased autonomy of enforcement regimes from those who wield power should result in greater compliance.

In the shorthand we have employed in this volume, then, stable democracy and the pluralization of politics should make institutional change more difficult, increasing C, and should also strengthen enforcement mechanisms, increasing V. We would therefore expect, ceteris paribus, higher levels of institutional stability, greater compliance, and the activation of previously dormant institutions – in other words, stronger institutions across the board.

Indeed, political institutions *have* strengthened in much of Latin America. In many countries, courts are stronger (Sieder and Angel 2005; Couso, Huneeus, and Sieder 2010; Rodríguez Garavito 2011), electoral laws are better enforced (Mozaffar and Schedler 2002), social policies are increasingly implemented in accordance with universalistic rules (De la O 2015; Garay 2016), participatory institutions have empowered indigenous groups (Falleti and Riofrancos 2018), some bureaucracies are stronger (Dargent 2015), and, in a few cases, enforcement of labor and environmental regulation has improved dramatically (Hochstetler and Keck 2007; Schrank 2011; Amengual 2016).

Overall, however, institutional strengthening has been modest in third-wave Latin America. Problems of institutional instability and low compliance persist throughout much of the region. Constitutions and electoral institutions remain remarkably unstable (Elkins 2017; Calvo and Negretto, this volume); labor, environmental, and other regulations remain unevenly enforced (Amengual 2016; Amengual and Dargent, this volume); and the number of dubiously constitutional presidential reelections, irregular removals of presidents, and other constitutional crises continues to be strikingly high (Helmke, this volume).

What explains the persistence of weak institutions in much of Latin America? Three long-standing and interconnected factors appear to reinforce institutional weakness in the region. The first is socioeconomic inequality. Extreme inequality often results in uneven compliance (O'Donnell 1993, 1999a; Lieberman 2003). Where social, economic, racial, and gender inequality is high, wealthier and higher-status individuals are more likely to have both an interest in and the means to evade laws – including everything from tax laws and labor regulations to abortion laws and military conscription – that apply to lower- and middle-income citizens (see Lieberman 2003). In other cases, like that of violence against women laws in Mexico, only wealthy and well-educated individuals possess the resources to comply with (and thus benefit from) what are widely understood to be aspirational law (Htun and Jensenius, this volume).

As Holland's chapter on forbearance makes clear, uneven compliance does not always favor the rich. Inequality reduces the likelihood that the poor will exert influence in the national-level arenas where laws are designed. However, the all-too-visible cost of actually enforcing laws that impose great harm on poor people – like laws prohibiting squatting and street vending – generates powerful pressure for local governments to engage in forbearance. In this case, then, selective enforcement favors the poor in the short term while reducing incentives for redistribution through public policy in the longer term.

A second factor reinforcing institutional weakness is the persistence of low state capacity (Centeno 2002; O'Donnell 2004a). In terms of fiscal capacity, Latin American states remain considerably weaker than their counterparts in Europe and East Asia (Cardenas 2010). Early patterns of state weakness, rooted in factors such as social inequality, the nature of interstate conflict, and the timing of the region's insertion into the global economy, have persisted over time.[4] Limited state capacity thus helps explain the "standoffish" nature of many Latin American states (Amengual and Dargent, this volume), as well as the incentives for governments to use forbearance as an informal social policy instead of investing in formal welfare states (Holland, this volume). Weak states with limited revenues must pick and choose their enforcement battles and are more dependent on societal coproduction to achieve compliance.

Third, institutional weakness is reinforced by persistent economic and political volatility. Economic shocks such as high inflation, recession, and commodity boom and bust cycles remain a common occurrence in most of Latin America. As a producer of natural resources dependent on external capital, the region has long been vulnerable to boom and bust cycles (Campello and Zucco 2015). Economic shocks disrupt distributive coalitions and generate higher levels of public discontent, which contribute to higher levels of institutional instability. Economic shocks have hardly diminished during the democratic era. Indeed, in the last thirty-five years alone, Latin America has experienced the debt crisis and soaring inflation of the 1980s, the "lost half-decade" of 1998–2002, and the extraordinary commodities boom and

---

[4] On the origins of state weakness in the region, see Centeno (2002); Coatsworth (2008); Mahoney (2010); Kurtz (2013); Soifer (2015).

bust cycle of 2002–2014 (Bértola and Ocampo 2012). As a result, pressure for policy and institutional change remains high.

Historically, political volatility has also been high in Latin America. In much of the region, military coups and other irregular seizures of power brought frequent, sudden, and often dramatic reshufflings of rule-writing coalitions. The Mexican presidency changed hands a stunning thirty-six times between 1835 and 1863. Bolivia and Paraguay each experienced more than a dozen coups in the twentieth century alone. Although the post-1978 third wave brought an unprecedented level of democratic stability to the region, electoral volatility remains extraordinarily high (Roberts 2014; Mainwaring 2018),[5] and a striking number of elected presidents have been unable to finish their term in office: *twenty-five* Latin American presidents were either impeached or forced to resign amid protest and impeachment threats between 1978 and 2018 (Pérez-Liñán and Polga-Hecimovich 2018).[6]

Contra widespread expectations, few Latin American party systems stabilized over the course of the third wave. Levels of electoral volatility, which were among the highest in the world in the 1990s, remained strikingly high (Roberts 2014; Mainwaring 2018). Indeed, many of the region's party systems (e.g., Argentina, Colombia, Costa Rica, Guatemala, Honduras, Mexico, Peru, Venezuela) grew considerably *more* fragmented and volatile during the early twenty-first century. Although healthy political pluralism may contribute to institutional strength, extreme fragmentation and electoral volatility can be an important source of institutional instability. As long as Latin American democracies are characterized by frequent and far-reaching shifts in governing coalitions, and therefore rule makers, many political institutions are likely to remain unstable.

These observations suggest that the persistence of institutional weakness in Latin America is rooted in economic and political conditions that have long afflicted the region: state weakness, high socioeconomic inequality, and economic and political volatility. Worse, there is reason to think that these conditions are, at least in part, a function of institutional weaknesses. Thus, much of Latin America may be suffering from a self-reinforcing cycle in which social inequality and economic and political instability generate institutional weakness, which, in turn, reinforces inequality and instability.

A final, somewhat paradoxical, factor reinforcing institutional weakness in Latin America may be democracy itself. Latin America is more democratic

---

[5] There is also evidence that this electoral volatility is rooted in unstable economic conditions. See Roberts and Wibbels (1999); Campello and Zucco (2015); Murillo and Visconti (2017).

[6] Not all coalitions are unstable in Latin America. For example, Albertus and Menaldo's (this volume) analysis of authoritarian constitutions highlights the role of coalitional stability. One of the factors sustaining holdover constitutions, they argue, is the survival of old-guard authoritarian elites and their economic allies. For authoritarian constitutions to break down, they find, the old elite must be "dead and gone."

today than at any other period in history. Civilian rule and competitive elections are solidly in place in nearly every country in the region – and have been for more than a generation. However, democracy itself may reinforce institutional weakness in Latin America – by generating pressure for the design of more ambitious institutions. Democratization permitted the emergence of a revitalized civil society. Free to organize without fear of repression, a diversity of civic groups mobilized in pursuit of ambitious socioeconomic and political goals during the late twentieth and early twenty-first centuries. Whether it was indigenous groups in Bolivia and Ecuador, landless and environmental movements in Brazil, unemployed workers in Argentina, or students in Chile, social movements across Latin America pushed governments to adopt new rights, protections, and other inclusionary reforms (Garay 2016; Falleti and Riofrancos 2018; Silva and Rossi 2018). At the same time, electoral competition – in a context of extreme social inequality – generated incentives for politicians to embrace and advance these reforms.

Indeed, Latin America's electoral turn to the Left in the early twenty-first century gave rise to a range of new policies and institutions aimed at appealing to previously marginalized constituencies (Levitsky and Roberts 2011). Examples include the inclusion of diverse social rights (Gauri and Brinks 2008; Elkins, Ginsburg, and Melton 2009) and indigenous rights (Yashar 2005) in new constitutions, the creation of new participatory institutions (Wampler 2009; Mayka 2019) and mechanisms of prior consultation (Falleti and Riofrancos 2018), the expansion of social policy to include the informal poor (Garay 2016), and the adoption of gender and racial quota laws (Htun 2016), anti–domestic violence laws (Htun and Jensenius this volume), and laws protecting the rights of domestic workers. Whether these laws were meant as window dressing or as aspirational, the fact remains that they sought to produce great social change, and their ambition often outstripped their effectiveness.

In sum, democratic politics amid extreme social inequality creates incentives for the design of institutions that pursue far-reaching goals. In other words, it gives rise to institutions that are highly ambitious – io' in Figure 1.1 (see Chapter 1). As we argued above, however, extreme inequality creates obstacles to compliance. Inequality creates incentives for privileged sectors to avoid compliance and endows them with the resources to do it. Where wealth is highly concentrated, economic elites tend to exert vast influence over state officials – via campaign contributions, bribes, media ownership, the contracting of high-powered lawyers, and gatekeeping in elite social circles. In extreme cases, legislators, governors, mayors, judges, public prosecutors, and bureaucrats become agents of the rich. The result, in many cases, is uneven compliance with laws aimed at taxing and regulating the rich or protecting and expanding the rights of historically excluded sectors. Consequently, ambitious laws are weakly enforced. Thus, unequal democracies are more likely to give rise to window dressing institutions, aspirational rights, and ambitious laws and regulations that fail to elicit widespread compliance.

Compliance with new institutions has, however, varied significantly across early twenty-first-century Latin America. As the chapters by Amengual and Dargent, Falleti, Fernández Milmanda and Garay, and Schrank make clear, ambitious new institutions were not uniformly confined to aspirational or window dressing status. Under pressure from civil society, the courts, and international actors, governments at times invested heavily in enforcement. The result, in many cases, was a surprising degree of behavioral change. To use the terms employed in Figure 1.1 in Chapter 1, these institutions moved *io* quite far from *po*, so that *S* increased, sometimes quite impressively. Nevertheless, even where enforcement efforts and compliance were substantial, the gap between institutional ambition (*io´*) and actual compliance (*io*) remained vast. Democratic competition encouraged politicians to raise the institutional bar, but due to long-standing obstacles such as inequality and state weakness, even heroic efforts to clear the bar often failed. Democratization in unequal societies has thus given rise to highly ambitious institutions that, in many instances, have brought real behavioral change. But at the same time, gaps between ambition and outcomes have persisted and even grown, giving the impression of continued institutional weakness. In many cases, then, it is the ambition–compliance gap that drives perceptions of institutional weakness, despite some very real advances in changing outcomes.

CONCLUSION: FROM INSTITUTIONAL WEAKNESS TO INSTITUTIONAL WEAKENING

In this volume we have told a story of long-standing institutional weakness that persists despite conditions that we might expect to be conducive to institutional strengthening. We have drawn attention to the political logics underlying institutions that are designed to be weak, or that endure despite a long history of weakness. Yet the chapters in this volume also examined conditions under which institutions activate or strengthen. Whether it is property rights institutions in Porfirian Mexico (Saffón and Gonzalez Bertomeu), mechanisms of indigenous consultation in early twenty-first-century Bolivia (Falleti), environmental regulation in Argentina (Amengual and Dargent; Fernández Milmanda and Garay), an imported labor inspection regime in the Dominican Republic (Schrank), or, more distressingly, constitutional mechanisms protecting authoritarian elites (Albertus and Menaldo), the chapters in this volume have begun to identify some of the conditions that generate compliance and stability where they had long been absent.

Yet there is also a need to think about movement in the opposite direction. In several parts of the world, including some of history's most established democracies, there are troubling signs of institutional *weakening*. In Central Europe, democratic institutions that were widely thought consolidated have come unmoored; in Hungary and Poland, for example, once independent judiciaries have weakened dramatically (Scheppele 2015). In Spain, the Catalan nationalist movement's push for independence triggered a constitutional crisis and temporary breakdown of the regional institutional order in 2017–2018. In Great Britain, the political crisis triggered by the 2016 Brexit referendum weakened a range of established parliamentary norms and procedures, leaving British democracy more dysfunctional than at any time since World War II. And in the United States, established institutions of legislative oversight, judicial independence, bureaucratic autonomy, and even voting rights have come under threat over the last decade.

In established democracies such as Britain and the United States, institutions have not, for the most part, collapsed or been openly violated. Rather, the informal norms underlying – and governing – them have eroded, resulting in growing partisan contestation over what it means to comply, and, ultimately over the institutions themselves, threatening instability. In the United States, for example, Republicans' refusal to allow President Obama to fill a Supreme Court vacancy in 2016 and growing calls for Democrats to expand (or "pack") the court do not violate the formal terms of the Constitution. They do, however, challenge the long-standing informal institutions governing the judicial nomination process that gave the Constitution meaning, expanding quite dramatically the range of acceptable behavior (Levitsky and Ziblatt 2018). This, in turn, has both eroded public confidence in the court and triggered growing calls for judicial reform. Thus, both compliance with and the stability of key judicial institutions are now in question.

It may be time, therefore, to begin thinking about the causes of institutional weakening – or the conditions under which previously strong institutions grow weaker. Weakening may take various forms. One is destabilization, or an increased rate of change, such that institutions no longer survive modest shifts in underlying preferences or power distributions. This sort of "repeal and replace" pattern has emerged in US labor, environmental, and immigration rules in the early twenty-first century.

A second form of institutional weakening is deactivation, which is characterized by either reduced state enforcement or declining societal compliance or cooperation with enforcement (Levitsky and Murillo 2014; Dargent, Feldmann, and Luna 2017). In China and Vietnam, for example, many communist rules remained on the books in the 1990s, even as (formally prohibited) private economic activities proliferated (Tsai 2007; Malesky 2005).[7]

---

[7] According to Tsai (2007), laws banning private property remained on the books in China although economic actors with the connivance of local state officials adopted alternative norms to operate private firms, which were always dependent on public discretion to subsist. Similarly, Malevsky (2005) argues that restrictions on foreign investment in Vietnam were purposely not enforced in the 1990s to allow for economic liberalization.

Thus, whereas economic liberalization in Latin America occurred via formal institutional change, early economic liberalization in China and Vietnam was largely informal, taking the form of growing noncompliance with the formal communist system. In the United States, where enforcement of labor safety regulations once relied on union coproduction, with floor plant delegates playing a crucial monitoring role (Huber 2007), declining unionization is likely to weaken compliance with labor safety regulations even in the absence of changes in the formal rules.

Third, institutions may drift into insignificance, in that compliance remains unchanged but the institution's failure to adapt to a changing environment renders it insignificant (see especially Hacker 2005).[8] As noted in the introduction, the United States establishes the minimum wage via legislation; keeping these laws on the books as inflation rises, such that the minimum wage falls well below market wages, may therefore render them insignificant.

What causes institutional weakening? Under what conditions do previously strong institutions experience an erosion of compliance, stability, or significance? We have suggested, in general terms, that institutional weakness is a function of diverging preferences between the coalition that supports institutional creation and the set of actors that participates in enforcement and compliance, in the case of noncompliance; or between the coalition that crafts an institution at time t and the one in charge of institutional creation and change at $t+x$, in the case of instability. The converse must therefore be true for institutional strength. Institutions are strong when there is a persistent, sufficiently broad consensus – despite alternation in office and the division of labor between institutional creation and enforcement – that S is always a net positive for those who hold power. That is to say, institutions are strong when key actors consider that, regardless of short-term costs, they ultimately generate more benefits than costs.

By this we do not mean to suggest that everyone must support an institution for it to work. That sort of generalized consensus is rare, especially in the political world. It may be the case, however, that institutions work best when preferences over them are dispersed across partisan boundaries. We might therefore expect institutional stability where support for the basic institutional framework cuts across partisan cleavages, such that there are veto players in place to prevent wholesale change no matter who is in office. And we can expect greater compliance where there is enough cross-cutting support for the institutional framework to build state enforcement capacity over multiple administrations, to roughly align social norms and expectations with the institutional mandates, and to quell pockets of resistance within

---

[8] On institutional drift and hidden institutional change, also see Streeck and Thelen (2005); Mahoney and Thelen (2010).

the state. In other words, political institutions will be strongest where institutional winners and losers are distributed across partisan boundaries, rather than concentrated on one side or the other.

Under what conditions, then, might we see well-established institutions begin to weaken? One is extreme partisan polarization. If the argument made in the previous paragraph is correct, then we could see weakening when institutional preferences begin to align closely with partisan cleavages and we have alternation in office, or a division of labor, across these cleavages. When partisan identity easily predicts preferences across not only a broad range of outcomes but also the institutional arrangements that help produce them, we should expect to see greater instability – as seen in the "repeal and replace" dynamic that has emerged in the United States in recent electoral cycles. Extreme polarization also raises the stakes of the politics. When partisan preferences over policy are vastly different, the perceived cost of partisan rivals' ascent to power can rise dramatically, to the point where parties grow willing to use "any means necessary" – including breaking, bending, or changing the rules – to defeat them. And as Svolik (2019) has shown, polarized electorates are more likely to accept such abuse. Indeed, deepening polarization contributed to the weakening of established institutions in Chile in the 1960s and early 1970s (Valenzuela 1978) and Venezuela in the 1990s and early 2000s, and it may be doing so in the contemporary United States (Levitsky and Ziblatt 2018).

A second condition that may erode the foundations of established institutions is increased coalitional instability. The collapse of established parties and the relatively rapid emergence of new partisan actors may shake the foundations of the multiparty consensus undergirding institutions. Thus, just as party system collapse brought a dramatic institutional upheaval in Venezuela, the weakening of established parties in Central and Southern Europe, India, Israel, and even France and Great Britain is likely to bring greater contestation over the existing rules of game. The weakening of established players generates new winners and losers, which may weaken support for existing institutions, leaving them vulnerable to replacement or less capable of gaining the societal and bureaucratic cooperation necessary to sustain compliance.

Coalitional instability is especially likely to challenge existing institutions when it is accompanied by the rise of outsider and antiestablishment forces. Populist outsiders such as Donald Trump in the United States and antiestablishment-movement parties such as Italy's Five Star Movement, Spain's Podemos and Vox, or Britain's Brexit Party win votes with populist, antielite appeals. Outsiders who win power are more likely to challenge established institutions than are establishment politicians (Weyland 2002), and successful populists – who have just attacked and defeated the established parties that created and sustained the old rules – have an especially strong incentive to rewrite them. And having campaigned on the idea that the existing institutional order is rigged in favor of the established parties, successful populists earn a popular mandate to challenge that order (Levitsky and Loxton 2013).

Polarization, increased political volatility, and populism are, of course, proximate causes of institutional weakening. A deeper understanding of contemporary patterns of institutional weakening thus requires exploration of the causes of polarization, party system decline, and populism. These likely include exogenous shocks such as globalization, technological change, rising inequality, and migration. These changes appear to have cut across and divided many of the coalitions that sustained key institutional arrangements during the post–World War II era.

***

In sum, this volume has proposed a conceptualization of institutional weakness based on the behavioral effects of rules. We introduced a typology that highlights the varying effects of ambition, compliance, and stability. The chapters in the volume explored many of the political conditions that lead to the adoption of weak institutions or changes in levels of compliance. Drawing on those chapters, the introduction developed a set of hypotheses regarding the sources of institutional weakness. In this concluding chapter, we explored some of the empirical challenges involved in measuring institutional weakness. We also examined why institutions remain weak in much of Latin America, and why they may be weakening elsewhere in the world. These remain critical questions for future research.

Bibliography

"Abortion in El Salvador: Miscarriage of Justice." 2016. *Economist*, December 1. Available at: www.economist.com/international/2016/12/01/miscarriage-of-justice [Accessed January 20, 2020].

Acemoglu, Daron, and Matthew O. Jackson. 2017. "Social Norms and the Enforcement of Laws." Working Paper 20369. Cambridge, MA: National Bureau for Economic Research.

Acemoglu, Daron, Simon Johnson, and James A. Robinson. 2001. "The Colonial Origins of Comparative Development: An Empirical Investigation." *American Economic Review* 91(5): 1369–1401.

2002. "Reversal of Fortune: Geography and Institutions in the Making of the Modern World Income Distribution." *The Quarterly Journal of Economics* 117(4): 1231–1294.

La Agencia Latinoamericana de Expertos en Planificación H, SA (ALEPH SA). 2002. *Evaluacion de sistemas de servicio civil: Estudio de caso: República Dominicana.* Santo Domingo: Banco Interamericano de Desarrollo.

Aisen, Ari, and Francisco Veiga. 2013. "How Does Political Instability Affect Economic Growth?" *European Journal of Political Economy* 29(1): 151–167.

Albertus, Michael. 2015. *Autocracy and Redistribution.* New York: Cambridge University Press.

Albertus, Michael, and Victor Menaldo. 2012. "Coercive Capacity and the Prospects for Democratization." *Comparative Politics* 44(2): 151–169.

2014. "Gaming Democracy: Elite Dominance during Transition and the Prospects for Redistribution." *British Journal of Political Science* 44(3): 575–603.

2018. *Authoritarianism and the Elite Origins of Democracy.* New York: Cambridge University Press.

Alburquerque, Rafael. 1984 [1992]. "Administración del salario mínimo." In *Estudios de derecho del trabajo.* Edited by Rafael Alburquerque. Santo Domingo: Taller, 330–344.

2005. "La supervisión administrativa de las normas de trabajo." Paper presented at Massachusetts Institute of Technology, Cambridge, MA, January 21.

Alfonso, Tatiana. 2018. "Redistributing through Property Rights? Collective Land Tenure Systems and Welfare for the Rural Poor in Latin America." PhD dissertation, University of Wisconsin in Madison.

Altman, David. 2014. *Direct Democracy Worldwide*. New York: Cambridge University Press.

Amazon Conservation Association. 2014. "Fact Sheet: Illegal Gold Mining in Madre de Dios, Peru" [Online]. Available at: www.amazonconservation.org/pdf/gold_mining_fact_sheet.pdf [Accessed February 25, 2015].

Amengual, Matthew. 2013. "Pollution in the Garden of the Argentine Republic: Building State Capacity to Escape from Chaotic Regulation." *Politics and Society* 41(4): 527–560.

2014. "Pathways to Enforcement: Labor Inspectors Leveraging Linkages with Society in Argentina." *ILR Review* 67(1): 3–33.

2015. *Politicized Enforcement: Labor and Environmental Regulation in Argentina.* New York: Cambridge University Press.

2016. *Politicized Enforcement in Argentina: Labor and Environmental Regulation.* New York: Cambridge University Press.

2018. "Buying Stability: The Distributive Outcomes of Private Politics in the Bolivian Mining Industry." *World Development* 104(C): 31–45.

American Federation of Labor and Congress of Industrial Organizations (AFL-CIO). 1993. "Dominican Republic: Right to Organize in the Free Trade Zones." Unpublished document.

Amnesty International. 2003. "Mexico: Intolerable Killings: 10 Years of Abductions and Murders of Women in Ciudad Juárez and Chihuahua." Summary report and appeals cases. Available at: www.amnesty.org/en/documents/AMR41/027/2003/en/ [Accessed January 20, 2020].

Andersson, Krister, Clark C. Gibson, and Fabrice E. Lehoucq. 2005. "Municipal Politics and Forest Governance: Comparative Analysis of Decentralization in Bolivia and Guatemala." *World Development* 34(3): 576–595.

Andrews, Josephine T., and Robert W. Jackman. 2005. "Strategic Fools: Electoral Rule Choice under Extreme Uncertainty." *Electoral Studies* 24(1): 65–84.

Anguelovski, Isabelle, and Joan Martínez-Alier. 2014. "The 'Environmentalism of the Poor' Revisited: Territory and Place in Disconnected Global Struggles." *Ecological Economics* 102(C): 167–176.

Anria, Santiago. 2013. "Social Movements, Party Organization, and Populism: Insights from the Bolivian MAS." *Latin American Politics and Society* 55(3): 19–46.

2016. "Democratizing Democracy? Civil Society and Party Organization in Bolivia." *Comparative Politics* 48(4): 459–478.

2018. *When Movements Become Parties: The Bolivian MAS in Comparative Perspective.* New York: Cambridge University Press.

Ardanaz, Martín, Marcelo Leiras, and Mariano Tommasi. 2014. "The Politics of Federalism in Argentina and Its Implications for Governance and Accountability." *World Development* 53: 26–45.

Arias Aróstegui, Enrique. 2010. "El 'boom' de la construcción…y de las mafias también." Instituto de Defensa Legal – Seguridad Ciudadana [Online]. Available at: http://goo.gl/EkUIjc [Accessed February 24, 2014].

Aristotle. 1946. *The Politics of Aristotle.* Edited by Ernest Barker. Oxford: Clarendon Press.

Arjona, Ana. 2015. "Civilian Resistance to Rebel Governance." In *Rebel Governance in Civil War.* Edited by Ana Arjona, Nelson Kasfir, and Zachariah Mampilly. New York: Cambridge University Press, 180–202.

2016. *Rebelocracy: Social Order in the Colombian Civil War.* New York: Cambridge University Press.

Armstrong, Elia, and Yasuhiko Matsuda. 2003. "Depoliticising the Civil Service." Workshop Report, 11th International Anti-corruption Conference. Washington, DC: World Bank and United Nations Department of Economic and Social Affairs.

Auditoría General de la Nación (AGN). 2014. *Implementación de la Ley 26.331, 2007–2013.* Buenos Aires: AGN.

Ávila-Espinosa, Felipe Arturo. 2010. "El problema agrario a fines del Porfiriato y en los comienzos de la Revolución." In *La justicia durante el Porfiriato y la Revolución 1898–1914.* Volume 5. Edited by Suprema Corte de Justicia de la Nación (SCJN). Mexico: Suprema Corte de Justicia de la Nación, 3–179.

Avritzer, Leonardo. 2009. *Participatory Institutions in Democratic Brazil.* Washington, DC: Woodrow Wilson Center Press and Johns Hopkins University Press.

Babb, Sarah. 2013. "The Washington Consensus as Transnational Policy Paradigm: Its Origins, Trajectory, and Likely Successor." *Review of International Political Economy* 20(2): 268–297.

Badie, Bertrand. 2000. *The Imported State: The Westernization of the Political Order.* Palo Alto: Stanford University Press.

Baiocchi, Gianpaolo, Patrick Heller, and Marcelo Silva. 2011. *Bootstrapping Democracy: Transforming Local Governance and Civil Society in Brazil.* Stanford: Stanford University Press.

Bakke, Kristin, and Erik Wibbels. 2006. "Diversity, Disparity, and Civil Conflict in Federal States." *World Politics* 59(1): 1–50.

Baldez, Lisa. 2014. *Defying Convention: US Resistance to the UN Treaty on Women's Rights.* New York: Cambridge University Press.

Banco Central de la República Dominicana. 2003. "Tasas de cambio promedio para compra y venta de divisas, 1991." www.bancentral.gov.do/a/d/2538-mercado-cambiario.

2013. "Tasas de cambio del dólar de referencia del mercado spot, promedio trimestral." Unpublished data.

Banco Interamericano de Desarrollo – Secretaría de Estado de Trabajo (BID-SET). 2002. *Programa de capacitación y modernización laboral: Componente de fortalecimiento institucional: Informe de diagnóstico.* Santo Domingo: Secretaría de Estado de Trabajo.

Baraybar, Viviana, and Eduardo Dargent. 2019. State Responses to the Gold Rush in the Andes (2004–2018): The Politics of State Action (and Inaction). Cuaderno de Trabajo, no. 48. Lima, Peru: Departamento de Ciencias Sociales, PUCP. Available at: http://repositorio.pucp.edu.pe/index/handle/123456789/136973 [Accessed May 20, 2019].

Barsky, Osvaldo, and Leonardo Fernández. 2008. *Cambio técnico y transformaciones sociales en el agro extrapampeano.* Buenos Aires: Teseo.

Barsted, Leila de Andrade Linhares. 1994. *Violência contra a mulher e cidadania: Uma avaliação das políticas públicas.* Rio de Janeiro: Cidadania, Estudo, Pesquisa, Informação e Ação (CEPIA).

Bartolini, Stefano, and Peter Mair. 1990. *Identity, Competition, and Electoral Availability: The Stabilization of European Electorates.* Cambridge: Cambridge University Press.

Bas, Muhammet, and Randall Stone. 2017. "Probabilistic Democracy." Working paper.

Bascopé Sanjinés, Iván. 2010. *Lecciones aprendidas sobre consulta previa.* La Paz: Centro de Estudios Jurídicos e Investigación Social.

Bazant, Jan. 1971. *Los bienes de la iglesia en México (1856–1875): Aspectos económicos y sociales de la revolución liberal.* México: El Colegio de México.

Beck, Thorsten, Asli Demirgüç-Kunt, and Ross Levine. 2003. "Law and Finance: Why Does Legal Origin Matter?" *Journal of Comparative Economics* 31(4): 653–675.

Becker, Gary. 1968. "Crime and Punishment: An Economic Approach." *Journal of Political Economy* 76(2): 169–217.

Beer, Caroline. 2016. *Explaining Gender Violence Policies in the Mexican States.* Pittsburgh: Latin American Studies Association. https://lasa.international.pitt.edu/files/Final-MainIndex.pdf.

2017. "Left Parties and Violence against Women Legislation in Mexico." *Social Politics: International Studies in Gender, State and Society* 24(4): 511–537.

Benoit, Kenneth. 2004. "Models of Electoral System Change." *Electoral Studies* 23(3): 363–389.

Benoit, Kenneth, and John W. Schiemann. 2001. "Institutional Choice in New Democracies Bargaining over Hungary's 1989 Electoral Law." *Journal of Theoretical Politics* 13(2): 153–182.

Benson, David, and Andrew Jordan. 2011. "What Have We Learned from Policy Transfer Research? Dolowitz and Marsh Revisited." *Political Studies Review* 9(3): 366–378.

Bensusán, Graciela. 2000. *El modelo mexicano de regulación laboral.* Xochimilco: Plaza y Valdés.

Berggren, Niclas, Andreas Bergh, and Christian Bjornskov. 2009. "The Growth Effects of Institutional Instability." *Journal of Institutional Economics* 8(2): 187–224.

Bergman, Marcelo. 2009. *Tax Evasion and the Rule of Law in Latin America.* University Park: Pennsylvania State University Press.

Berkowitz, Daniel, Katharina Pistor, and Jean-François Richard. 2003a. "Economic Development, Legality, and the Transplant Effect." *European Economic Review* 47(1): 165–195.

2003b. "The Transplant Effect." *American Journal of Comparative Law* 51(1): 163–203.

Bértola, Luis, and José Antonio Ocampo. 2012. *The Economic Development of Latin America since Independence.* Oxford: Oxford University Press.

Bertucci, Guido. 2007. "Strengthening Public Sector Capacity for Achieving the Millennium Development Goals." In United Nations Department of Economic and Social Affairs and International Association of Schools and Institutes of Administration, *Excellence and Leadership in the Public Sector: The Role of Education and Training.* Edited by Allan Rosenbaum and John-Mary Kauzya. New York: United Nations, 1–10.

Bill Chavez, Rebecca. 2004. *The Rule of Law in Nascent Democracies: Judicial Politics in Argentina.* Redwood City: Stanford University Press.

Birch, Sarah, Frances Millard, Marina Popescu, and Kieran Williams. 2002. *Embodying Democracy: Electoral System Design in Post-Communist Europe.* Springer.

Black, Cyril. 1975. "Russian History in Japanese Perspective: An Experiment in Comparison." *Jahrbücher für Geschichte Osteuropas* 23: 481–488.

1978. "Japan and Russia: Bureaucratic Politics in a Comparative Context." *Social Science History* 2(4): 414–426.

Boix, Carles. 1999. "Setting the Rules of the Game: The Choice of Electoral Systems in Advanced Democracies." *American Political Science Review* 93(3): 609–624.

Boix, Carles, Michael Miller, and Sebastian Rosato. 2013. "A Complete Dataset of Political Regimes, 1800–2007." *Comparative Political Studies* 46(12): 1523–1554.

Boone, Catherine. 2003. *Political Topographies of the African State.* New York: Cambridge University Press.

Bourdieu, Pierre. 1984. *Distinction: A Social Critique of the Judgement of Taste.* Cambridge: Harvard University Press.

2010. "The Left Hand and the Right Hand of the State." In *Sociology Is a Martial Art.* Edited by Giséle Sapiro. New York: New Press, 67.

Bravo-Rodríguez, Alicia. 1990. "Perfil biográfico de los Ministros de la Suprema Corte de Justicia de la Nación, cuando fue su Presidente Ignacio L. Vallarta (1877–1882)." In *La Suprema Corte de Justicia a principios del Porfirismo (1877–1882).* Edited by Lucio Cabrera Acevedo. México: Supreme Court of Justice of Mexico, 1115–1144.

Brehm, John, and Scott Gates. 1997. *Working, Shirking, and Sabotage: Bureaucratic Response to a Democratic Public.* Ann Arbor: University of Michigan Press.

Brennan, Geoffrey, and Alan Hamilton. 2001. "Constitutional Choice." In *The Elgar Companion to Public Choice.* Edited by William Shughart and Laura Razzolini. Cheltenham: Edward Elgar, 117–139.

Brewer-Carías, Allan. 2009. *Constitutional Protection of Human Rights in Latin America.* New York: Cambridge University Press.

Brinks, Daniel M. 2003. "Informal Institutions and the Rule of Law: The Judicial Response to State Killings in Buenos Aires and São Paulo in the 1990s." *Comparative Politics* 36(1): 1–19.

2008. *The Judicial Response to Police Killings in Latin America: Inequality and the Rule of Law.* New York: Cambridge University Press.

2019. "Access to What? Legal Agency and Access to Justice for Indigenous Peoples in Latin America." *Journal of Development Studies* 55(3): 348–365.

Brinks, Daniel M., and Abby Blass. 2013. "Beyond the Façade: Institutional Engineering and Potemkin Courts in Latin America, 1975–2009." Unpublished manuscript. Available at: www.academia.edu/15429591/Beyond_the_Fac_ade_Institutional_ Engineering_and_Potemkin_Courts_in_Latin_America_1975-2009 [Accessed January 20, 2020].

2017. "Rethinking Judicial Empowerment: The New Foundations of Constitutional Justice." *International Journal of Constitutional Law* 15(2): 296–331.

2018. *The DNA of Constitutional Justice in Latin America: Politics, Governance, and Judicial Design.* Cambridge: Cambridge University Press.

Brinks, Daniel M., and Sandra Botero. 2014. "Inequality and the Rule of Law: Ineffective Rights in Latin American Democracies." In *Reflections on Uneven Democracies: The Legacy of Guillermo O'Donnell.* Edited by Daniel M. Brinks, Marcelo Leiras, and Scott Mainwaring. Baltimore: Johns Hopkins University Press, 214–239.

Brinks, Daniel M., and Varun Gauri. 2014. "The Law's Majestic Equality? The Distributive Impact of Judicializing Social and Economic Rights." *Perspectives on Politics* 12(2): 375–393.

Brinks, Daniel, Steven Levitsky, and M. Victoria Murillo. 2019. *Understanding Institutional Weakness: Power and Design in Latin American Institutions.* Cambridge: Cambridge University Press.

Buchanan, James M., and Gordon Tullock. 1962. *The Calculus of Consent.* Vol. 3 of *The Collected Works of James. M. Buchanan.* Ann Arbor: University of Michigan Press.

Buitrago, Miguel A. 2010. "Civil Society, Social Protest, and Presidential Breakdown in Bolivia." In *Presidential Breakdowns in Latin America.* Edited by Mariana Llanos and Leiv Marsteintredet. Basingstoke: Palgrave MacMillan, 91–110.

Büthe, Tim, and Helen Milner. 2008. "The Politics of Foreign Direct Investment into Developing Countries: Increasing FDI through Trade Agreements?" *American Journal of Political Science* 52(4): 741–762.

Cabrera Acevedo, Lucio. 1985. "La Revolución de 1910 y el poder judicial federal." In *La Suprema Corte de Justicia y el pensamiento jurídico.* Edited by Supreme Court of Justice of Mexico.

1990. *La Suprema Corte de Justicia a principios del Porfirismo (1877–1882).* México: Supreme Court of Justice of Mexico.

Caiden, Gerald. 1991. *Administrative Reform Comes of Age.* New York: De Gruyter.

Calderón Cockburn, Julio. 2006. *Mercado de tierras urbanas, propiedad y pobreza.* Cambridge, MA: Lincoln Institute of Land Policy.

2013. "La ciudad ilegal en el Perú." In *Perú hoy, el Perú subterráneo.* Edited by Werner Jungbluth. Lima: DESCO, 39–56.

Calvo, Ernesto. 2009. "The Competitive Road to Proportional Representation: Partisan Biases and Electoral Regime Change under Increasing Party Competition." *World Politics* 61(2): 254–295.

Calvo, Ernesto, and Juan Pablo Miccozi. 2005. "The Governor's Backyard: A Seat-Vote Model of Electoral Reform for Multiparty Races." *Journal of Politics* 67(4): 1050–1074.

Calvo, Ernesto, and María Victoria Murillo. 2004. "Who Delivers? Partisan Clients in the Argentina Electoral Market." *American Journal of Political Science* 48(4): 742–757.

2012. "When Parties Meet Voters: Assessing Political Linkages through Partisan Linkages and Distributive Expectations in Argentina and Chile." *Comparative Political Studies* 46(7): 851–882.

Cámara de Diputados. 2006. Diario de Sesiones (November 22th (session 29), November 23th (session 30), November 29th (session 30)).

Camara de Senadores, Diario de Asuntos Entrados, several years (2000–2014).

Cámara de Senadores. 2007. Diario de Sesiones (June 6th (session 7), August 22th (session 11), November 14th (session 13), November 21th (session 13)).

Camargo, Angélica, and Adriana Hurtado. 2011. *La urbanización informal en Bogotá: Panorama a partir del Observatorio.* Bogotá: Universidad Piloto de Colombia.

Cameron, Maxwell A., Eric Hershberg, and Kenneth E. Sharpe. 2012. *New Institutions for Participatory Democracy in Latin America: Voice and Consequence.* New York: Palgrave Macmillan.

Campello, Daniela, and Cesar Zucco Jr. 2014. "Merit, Chance, and the International Determinants of Government Success." Working paper, Getúlio Vargas Foundation.

2015. "Presidential Success and the World Economy." *Journal of Politics* 78(2): 589–602.

Cardenas, Mauricio. 2010. "State Capacity in Latin America." *Economia* 10(2): 1–45.

Carey, John M. 2005. "Presidential versus Parliamentary Government." In *Handbook of New Institutional Economics.* Edited by Claude Menard and Mary M. Shirley. Dordrecht: Springer, 91–122.

Carey, John M., and Matthew S. Shugart. 1995. "Incentives to Cultivate a Personal Vote." *Electoral Studies* 14(4): 417–439.

1998. *Executive Decree Authority.* New York: Cambridge University Press.

Carpenter, Daniel P. 2001. *The Forging of Bureaucratic Autonomy: Reputations, Networks, and Policy Innovation in Executive Agencies, 1862–1928*. Princeton: Princeton University Press.

2014. "Detecting and Measuring Capture." In *Preventing Regulatory Capture: Special Interest Influence and How to Limit It*. Edited by Daniel Carpenter and David A. Moss. New York: Cambridge University Press.

Carrubba, Clifford. 2009. "A Model of the Endogenous Development of Judicial Institutions in Federal and International Systems." *Journal of Politics* 71(1): 55–69.

Centeno, Miguel Angel. 2002. *Blood and Debt: War and the Nation-State in Latin America*. University Park: Pennsylvania State University Press.

Centeno, Miguel Angel, Atul Kohli, and Deborah J. Yashar. 2017. *States in the Developing World*. New York: Cambridge University Press.

Center for Reproductive Rights. 2014. *A Pivotal Moment: 2014 Annual Report*. New York: Center for Reproductive Rights. Available at: www.reproductiverights.org/sites/crr.civicactions.net/files/documents/CRR-2014-Annual-Report.pdf [Accessed January 20, 2020].

Centro de Estudios Jurídicos e Investigación Social (CEJIS). 2014. *El gas y el destino de Bolivia*. Santa Cruz: CEJIS.

Centro de Estudios para el Desarrollo Laboral y Agrario (CEDLA). 2015. *La Economía del Oro: Ensayos sobre la Explotación en Sudamérica*. La Paz: CEDLA.

Cepeda, Denisse. 2008. "Donde ir si tiene conflicto laboral." *Listín diario*, April 14.

Cepeda Espinosa, Manuel José. 2004. "Judicial Activism in a Violent Context: The Origin, Role and Impact of the Colombian Constitutional Court." *Washington University Global Studies Law Review* 3: 529.

Cheibub, José Antonio, Jennifer Gandhi, and James Raymond Vreeland. 2010. "Democracy and Dictatorship Revisited." *Public Choice* 143(1–2): 67–101.

Chêne, Marie. 2009. "Low Salaries, the Culture of Per Diems and Corruption." *Transparency International/U4*. Available at: www.u4.no/publications/low-salaries-the-culture-of-per-diems-and-corruption.pdf [Accessed January 20, 2020].

Chorev, Nitsan. 2007. *Remaking U.S. Trade Policy: From Protectionism to Globalization*. Ithaca: Cornell University Press.

Cleary, Matthew, and Susan Stokes. 2006. *Democracy and the Culture of Skepticism: Political Trust in Argentina and Mexico*. New York: Russell Sage.

Coatsworth, John. 1981. *Growth against Development: The Economic Impact of Railroads in Porfirian Mexico*. DeKalb: Northern Illinois University Press.

2008. "Inequality, Institutions, and Economic Growth in Latin America." *Journal of Latin American Studies* 40(3): 545–569.

Cohen, Stephen. 2000. *The Making of United States International Economic Policy: Principles, Problems, and Proposals for Reform*. Westport: Greenwood.

Collier, David. 1976. *Squatters and Oligarchs: Authoritarian Rule and Policy Change in Peru*. Baltimore: Johns Hopkins University Press.

Collier, Ruth B., and David Collier. 1991. *Shaping the Political Arena: Critical Junctures, the Labor Movement, and Regime Dynamics in Latin America*. Princeton: Princeton University Press.

Colomer, Josep M. 2004. "The Strategy and History of Electoral System Choice." In *The Handbook of Electoral System Choice*. Edited by Josep M. Colomer. London: Palgrave Macmillan, 3–78.

2005. "It's Parties That Choose Electoral Systems (or, Duverger's Laws Upside Down)." *Political Studies* 53(1): 1–21.

Conaghan, C. M. 2008. "Ecuador: Correa's Plebiscitary Presidency." *Journal of Democracy* 19(2): 46–60.

Conran, James, and Kathleen A. Thelen. 2016. "Institutional Change." In *The Oxford Handbook of Historical Institutionalism*. Edited by Orfeo Fioretos, Tulia G. Falleti, and Adam Sheingate. Oxford: Oxford University Press, 51–70.

Cook, María Lorena. 2007. *The Politics of Labor Reform in Latin America: Between Flexibility and Rights*. University Park: Pennsylvania State University Press.

Coolidge, Jacqueline. 2006. *Reforming Inspections*. June. Viewpoint Note no. 308. Washington, DC: World Bank.

Coppedge, Michael. 1997. "District Magnitude, Economic Performance, and Party-System Fragmentation in Five Latin American Countries." *Comparative Political Studies* 30(2): 156–185.

1998. "The Evolution of Latin American Party Systems." In *Politics, Society, and Democracy: Latin America*. Edited by Scott Mainwaring and Arturo Valuenzuela. New York: Routledge, 171–206.

Córdova, H. 2015. "¿Oro Boliviano?" In *La economía del oro: Ensayos sobre la explotación en Sudamérica*. Edited by CEDLA. La Paz: CEDLA, 61–75. http://extractivismo.com/wp-content/uploads/2016/07/EconomiaDelOro2015.pdf.

Corrales, Javier, and Michael Penfold. 2014. "Manipulating Term Limits in Latin America." *Journal of Democracy* 25(4): 157–168.

Correa, Rafael. 2012. "Ecuador's Path." *New Left Review* 77(September–October): 89–104.

Coslovsky, Salo V. 2011. "Relational Regulation in the Brazilian Ministerio Publico: The Organizational Basis of Regulatory Responsiveness." *Regulation and Governance* 5(1): 70–89.

Couso, Javier, Alexandra Huneeus, and Rachel Sieder, eds. 2010. *Cultures of Legality: Judicialization and Political Activism in Latin America*. Cambridge Studies in Law and Society. Cambridge: Cambridge University Press.

Cox, Gary W., and Scott Morgenstern. 2002. "Epilogue: Latin America's Reactive Assemblies and Proactive Presidents." In *Legislative Politics in Latin America*. Edited by Scott Morgenstern and Benito Nacif. New York: Cambridge University Press, 446–468.

Crawford, Sue E. S., and Elinor Ostrom. 1995. "A Grammar of Institutions." *American Political Science Review* 89(3): 582–600.

Crisp, Brian F., and Juan Carlos Rey. 2001. "The Sources of Electoral Reform in Venezuela." In *Mixed-Member Electoral Systems: The Best of Both Worlds?* Edited by Matthew Soberg Shugart and Martin P. Wattenberg. New York: Oxford University Press.

Cukierman, Alex, Steven B. Web, and Bilin Neyapti. 1992. "Measuring the Independence of Central Banks and Its Effect on Policy Outcomes." *World Bank Economic Review* 6(3): 353–398.

Dahl, Robert. 1973. *Polyarchy: Participation and Opposition*. New Haven: Yale University Press.

Damonte Valencia, Gerardo. 2013. "Formalizing the Unknown: The Stalemate over Formalizing Small-Scale Mining in Madre de Dios." The *Broker* [Online]. Available at: www.thebrokeronline.eu/Articles/Formalizing-the-unknown [Accessed February 23, 2015].

Dargent, Eduardo. 2015. *Technocracy and Democracy in Latin America*. New York: Cambridge University Press.

Dargent, Eduardo, Andreas E. Feldmann, and Juan Pablo Luna. 2017. "Greater State Capacity, Lesser Stateness: Lessons from the Peruvian Commodity Boom." *Politics and Society* 45(1): 3–34.

Dargent, Eduardo, and Madai Urteaga. 2017. "Adaptación estatal por presiones externas: Los determinantes de la respuesta estatal al boom del oro en el Perú (2004–2015)." *Revista de ciencia política* 36(3): 655–677.

Davies, Emmerich, and Tulia G. Falleti. 2017. "Poor People's Participation: Neoliberal Institutions or Left Turn?" *Comparative Political Studies* 50(12): 1699–1731.

De Jong, Martin, et al. 2007. "Cross-National Policy Transfer to Developing Countries: Prologue." *Knowledge, Technology, and Policy* 19(4): 3–8.

De la O, Ana. 2015. *Crafting Policies to End Poverty in Latin America: The Quiet Transformation*. New York: Cambridge University Press.

de la Riva Miranda, Polo. 2011. "Monitoreo socioambiental en territorio indígena Guaraní." *Industrias extractivas: Políticas y derechos, Artículo Primero. Revista de debate social y jurídico (CEJIS)* 14(21): 35–56.

De La Torre, Carlos. 2010. *Populist Seduction in Latin America*. Athens: Ohio University Press.

De Salvo, María A. 2014. "El MOCASE: Orígenes, consolidación y fractura del movimiento campesino de Santiago del Estero." *Astrolabio* 12: 271–300.

Defensoría del Pueblo. 2014. *Gestión del estado frente de la minería informal e ilegal en el Perú. Report no. 167*. Lima: Defensoría del Pueblo.

Deininger, Klaus, and Hans Binswager. 1999. "The Evolution of the World's Bank Land Policy: Principles, Experience, and Future Challenges." *The World Bank Research Observer* 14(2): 247–276.

Devisscher, Tahia. 2008. *Cinco siglos de acumulación de costos socio-ambientales: La actividad minera en Bolivia*. Documento de trabajo (Working paper). La Paz: Programa de las Naciones Unidas para el Desarrollo (PNUD).

Devlin, Robert, and Graciela Moguillansky. 2012. *What's New in the New Industrial Policy in Latin America?* Washington, DC: Inter-American Development Bank (IDB).

Díaz, Geovanny. 2010. "Funcionarios del MTSS participan en seminarios inspección de trabajo y responsabilidad social empresarial." *MTSS informa* 25(August 17): 1.

Dick, H.W. 1985. "The Rise of a Middle Class and the Changing Concept of Equity in Indonesia: An Interpretation." *Indonesia* 39(April): 71–92.

Dilulio, John D. 1994. "Principled Agents: The Cultural Bases of Behavior in a Federal Government Bureaucracy." *Public Administration* 4(3): 277–318.

Dimitrov, Martin K. 2009. *Piracy and the State: The Politics of Intellectual Property Rights in China*. New York: Cambridge University Press.

Dix, Robert. 1982. "The Breakdown of Authoritarian Regimes." *Western Political Quarterly* 35(4): 554–573.

Dobbins, Frank, Beth Simmons, and Geoffrey Garrett. 2007. "The Global Diffusion of Public Policies: Social Construction, Coercion, Competition, or Learning?" *Annual Review of Sociology* 33(1): 449–472.

Doebele, William A. 1977. "The Private Market and Low-Income Urbanization: The 'Pirate' Subdivisions of Bogota." *American Journal of Comparative Law* 25(3): 531–564.

Dolowitz, David. 1993. "A Policy-Maker's Guide to Policy Transfer." *Political Quarterly* 74(1): 101–108.

Dolowitz, David, and David Marsh. 1996. "Who Learns What from Whom: A Review of the Policy Transfer Literature." *Political Studies* 44(2): 343–357.

Dore, Ronald. 1973. *British Factory, Japanese Factory*. Berkeley: University of California Press.

Dosh, Paul. 2010. *Demanding the Land: Urban Popular Movements in Peru and Ecuador, 1990–2005.* University Park: Pennsylvania State University Press.

Downs, Anthony. 1957. *An Economic Theory of Democracy.* New York: HarperCollins.

Dublán, Manuel, and José María Lozano. [1911] 2004. *Legislación mexicana o Colección completa de las disposiciones legislativas expedidas desde la independencia de la República.* México: Suprema Corte de Justicia de la Nación-El Colegio de México-Escuela Libre de Derecho-Estado de México-Tribunal Superior de Justicia del Estado de México.

Ducey, Michael. 1997. "Liberal Theory and Peasant Practice: Land and Power in Northern Veracruz, Mexico (1826–1900)." In *Liberals, the Church, and Indian Peasants: Corporate Lands and the Challenge of Reform in Nineteenth-Century Spanish America.* Edited by Robert Jackson. Albuquerque: University of New Mexico Press, 65–93.

Dziuda, Wioletta, and William G. Howell. 2019. "Political Scandal: A Theory." Available at: https://cpb-us-w2.wpmucdn.com/voices.uchicago.edu/dist/5/539/files/2019/01/Political-Scandal-website-Dec-2018-xg88lx.pdf.

Eaton, Kent. 2012. "The State of the State in Latin America: Challenges, Challengers, Responses and Deficits." *Revista de ciencia política* 32(3): 643–657.

Echebarría, Koldo, and Juan Carlos Cortázar. 2006. "Las reformas de la administración y el empleo públicos en América Latina." In *El estado de la reforma del estado en América Latina.* Edited by Eduardo Lora. Washington, DC: Banco Interamericano de Desarrollo (BID), 139–173.

Edwards, Sebastian. 2010. *Left Behind: Latin America and the False Promise of Populism.* Chicago: University of Chicago Press.

Eeckhout, Jan, Nicola Persico, and Petra E. Todd. 2010. "A Theory of Optimal Random Crackdowns." *American Economic Review* 100(3): 1104–1135.

Elkins, Zachary. 2017. "A Militant Defense of Term Limits in Bolivia." Paper presented at the Conference on Weak Institutions, University of Texas at Austin, September 28.

Elkins, Zachary, Tom Ginsburg, and James Melton. 2009. *The Endurance of National Constitutions.* New York: Cambridge University Press.

2010. "The Comparative Constitutions Project." Available at: https://comparative-constitutionsproject.org [Accessed January 20, 2020].

Elkins, Zachary, Andrew Guzman, and Beth Simmons. 2006. "Competing for Capital: The Diffusion of Bilateral Investment Treaties, 1960–2000." *International Organization* 60(4): 811–846.

Ellermann, Antje. 2005. "Coercive Capacity and the Politics of Implementation: Deportation in Germany and the United States." *Comparative Political Studies* 38(10): 1219–1244.

2009. *States against Migrants: Deportation in Germany and the United States.* New York: Cambridge University Press.

Ellickson, Robert C. 1991. *Order without Law.* Cambridge: Harvard University Press.

Elster, Jon. 1995. "Forces and Mechanisms in the Constitution-Making Process." *Duke Law Journal* 45(2): 364–396.

Epp, Charles R. (1998). *The Rights Revolution: Lawyers, Activists, and Supreme Courts in Comparative Perspective.* New York: Cambridge University Press.

Epstein, Lee, Olga Shvetsova, and Jack Knight. 2001. "The Role of Constitutional Courts in the Establishment and Maintenance of Democratic Systems of Government." *Law and Society Review* 35(1): 117–164.

Escobar-Ohmstede, Antonio (coord). 1993. *Indio, nación y comunidad en el México del siglo XIX*. México: Centro de Estudios Mexicanos y Centroamericanos.

Estado de Veracruz. 2016. *Declaración de alerta de violencia de género contra las mujeres*.

Etchemendy, Sebastian, and Ruth Collier. 2007. "Down but Not Out: Union Resurgence and Segmented Neocorporatism in Argentina (2003–2007)." *Politics and Society* 35(3): 363–401.

Etchemendy, Sebastian, and Candelaria Garay. 2011. "Argentine Left Populism in Comparative Perspective." In *The Resurgence of the Latin American Left*. Edited by Steve Levitsky and Kenneth Roberts. Baltimore: Johns Hopkins University Press, 283–305.

Evans, Peter. 1995. *Embedded Autonomy: States and Industrial Transformation*. Princeton: Princeton University Press.

"Development as Institutional Change: The Pitfalls of Monocropping and the Potentials of Deliberation." *Studies in Comparative International Development* 38(4): 30–52.

2005. "Harnessing the State: Rebalancing Strategies for Motivating and Monitoring." In *States and Development: Historical Antecedents of Stagnation and Advance*. Edited by Matthew Lange and Dietrich Rueschemeyer. Gordonsville: Palgrave Macmillan, 26–47.

Fairfield, Tasha. 2015. *Private Wealth and Public Revenue in Latin America*. New York: Cambridge University Press.

Falcón, Romana. 2015. *El jefe político*. México: El Colegio de México/El Colegio de Michoacán/CIESAS.

Falleti, Tulia. 2010. *Decentralization and Subnational Politics in Latin America*. New York: Cambridge University Press.

Falleti, Tulia, and James Mahoney. 2015. "The Comparative Sequential Method." In *Advances in Comparative-Historical Analysis*. Edited by James Mahoney and Kathleen Thelen. Cambridge: Cambridge University Press, 211–239.

Falleti, Tulia, and Thea Riofrancos. 2018. "Endogenous Participation: Strengthening Prior Consultation in Extractive Economies." *World Politics* 70(1): 86–121.

Fernández Milmanda, Belén, and Candelaria Garay. 2019. "Subnational Variation in Forest Protection in the Argentine Chaco." *World Development* 118: 79–94.

Fishkin, Joseph, and David E. Pozen. 2018. "Asymmetric Constitutional Hardball." *Columbia Law Review* 118(3): 915–982.

Flemmer, Ricarda, and Almut Schilling-Vacaflor. 2016. "Unfulfilled Promises of the Consultation Approach: The Limits to Effective Indigenous Participation in Bolivia's and Peru's Extractive Industries." *Third World Quarterly* 37(1): 172–188.

Franceschet, Susan. 2010. "Explaining Domestic Violence Policy Outcomes in Chile and Argentina." *Latin American Politics and Society*, 52(3): 1–29.

Francescone, Kirsten. 2015. "Cooperative Miners and the Politics of Abandonment." *The Extractive Industries and Society* 2(4): 746–755.

Franco-Vivanco, Edgar. 2018. "Justice as Checks and Balances: Indigenous Claims in the Courts of Colonial Mexico." Paper prepared for the LSE – Stanford – Universidad de los Andes Long-Run Development in Latin America Conference, London, May 16–17. Available at: www.lse.ac.uk/lacc/publications/PDFs/Franco-Vivanco-JusticeAndChecks-May-2018.pdf [Accessed January 20, 2020].

Franks, Julie. 1997. "The Dominican Republic." NACLA Report on the Americas, New York City.

Fraser, Donald J. 1972. "La Política de desamortización en las comunidades indígenas, 1856–1872." *Historia Mexicana* 21(4): 615–652.

Fraser, Nancy. 2003. "Social Justice in the Age of Identity Politics: Redistribution, Recognition, and Participation." In *Redistribution or Recognition? A Political-Philosophical Exchange.* Edited by Nancy Fraser and Axel Honneth. New York: Verso, 7–109.

Freidenberg, Flavia, and Tomas Došek. 2015. "Las reformas electorales en América Latina (1978–2015)." In *Reformas políticas en América Latina: Tendencias y casos.* Edited by Kevin Casas-Zamora, Marian Vidaurri, Betilde Muñoz-Pogossian, and Raquel Chanto. Washington, DC: Organizacion de Estados Americanos, 25–92.

Frías, Sonia M. 2010. "Resisting Patriarchy within the State: Advocacy and Family Violence in Mexico." *Women's Studies International Forum* 33(6): 542–551.

2013. "¿Protección de derechos o búsqueda de legitimidad? Violencia de pareja contra las mujeres en México." *Journal of the Institute of Iberoamerican Studies* 15(2): 233–270.

2014. "Ámbitos y formas de violencia contra mujeres y niñas: Evidencias a partir de las encuestas." *Acta Sociológica* 65: 11–36.

Frundt, Henry. 1998. *Trade Conditions and Labor Rights: U.S. Initiatives, Dominican and Central American Responses.* Gainesville: University Press of Florida.

Fukuyama, Francis. 2004. *La construcción del Estado: Hacia un nuevo orden mundial en el siglo XXI.* Barcelona: Ediciones B.

Fung, Archon, and Erik Olin Wright, eds. 2003. *Deepening Democracy: Institutional Innovations in Empowered Participatory Governance.* New York: Verso Books.

Galanter, Marc. 1974. "Why the 'Haves' Come Out Ahead: Speculations on the Limits of Legal Change." *Law and Society Review* 9(1): 95–160.

Gallagher, Michael, and Paul Mitchell, eds. 2005. *The Politics of Electoral Systems.* Oxford and New York: Oxford University Press.

Galligan, Denis, and Mila Versteeg, eds. 2013. *Social and Political Foundations of Constitutions.* New York: Cambridge University Press.

Gandarillas, Marco, Georgina Jiménez, and Jorge Campanini. 2013. *Arcopongo: La actual política minera alienta los conflictos mineros.* Dossier CEDIB (Centro de Documentación e Información Bolivia). Cochabamba: CEDIB.

Garay, Candelaria. 2016. *Social Policy Expansion in Latin America.* New York: Cambridge University Press.

García Ayala, Luis, and Esteban Valle-Riestra. 2015. "¿Cómo responde un 'estado anémico'? Empresarios, policías y crimen organizado en el 'boom' de la construcción en Perú." Paper prepared for Asociación Latinoamericana de Ciencia Política, Lima, July 22–24 [Online]. Available at: http://congreso.pucp.edu.pe/alacip2015/ponencias/?pagina=3.

García Collazo, María Agustina, Amalia Panizza, and José María Paruelo. 2013. "Ordenamiento territorial de bosques nativos: Resultados de la zonificación realizada por provincias del Norte Argentino." *Ecología austral* 23(2): 97–107.

García-Moreno, Claudia, Henrica A. F. M. Jansen, Mary Ellsberg, Lori Heise, and Charlotte H. Watts. 2006. "Prevalence of Intimate Partner Violence: Findings from the WHO Multi-country Study on Women's Health and Domestic Violence." *Lancet* 368(9543): 1260–1269.

Gauri, Varun, and Daniel M. Brinks, eds. 2008. *Courting Social Justice: Judicial Enforcement of Social and Economic Rights in the Developing World.* Cambridge: Cambridge University Press.

Geddes, Barbara. 1996. "Initiation of New Democratic Institutions in Eastern Europe and Latin America." In *Institutional Design in New Democracies Eastern Europe and Latin America*. Edited by Arend Lijphart and Carlos Waisman. Boulder: Westview Press.

General Accounting Office (GAO). 1998. *Caribbean Basin: Worker Rights Progress Made, but Enforcement Challenges Remain*. Washington, DC: GAO.

Gerring, John. 2007. "Is There a (Viable) Crucial-Case Method?" *Comparative Political Studies* 40(3): 231–253.

Gerring, John, Strom Thacker, and Carola Moreno. 2005. "Centripetal Democratic Governance: A Theory and Global Inquiry." *American Political Science Review* 99(4): 567–581.

Gerschenkron, Alexander. 1962. *Economic Backwardness in Historical Perspective*. Cambridge: Belknap Press.

Gerth, Hans, and C. Wright Mills. 1946. *For Max Weber*. London: Routledge.

Gibson, Edward, ed. 2004. *Federalism and Democracy in Latin America*. Baltimore: Johns Hopkins University Press.

Gibson, Edward. 2005. "Boundary Control: Subnational Authoritarianism in Democratic Countries." *World Politics* 58(1): 101–132.

Gilbert, Alan, and Peter Ward. 1985. *Housing, the State and the Poor: Policy and Practice in Three Latin American Cities*. New York: Cambridge University Press.

Gingerich, Daniel. 2010. "Understanding Off-the-Books Politics: Conducting Inference on the Determinants of Sensitive Behavior with Randomized Response Surveys." *Political Analysis* 18(3): 349–380.

2013. "Governance Indicators and the Level of Analysis Problem: Empirical Findings from South America." *British Journal of Political Science* 43(3): 505–540.

Ginsburg, Tom. 2003. *Judicial Independence in New Democracies: Constitutional Courts in Asian Cases*. New York: Cambridge University Press.

Giusti-Rodríguez, Mariana. 2017. "Going beyond Co-ethnicity: Assessing the Programmatic Reach of Ethnic Cleavages." Manuscript, Cornell University.

Glade, William. 1989. "Economy, 1870–1914." In *Latin America: Economy and Society, 1870–1930*. Edited by Leslie Bethell. New York: Cambridge University Press, 1–56.

Goemans, Hein, Kristian Skrede Gleditsch, and Giacomo Chiozza. 2009. "Introducing Archigos: a Dataset of Political Leaders." *Journal of Peace Research* 46(2): 269–283.

Goldfrank, Benjamin. 2007. "The Politics of Deepening Local Democracy: Decentralization, Party Institutionalization, and Participation." *Comparative Politics* 39(2): 147–168.

Gomera, Federico. 2012. "La institucionalidad nacional y el funcionamiento de la seguridad social en la República Dominicana." Address to the ILO, Santiago, Chile.

González Ocantos, Ezequiel, Chad Kiewiet de Jonge, and David W. Nickerson. 2014. "The Conditionality of Vote-Buying Norms: Experimental Evidence from Latin America." *American Journal of Political Science* 58(1): 197–211.

González-Navarro, Moisés. 1985. "El maderismo y la revolución agraria." Presented at the Coloquio Internacional México al Filo del Siglo XXI. La Revolución Hoy, City University, Mexico City, November 4.

1990. "Vallarta, indios y extranjeros en la Suprema Corte de Justicia de la Nación (1877–1887)." In *La Suprema Corte de Justicia a principios del Porfirismo (1877–1882)*. Edited by Lucio Cabrera Acevedo. Mexico: Supreme Court of Justice of Mexico, 1075–1092.

González-Roa, Fernando. 1919. *El aspecto agrario de la Revolución Mexicana*. Mexico City: Poder Ejecutivo–Dirección de Talleres Gráficos.

Government of Mexico. 1885. *Legislación de terrenos baldíos: ó sea completa colección de leyes, decretos, órdenes, circulares, reglamentos, contratos y demás disposiciones supremas, relativas a terrenos baldíos de la República, publicadas hasta el mes de setiembre de 1885*. Chihuahua: Imprenta y Librería Donato Miramontes.

Greif, Avner, and David D. Laitin. 2004. "A Theory of Endogenous Institutional Change." *American Political Science Review* 98(4): 633–652.

Grindle, Merilee. 2007. *Going Local: Decentralization, Democratization, and the Promise of Good Governance*. Princeton: Princeton University Press.

— 2009. "La brecha de la implementación." In *Política pública y democracia en América Latina: Del análisis a la implementación*. Edited by Freddy Mariñez Navarro and Vidal Garza Cantú. Mexico: Miguel Angel Porrúa, 33–57.

— 2012. "Good Governance: The Inflation of an Idea." In *Planning Ideas That Matter: Livability, Territoriality, Governance, and Reflective Practice*. Edited by Bishwapriya Sanyal, Lawrence J. Vale, and Christina D. Rosan. Boston: MIT Press, 259–282.

Grueso, Libia, Carlos Rosero, and Arturo Escobar. 1998. "The Process of Black Community Organizing in the Southern Pacific Coast of Colombia." In *Cultures of Politics and Politics of Cultures: Re-visioning Latin American Social Movements*. Edited by Sonia Alvarez, Evelina Dagnino, and Arturo Escobar. Boulder: Westview Press.

Gryzmala-Busse, Anna. 2011. "Time Will Tell? Temporality and the Analysis of Causal Mechanisms and Processes." *Comparative Political Studies* 44 (9), 1267–1297.

Guerra, François-Xavier. 1985. *Le Méxique: De l'Ancien Régime a la Revolution*. Paris: L'Harmattan.

Guerrero Lara, Ezequiel, Santamaria Gonzalez, and Luis Felipe. 1990. "La publicidad de la jurisprudencia en el periodo 1877–1882." In *La Suprema Corte de Justicia a principios del Porfirismo (1877–1882)*. Edited by Lucio Cabrera Acevedo. Mexico: Supreme Court of Justice of Mexico, 983–1000.

Haber, Stephen, and Victor Menaldo. 2011. "Do Natural Resources Fuel Authoritarianism? A Reappraisal of the Resource Curse." *American Political Science Review* 105(1): 1–26.

Haber, Stephen, Armando Razo, and Noel Maurer. 2003. *The Politics of Property Rights: Political Instability, Credible Commitments, and Economic Growth in Mexico, 1876–1929*. Cambridge: Cambridge University Press.

Hacker, Jacob S. 2005. "Policy Drift: The Hidden Politics of US Welfare State Retrenchment." In *Beyond Continuity: Institutional Change in Advanced Political Economies*. Edited by Wolfgang Streeck and Kathleen Ann Thelen. Oxford: Oxford University Press, 40–82.

Hacker, Jacob, and Paul Pierson. 2002. "Business Power and Social Policy." *Politics and Society* 30(2): 277–325.

Haggard, Stephan. 1990. *Pathways from the Periphery: The Politics of Growth in the Newly Industrializing Countries*. Ithaca: Cornell University Press.

Haggard, Stephan, and Robert Kaufman. 2016. *Dictators and Democrats: Masses, Elites, and Regime Change*. Princeton: Princeton University Press.

Hale, Charles A. 1968. *Mexican Liberalism in the Age of Mora, 1821–1853*. New Haven: Yale University Press.

2005. "Neoliberal Multiculturalism: The Remaking of Cultural Rights and Racial Dominance in Central America." *Political and Legal Anthropology Review* 28(1): 10–28.

Hall, Peter A. 2016. "Politics as a Process Structured in Space and Time." In *Handbook of Historical Institutionalism*. Edited by Orfeo Fioretos, Tulia G. Falleti, and Adam Sheingate. Oxford: Oxford University Press.

Hardin, Garrett. 1968. "The Tragedy of the Commons." *Science* 162(3859): 1243–1248.

Hart, H.L.A. 1961. *The Concept of Law*. Oxford: Oxford University Press.

Hartlyn, Jonathan. 1998. *The Struggle for Democratic Politics in the Dominican Republic*. Chapel Hill: University of North Carolina Press.

Harvey, Philip. 2004. "Aspirational Law." *Buffalo Law Review* 52(3): 701–726.

Hathaway, Oona. 2002. "Do Human Rights Treaties Make a Difference?" *Yale Law Journal* 111(8): 1935–2042.

Heise, L.L. 1998. "Violence against Women: An Integrated, Ecological Framework." *Violence against Women* 4(3): 262–290.

Helmke, Gretchen. 2004. *Courts under Constraints: Judges, Generals, and Presidents in Argentina*. Cambridge: Cambridge University Press.

2010. "The Origins of Institutional Crises in Latin America." *American Journal of Political Science* 54(3): 737–750.

2017. *Institutions on the Edge: The Origins and Consequences of Inter-branch Crises in Latin America*. Cambridge: Cambridge University Press.

2018. "Puzzle of Purges: Presidential Instability and Judicial Manipulation in Latin America." Working paper. Available at: www.gretchenhelmke.com/uploads/7/0/3/2/70329843/helmke_puzzleofpurges_2018.pdf [Accessed January 20, 2020].

Helmke, Gretchen, and Steven Levitsky. 2004. "Informal Institutions and Comparative Politics: A Research Agenda." *Perspectives on Politics* 2(3): 725–740.

eds. 2006. *Informal Institutions and Democracy: Lessons from Latin America*. New York: Cambridge University Press.

Helmke, Gretchen, and Julio Ríos-Figueroa, eds. 2011. *Courts in Latin America*. Cambridge: Cambridge University Press.

Henisz, Witold. 2000. "The Institutional Environment for Multinational Investment." *Journal of Law, Economics, and Organization* 16(2): 334–364.

Henisz, Witold. 2002. *Politics and International Investment: Measuring Risk and Protecting Profits*. Cheltenham: Edward Elgar.

Henisz, Witold, and Bennet Zelner. 2005. "Legitimacy, Interest Group Pressures, and Change in Emergent Institutions: The Case of Foreign Investors and Host Country Governments." *Academy of Management Review* 30(2): 361–382.

Henisz, Witold, Bennet Zelner, and Mauro Guillen. 2005. "The Worldwide Diffusion of Market-Oriented Infrastructure Reform, 1977–1999." *American Sociological Review* 70(6): 871–897.

Herbst, Jeffrey. 2000. *States and Powers in Africa*. Princeton: Princeton University Press.

Heredia, Blanca, and Ben Ross Schneider. 1998. "The Political Economy of Administrative Reform: Building State Capacity in Developing Countries." Paper presented at the Latin American Studies Association. Available at: http://citeseerx.ist.psu.edu/viewdoc/download?doi=10.1.1.464.6424&rep=rep1&type=pdf [Accessed January 20, 2020].

Hernández, Alicia. 1993. *Anenecuilco: Memoria y vida de un pueblo*. México: Colegio de México-Fondo de Cultura Económica.

Herring, Ronald. 1999. "Political Conditions for Agrarian Reform and Poverty Alleviation." Prepared for the DFID Conference on 2001 World Development Report on Poverty, Birmingham, August 16–17.

Hirschl, Ran. 2004. *Towards Juristocracy: The Origins and Consequences of the New Constitutionalism.* Cambridge: Harvard University Press.

2009. "The 'Design Sciences' and Constitutional Success." *Texas Law Review* 87(7): 1339–1374.

Hirschman, Albert. 1978. "Beyond Asymmetry: Critical Notes on Myself as a Young Man and on Some Other Old Friends." *International Organization* 32(1): 45–50.

Hochstetler, Kathryn. 2006. "Rethinking Presidentialism: Challenges and Presidential Falls in South America." *Comparative Politics* 38(4): 401–418.

Hochstetler, Kathryn, and Margaret E. Edwards. 2009. "Failed Presidencies: Identifying and Explaining a South American Anomaly." *Journal of Politics in Latin America* 1(2): 31–57.

Hochstetler, Kathryn, and Margaret Keck. 2007. *Greening Brazil: Environmental Activism in State and Society.* Durham: Duke University Press.

Hochstetler, Kathryn, and David Samuels. 2011. "Crisis and Rapid Reequilibration: The Consequences of Presidential Challenge and Failure in Latin America." *Comparative Politics* 43(2): 127–145.

Holden, Robert. 1994. *Mexico and the Survey of Public Lands.* DeKalb: Northern Illinois University Press.

Holland, Alisha C. 2015. "The Distributive Politics of Enforcement." *American Journal of Political Science* 59(2): 357–371.

2016. "Forbearance." *American Political Science Review* 110(2): 232–246.

2017. *Forbearance as Redistribution: The Politics of Informal Welfare in Latin America.* Cambridge: Cambridge University Press.

Holmes, Stephen, and Cass R. Sunstein. 2000. *The Cost of Rights: Why Liberty Depends on Taxes.* New York: W. W. Norton.

Howard, Dick. 1991. "The Essence of Constitutionalism." In *Constitutionalism and Human Rights: America, Poland, and France.* Edited by Kenneth Thompson and Rett Ludwikoski. London: Lanham, 3–41.

Htun, Mala. 2003. *Sex and the State: Abortion, Divorce, and the Family under Latin American Dictatorships and Democracies.* Cambridge: Cambridge University Press.

2016. *Inclusion without Representation in Latin America: Gender Quotas and Ethnic Reservations.* New York: Cambridge University Press.

Htun, Mala, Cheryl O'Brien, and S. Laurel Weldon. 2014. "Movilización feminista y políticas sobre violencia contra las mujeres." *Foreign Affairs Latinoamérica* 14(1): 2–13.

Htun, Mala, and S. Laurel Weldon. 2012. "The Civic Origins of Progressive Policy Change: Combating Violence against Women in Global Perspective, 1975–2005." *American Political Science Review* 106(3): 548–569.

2018. *States and the Logics of Gender Justice: State Action on Women's Rights around the World.* New York: Cambridge University Press.

Huber, Gregory A. 2007. *The Craft of Bureaucratic Neutrality: Interests and Influence in Governmental Regulation of Occupational Safety.* Cambridge: Cambridge University Press.

Huber, John, and Nolan McCarty. 2004. "Bureaucratic Capacity, Delegation, and Political Reform." *American Political Science Review* 98(3): 481–494.

Huber, John D., and Charles R. Shipan. 2002. *Deliberate Discretion? The Institutional Foundations of Bureaucratic Autonomy.* Cambridge: Cambridge University Press.

Humphreys Bebbington, Denise. 2012. "Consultation, Compensation and Conflict: Natural Gas Extraction in Weenhayek Territory, Bolivia." *Journal of Latin American Geography* 11(2): 49–71.

Huntington, Samuel. 1966. "Political Modernization: Europe vs. America." *World Politics* 18 (3): 378–414.

1968. *Political Order in Changing Societies.* New Haven: Yale University Press.

1996. "The West: Unique, Not Universal." *Foreign Affairs*, November/December, p. 35.

Iacoviello, Mercedes, and Laura Zuvanic. 2006. "Desarrollo e Integración de la Gestión Recursos Humanos en los Estados Latinoamericanos." In *Documentos y Aportes en Administración Pública y Gestión Estatal*, vol. 6, núm. 7. Santa Fe: Universidad Nacional del Litoral, 45–92.

Iacoviello, Mercedes, and Ana Rodriguez-Gustá. 2006. "Síntesis de diagnóstico: Caso República Dominicana." In *Informe de la situación del servicio civil en América Latina.* Edited by Koldo Echebarría. Washington, DC: Banco Interamericano de Desarrollo, 447–472.

Instituto Azucarero Dominicano (INAZUCAR). 2018. "Historia de la producción de caña de azúcar en la República Dominicana." Available at: www.inazucar.gov.do/index.php/noticias/41-historia-de-la-produccion-de-cana-de-azucar-en-la-republica-dominicana [Accessed January 20, 2020].

Instituto Nacional de Estadística y Censos (INDEC). 2002. *Censo nacional agropecuario.* Buenos Aires: INDEC.

Itzigsohn, José. 2000. *Developing Poverty: The State, Labor Market Deregulation, and the Informal Economy in Costa Rica and the Dominican Republic.* University Park: Pennsylvania State University Press.

Jácome, Luis I., and Fernando Vázquez. 2008. "Is There Any Link between Legal Central Bank Independence and Inflation? Evidence from Latin America and the Caribbean." *European Journal of Political Economy* 24(4): 788–801.

James, Timothy. 2013. *Mexico's Supreme Court: Between Liberal Individual and Revolutionary Social Rights, 1867–1934.* Albuquerque: University of New Mexico Press.

Jordana, Jacint, and David Levi-Faur. 2005. "The Diffusion of Regulatory Capitalism in Latin America: Sectoral and National Channels in the Making of New Order." *Annals of the American Academy of Political and Social Science* 598: 102–124.

Jung, Courtney, Ran Hirschl, and Evan Rosevear. 2014. "Economic and Social Rights in National Constitutions." *American Journal of Comparative Law* 62(4): 1043–1094.

Kapiszewski, Diana. 2012. *High Courts and Economic Governance in Argentina and Brazil.* Cambridge: Cambridge University Press.

Katz, Richard S. 2005. "Why Are There So Many (or So Few) Electoral Reforms." In *The Politics of Electoral Systems.* Edited by Michael Gallagher and Paul Mitchell. New York: Oxford University Press, 57–76.

Keck, Margaret, and Kathryn Sikkink. 1998. *Activists beyond Borders: Advocacy Networks in International Politics.* Ithaca: Cornell University Press.

Keefer, Philip, and David Stasavage. 2003. "The Limits of Delegation: Veto Players, Central Bank Independence, and the Credibility of Monetary Policy." *American Political Science Review* 97(3): 407–423.

Keyssar, Alexander. 2000. *The Right to Vote: The Contested History of Democracy in the United States.* New York: Basic Books.

Kiely, Ray. 1999. "The Last Refuge of the Noble Savage? A Critical Assessment of Post-development Theory." *European Journal of Development Research* 11(1): 30–55.

Kim, Youngh Hun, and Donna Bahry. 2008. "Interrupted Presidencies in Third Wave Democracies." *Journal of Politics* 70(3): 807–822.

Kitschelt, Herbert. 2000. "Linkages between Citizens and Politicians in Democratic Polities." *Comparative Political Studies* 33(6/7): 845–879.

Klingner, Donald, and David Arrellano Gault. 2006. "Mexico's Professional Career Civil Service Law: Governance, Political Culture, and Public Administrative Reform." *International Public Management Review* 7(1): 70–97.

Klug, Heinz. 2000. *Constituting Democracy: Law, Globalism and South Africa's Political Reconstruction.* New York: Cambridge University Press.

Knight, Alan. 1986. *The Mexican Revolution. Vol. 1, Porfirians, Liberals and Peasants.* Cambridge: Cambridge University Press.

Knight, Jack. 1992. *Institutions and Social Conflict.* New York: Cambridge University Press.

Knowlton, Robert. 1976. *Church Property and the Mexican Reform, 1856–1910.* Illinois: Northern Illinois University Press.

——— 1990. "La división de las tierras de los pueblos durante el siglo XIX: El caso de Michoacán." *Historia mexicana* 40(1): 3–25.

——— 1996. "Tribunales federales y terrenos federales en el México del siglo XIX: El semanario judicial de la federación." *Historia mexicana* 46(1): 71–98.

——— 1998. "El ejido mexicano en el siglo XIX." *Historia Mexicana* 48(1): 71–96.

Kogut, Bruce. 2012. *Small Worlds of Corporate Governance.* Cambridge: MIT Press.

Kourí, Emilio. 2004. *A Pueblo Divided: Business, Property, and Community in Papantla, Mexico.* Stanford: Stanford University Press.

——— n.d. Making the Ejido, unpublished book manuscript (date of version cited: 2011).

Krasner, Stephen D. 1988. "Sovereignty: An Institutional Perspective." *Comparative Political Studies* 21(1): 66–94.

Krauze, Léon. 2016. "Los Porkys: The Sexual-Assault Case That's Shaking Mexico." *New Yorker*, April 14, 2016.

Kuczynski, Pedro Pablo, and John Williamson. 2003. *After the Washington Consensus: Restarting Growth and Reform in Latin America.* Washington, DC: Peterson Institute for International Economics.

Kuntz, Sandra. 2010a. "De las reformas liberales a la Gran Depresión, 1856–1929." In *Historia económica general de México. De la Colonia a nuestros días.* Edited by Sandra Kuntz. México: El Colegio de México-Secretaría de Economía, 305–352.

Kuntz, Sandra. 2010b. "Los ferrocarriles y tierras a través de los expedientes de la Suprema Corte de Justicia." In *La justicia durante el Porfiriato y la Revolución 1898–1914.* Edited by Suprema Corte de Justicia de la Nación (SCJN). Mexico: SCJN, 5, 329–331.

Kurtz, Marcus J. 2013. *Latin American State Building in Comparative Perspective: Social Foundations of Institutional Order.* Cambridge: Cambridge University Press.

Kymlicka, Will. 1995. *Multicultural Citizenship: A Liberal Theory of Minority Rights.* Oxford, New York: Clarendon-Oxford University Press.

Landau, David, and Manuel José Cepeda, eds. 2017. *Colombian Constitutional Law: Leading Cases.* New York: Oxford University Press.

Lang, Miriam. 2003. "¿Todo el poder? Políticas públicas, violencia de género y feminismo en México." *Iberoamericana* 3(12): 69–90.

Langford, Malcolm. 2009. *Social Rights Jurisprudence: Emerging Trends in Comparative and International Law.* New York: Cambridge University Press.

Langford, Malcolm, Ben Cousins, Jackie Dugard, and Tshepo Madlingozi, eds. 2011. *Symbols or Substance? The Role and Impact of Socio-economic Rights Strategies in South Africa.* Cambridge: Cambridge University Press.

Langston, Joy. 2006. "The Birth and Transformation of the Dedazo in Mexico." In *Informal Institutions and Democracy: Lessons from Latin America.* Edited by Gretchen Helmke and Steven Levitsky. Baltimore: Johns Hopkins University Press.

La Porta, Rafael, Florencio Lopez-de-Silanes, and Andrei Shleifer. 2008. "The Economic Consequences of Legal Origins." *Journal of Economic Literature* 46(2): 285–332.

Lapegna, Pablo. 2016. *Soybeans and Power.* New York: Oxford University Press.

Latin American Public Opinion Project (LAPOP). AmericasBarometer 1997. Available at: www.LapopSurveys.org

2004. *Dominican Republic: Encuesta nacional de cultura política y democracia.* Nashville: Vanderbilt. Available at: www.lapopsurveys.org.

Latinobarómetro. 2005. *Latinobarómetro 2005.* Santiago: Latinobarómetro.

Leake, Andrés, and María de Ecónomo. 2008. *La Deforestación de Salta 2004–2007.* Salta: Fundación Asociana.

Levi, Margaret. 1997. *Consent, Dissent, and Patriotism.* New York: Cambridge University Press.

1988. *Of Rule and Revenue.* Berkeley: University of California Press.

Levitsky, Steven, and James Loxton. 2013. "Populism and Competitive Authoritarianism in the Andes." *Democratization* 20(1): 107–136.

Levitsky, Steven, and María Victoria Murillo. 2005. "Building Castles in the Sand? The Politics of Institutional Weakness in Argentina." In *Argentine Democracy: The Politics of Institutional Weakness.* Edited by Steven Levitsky and Maria Victoria Murillo. State College: Pennsylvania State University Press.

2009. "Variation in Institutional Strength." *Annual Review of Political Science* 12: 115–133.

2013. "Building Institutions on Weak Foundations." *Journal of Democracy* 24(2): 93–107.

2014. "Building Institutions on Weak Foundations: Lessons from Latin America." In *Reflections on Uneven Democracies: The Legacy of Guillermo O'Donnell.* Edited by Daniel M. Brinks, Marcelo Leiras, and Scott Mainwaring. Baltimore: Johns Hopkins University Press, 189–213.

Levitsky, Steven, and Kenneth M. Roberts. 2011. *The Resurgence of the Latin American Left.* Baltimore: Johns Hopkins University Press.

Levitsky, Steven, and Dan Slater. 2011. "Ruling Politics: The Formal and Informal Foundations of Institutional Reform." In Workshop on Informal Institutions, Harvard University, Cambridge, MA, November. Available at: http://conferences.wcfia.harvard.edu/ruling_politics/files/ruling_politics_intro-finalcompletedraft.pdf.

Levitsky, Steven, and Daniel Ziblatt. 2018. *How Democracies Die.* New York: Crown.

Levy, Brian, and Pablo Spiller, eds. 1996. *Regulations, Institutions, and Commitment: Comparative Studies of Telecommunications.* New York: Cambridge University Press.

Lewis, W. Arthur. 1961. "Education and Economic Development." *Social and Economic Studies* 10(2): 113–127.

Ley 26331. Presupuestos Mínimos Ambientales para la Protección de los Bosques Nativos. El Senado y Cámara de Diputados de la Nación Argentina.

Lieberman, Evan S. 2003. *Race and Regionalism in the Politics of Taxation in Brazil and South Africa*. Cambridge: Cambridge University Press.

Lijphart, Arend, and Don Aitkin. 1994. *Electoral Systems and Party Systems: A Study of Twenty-Seven Democracies, 1945–1990*. Oxford and New York: Oxford University Press.

Lindblom, Charles. 1977. *Politics and Markets*. New York: Basic Books.

Linz, Juan J. 1994. "Presidential or Parliamentary Democracy: Does It Make a Difference?" In *The Failure of Presidential Democracy*. Edited by Juan J. Linz and Arturo Valenzuela. Baltimore: Johns Hopkins University Press, 3–87.

Linz, Juan J., and Alfred Stepan. 1996. *Problems of Democratic Transition and Consolidation: Southern Europe, South America, and Post-communist Europe*. Baltimore: Johns Hopkins University Press.

Lipsky, Michael. 1980. *Street Level Bureaucracy: Dilemmas of the Individual in Public Services*. New York: Russell Sage Foundation.

———. 1983. *Street-Level Bureaucracy: The Dilemmas of the Individual in Public Service*. New York: Russell Sage Foundation.

Llanos, Mariana, and Leiv Marsteintredet. 2010. "Conclusions: Presidential Breakdowns Revisited." In *Presidential Breakdowns in Latin America: Causes and Outcomes of Executive Instability in Developing Democracies*. Edited by Mariana Llanos and Leiv Marsteintredet. New York: Palgrave Macmillan, 213–228.

Loewenstein, Karl. 1949. "The Presidency Outside the United States: A Study in Comparative Political Institutions." *Journal of Politics* 11(3): 447–496.

Longo, Francisco. 2005. *Diagnóstico institucional comparado de sistemas de servicio civil: Informe final de síntesis*. Washington, DC: Inter-American Development Bank. https://publications.iadb.org/es/publicacion/14595/diagnostico-institucional-comparado-de-sistemas-de-servicio-civil-informe-final.

Lucero, Antonio. 2008. *Struggles of Voice: The Politics of Indigenous Representation*. Pittsburgh: University of Pittsburgh Press.

Luft, John. 2013. "Moving Floors, the Obstacles to guaranteeing Environmental Protection of Native Forest in the Context of Argentina's Federalism." MA dissertation, Graduate School of Arts and Sciences, Georgetown University.

Lundahl, Mats, and Claudio Vedovato. 1989. "The State and Economic Development in Haiti and the Dominican Republic." *Scandinavian Economic History Review* 37(3): 39–59.

MacKinnon, Catherine A. 1991. "Reflections on Sex Equality under Law." *Yale Law Journal* 100(5): 1281–1328.

Madrid, Raúl L. 2012. *The Rise of Ethnic Politics in Latin America*. New York: Cambridge University Press.

Maeda, Ko. 2010. "Two Modes of Democratic Breakdown: A Competing Risks Analysis of Democratic Durability." *Journal of Politics* 72(4): 1129–1143.

Magaloni, Beatriz. 2003. "Authoritarianism, Democracy and the Supreme Court: Horizontal Exchange and the Rule of Law in Mexico." In *Democratic Accountability in Latin America*. Edited by Scott Mainwaring and Christopher Welna. Oxford: Oxford University Press, 266–305.

Mahoney, James. 2000. "Path Dependence in Historical Sociology." *Theory and Society* 29(4): 507–548.

2010. *Colonialism and Postcolonial Development: Spanish America in Comparative Perspective.* New York: Cambridge University Press.

Mahoney, James, and Kathleen Thelen. 2010. "A Theory of Gradual Institutional Change." In *Explaining Institutional Change: Ambiguity, Agency, and Power.* Edited by James Mahoney and Kathleen Thelen. Cambridge: Cambridge University Press, 1–37.

2015. *Advances in Comparative-Historical Analysis.* New York: Cambridge University Press.

Mainwaring, Scott. 1990. "Presidentialism in Latin America." *Latin American Research Review* 25(1): 157–179.

1997. "Multipartism, Robust Federalism, and Presidentialism in Brazil." In *Presidentialism and Democracy in Latin America.* Edited by Scott Mainwaring and Matthew Soberg Shugart. Cambridge: Cambridge university Press, 55–109.

2018. "Party System Institutionalization in Contemporary Latin America." In *Party System in Latin America: Institutionalization, Decay and Collapse.* Edited by S. Mainwaring. New York: Cambridge University Press, 34–70.

Mainwaring, Scott, Daniel Brinks, and Aníbal Pérez-Liñán. 2001. "Classifying Political Regimes in Latin America, 1945–1999." *Studies in Comparative International Development* 36 (1): 37–65.

Mainwaring, Scott, and Aníbal Pérez-Liñán. 2013. *Democracies and Dictatorships in Latin America: Emergence, Survival, and Fall.* New York: Cambridge University Press.

Mainwaring, Scott, and Matthew S. Shugart. 1997. *Presidentialism and Democracy in Latin America.* New York: Cambridge University Press.

Mainwaring, Scott, and Christopher Welna, eds. 2003. *Democratic Accountability in Latin America.* Oxford: Oxford University Press.

Malesky, Edmund. 2005. "Straight Ahead on Red: The Impact of Foreign Direct Investment on Local Autonomy in Vietnam." Paper presented at the annual meeting of the Midwest Political Science Association Chicago, April 3–7.

Mamadouh, Virginie, Martin De Jong, and Konstantinos Lalenis. 2003. "An Introduction to Institutional Transplantation." Department of Planning and Regional Development, School of Engineering, University of Thessaly. Discussion Paper Series 9(13): 273–292.

Mann, Michael. 1984. "The Autonomous Power of the State: Its Origins, Mechanisms and Results." *European Journal of Sociology* 25(2): 185–213.

Mares, Isabela. 2005. Social Protection around the World: External Insecurity, State Capacity and Domestic Political Cleavages. *Comparative Political Studies* 38(6): 623–651.

Marino, Daniela. 2001. "La desamortización de las tierras de los pueblos (centro de México, siglo XIX). Balance historiográfico y fuentes para su estudio." *América Latina en la historia económica* 8(16): 33–43.

2006. "La modernidad a juicio: Los pueblos de Huixquilucan en la transición jurídica (Estado de México, 1856–1911)." PhD dissertation, El Colegio de México.

2016. "La medida de su existencia. La abolición de las comunidades indígenas y el juicio de amparo en el contexto desamortizador (centro de México, 1856–1910)." *Revista de Indias* 76(266): 287–313.

Márquez, Daniel. 2015. "La evolución histórica del juicio de amparo mexicano (reflexión crítica)." In *Historia y constitución. Homenaje a José Luis Soberanes Fernández.* Edited by Miguel Carbonell and Cruz Barney Oscar. Mexico: UNAM, 337–365.

Marsteintredet, Leiv, and Einar Berntzen. 2008. "Reducing the Perils of Presidentialism in Latin America through Presidential Interruptions." *Comparative Politics* 41(1): 83–101.

Martínez-Alier, Joan. 2013. "The Environmentalism of the Poor." *Geoforum* 54: 239–241.

Martínez-Godínez, María. 2009. "Orígenes y antecedentes legislativos de la jurisprudencia." *Praxis de la justicia fiscal y administrativa*, no. 3, año 2010, 44–74.

Mayka, Lindsay. 2019. *Building Participatory Institutions in Latin America: Reform Coalitions and Institutional Change*. Cambridge: Cambridge University Press.

McAdams, Richard H. 1997. "The Origin, Development, and Regulation of Norms." *Michigan Law Review* 96: 338–433.

McBride, George McCutchen. 1923. *The Land Systems of Mexico*. New York: American Geographical Society.

McCubbins, Mathew D., Roger G. Noll, and Barry R. Weingast. 1987. "Administrative Procedures as Instruments of Political Control." *Journal of Law, Economics, and Organization* 3(2): 243–277.

McKie, Kristin. Forthcoming. "Presidential Term Limit Contravention: Abolish, Extend, Fail, or Respect?" *Comparative Political Studies*. https://doi.org/10.1177/0010414019830737.

McNulty, Stephanie L. 2011. *Voice and Vote: Decentralization and Participation in Post-Fujimori Peru*. Stanford: Stanford University Press.

Mecham, Lloyd. 1986. "El jefe político en México." *Secuencia* 4: 143–156.

Mejía Acosta, Andrés, and John Polga-Hecimovich. 2010. "Parliamentary Solutions to Presidential Crises in Ecuador." In *Presidential Breakdowns in Latin America*. Edited by Mariana Llanos and Leiv Marsteintredet. New York: Palgrave Macmillan, 73–90.

Menaldo, Victor. 2016. *The Institutions Curse*. New York: Cambridge University Press.

Méndez, Juan E., Guillermo O'Donnell, and Paulo Sérgio Pinheiro, eds. 1999. *The (Un)Rule of Law and the Underprivileged in Latin America*. Notre Dame: Notre Dame University Press.

Méndez, Mario. 1993. *Reformas y lucha de intereses*. Santo Domingo: Editora Corripio.

Mendoza-García, Edgar. 2011. *Municipios, cofradías y tierras comunales: Los pueblos chocholtecos de Oaxaca en el siglo XIX*. Oaxaca: Universidad Autónoma "Benito Juárez" de Oaxaca, Universidad Nacional Autónoma de México, Universidad Autónoma Metropolitana-Azcapotzalco, Centro de Investigaciones y Estudios Superiores en Antropología Social.

Merryman, John Henry. 1996. "The French Deviation." *American Journal of Comparative Law* 44(1): 109–119.

Migdal, Joel S. 1988. *Strong Societies and Weak States: State-Society Relations and State Capabilities in the Third World*. Princeton: Princeton University Press.

Migdal, Joel, Atul Kohli, and Vivienne Shue. 1994. Introduction to *State Power and Social Forces: Struggles and Accommodation*. Edited by Joel Migdal, Atul Kohli, and Vivienne Shue. New York: Cambridge University Press, 1–4.

Ministerio del Administración Pública (MAP). 2014. "Análisis del BID refleja avances de la República Dominicana en índices del servicio civil." Diario Libre. Available at: www.diariolibre.com/actualidad/anlisis-del-bid-refleja-avances-de-la-repblica-dominicana-en-ndices-del-servicio-civil-KADL910831 [Accessed January 20, 2020].

Ministerio de Ambiente y Desarrollo Sustentable (MAyDS). 2016. *Ley 26.331. Informe de Estado de Implementación 2010–2015*. Buenos Aires: MAyDS-Dirección de Bosques.

Ministerio de Economía y Finanzas Públicas. 2015. "Chaco. Ficha provincial." Secretaría de Política Económica y Planificación del Desarrollo, Buenos Aires, October 2015. Available at: www.economia.gob.ar/peconomica/dnper/fichas_provinciales/Chaco.pdf.

Ministerio de Trabajo. 2015. *Boletín estadístico 2015*. Santo Domingo: Ministerio de Trabajo.

Mockus, Antanas. 2012. "Make Unfamiliar the Familiar." Paper presented at Reframing International Development conference, Massachusetts Institute of Technology Department of Urban Studies and Planning, Cambridge, MA, April.

Moe, Terry. 1990. "Political Institutions: The Neglected Side of the Story." Special issue, *Journal of Law, Economics and Organization* 6: 213–253.

2005. "Power and Political Institutions." *Perspectives of Politics* 3(2): 215–233.

Moncada, Eduardo. 2016. *Cities, Business, and the Politics of Urban Violence in Latin America*. Palo Alto: Stanford University Press.

Moore, Barrington Jr. 1966. *Social Origins of Dictatorship and Democracy: Lord and Peasant in the Making of the Modern World*. Boston: Beacon Press.

Motta Ferraz, Octávio. 2010. "Harming the Poor through Social Rights Litigation: Lessons from Brazil." *Texas Law Review* 89: 1643–1668.

Mozaffar, Shaheen, and Andreas Schedler. 2002. "The Comparative Study of Electoral Governance." *International Political Science Review* 23(1): 5–27.

Murillo, María Victoria. 2001. *Labor Unions, Partisan Coalitions, and Market Reforms in Latin America*. New York: Cambridge University Press.

2005. "Partisanship Amidst Convergence: Labor Market Reforms in Latin America." *Comparative Politics* 37(4): 441–458.

2009. *Political Competition, Partisanship, and Policymaking in Latin America*. New York: Cambridge University Press.

Murillo, María Victoria, Lucas Ronconi, and Andrew Schrank. 2011. "Latin American Labor Reforms: Evaluating Risk and Security." In *The Oxford Handbook of Latin American Economics*. Edited by José Antonio Ocampo and Jaime Ros. Oxford: Oxford University Press, 790–812.

Murillo, María Victoria, and Andrew Schrank. 2005. "With a Little Help from My Friends: Partisan Politics, Transnational Alliances, and Labor Rights in Latin America." *Comparative Political Studies* 38(8): 971–999.

Murillo, María Victoria, and Giancarlo Visconti. 2017. "Economic Performance and Incumbents' Support in Latin America." *Electoral Studies* 45: 180–190.

Murray, Rainbow. 2007. "How Parties Evaluate Compulsory Quotas: A Study of the Implementation of the 'Parity' Law in France." *Parliamentary Affairs* 60(4): 568–584.

Mustapic, Ana María. 2010. "Presidentialism and Early Exits: The Role of Congress." In *Presidential Breakdowns in Latin America: Causes and Outcomes of Executive Instability in Developing Democracies*. Edited by Mariana Llanos and Leiv Marsteintredet. New York: Palgrave Macmillan, 17–32.

Nalepa, Monika, Georg Vanberg, and Caterina Chiopris. 2018. "Authoritarian Backsliding." Unpublished manuscript, University of Chicago and Duke University. www.monikanalepa.com/uploads/6/6/3/1/66318923/auth_back_chicago.pdf.

Negretto, Gabriel. 2006. "Choosing How to Choose Presidents." *Journal of Politics* 68(2): 421–433.

2009. "La reforma electoral en América Latina: Entre el interés partidario y las demandas ciudadanas." In *Reforma del sistema electoral chileno*. Edited by Arturo Fontaine, Cristian Larroulet, Jorge Navarrete, and Ignacio Walker. Santiago de Chile: PNUD-CIEPLAN-CEP, 63–103 [Accessed January 20, 2020].

2013. *Making Constitutions: Presidents, Parties, and Institutional Choice in Latin America*. Cambridge: Cambridge University Press.

2015. "From Duverger to Rokkan and Back: Progress and Challenges in the Study of Electoral Systems." In *Routledge Handbook of Comparative Political Institutions*. Edited by Jennifer Gandhi and Ruben Rufino. London: Routledge, 113–128.

Negretto, Gabriel, and José Antonio Aguilar-Rivera. 2000. "Rethinking the Legacy of the Liberal State in Latin America: The Cases of Argentina (1853–1916) and Mexico (1857–1910)." *Journal of Latin American Studies* 32(2): 361–397.

N'gweno, Bettina. 2000. *On Titling Collective Property, Participation, and Natural Resource Management: Implementing Indigenous and Afro-Colombian Demands*. Washington, DC: The World Bank. Available at: http://documents.worldbank.org/curated/en/868771468770446387/On-titling-collective-property-participation-and-natural-resources-management-implementing-indigenous-and-Afro-Colombian-demands.

Nichter, Simeon. 2011. "Vote Buying in Brazil: From Impunity to Prosecution." Unpublished. Available at: https://projects.iq.harvard.edu/files/ruling_politics/files/nichter_-_vote_buying_in_brazil_-_from_impunity_to_prosecution.pdf [Accessed January 20, 2020].

Nohlen, Dieter. 1994. *Institutional Reform in Latin America from the Perspective of Political Engineering*. Heidelberg.

North, Douglass C. 1990. *Institutions, Institutional Change and Economic Performance*. Cambridge: Cambridge University Press.

North, Douglass C., and Barry R. Weingast. 1989. "Constitutions and Commitment: The Evolution of Institutions Governing Public Choice in Seventeenth-Century England." *Journal of Economic History* 49(4): 803–832.

Nuñez, Jeremias. 2011. "RD avanza en la descentralización de la labor de inspección." El *puerto*, May 12.

O'Brien, Kevin, and Lianjiang Li. 1999. "Selective Policy Implementation in Rural China." *Comparative Politics* 31(2): 167–181.

O'Donnell, Guillermo A. 1993. "On the State, Democratization and Some Conceptual Problems: A Latin American View with Glances at Some Postcommunist Countries." *World Development* 21(8): 1355–1369.

1994. "Delegative Democracy." *Journal of Democracy* 5(1): 55–69.

1998. "Horizontal Accountability in New Democracies." *Journal of Democracy* 9(3): 112–126.

1999a. *Counterpoints: Selected Essays on Authoritarianism and Democratization*. Notre Dame: University of Notre Dame Press.

1999b. "Polyarchies and the (Un)Rule of Law in Latin America." In *The (Un)rule of Law and the Underprivileged in Latin America*. Edited by Juan E. Méndez.

O'Donnell, Guillermo, and Paulo Sérgio Pinheiro. Notre Dame: University of Notre Dame Press, 303–337.

2004. "Why the Rule of Law Matters." *Journal of Democracy* 15(4): 32–46.

O'Donnell, Guillermo, and Philippe Schmitter. 1986. *Transitions from Authoritarian Rule*. Baltimore: Johns Hopkins University Press.

Oficina Nacional de Administración Publica (ONAP). 2004. *ONAP informa*. April.

Olson, Mancur. 2000. *Power and Prosperity: Outgrowing Communist and Capitalist Dictatorships*. New York: Basic Books.

Onoma, Ato. 2010. *The Politics of Property Rights Institutions in Africa*. Cambridge: Cambridge University Press.

Oquendo, Angel. 2006. *Latin American Law*. New York: Foundation Press; Thomson/ West.

Organismo de Evaluación y Fiscalización Ambiental (OEFA). 2013. *Fiscalización ambiental a la pequeña minería y minería artesanal*. Lima: OEFA.

Orozco, Wistano Luis. 1898. *Legislación y jurisprudencia sobre terrenos baldíos*. México: Ediciones el Caballito.

Ostrom, Elinor. 1986. "An Agenda for the Study of Institutions." *Public Choice* 48(1): 3–25.

   1996. "Crossing the Great Divide: Co-production, Synergy, and Development." *World Development* 24(6): 1073–1087.

Oviedo, José, et al. 2007. *Índice de transparencia de las entidades públicas*. Santo Domingo: Participación Ciudadana.

Owensby, Brian. 1999. *Intimate Ironies: Modernity and the Making of Middle-Class Lives in Brazil*. Stanford: Stanford University Press.

Ozarow, Daniel. 2014. "When All They Thought Was Solid Melted into Air: Resisting Pauperization in Argentina during the 2002 Crisis." *Latin American Research Review* 49 (1): 178–202.

Palacio (Santo Domingo). 2008. "Vicepresidente dictó conferencias en México y España." 4, 182: 6.

Parrado, Salvador, and Miquel Salvador. 2011. "The Institutionalization of Meritocracy in Latin American Regulatory Agencies." *International Review of Administrative Sciences* 77(4): 687–712.

Pellegrini, Lorenzo, and Marco Octavio Ribera Arismendi. 2012. "Consultation, Compensation and Extraction in Bolivia after the 'Left Turn': The Case of Oil Exploration in the North of La Paz Department." *Journal of Latin American Geography* 11(2): 103–120.

Peña, Ximena, María Alejandra Vélez, Natalia Perdomo, and Juan Camilo Cárdenas. 2017. "Collective Property Leads to Household Investments: Lessons from Land Titling in Afro-Colombian Communities." *World Development* 97(C): 27–48.

Pérez Castellón, Ariel. 2013. "Justicia constitucional en Bolivia: Desafíos y oportunidades para la tutela de los derechos de los pueblos indígenas en conflictos socioambientales." *Revista catalana de dret ambiental* 4(2): 1–47.

Pérez-Liñán, Aníbal. 2005. "Latin American Democratization since 1978: Democratic Transition, Breakdowns and Erosions." In *The Third Wave of Democratization in Latin America: Advances and Setbacks*. Edited by Frances Hagopian and Scott Mainwaring. Cambridge: Cambridge University Press, 14–59.

   2007. *Presidential Impeachment and the New Political Instability in Latin America*. New York: Cambridge University Press.

Pérez-Liñán, Aníbal, and John Polga-Hecimovich. 2018. "Executive Exits in the Americas." Unpublished manuscript, last modified June 6, 2018.

Peters, B. Guy. 2011. *Institutional Theory in Political Science: The New Institutionalism*. London: Bloomsbury.

Pierson, Paul. 1994. *Dismantling the Welfare State? Reagan, Thatcher, and the Politics of Retrenchment*. Cambridge: Cambridge University Press.

2000. "Increasing Returns, Path Dependence, and the Study of Politics." *American Political Science Review* 94(2): 251–267.

2004. *Politics in Time: History, Institutions, and Social Analysis.* Princeton: Princeton University Press.

2016. "Power in Historical Institutionalism." In *The Oxford Handbook of Historical Institutionalism.* Edited by Orfeo Fioretos, Tulia G. Falleti, and Adam Sheingate. Oxford: Oxford University Press, 124–141.

Piore, Michael J., and Andrew Schrank. 2008. "Toward Managed Flexibility: The Revival of Labour Inspection in the Latin World." *International Labour Review* 147(1): 1–23.

2018. *Root-Cause Regulation: Protecting Work and Workers in the Twenty-First Century.* Cambridge: Harvard University Press.

Pizaro, Cynthia. 2008. *La Vulnerabilidad de los Inmigrantes Bolivianos Como Sujetos de Derechos Humanos: Experimentando la Exclusión y la Discriminación en la Región Metropolitana de la Ciudad de Córdoba.* Instituto Nacional contra la Discriminación, la Xenofobia y el Racismo Ministerio de Justicia, Seguridad y Derechos Humanos Gobierno de la República Argentina.

Portes, Alejandro. 2006. "Institutions and Development: A Conceptual Reanalysis." *Population and Development Review* 32(2): 233–262.

Posada-Carbó, Eduardo. 2011. "Latin America: Colombia after Uribe." *Journal of Democracy* 22(1): 137–151.

Posner, Daniel, and Daniel Young. 2007. "The Institutionalization of Political Power in Africa." *Journal of Democracy* 18(3): 126–140.

Post, Alison E. 2014. *Foreign and Domestic Investment in Argentina: The Politics of Privatized Infrastructure.* Cambridge: Cambridge University Press.

Post, Alison E., and Maria Victoria Murillo. 2016. "How Investor Portfolios Shape Regulatory Outcomes: Privatized Infrastructure after Crises." *World Development* 77(C): 328–345.

Poveda, Pablo. 2015. "El oro en la economía internacional." In *El oro en Bolivia: Mercado, producción y medio ambiente.* Edited by Pablo Poveda, Neyer Nogales, and Ricardo Calla. La Paz: CEDLA, 1–100.

Powell, Robert. 1999. *In the Shadow of Power: States and Strategies in International Politics.* Princeton: Princeton University Press.

Powell, T.G. 1972. "Los liberales, el campesinado indígena y los problemas agrarios durante la Reforma." *Historia mexicana* 21(4): 653–675.

Pritchett, Lant, and Michael Woolcock. 2002. "Solutions When the Solution Is the Problem: Arraying the Disarray in Development." CGD Working Paper 10. www.sciencedirect.com/science/article/abs/pii/S0305750X03002201.

Pritchett, Lant, et al. 2012. "Looking Like a State: Techniques of Persistent Failure in State Capability for Implementation." UNU/WIDER Working Paper 2012/63. www.tandfonline.com/doi/abs/10.1080/00220388.2012.709614.

Programa Naciones Unido de Desarrollo (PNUD). 2008. *Informe sobre desarrollo humano República Dominicana 2008: Desarrollo humano, una cuestión de poder.* Santo Domingo: PNUD.

Przeworski, Adam. 1991. *Democracy and the Market.* New York: Cambridge University Press.

Przeworski, Adam, Michael E. Alvarez, José Antonio Cheibub, and Fernando Limongi. 2000. *Democracy and Development: Political Institutions and Well-Being in the World, 1950–1990.* New York: Cambridge University Press.

Ramírez Corzo, Daniel, and Gustavo Riofrío. 2006. *Formalización de la propiedad y mejoramiento de barrios: Bien legal, bien informal.* Lima: DESCO.

Ramírez, Karla, and Carlos Echarri. 2010. "Mapeo de procesos de atención y construcción de indicadores sobre casos de violencia contra las mujeres." Inmujeres Cuaderos de Trabajo 17. Mexico City: INMUJERES. Available at: http://web.inmujeres.gob.mx/transparencia/archivos/estudios_opiniones/cuadernos/ct17.pdf .

Red Agroforestal Chaco Argentina (REDAF). 2008. *Informe monitoreo OTBN: Salta.* Available at: http://redaf.org.ar/descargas/ [Accessed January 20, 2020].

Red Interamericana de la Cooperación Laboral (RIAL). 2009. *Informe de la cooperación entre la secretaría de trabajo (SET) República Dominicana y el ministerio de trabajo, empleo y seguridad social (MTEySS) de Argentina sobre "el plan nacional de trabajo decente en Argentina."* http://rialnet.org/sites/default/files/Informe%20Final_19.pdf.

Reina, Leticia. 1980. *Las rebeliones campesinas en México (1819–1906).* Mexico City: Siglo XXI.

2013. *Historia del Istmo de Tehuantepec: dinámica del cambio sociocultural, siglo XIX.* México: Instituto Nacional de Antropología e Historia.

Remmer, Karen. 1991. "The Political Impact of Economic Crisis in Latin America in the 1980s." *American Political Science Review* 85(3): 777–800.

2008. "The Politics in Institutional Change: Electoral Reform in Latin America, 1978–2002." *Party Politics* 14(1): 5–30.

Rich, Jessica A.J. 2013. "Grassroots Bureaucracy: Intergovernmental Relations and Popular Mobilization in Brazil's AIDS Policy Sector." *Latin American Politics and Society* 55(2): 1–25.

Ridgeway, Cecilia L. 2001. "Gender, Status, and Leadership." *Journal of Social Issues* 57(4): 637–655.

Riedl, Rachel Beatty. 2014. *Authoritarian Origins of Democratic Party Systems in Africa.* New York: Cambridge University Press.

Rivera Cusicanqui, Silvia. 1990. "Liberal Democracy and Ayllu Democracy in Bolivia: The Case of Northern Potosí." *Journal of Development Studies* 26(4): 97–121.

2004. "Reclaiming the Nation." NACLA Report on Bolivia (November–December), 19–23. North American Congress on Latin America, New York City.

Roberts, Kenneth M. 2014. *Changing Course in Latin America.* Cambridge: Cambridge University Press.

Roberts, Kenneth M. and Erik Wibbels. 1999. "Party Systems and Electoral Volatility in Latin America: A Test of Economic, Institutional, and Structural Explanations." *American Political Science Review* 93(3) (September): 575–590.

Rodríguez-Franco, Diana. 2017. "Participatory Institutions and Environmental Protection: Popular and Prior Consultations in Latin America." PhD dissertation, Northwestern University.

Rodríguez Garavito, César. 2011a. "Beyond the Courtroom: The Impact of Judicial Activism on Socioeconomic Rights in Latin America." *Texas Law Review* 89(7): 1669–1698.

2011b. "Ethnicity.gov: Global Governance, Indigenous Peoples, and the Right to Prior Consultation in Social Minefields." *Indiana Journal of Global Legal Studies* 18(1): 263–305.

2012. *Etnicidad.gov. Los recursos naturales, los pueblos indígenas y el derecho a la consulta previa en los campos sociales minados.* Bogotá: Centro de Estudios de Derecho, Justicia y Sociedad, Dejusticia.

Rodrik, Dani. 2007. *One Economics, Many Recipes: Globalization, Institutions, and Economic Growth.* Princeton: Princeton University Press.

Rogowski, Ronald. 1987. "Trade and the Variety of Democratic Institutions." *International Organization* 41(2): 203–223.

　1989. *Commerce and Coalitions: How Trade Affects Domestic Political Alignments.* Princeton: Princeton University Press.

Rokkan, Stein. 1970. *Citizens, Elections, Parties: Approaches to the Comparative Study of the Process of Development.* Oslo: Universitetsforlaget.

Ronconi, Lucas. 2010. "Enforcement and Compliance with Labor Regulations in Argentina." *Industrial and Labor Relations Review* 63(4): 719–736.

Rose-Ackerman, Susan. 2007. "Public Administration and Institutions in Latin America." Paper prepared for Copenhagen Consenso, Consulta de San José de Costa Rica, San José, October 21–25 [Online]. Available at: www.copenhagenconsensus.com/sites/default/files/publ_adm_sp_ackerman_final.pdf [Accessed January 1, 2016].

Rosenberg, Tina. 1992. "Latin America's Magical Realism." *Wilson Quarterly* 16(4): 58–74.

Royo, Sebastián. 2003. *Review of Clientelism, Interests, and Democratic Representation: The European Experience in Historical and Comparative Perspective.* Perspectives on Politics. Edited by Simona Piattoni, ed. 1(1): 217–218.

Rueschemeyer, Dietrich. 1986. *Power and the Division of Labor.* Stanford: Stanford University Press.

　2005. "Building States – Inherently a Long-Term Process? An Argument from Theory." In *States and Development: Historical Antecedents of Stagnation and Advance.* Edited by Matthew Lange and Dietrich Rueschemeyer. London: Palgrave Macmillan, 143–164.

Ruiz, Ethelia. 2010. *Mexico's Indigenous Communities: Their Lands and Histories, 1500-2010.* Boulder: University Press of Colorado.

Ruíz Muller, Manuel. 2011. "Análisis del proceso de implementación del capítulo ambiental del acuerdo de promoción comercial entre Estados Unidos y Perú: La situación peruana." In *Resumen de Políticas.* Lima: Banco Interamericano de Desarrollo.

Sabet, Daniel M. 2014. "Co-production and Oversight: Citizens and Their Police." Working Paper Series on Civic Engagement and Public Security in Mexico. Available at: www.wilsoncenter.org/sites/default/files/sabet_co-production_oversight_0.pdf [Accessed January 20, 2020].

Saffon, María Paula. 2015. "When Theft Becomes Grievance: Dispossessions as a Cause of Redistributive Land Claims in 20th Century Latin America." PhD dissertation, Columbia University.

　Forthcoming. "Property and Land." In *The Oxford Handbook of Constitutional Law in Latin America.* Edited by Conrado Hübner Mendes and Roberto Gargarella.

　n.d. "When Theft Becomes Grievance: The Violation of Land Rights as a Cause of Agrarian Reform Claims in Latin America." Unpublished manuscript.

Salman, Ton, Felix Carrillo, and Carola Soruco. 2015. "Small-Scale Mining Cooperatives and the State in Bolivia: Their Stories, Memories, and Negotiation Strategies." *The Extractive Industries and Society* 2(2): 360–367.

Samuels, David, and Richard Snyder. 2001. "The Value of a Vote: Malapportionment in Comparative Perspective." *British Journal of Political Science* 31(4): 651–671.

Sánchez-Ancochea, Diego. 2005. "Domestic Capital, Civil Servants and the State: Costa Rica and the Dominican Republic under Globalisation." *Journal of Latin American Studies* 37(4): 693–726.

2013. "Does Globalization Help to Overcome the 'Crisis of Development?' Political Actors and Economic Rents in Central America and the Dominican Republic." In *Getting Development Right: Structural Transformation, Inclusion, and Sustainability in the Post-crisis Era*. Edited by Eva Paus. New York: Palgrave, 117–136.

Sandoval Rojas, Nathalia, and Daniel M. Brinks. Forthcoming 2020. "Entrenching Social Constitutionalism? Contributions and Challenges of the Left in Latin American Constitutionalism." In *Legacies of the Left Turn in Latin America: The Promise of Inclusive Citizenship*. Edited by Manuel Balán and Françoise Montambeault. Notre Dame: Notre Dame University Press.

Saravia, Gerardo, and Patricia Wiesse. 2014. "El ¡bum! de la construcción." *Ideele revista* [Online]. Available at: http://goo.gl/WMnPRX [Accessed November 10, 2014].

Schavelzon, Salvador. 2012. *El nacimiento del Estado Plurinacional de Bolivia: Etnografía de una asamblea constituyente*. La Paz: CEJIS and Plural Editores.

Schedler, Andreas, Larry Jay Diamond, and Marc F. Plattner. 1999. *The Self-Restraining State: Power and Accountability in New Democracies*. Boulder: Lynne Rienner.

Schenk, Frank, and Orensanz, Lucrecia. 1995. "La desamortización de las tierras comunales en el Estado de México (1856–1911): El caso del distrito de Sultepec." *Historia mexicana* 45(1): 3–37.

Scheppele, Kim Lane. 2015. "Understanding Hungary's Constitutional Revolution." In *Constitutional Crisis in the European Constitutional Area: Theory, Law and Politics in Hungary and Romania*. Edited by Armin von Bogdandy and Pál Sonnevend. Oxford: Hart, 111–124.

Schickler, Eric. 2001. *Disjointed Pluralism: Institutional Innovation and the Development of the U.S. Congress*. Princeton: Princeton University Press.

Schilling-Vacaflor, Almut. 2012. Democratizing Resource Governance Through Prior Consultations? Lessons from Bolivia's Hydrocarbon Sector (January 12, 2012). GIGA (German Institute of Global and Area Studies) Working Paper No 184. Available at SSRN: https://ssrn.com/abstract=1984033 or http://dx.doi.org/10.2139/ssrn.1984033. The paper is available here: https://papers.ssrn.com/sol3/papers.cfm?abstract_id=1984033.

Schmidt, Mariana. 2010a. *Crónicas de un (des)ordenamiento territorial*. Buenos Aires: TeseoPress.

2010b. "Ordenamiento territorial de bosques nativos: definiciones y debates en la provincia de Salta." *Proyección* 8: 114–140.

Scholz, John T., and B. Dan Wood. 1998. "Controlling the IRS: Principals, Principles, and Public Administration." *American Journal of Political Science* 42(1): 141–162.

Schrank, Andrew. 2003. "Foreign Investors, 'Flying Geese,' and the Limits to Export-Led Industrialization in the Dominican Republic." *Theory and Society* 32(4): 415–443.

2009. "Professionalization and Probity in a Patrimonial State: Labor Inspectors in the Dominican Republic." *Latin American Politics and Society* 51(2): 91–115.

2011. "Co-producing Workplace Transformation: The Dominican Republic in Comparative Perspective." *Socio-Economic Review* 9(2): 419–445.

2013. "From Disguised Protectionism to Rewarding Regulation: The Impact of Trade-Related Labor Standards in the Dominican Republic." *Regulation and Governance* 7(3): 299–320.

Schuster, Christian. 2012. *Tenure vs. Merit? The Sequential Politics of Reforming Patronage Bureaucracies*. London: London School of Economics. http://docplayer.net/102116419-Tenure-vs-merit-the-sequential-politics-of-reforming-patronage-bureaucracies-1.html.

2014. *Strategies to Professionalize the Civil Service: Lessons from the Dominican Republic.* Technical Note no. IDB-TN-688. Washington, DC: IDB.

SDP (Secretaría Distrital de Planeación). 2011. *Base de Legalización de Barrios.* Bogotá: SDP, and Observatorio del Mercado Informal de Suelo y Vivienda.

Secretaría de Ambiente de la Provincia de Salta (SAS). 2014. *Informe anual sobre el estado general del ambiente: Año 2014.* Salta: Secretaría de Ambiente.

2015. *Informe Anual Sobre el Estado General del Ambiente. Año 2015.* Salta: Secretaría de Ambiente.

Secretaría de Ambiente y Desarrollo Sustentable (SAyDS). 2013. "Informe sobre el estado del ambiente 2012." SAyDS.

2015. "Monitoreo de la superficie de bosque nativo de la República Argentina: Periodo 2013–2014." Dirección de Bosques, SAyDS, Buenos Aires.

Secretaría de Estado de Trabajo (SET). 2000. *Proceso de reforma y modernización de la administración del trabajo en República Dominicana: Memoria de una gestión, 1991–2000.* Santo Domingo: SET.

2005a. *Boletín estadístico no. 5.* Santo Domingo: SET.

2005b. Unpublished data on individual inspectors.

Secretaría de Gobernación. 2016. "Declaratoria de Alerta de Violencia de Género contra las Mujeres. Estado de Veracruz." Mexico City, November 23.

Secretaría Técnica de la Presidencia (STP). 2005. *Programa de apoyo a la reforma y modernización del poder ejecutivo (pro-reforma).* Santo Domingo.

Serra, Narcís, and Joseph Stiglitz. 2008. *The Washington Consensus Reconsidered: Towards a New Global Governance.* Washington, DC: IPD.

Shearer, Matthew, and Joaquim Tres. 2013. "South-South and Triangular Cooperation in Latin America and the Caribbean: Much Ado about Nothing?" *Integration and Trade* 36 (January–June): 1–10.

Shefter, Martin. 1977. "Party and Patronage: Germany, England, and Italy." *Politics and Society* 7(4): 403–451.

Shepherd, Geoffrey. 2003. *Understanding Public Organizations: An Aid to Reform in Developing Countries.* Washington, DC: World Bank.

Shepherd, Geoffrey, and Sophia Valencia. 1996. "Modernizing the Public Administration in Latin America: Common Problems, No Easy Solutions." Paper presented at Reforma del Estado en America Latina y Caribe Conference, Madrid, October 14–17.

Shugart, Matthew S. 1995. "The Electoral Cycle and Institutional Sources of Divided Presidential Government." *American Political Science Review* 89(2): 327–343.

2001. "Extreme Electoral Systems and the Appeal of the Mixed-Member Alternative." In *Mixed-Member Electoral Systems: The Best of Both Worlds?* Edited by Matthew Soberg Shugart and Martin P. Wattenberg. Oxford: Oxford University Press, 25–51.

2005. "Comparative Electoral Systems Research: The Maturation of the Field and New Challenges Ahead." In *The Politics of Electoral Systems.* Edited by Michael Gallagher and Paul Mitchell. Oxford: Oxford University Press, 24–55.

Shugart, Matthew S., and John M. Carey. 1992. *Presidents and Assemblies: Constitutional Design and Electoral Dynamics.* Cambridge: Cambridge University Press.

Shugart, Matthew S., Melody E. Valdini, and Kati Suominen. 2005. "Looking for Locals: Voter Information Demands and Personal Vote-Earning Attributes of Legislators under Proportional Representation." *American Journal of Political Science* 49(2): 437–449.

Sieder, Rachel, Line Schjolden, and Alan Angell, eds. 2005. *The Judicialization of Politics in Latin America*. New York: Palgrave Macmillan.

Silva, Patricio. 2009. *In the Name of Reason: Technocrats and Politics in Chile*. University Park: Pennsylvania State University Press.

Silva-Herzog, Jesús. 1959. *El agrarismo mexicano y la reforma agraria: Exposición y crítica*. Mexico City: Fondo de Cultura Económica.

   1972. *Breve historia de la Revolución Mexicana: Los antecedentes y la etapa maderista*. Mexico City: Fondo de Cultura Económica.

Silva, Eduardo and Federico Rossi, eds. 2018. *Reshaping the Political Arena: From Resisting Neoliberalism to the Second Incorporation*. Pittsburgh: University of Pittsburgh Press.

Simpson, Eyler. 1937. *The Ejido: Mexico's Way Out*. Chapel Hill: University of North Carolina Press.

Skocpol, Theda. 1979. *States and Social Revolutions: A Comparative Analysis of France Russia, and China*. Cambridge: Cambridge University Press.

   1985. "Bringing the State Back In: Strategies of Analysis in Current Research." In *Bringing the State Back In*. Edited by Peter B. Evans, Dietrich Rueschemeyer, and Theda Skocpol. New York: Cambridge University Press, 3–43.

Skocpol, Theda, and Ellen Kay Trimberger. 1977–78. "Revolutions and the World-Historical Development of Capitalism." *Berkeley Journal of Sociology* 22: 101–113.

Skrentny, John D. 2002. *The Minority Rights Revolution*. Cambridge: Harvard University Press.

Slater, Dan, and Diana Kim. 2015. "Standoffish States: Nonliterate Leviathans in Southeast Asia." *TRaNS: Trans-regional and -National Studies of Southeast Asia* 3(1): 25–44.

Slater, Dan, and Joseph Wong. 2013. "The Strength to Concede: Ruling Parties and Democratization in Developmental Asia." *Perspectives on Politics* 11(3): 717–733.

Smulovitz, Catalina. 2015. "Legal Inequality and Federalism: Domestic Violence Laws in the Argentine Provinces." *Latin American Politics and Society* 57(3): 1–26.

Sociedad Peruana de Derecho Ambiental (SPDA). 2015. *Las rutas del oro ilegal: Estudios de caso en cinco países amazónicos*. Lima: SPDA.

Soifer, Hillel. 2008. "State Infrastructural Power: Approaches to Conceptualization and Measurement." *Studies in Comparative International Development* 43(3): 231–251.

   2015. *State Building in Latin America*. Cambridge: Cambridge University Press.

Souza, Celina. 2001. "Participatory Budgeting in Brazilian Cities: Limits and Possibilities in Building Democratic Institutions." *Environment and Urbanization* 13(1): 159–184.

Spiller, Pablo T., and Mariano Tommasi. 2007. *The Institutional Foundations of Public Policy in Argentina*. Cambridge: Cambridge University Press.

Steinmo, Sven, Kathleen Thelen, and Frank Longstreth, eds. 1992. *Structuring Politics: Historical Institutionalism in Comparative Analysis*. New York: Cambridge University Press.

Stepan, Alfred. 1999. "Federalism and Democracy: Beyond the U.S. Model." *Journal of Democracy* 10(4): 19–34.

Stevenson, Linda. 1999. "Gender Politics in the Mexican Democratization Process." In *Toward Mexico's Democratization*. Edited by Jorge I. Domínguez and Alejandro Poiré. New York: Routledge, 57–87.

Stiglitz, Joseph. 2013. "Institutional Design for China's Innovation System: Implications for Intellectual Property Rights." In *Law and Economics with Chinese Characteristics: Institutions for Promoting Development in the Twenty-First Century*. Edited by David Kennedy and Joseph E. Stiglitz. Oxford: Oxford University Press, 247–277.

Streeck, Wolfgang, and Kathleen Thelen. 2005. "Introduction: Institutional Change in Advanced Political Economies." In *Beyond Continuity: Institutional Change in Advanced Political Economies*. Edited by Wolfgang Streeck and Kathleen Thelen. New York: Oxford University Press, 1–39.

Sunstein, Cass R. 2017. *Impeachment: A Citizen's Guide*. Cambridge: Harvard University Press.

Svampa, Maristella. 2015. "Commodities Consensus: Neoextractivism and Enclosure of the Commons in Latin America." *South Atlantic Quarterly* 114(1): 65–82.

Svolik, Milan. 2019. "Polarization versus Democracy." *Journal of Democracy* 30(3): 20–32.

Swenson, Jennifer J., Catherine E. Carter, Jean-Christophe Domec, and Cesar I. Delgado. 2011. "Gold Mining in the Peruvian Amazon: Global Prices, Deforestation, and Mercury Imports." *PLOS ONE* 6(4): 1–7.

Taagepera, Rein, and Matthew S. Shugart. 1989. *Seats and Votes: The Effects and Determinants of Electoral Systems*. New Haven: Yale University Press.

Takao, Yasuo. 2014. "Policy Learning and Diffusion of Tokyo's Metropolitan Cap-and-Trade: Making a Mandatory Reduction of Total CO_2 Emissions Work at Local Scales." *Policy Studies* 35(4): 319–338.

Tanck, Dorothy. 2005. *Atlas ilustrado de los pueblos de Indios*. Mexico City: Colegio de México.

Tannenbaum, Frank. 1930. *The Mexican Agrarian Revolution*. Washington, DC: Brookings Institution.

Tendler, Judith. 2002a. "Small Firms, the Informal Sector, and the Devil's Deal." *IDS Bulletin* 33(3): 1–15.

2002b. "Why Social Policy Is Condemned to a Residual Category of Safety Nets and What to Do about It." Geneva: United Nations Research for Social Development (UNRISD).

Thelen, Kathleen. 2004. *How Institutions Evolve: The Political Economy of Skills in Germany, Britain, the United States and Japan*. New York: Cambridge University Press.

Thelen, Kathleen, and Wolfgang Streeck. 2005. "Institutional Change in Advanced Political Economies." In *Beyond Continuity: Institutional Change in Advanced Political Economies*. Edited by Wolfgang Streeck and Kathleen Ann Thelen. Oxford: Oxford University Press, 1–39.

Therborn, Göran. 1979. "The Travail of Latin American Democracy." *New Left Review* 113–114: 71–109. https://newleftreview.org/issues/I113/articles/goran-therborn-the-travail-of-latin-american-democracy.

Thompson, José. 2016. *El Derecho a la Consulta Previa, Libre e Informada: una mirada crítica desde los pueblos indígenas*. San José: Instituto Interamericano de Derechos Humanos.

Torres Tovar, Carlos Alberto. 2009. *Ciudad informal colombiana: Barrios construidos por la gente*. Bogotá: Universidad Nacional de Colombia.

Torres Wong, Marcela. 2018a. *Natural Resources, Extraction and Indigenous Rights in Latin America*. New York: Routledge.

2018b. "Prior Consultation and the Defence of Indigenous Lands in Latin America." In *Crisis and Conflict in Agriculture*. Edited by Rami Zurayk, Eckart Woertz, and Rachel Bahn. Boston: CAB International, 247–260.

Towns, Ann E. 2010. *Women and States: Norms and Hierarchies in International Society*. New York: Cambridge University Press.

Tranjan, Ricardo J. 2016. *Participatory Democracy in Brazil: Socioeconomic and Political Origins*. Notre Dame: University of Notre Dame Press.

Trucchi, Giorgio. 2015. "OIT resuelve sobre queja por discriminación a inspectores de trabajo." Available at: www.rel-uita.org/index.php/es/sindicatos/item/6929-oit-resuelve-sobre-queja-por-discriminacion-a-inspectores-de-trabajo [Accessed January 31, 2016].

True, Jacqui. 2012. *The Political Economy of Violence against Women*. Oxford: Oxford University Press.

Tsai, Kellee S. 2007. "Adaptive Informal Institutions and Endogenous Institutional Change in China." *World Politics* 59(1): 116–141.

Tushnet, Mark. 2003. "Constitutional Hardball." *John Marshall Law Review*: 37(3): 523–553.

Tyler, Tom R. 2006. *Why People Obey the Law*. Princeton: Princeton University Press.

Twain, Mark. 1905 [1899]. *The Man That Corrupted Hadleyburg and Other Stories and Essays*. New York and London: Harper & Collins (page 66).

Valencia Arroyo, Lenin. 2014. *Madre de dios: ¿Podemos evitar la tragedia? Políticas de ordenamiento de la minería aurífera*. Lima: Sociedad Peruana de Derecho Ambiental.

Valenzuela, Arturo. 1978. *The Breakdown of Democratic Regimes*. Chile: Johns Hopkins University Press.

2004. "Latin American Presidencies Interrupted." *Journal of Democracy* 15(4): 5–19.

Van Cott, Donna Lee. 2005. *From Movements to Parties in Latin America: The Evolution of Ethnic Politics*. New York: Cambridge University Press.

2008. *Radical Democracy in the Andes*. New York: Cambridge University Press.

Versteeg, Mila, Timothy Horley, Anne Meng, Mauricio Guim, and Marilyn Guirguis. Forthcoming 2020. "The Law and Politics of Presidential Term Limit Evasion." *Columbia Law Review*. SSRN: https://ssrn.com/abstract=3359960 [Accessed January 20, 2020].

Villarreal, Andrés. 2007. "Women's Employment Status, Coercive Control, and Intimate Partner Violence in Mexico." *Journal of Marriage and Family* 69(2): 418–434.

Viterna, Jocelyn. 2012. "The Left and 'Life' in El Salvador." *Politics and Gender* 8(2): 248–254.

Wade, Robert. 1990. *Governing the Market: Economic Theory and the Role of Government in East Asian Industrialization*. Princeton: Princeton University Press.

Washington Office on Latin America (WOLA). 2011. "Tackling Urban Violence in Latin America: Reversing Exclusion through Smart Policing and Social Investment." Report. Available at: www.wola.org/sites/default/files/downloadable/Citizen%20Security/2011/Tackling_Urban_Violence_in_Latin_America.pdf [Accessed January 20, 2020].

Weaver, Julie Anne. 2017. "Voting, Citizen Engagement and Political Accountability in Municipal Politics: The Case of Peru." Paper presented at the Latin American Studies Association (LASA) International Congress, Lima, Peru, April.

Weber, Max. 1978 [1922]. *Economy and Society: An Outline of Interpretive Sociology*. Berkeley: University of California Press.

Weingast, Barry R. 1997. "The Political Foundations of Democracy and the Rule of Law." *American Political Science Review* 91(2): 245–263.

Weingast, Barry R., and Mark J. Moran. 1983. "Trade Commission Bureaucratic Discretion or Congressional Control? Regulatory Policymaking by the Federal Trade Commission." *Journal of Political Economy* 91(5): 765–800.

Weinstein, Barbara. 1990. "The Industrialists, the State, and the Issues of Worker Training and Social Services in Brazil, 1930–50." *Hispanic American Historical Review* 70(3): 379–404.

Weitz-Shapiro, Rebecca. 2014. *Curbing Clientelism in Argentina: Politics, Poverty, and Social Policy*. Cambridge: Cambridge University Press.

Weldon, Jeffrey. 1997. "Political Sources of Presidencialismo in Mexico." In *Presidentialism and Democracy in Latin America*. Edited by Scott P. Mainwaring and Matthew S. Shugart. Cambridge: Cambridge University Press, 225–259.

Weldon, S. Laurel. 2002. *Protest, Policy, and the Problem of Violence against Women: A Cross-National Comparison*. Pittsburgh: University of Pittsburgh Press.

Wells, Harwell. 2001. "The End of the Affair? Anti-dueling Laws and Social Norms in Antebellum America." *Vanderbilt Law Review* 54(4): 1805–1847.

Westney, Eleanor. 1987. *Imitation and Innovation: The Transfer of Western Organizational Practices to Japan*. Cambridge: Harvard University Press.

Weyland, Kurt. 2002. "Limitations of Rational-Choice Institutionalism for the Study of Latin American Politics." *Studies in Comparative International Development* 37(1): 57–85.

2009. "Institutional Change in Latin America: External Models and Their Unintended Consequences." *Journal of Politics in Latin America* 1(1): 37–66.

Wiles, Ellen. 2006. "Aspirational Principles or Enforceable Rights? The Future for Socio-economic Rights in National Law." *American University International Law Review* 22(1): 35–64.

Wilkie, James W. 1967. *The Mexican Revolution: Federal Expenditure and Social Change since 1910*. Berkeley: University of California Press.

1998. "Primera reforma agraria en Mexico, 1853–1909, a través de la estadística nacional." *Mexico and the World* 3(3). www.profmex.org/mexicoandtheworld/ volume3/3summer98/ laestadistica_economicap2.html.

Wilson, James Q. 1980. *The Politics of Regulation*. New York: Basic Books.

Womack, John. 1968. *Zapata and the Mexican Revolution*. New York: Vintage.

World Bank. 1993. *The East Asian Miracle: Economic Growth and Public Policy*. Oxford: World Bank/Oxford University Press.

1997. *World Development Report: The State in a Changing World*. Washington, DC: World Bank.

2004. *Doing Business in 2004: Understanding Regulation*. Washington, DC: World Bank.

Yashar, Deborah J. 2005. *Contesting Citizenship in Latin America: The Rise of Indigenous Movements and the Postliberal Challenge*. New York: Cambridge University Press.

2018. *Homicidal Ecologies: Illicit Economies and Complicit States in Latin America*. Cambridge: Cambridge University Press.

Ziblatt, Daniel. 2017. *Conservative Political Parties and the Birth of Modern Democracy in Europe*. New York: Cambridge University Press.

Zovatto, G., and Jesús Orozco Henriquez. 2008. *Reforma política y electoral en America Latina 1978–2007* (No. 324 (7/8) 342.807).

Index